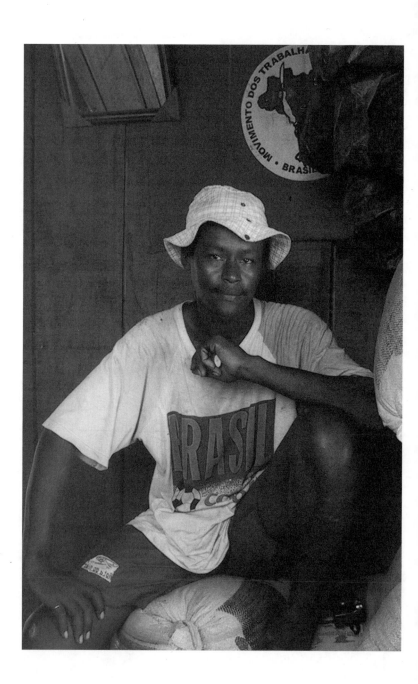

# To Inherit the Earth

## The Landless Movement and the Struggle for a New Brazil

Angus Wright and Wendy Wolford

Food First Books
*Oakland, California*

Food First Books
398 60th Street
Oakland, CA 94618
510-654-4400
www.foodfirst.org

Cover and text design by Amy Evans McClure
Cover photograph by Sebastião Salgado
Cartographer: Thomas Leroe-Munoz
Copy editor: Tamar Love
Proofreader: Wade Fox
Indexer: Ken Della Penta
Interior photographs by Angus Wright (pages: ii, xxxii, 41, 69, 92, 100,
172, 175, 180, 190, 201, 215, 226, 248, 251, 262, 270, 295, 308); Peter
Rosset (page: 49); and Wendy Wolford (pages: 136, 137)

*Library of Congress Cataloging-in-Publication Data*
Wright, Angus Lindsay.
    To inherit the earth : the landless movement and the struggle for a new
    Brazil / by Angus Wright and Wendy Wolford.
        p. cm.
    ISBN 0-935028-90-0
    1. Land reform—Brazil—History—20th century. 2. Movimento dos
    Trabalhadores Rurais sem Terra (Brazil)—History. 3. Peasantry—Brazil—
    Political activity—History—20th century. 4. Agricultural laborers—Brazil—
    Political activity—History—20th century. I. Wolford, Wendy. II. Title.
    HD1333.B6W74 2003
    333.3'181—dc21                                              2003014764

Food First Books are distributed by:
Client Distribution Services (CDS)
425 Madison Avenue, 3rd Floor
New York, NY 10017
800-343-4499
www.cdsbooks.com

Printed in Canada

5 4 3 2 1 – 03 04 05 06 07

# Contents

# Preface

THIS BOOK DEALS WITH ONE of the most important new social movements in contemporary Latin America: Brazil's Landless Workers Movement, or MST. But in discussing this movement, we are in truth referring to something much bigger than any single organization: the MST's rapid development speaks to the urgent need in Brazil to find an alternative system of politics, a different way of organizing the fight for the "right to have rights." Brazilians' search for—and belief in—such an alternative system is also the subject of this book.

We began to work on this project together in the summer of 2000, when we met at an international rural sociology conference in Rio de Janeiro, but both of us had studied Brazil and the MST for many years. We agreed to work together because we share a love for Brazil, and because we believe that the rise of MST is a phenomenal story, one that needs to be told in some detail to people interested in hunger, social change, poverty, environmental conservation and Latin America.

Wendy was first introduced to the movement in 1993, when she took a year off from college to volunteer as a construction worker on an MST settlement in the northeastern state of Sergipe. Despite some initial language difficulties, she learned enough to realize that the MST was an important movement fighting for social change in Brazil. She entered the doctoral program in the Department of Geography at the University of California at Berkeley in 1995, intending to study the MST further. In 1997, Wendy spent seven months in São Paulo on a Social Science Research Council Pre-Dissertation Fellowship. She studied at the University of São Paulo with Professors José Eli da Veiga (economics) and Ariovaldo Umbelino (geography) and spent three days a week working in the MST's national headquarters, located in the city. During that time, Wendy was able to examine the movement's archives and meet with important movement members and leaders. In 1998, Wendy returned to Brazil for fourteen months of field research, during which time she conducted over 200 interviews in Santa Catarina and Pernambuco (see http://globetrotter.berkeley.edu/DissPropWorkshop for comments on that field experience). Wendy earned her PhD in 2001, and began work that year as an assistant professor in the Geography Department at the University of North Carolina at Chapel Hill. She continues to work on the MST as well as more broadly on developing research on geographies of resistance.

Angus began his study of Brazilian history as an undergraduate at the University of Kansas, and continued at Cornell and the University of Michigan, where he earned a PhD in Latin American history in 1976. He spent 1970–1971 in Brazil, doing research for his dissertation on the social and environmental problems created by plantation export agriculture in southern Bahia. In 1991 and 1992, he worked in the same region, analyzing the problems of biological conservation as they related to the regional economy. It was in Bahia that he first encountered organizations of landless people working for agrarian reform. In the year 2000, he began work on this book, making four research trips to Brazil over a two-year period. Angus has taught environmental studies at California State University, Sacramento, since 1972 and is the author of *The Death of Ramón González: The Modern Agricultural Dilemma* (University of Texas Press, 1990).

Most of the information from field studies carried out for this book was collected at different times over a period of three years. Wendy worked in settlements in the southern state of Santa Catarina and the northeastern state of Pernambuco. She interviewed MST settlers, MST leaders, large farmers, rural workers, urban residents and government

officials. Because of the agreement she made with the people she interviewed, the names of Wendy's informants—with the exception of very
high-profile movement leaders—have been changed to preserve their
owners' anonymity. Angus worked in settlements in the southernmost
state of Rio Grande do Sul, the northern state of Pará and the northeastern states of Bahia and Pernambuco. He also interviewed MST settlers and MST leaders. The names of Angus's informants have not been
changed or obscured, except in certain sensitive instances. The quotes
in the book, from the people we interviewed, were either taped or reconstructed from field notes.

We have many people to thank for their assistance in writing this
book. First of all, we wish to thank those people in the MST who were
always extraordinarily gracious about giving up their valuable time to
help us find information and talk with us about their experiences. This
book is *for* them as much as it is *about* them. We also learned a great
deal about the MST and the situation in Brazil from colleagues both in
Brazil and in the United States. We would particularly like to thank
Bernardo Fernandes Mançano for the work he has done on the movement and for providing us with helpful comments during a visit to
the United States in 2001. Tamara Benakouche, Maria Ignez Silveira
Paulilo, Mana, Valéria Gonçalvez, Peter May, John Wilkinson and the
Araújo family were all invaluable sources of information and friendship
for Wendy. José Augusto Pádua, Rosineide Bentes da Silva, Keith Alger,
Cristina Alves and Salvador Trevizan each deserve our thanks for many
forms of assistance. The project would not have been possible without
their help.

The ideas and writing in this book also benefited from comments
and suggestions made by Carmen Diana Deere, Peter Evans, Julie Guth-
man, Gillian Hart, Michael Johns, Mary Mackey, Douglas Murray,
Charles Postel, Jessica Teisch and Michael Watts. Research for the work
was funded by Food First, the National Science Foundation, the Social
Science Research Council, the Institute for the Study of World Peace
and the Institute of International Studies at the University of California
at Berkeley.

We want to thank Clancy Drake, the managing editor at Food First,
for her Herculean efforts in improving the manuscript and seeing it to

print. Peter Rosset and Anuradha Mittal, also at Food First, provided invaluable advice and assistance.

Finally, both authors would like to thank Mary, Joe, Jessica and John for their advice, indulgence and continual support.

# Publisher's Note

Food First Books is publishing this book as part of the Land Research Action Network (www.landaction.org), a program funded by the Ford, Pond and C. S. Mott Foundations, and by the Kaplan Fund. The publisher wishes to thank Maisa Mendonça and Friends of the MST for their help with this book.

# About the Authors

Angus Wright teaches Environmental Studies at California State University at Sacramento. His Ph.D. in Brazilian History is from the University of Michigan. Angus is the author of *The Death of Ramon Gonzalez: The Modern Agricultural Dilemma* (University of Texas Press).

Wendy Wolford teaches Geography at the University of North Carolina at Chapel Hill. She received her Ph.D. in Geography from the University of California at Berkeley. Wendy's research interests include the political economy of development, agrarian societies, and the struggle for land in Brazil.

# Introduction

## To Inherit the Earth

THIS IS THE STORY OF more than one million people in Brazil who have transformed their lives. They have done so by organizing peaceful protests that have forced the Brazilian government to redistribute twenty million acres of agricultural land to 350,000 families and to assist them further in creating new livelihoods. These people have vastly improved the quality of education and health care available to their families, achieving these gains by successfully challenging the dominant institutions and some of the most powerful people of Brazil, a nation of more than 175 million people and one of the world's ten largest economies.

The million people—men, women and children—who are members of the MST (*O Movimento dos Trabalhadores Rurais Sem-Terra*, the Landless Workers Movement) have faced down police, the military and private gangs of hired gunmen. They have suffered imprisonment, beatings and, sometimes, death. Instead of waiting for the government to meet its long-standing promises to redistribute land, members of the MST have occupied land claimed by wealthy landowners, continuing the occupations until the government met their immediate needs for land. Before and after receiving land, they continued to insist that the government go beyond land distribution to pursue a broader program of agrarian reform and social change. They have continued to organize and press for their demands in spite of the assassinations of hundreds of their leaders and members. In committing themselves to the long and difficult struggles that participation in the MST brings to virtually all who join, many MST members have undergone a profound personal transformation from passive and victimized people to highly energized agents of change. They have become real citizens. They have also demonstrated that solutions can be found to some of the world's most stubborn problems of poverty and wasteful use of land.

The MST has worked through collective leadership, scrupulously avoiding dependence on a single leader. While the movement has been very effective at building alliances and working in a variety of coalitions, it has maintained its independence. At this writing, more than eighty thousand MST families who have not yet benefited from land distributions are occupying land in the continuing battle to make agrarian reform an enduring reality in Brazil. The MST has shown clearly that the landless need not be compelled to journey to the Amazon forest and other environmentally sensitive areas in order to carve out farms, as the government has tried to convince them to do. Many MST farmers are pioneering more ecologically sound means of production on land long available for agriculture.

The MST has seen to it that 150,000 children are attending elementary and secondary schools. Many teachers in the settlement schools, who must meet standards determined by the government, have been trained by the MST itself. The organization has established teacher-training programs with seven national universities and works with UNESCO, UNICEF and the Catholic Church on joint educational projects. The movement has a national high school and a school for training organizers and is building a university near São Paulo, called *A Universidade da Terra* (the University of the Land). The MST has itself obtained, or pressured the government into providing, health and other social services for poor rural people on MST settlements throughout Brazil. Few of these people previously had access to such services.

People from nations around the world have been inspired by the Brazilian landless movement and have studied its example to see what can be learned about confronting their own social and environmental problems. European governments, the United Nations and other international organizations have given special awards to the MST for its accomplishments in agrarian reform, innovative education, rural health care and ecological farming. The Swedish Parliament awarded the MST the Right Livelihood Award (often called the alternative Nobel Prize), and many observers consider the MST to be the most important social movement in Latin America today.

## The Frustrating Trap of Inequality

It is especially heartening that the story of the MST is taking place in Brazil. Most people who have thought seriously about Brazil have concluded that the country's fundamental problem is inequality: as Brazilian journalist Wilson Braga wrote in 1985, "We have two countries here under one flag, one constitution and one language. One part of Brazil is in the twentieth century, with high-technology computers and satellite launches. And, beside that, we have another country where people are eating lizards to survive." Even casual visitors tend to agree with the sentiment of Albert Camus, who, after touring Brazil in 1949, wrote, "I have never seen luxury and misery so insolently mixed."

The deep social inequalities built into Brazilian society over the past five hundred years have sometimes seemed nearly impossible to overcome. Until 1888, Brazil was a society built on slavery. The historic and continuing control of the land by a very small minority of landowners has led to systematic, rapacious exploitation of the poor and of the nation's soils and forests. More than 50 percent of the nation's agricultural land is controlled by just 4 percent of landowners.[1] The pattern of unequal land ownership has been the foundation for the growth of stark inequities in income, social status, education, health care, social services, participation in community affairs and access to the courts. After five centuries of dominance over people and institutions, landowners have learned that they can often operate as a law unto themselves, literally committing murder with impunity and undoing reform efforts time and time again.

It is difficult to summarize the depth of Brazil's problem with inequality because it is so pervasive in the life and culture of the nation.

However, we can begin with some general statistics on inequality. One telling measurement compares the income of the richest 20 percent of the population to that of the poorest 20 percent:

- In Western Europe, the richest fifth of the population receive four times as much income as the poorest fifth.
- In the United States, the ratio is eight to one.
- In Brazil, the richest fifth receive thirty-four times as much income as the poorest fifth of the population.

A recent United Nations study showed that nearly a third of all Brazilians, approximately fifty-five million people, live on less than two dollars a day. Brazil also suffers by comparison to other countries in its same average per capita income bracket: a third of Brazilians live in absolute poverty, while only 15 percent of Mexicans fall into this category. By most measures, Brazil has the largest gap between rich and poor of any sizable nation on Earth.[2]

In spite of the poverty that afflicts so many Brazilians, the country is rich in many ways. Brazil has a highly favorable ratio of productive agricultural land to people, comparable to the United States as one of the nations best endowed with the ability to produce food. It is among the top producers and exporters of many agricultural commodities, notably soybeans, poultry, sugar, coffee, cacao, orange juice concentrates, corn and cotton. It has the world's largest reserves of iron ore and quite likely the largest reserves of bauxite for making aluminum. It is richly endowed with gold, silver, manganese and copper. While only modestly endowed with fossil fuels, the nation has already developed a large portion of its enormous hydroelectric potential. Brazil has become one of the top ten industrial economies in the world, manufacturing steel, automobiles, ships, airplanes, farm implements, industrial and agricultural chemicals, light armaments, computers and a vast array of basic consumer goods.

For several decades in the mid-twentieth century, Brazilians and foreigners alike talked excitedly about this rich and diverse nation as "the country of the future." The future arrived in the form of huge new factories, freeways and skyscrapers, but so few enjoyed the benefits of growth—and so many paid its high price—that talk of "the country of the future" came to be understood as the starting point for a series of sour jokes.

While there is no doubt that economic growth and technological progress have improved the lives of most Brazilians in many ways over the last century, inequality persists, and by most measures has even increased during the same period. Growth and technological change in conditions of severe inequality have tended to exacerbate rather than reduce inequalities, making the rich richer and the poor at least relatively poorer. There is also no doubt that social inequality has undermined the development potential of these economic and technological gains, as well as fashioned new opportunities for exploitation and squandered countless opportunities to create a far happier society.

No class of Brazilians is unaffected by the effects of inequality. Living in fabulous privilege among so many desperately poor people, the Brazilian rich have found it increasingly necessary to isolate themselves from their fellow citizens. One example of the ironies of inequality comes from a *Washington Post* story dated June 1, 2002, which documents the rise of helicopter travel in Brazil's largest city, São Paulo, during a period when its economy had been in recession. Poverty and insecurity had pushed the city's crime rate to record levels—sixty homicides per year per 100,000 people in São Paulo compared to seven per 100,000 in New York City (in 2001, the homicide rate in Rio de Janeiro was approximately nine times higher than in New York City). The fear of violence and kidnappings, combined with the everyday hassles of getting around in São Paulo—including long traffic jams and dangerous road conditions—have encouraged Brazil's elite to take to the skies. An estimated 240 helipads (compared to 10 in New York City) carry politicians, business executives and the simply wealthy to their gated communities, which they consider relatively safe because of the presence of armed guards patrolling the perimeter. When forced to the ground, many of Brazil's wealthy travel in armored vehicles with bulletproof glass; drivers take special courses in escaping ambushes and foiling kidnappings.

The rich fear the desperation and anger of the poor, who are living in some of the world's most troubled and violent urban slums, called *favelas*. In forty years, Brazil went from a country that was two-thirds rural to one that was more than two-thirds urban. A growing industrial economy and the persistence of rural poverty sent great waves of people to the cities. Brazil's many large cities, especially Rio de Janeiro and São Paulo, have mushroomed so rapidly that there is insufficient infrastructure to accommodate everyone—in poor neighborhoods there are too few buses, inadequate provision of drinking water and almost no sewage lines. Compared to the demand, jobs are scarce, ill paid and often temporary. People build houses from whatever they can find: slabs of metal siding, cardboard boxes, wooden posts, mud and adobe—whatever is lying around that they can turn into a shelter. Houses are often piled crazily on top of each other, without effective zoning or community associations to oversee new development. These houses are often built illegally, and residents illegally tap into electrical lines and other utility services. There is little or no garbage service, so trash piles up and creates centers of infection and toxic pollution. Some favelas have been built around garbage dumps because of the food and materials that people can extract from the garbage. Such is the desperation of the residents that they have even fought pitched battles with police and military sent to remove them from the dangerous dumps. In some lowland marshy areas, slum dwellers have used cheap liquor and parties to bribe garbage truck drivers from elsewhere in the city to dump garbage in the marshes, making landfill to accommodate more shacks.

Poverty, despair and exploitation create ideal breeding grounds for crime. Thieves and drug dealers live side by side with the majority of people, who are just trying to earn enough for a better place to live or to keep families together. Although many favela dwellers have proven amazingly resilient and ingenious in finding ways to improve their houses and their lives, for most urban poor people, life is full of disappointments, insults and injuries. Recently, many of the political machines that have controlled the slums have given way to well-armed drug gangs, who bring a certain sort of limited peace, and even drug-financed social programs, in exchange for submission to the drug lords. Politicians and criminal bosses alike exploit the people's needs and their dependence on extralegal stratagems of survival, creating networks of obligations and favors. Though politicians and political movements have promised a great deal, they have yet to provide real alternatives for the great majority of people mired in poverty.

For poor people who stayed in the countryside, the situation mostly remains as bad or worse. Because the situation of rural poverty is a large share of the subject of this book, we will be very brief in our treatment of it here. In the last half of the twentieth century, hunger and malnutrition continued to stalk Brazil's rural poor. (These same hungry people, paradoxically, were doing the work of planting and harvesting crops that fed and clothed tens of millions of Brazilians and foreigners.) Illiteracy rates remained high. Health care and disease control improved only very modestly, and in some important ways worsened. Experts frequently classify the poor of Brazil's Northeast as the largest group of severely malnourished and disease-ridden people in the Western Hemisphere.

The economic "modernization" programs of the Brazilian government in the last half of the twentieth century brought widespread, capital-intensive mechanization and chemical dependence to Brazilian agriculture. A sizable group of rural people, who had managed in earlier years to improve their lot through control of small holdings of land or through organizing for better labor contracts, lost their land or their jobs to large, mechanized operations. Even rural people who may have thought they had succeeded in making themselves the exception to the rule of Brazilian rural poverty found that they had been cast down into a nightmare of unemployment and dispossession. For two decades, a military government practiced severe and violent repression against those who attempted to protest growing misery in rural Brazil. That so many people were willing to go to the cities in spite of the increasingly well-known horrors of slum life that awaited most of them is powerful testimony to the difficult situation in the countryside.

Brazil is large enough and rich enough to have a substantial middle class, composed of perhaps thirty-five to forty million people. Even this relatively comfortable 20 to 25 percent of the population suffers from the effects of the great inequalities of the society. It is politically very difficult to tax the powerful rich, and the poor majority have little income to tax. As a consequence, social services of all kinds, including health and education, are chronically starved for funds, which, in turn, limits the growth of professional and semiprofessional occupations. Because of the poverty of the majority of Brazil's population, the domestic market for goods and services is much smaller than it could be. The small national market restricts opportunities for economic growth and investment. Severe inequality also creates myriad opportunities for corruption in business and government in ways that generate continual injustices and frustrations, great and small. These injustices harm everyone.

## A Way Out of the Trap?

From the poor, who suffer its most painful consequences, to rich investors, who fear kidnapping and would like to see greater opportunities for stable economic growth, to the economically pressured middle class, most Brazilians feel in some way trapped by the great national problem of inequality. Many are also profoundly discouraged by the long and sad history of unsuccessful attempts to reduce the severity of the problem; a variety of political movements and initiatives throughout the twentieth century failed at breaking Brazil out of the inequality trap. There has long been substantial agreement among Brazilians that a key part of reducing inequality must involve addressing the needs of the rural poor through agrarian reform, a goal that has seemed impossible to achieve in the face of the entrenched opposition of a small minority of powerful landowners.

It is within this context of frustration that the MST has attracted so much interest and enthusiasm. Working with the landless, the dispossessed, the unemployed and the migrant or day laborer—in short, the poorest people in Brazilian society—the MST has achieved what few believed possible. It has mobilized the very poorest and most desperate people to change their lives dramatically and forced the government to live up to previously hollow promises to initiate agrarian reform. The MST has acted aggressively and persistently, even to the point where it has clashed with people who consider themselves supporters of the movement. In hindsight, it seems unlikely that any movement less aggressive, less persistent and less independent of its friends could have finally gotten the ball rolling for agrarian reform in Brazil.

The MST has created this momentum for change by taking advantage of Brazil's most profound legal contradiction: the contrast between laws mandating good land use and large landowners' actual, wasteful practices. Early in Brazil's European history, the Portuguese monarchy created the foundation for these wasteful practices by giving away vast tracts of land to royal favorites. The crown was eager to nail down claims to a vast territory at a time when there were relatively few potential Portuguese emigrants to actually settle the land. With the English, French, Dutch and Spanish in competition for the same area, the Portuguese crown gave its favorites not only land, but also much of the responsibility of defending and administering it. Though Portugal's rulers were warned by royal officials that this practice would lead to abuses and arrogance that would threaten both the authority of the crown and the good use of the land, the monarchs ignored these warnings in order to achieve a strong Portuguese presence in Brazil.

As we will explore in much greater detail later in subsequent chapters, this practice led to the very abuses of land and people that royal administrators had feared. Landowners relied on having a great deal of land rather than on administering it or using it well. They did very little to distribute the benefits of their plantations among their slaves, employees and dependents. If they damaged the land under production, new land was always available.

From the colonial period on, Portuguese officials and the later Brazilian national governments tried in various ways to resolve the problems of inequality and poor land use—to little avail. One principle of law that was originally intended to deal with these problems was that of effective use; that is, if land were not being put to good use by its owner, then others could make a competing claim and acquire title to the land for themselves. This principle, not unknown in Anglo-American law, is often known as "use it or lose it" or "squatter's rights."

Unfortunately, as we will see, the powerful landholders learned how to use this principle to manipulate the law on their own behalf, driving others off the land. However, the principle remained part of Brazilian law and was even strengthened over time, becoming enshrined in Brazilian constitutions as the idea that land, in order to be claimed by an owner, has to "serve its social function." Successive Brazilian governments promised to make this concept meaningful by redistributing land to the poor, but for a variety of reasons, the governments always failed to make good on the promises. The contradiction was clear: there was a legal requirement that the land serve a positive social function, yet the landowners generally and systematically abused the real potential of the land, with a negative effect on general prosperity.

The MST discovered how to make the idea of the "social function of land" into a mighty tool to push forward real agrarian reform. As we will see in the chapters that follow, the MST did not approach the effective use principle simply through abstract theorizing and planning. Rather, it was in seeking solutions for the terrible dilemmas of landlessness that it became clear to them how the old paradox of land law could be used on their behalf.

Throughout Brazilian history, desperate people had sometimes settled on little-used land claimed by others, with the goal of trying to gain ownership for themselves. These people had remained isolated, and in their isolation, they were usually defeated—driven off the land and forced to seek work as landless laborers. It was only as various movements grew in resistance to Brazil's military dictatorship that landless people began to see the possibilities of organizing in support of their own cause. As we will see in the first chapter of this book, landless people learned how to turn the occupation of land into immediate victory for themselves and into an enduring movement for agrarian reform and even broader social changes. They broke apart a contradiction and, in doing so, created possibilities for a new future for themselves and for their country.

## History's Geography
### The Organization of This Book

We have chosen to tell the story of the MST in three main chapters, followed by a fourth that assesses the successes, failures and challenges of the movement's first decades. Throughout, we tell stories from our field research that we believe represent important parts of the MST's story. While we have had to leave out many fascinating and valuable narratives, we hope we have told enough to give some insights into the diverse issues Brazilian rural people face throughout the country. Those who shared their stories with us were brave and generous in doing so, and even where we may take a critical perspective on their actions, we have sought to understand their choices.

The first three chapters are organized both geographically and historically. The accomplishments and shortcomings of the MST cannot be properly assessed without an understanding of the historical roots and geographical circumstances of the struggle for land and rural equality. The MST is a Brazilian movement, and without some knowledge of Brazil's social and political history, any appreciation or evaluation of the MST would be skewed and incomplete. We ask the reader to follow us down some of the paths of Brazilian history so that we can arrive at a better understanding of the MST's remarkable journey.

One of Brazil's most obvious but profound realities is its sheer size and diversity—the nation is as large as the lower forty-eight states of the United States, with an additional Texas thrown in. Brazilian rulers have always been preoccupied with the need to bring the country together into a more meaningful single entity. For much of its history, Brazil hardly seemed a nation at all because its several regions were so distinct from one another. The MST has not escaped the geographical influences of regions widely separated by distance and diversity of history, culture and economic activities. In each region, the movement has faced different challenges; it has had to work in different ways and has had different measures of success. It is not possible to understand the MST properly without recognizing these geographic realities.

Chapter 1 tells how people in Rio Grande do Sul, the southernmost state, organized to fight for land and created the foundations for a regional and then a national movement during the period when Brazil was just starting to emerge from the most repressive years of the military regime. Part of this chapter tells the story of government repression and the resistance to it; it recounts the movement's roots in liberation theology, and the transformation of the Brazilian Left under the dictatorship. The chapter also describes how, in extreme southern Brazil, a tradition of small family farms created a special context for agrarian reform. Here farm families faced the possible destruction of the smallholder tradition as mechanization and government policies drove them from the land. We learn how one such family, the Placotniks, became swept up in these events and how their lives were changed. The chapter concludes with the reflections of successful MST settlers enjoying the fruits of their victory while continuing to face very difficult economic, political and environmental challenges.

Chapter 2 begins with an examination of how the new civilian governments that took power after the demise of the military dictatorship took up the intense national debate over agrarian reform. We see that the debate is critically shaped by the five-century history of rural inequality in Brazil, and we move on to consider the difficulties of agrarian reform in Brazil's poorest region, the Northeast, where the foundations for inequality were laid from the earliest days of the Portuguese colony, through a long history of slavery and plantations producing for export. The history of the Northeast has shaped Brazilian culture and politics in ways that have persisted until the current day, and Chapter 2 discusses how that history has affected Brazilians' image of themselves and of the nation's problems. We then see how the MST has worked for agrarian reform in the Northeast, and examine some of the movement's most severe challenges and shortcomings through the lens of an especially burdensome regional history.

Chapter 3 takes us to the Amazon, where we consider the relationship between the landless and the forest. This chapter examines the history of Amazon development, especially in the last four decades, showing how the desperation of the landless has been manipulated and exploited for purposes that have very little to do with meeting their needs. We show how settlers become caught up in traps that they cannot escape alone. We visit settlements where settlers have joined the MST to find a way out of those traps. We also visit the world's largest iron mine, which represents a key part of the dynamic that is shaping the future of the forest and of the settlers. The relatively recent arrival of the MST in the area we visit has begun to create an alternative vision for a solution to the dilemmas of forest preservation and landlessness.

In all three of these chapters, a continuing theme is the recognition by the MST and by a large share of its members that the movement, and agrarian reform in general, cannot by itself accomplish all the goals the landless have set for themselves. Throughout this part of the book, we show how critical are the MST's connections and alliances with other social movements, political parties and civic organizations. Questions of human rights, environmental conservation, union organization, the role of political parties and government policy are woven into the narrative. By continually returning to themes of the MST's engagement with other social movements and political forces, we hope to provide one kind of lens through which to look at Brazil's history and its contemporary dilemmas.

Chapter 4 undertakes an overall assessment of the history and meaning of the movement's formation and actions. We address a series of questions as part of our assessment: Is life better for MST settlers now than it was before they became part of the movement? What has been the role of government policy in agrarian reform, and what are the issues before future administrations? What has been the role of the United States in agrarian reform throughout the world, and what are the implications for the future of agrarian reform in Brazil? How is agrarian reform linked to broader issues of national development? What has been the role of the MST in reducing the legal impunity of powerful landholders, and what is the significance of holding landholders accountable in creating new alternatives for conservation of forests, wildlife and soils? What is the relationship between the MST and the Brazilian state? How successful has the MST been in transforming people into active citizens, and how significant has the movement been in the overall rebirth of Brazilian civil society since the end of the military dictatorship?

We close with reflections on the future of the MST and its children and with a postscript on the recent election of a new Brazilian government more sympathetic to the MST than previous administrations.

We believe that the MST—or a movement much like it—was necessary to begin a process of agrarian reform in Brazil. We also believe that the MST has played a very positive role in wider social changes occurring in Brazil, and that it is a movement worthy of serious study by all those interested in improving human life and the human relationship to nature. We have also been forthright in pointing out what we see as the shortcomings of the movement and of people involved in it. The MST has long maintained that honest criticism is vital to the life of a healthy movement, and we agree. It is our hope that this book will be read in the spirit of enthusiastic participation in a task that joins critical thought and citizen action, a task performed continuously by the members of the MST.

The story of the MST is a remarkable and complicated one, encompassing both victories and defeats, brilliant solutions and ongoing dilemmas. Many elements of the story would never happen in quite the same way outside Brazil. There are also inherent limits to what the organization can accomplish on its own. The MST, an organization based on agriculture, farmers and farmworkers, can hardly be expected by itself to transform a Brazilian society that is now predominantly urban and industrial. However, in its special Brazilian character and in its shortcomings and successes, the story of the MST invites us to reflect on the possibilities for positive social change. This is especially important in an era when many seem to doubt that the poor can organize effectively on their own behalf, much less create genuinely fresh approaches to familiar problems, as the people of the MST have done. The members of the MST, while recognizing many of the organization's limitations, dare to believe that it can provide the impetus for much broader change that would involve all of society.

This book is a history of the MST, but it is also a reflection both on what the organization has accomplished in the area of agrarian reform and on its chances for achieving its ambition for sweeping social transformations beyond the boundaries of the land itself.

# Chronology

*Some Important Dates in Brazilian and MST History*

1500  Pedro Álvares Cabral is the first European to sight and land on Brazilian territory.

1530  First Portuguese expedition to colonize Brazil.

1534–1536  Portuguese king grants land in Brazil to twelve "captains," beginning tradition of large estates and plantations.

1549  First centralized government in Brazil founded in Salvador da Bahia under Tomé de Souza.

1697  Colonial planters and army destroy Palmares, a large, fortified *quilombo* (settlement of escaped slaves) founded nearly sixty-eight years earlier.

1763  Colonial capital of Brazil moved from Salvador da Bahia to Rio de Janeiro.

1808  Portuguese king and court move to Brazil to escape Napoleon, who occupies Portugal.

1822  Prince Pedro of Portugal remains in Brazil, declares it an independent empire, with himself as emperor, Pedro I.

1823  First Brazilian constitution proclaimed.

1850  New land law (*lei da terras*) makes it yet more difficult for small farmers to obtain land.

1888  Slavery abolished.

1889 Emperor Pedro II (1840–1889) dethroned by the army; creation of the first Brazilian republic.

1891 New constitution gives states power to write their own land laws.

1897 Destruction of Canudos, a settlement of rural poor, by the fourth armed force sent against it, and death of its leader, Antônio Conselheiro.

1912–1915 Revolt in the *Contestado* in Rio Grande do Sul; João Maria, "the Monk," leads peasant farmers and rural poor in protest against exclusion from land conceded to United States investors.

1924–1927 Young army officer Luis Carlos Prestes, later head of the Brazilian Communist Party, leads revolutionary column through rural Brazil, is defeated by force organized by planters.

1930 Revolt brings Getúlio Vargas to power, which he holds until deposed in 1945 (he holds power again 1950–1954).

1955 First Peasant League established in Pernambuco.

1961 National capital moved to new city of Brasília. Election and resignation of President Jânio Quadros. Vice-President João Goulart becomes president.

1962 Legalization of rural labor unions.

1963 President Goulart proposes land reform, which fails to get the two-thirds vote needed in Congress; he submits a more modest proposal in 1964.

1964 Brazilian military deposes Goulart and takes power.

1968 Institutional Act No. 5 establishes greatly increased dictatorial powers.

1974 Rapid economic growth, aka "the Brazilian miracle," falters and begins decline.

1975 Conference of Brazilian Bishops (CNBB) establishes Pastoral Commission on Lands (CPT), largely in response to land conflicts in the Amazon region.

1975 Widespread protests over death of journalist Vládimir Herzog.

1977 Student strikes and call for restoration of political liberties by prominent businessmen and industrialists.

1978 Strike of *metalurgicos*, workers in the automobile and related industries in the state of São Paulo; first major challenge to military regime.

1978–1979 First land occupations in various states that will lead to the formation of the MST (Movimento dos Trabalhadores Rurais Sem-Terra); includes occupations at Brilhante, Macali, and Encruzilhada Natalino.

1983 Workers' Party (PT) formed.

1984 Families at Encruzilhada Natalino win land. First national organizing meeting of MST, Cascavel, Paraná.

1985 First National Congress of MST, Curitiba, Paraná. Military leaves power; civilian Tancredo Neves becomes president, dies. Vice President José Sarney becomes president.

1985–1988 National political debate over provisions of new constitution, including land reform provisions, which languish.

1988 Adoption of new constitution. Chico Mendes assassinated.

1990 Second National MST Congress, with over five thousand delegates attending.

1990–1992 Fernando Collor is president.

1992 MST creates a national confederation of agrarian reform cooperatives to work on production issues.

1992–1994 Former vice-president Itamar Franco is president (takes office after Collor impeached).

1994–2002 Fernando Henrique Cardoso is president.

1995 Third National MST Congress; the MST adopts a new motto, "Agrarian Reform: Everyone's Struggle," and takes its message to the cities.

1996 On April 17, nineteen MST members are killed during a peaceful march to the governor's office in the state of Pará.

1997 After marching for over two months, one thousand MST members enter Brasília on April 17 and are welcomed by tens of thousands of supporters.

2000 MST's Fourth National Congress; over eleven thousand people attend.

2002 Luis Inácio da Silva, "Lula," is elected as Brazil's first working-class president.

# Glossary

## Acronyms

**CEB** Comunidade Eclesial do Base; Christian Ecclesiastical Base Community

**CNBB** Conferência Nacional dos Bispos do Brasil; National Conference of Bishops

**CNS** Conselho Nacional de Seringueiros; National Rubber Tappers' Union

**CPT** Comissão Pastoral das Terras; Pastoral Commission on Lands

**FAO** Food and Agricultural Organization of the United Nations

**FETAPE** Federação de Trabalhadores na Agricultura de Pernambuco; Rural Trade Union of Pernambuco

**FUNAI** Fundação Nacional do Índio; National Indian Foundation

**INCRA** Instituto Nacional de Colonização e Reforma Agrária; National Institute for Colonization and Land Reform

**IMF** International Monetary Fund

**MST** Movimento dos Trabalhadores Rurais Sem-Terra; Landless Workers' Movement

**PNRA** Plano Nacional de Reforma Agrária; National Plan for Agrarian Reform

**PT** Partido dos Trabalhadores; Workers' Party

**UDR** União Democrática Rural; Rural Democratic Union

# Portuguese Terms

abertura: a policy of political "opening"

acampado: encampment dweller

agreste: transition zone in Brazil's Northeast

agrovila: small rural village

animação: fun activities

assentamento: settlement

bolsa escola: school scholarship policy

caboclo: mixed-race person

chimarrão: large decorated gourd in which erva mate is brewed

despachante: intermediary used to expedite business transactions

distensão: "loosening up" of the military dictatorship

erva mate: mildly caffeinated tea

favela: urban slum

fazenda: rural estate

fazendeiro: rural landowner

garimpeiro: gold prospector

gaúcho: cowboy; inhabitant of Rio Grande do Sul

grilagem: land fraud; named for a technique using crickets (*grilos*) to give new documents an antique look; grilado: fraudulently claimed

jagunço: hired gunman

latifúndio: large rural landholding

morador: resident of a plantation

mística: MST collective entertainment and theater

município: county

queimando o arquivo: "burning the archives," a technique of land fraud involving destroying land title archives; more broadly, killing anyone for the sake of eliminating witnesses in court cases

quilombo: settlement of runaway slaves

ribeirinho: river dweller

saque: incidence of looting

sem-terra: without land; a landless person, or landess people collectively

sertão: arid interior zone of the Northeast

zona da mata: coastal forest zone of the Northeast

José and Anir Placotnik, veterans of the MST from its earliest days,
with a statuette of the Brazilian saint Dona Aparecida, a campaign sticker
for Lula and a *chimarrão*.

## CHAPTER ONE

# Fulfilling a Promise

## The Beginnings of the Landless Movement
## in Rio Grande Do Sul

FOR NEARLY A WEEK BEFORE THE FESTIVAL, José and Anir Placotnik and their three daughters work to prepare the feast. They start
by selecting two cattle for slaughter. As the day of the festival approaches, neighbors of the Placotnik family begin to lend a hand, helping cut and collect the firewood that will be necessary for the long day's
barbecue. Using homemade ladders, teenaged boys and girls put up
lines of colorful pennants around the picnic grounds. Women count
the sausages and wheels of cheese they have made in previous months
and select some of the best to bring to the festival. They will also bring
fruit and jams they have canned and vegetables they have put up in
vinegar. On the day of the party, they will make great mounds of potato
salad. The festival will honor Our Lady of the Apparition—Nossa Senhora da Aparecida—Brazil's national patron saint, whose existence became known in the eighteenth century, when fishermen fished a small
statute of Our Lady from a lake in what is now the state of São Paulo.

October is springtime here in Brazil's southernmost state, Rio
Grande do Sul; on this highland plateau the warm afternoons are a welcome relief from the cold and rainy days of the Southern Hemisphere's
winter. In Brazil's south, winter even brings an occasional dusting of

snow—national television programs periodically film the thin ice on the surface of small ponds to show the harsh miracle of cold weather to the majority of Brazilians, for whom such cold weather is nearly unimaginable. With winter past, October 12, the day of Our Lady, is a little like Easter, a celebration of the rebirth that is evident as the plants begin to flourish again and the animals give birth. The soil warms and is ready to receive the seeds for the bean and corn crops to come months later.

This is lovely country, the kind a farmer from anywhere in the world would instantly desire: a well-watered plateau cut by ancient stream-ways, with softly rounded hillsides planted to row crops and intensely green woods in the creek bottoms. Here and there, forest remnants also spill across the tops of some of the ridges. The Araucarian pine, with its long needles and limbs jutting sharply up, the longest branches at the top, adds a touch distinctive of South America's southern regions. The soil is good: a rich topsoil of six to twelve inches, more in the bottom-lands, with bedrock as much as twenty to thirty feet down. Springtime means planting crops and calving, so it is a busy time for these farmers, but there is still time to express faith in the harvests that will come by feasting on what has been saved from the last harvest. There is time to sing and dance as the promise of the eternal return of life and the sea-son in this rich land is fulfilled.

José Placotnik is fulfilling another promise in preparing the feast, a promise he made to Dona Aparecida—that if she answered his prayer, he would hold a yearly feast in her honor. His promise and its fulfill-ment is the story of one family's participation in what would become a much larger story of transformation in Brazilian rural life.

José's Portuguese-speaking neighbors cannot pronounce his Russian-Polish name, so they learned to call him by the similar-sounding nick-name, Pacote (pah-*koh*-chi), meaning "package." Though there's no deeper reason for his having been given the name, one inevitably thinks of him as a package of enthusiasm and energy, with a high intensity that shines through his brown eyes and is expressed in his normal walk, which is nearly jogging speed. He is small and wiry and graceful in his self-assured movements. Pacote's paternal grandfather came to Brazil from Russia, probably from an area bordering on Poland, a few years after the Russian Revolution of 1917. Like many other European immi-

grants, he was looking for one of the small farm plots the Brazilian government was dangling to attract immigrants to what was then considered a frontier of European settlement.[1]

Pacote's grandfather did eventually find a piece of land, and he married a local woman who had strong roots in the region's indigenous
communities. The land was not sufficient in quantity to be divided for
children and grandchildren, so Pacote's parents had to work as day laborers, rent land and sharecrop. It was a life of poverty and insecurity,
as landowners forced sharecroppers to move frequently so that they
would establish no claims to the land. It was foolish for a sharecropper
to invest in the land, because a barn built would have to be abandoned
and an orchard planted would not yield fruit to the family who nurtured it. Under such conditions, farmers had little incentive to invest in
the care of the soil.

A sharecropper can't afford to leave land fallow and must usually
plant what the landowner considers most profitable, regardless of its
consequences for the soil. Just as in the sharecropping country of the
American South, environmental degradation was widespread here in
southern Brazil, undermining the productive quality of the land over
decades and generations. The sharecroppers' crops often failed to meet
the nutritional needs of the family. Poor harvests meant hunger—and
devastating debt, because it was up to the sharecropper to finance all
the costs of putting in the crop, cultivating it and harvesting it. After
the harvest, a large share—usually half—went to the landowner.

To make matters worse, the Brazilian government was promoting
investment by large syndicates from Japan, Europe and the US, which
were interested in highly mechanized, chemical-dependent wheat, corn
and soybean production in Brazil's southern states. These syndicates
were buying up land, soaking up the available agricultural credit and
producing local surpluses that drove crop prices down, thus forcing
small farm families from the land.[2] It was doubly difficult for sharecroppers to obtain land when even those family farmers who already
owned land were losing it. Pacote, like most of his friends, looked for a
way to escape from the miserable treadmill existence of sharecropping.
It was this search that would eventually lead to the promise he made to
Dona Aparecida, to the special and terrible circumstances that led him
to make it and, finally, to the fulfillment of his promise.

## Decades of Dictatorship
*Repression, Religion and Resistance*

Pacote grew up in the repressive atmosphere of a military dictatorship, a brutal national government such as Brazil had seldom experienced.[3] The military took power in 1964 in response to fears by Brazilian elites that Brazil's poor were finally getting organized, demanding land reform and expanded rights for urban workers. Some of the peasant and worker organizations used the rhetoric of socialism or communism and the Brazilian Communist Party played a role—though usually a minor one—in some of the unions and peasant coalitions.

In retrospect, it is clear that the demands of these poor peoples' movements were modest and their organizations weak. The Communist Party's role was minimal, and in many cases, it actually slowed down or moderated more radical organizations and activists, as the party had become a sluggish, bureaucratic organization with a very long-range vision that made it uninterested in immediate revolutionary possibilities. But in the Cold War climate of the time—and in the wake of the rise to power of Fidel Castro in Cuba—even modest initiatives by the poor loomed large and threatening in the eyes of conservative Brazilian landowners, businessmen and military officers. Sharing their fears, the United States government connived with the military to plan a coup d'etat to overthrow President João Goulart who, as vice-president, had come to power upon President Janio Quadros's resignation. Goulart's indecisiveness and occasional ineptitude, like that of his predecessor, Quadros, compounded the fears and confusion of Brazilians and facilitated the coup. Shortly after the introduction of a moderate land-reform program in the Brazilian Congress, the military struck, and President Goulart went into exile.

Immediately after the coup, the new military rulers of Brazil began to attack and dismantle peasant groups, trade unions and student organizations, imprisoning many of the organizations' leaders and exiling, torturing or executing many others. When protests against the military government took fire in 1968, the government became even more repressive, passing Institutional Act No. 5, which banned virtually all criticism and opposition to the government, suspending Brazilian citizens' few remaining civil liberties. Censorship of the press prior to publication was strict and thorough. Police and military intelligence organizations carried out fierce attacks on individuals and organizations; exile, imprisonment, torture and disappearance carried out by officials reached a fever pitch. Conventional politics hardly existed—the government set up an official political party and even established a government-controlled opposition party to present a thin and unconvincing façade of democracy. Brazilians learned to speak with caution. For more than a decade, a kind of collective hush ruled the public life of Brazilian cities. The government permitted public assembly only with special permission, and permission was granted sparingly. Political rallies and demonstrations were forbidden. The military did not flinch at using ghastly means to obtain information; in some cases, for example, police tortured children to obtain information from their parents.[4]

Some opponents of the regime engaged in urban guerrilla warfare, robbing banks to finance their activities and kidnapping diplomats, including the Swiss and American ambassadors, to obtain the release of political prisoners. Although these actions garnered widespread attention and a certain admiration from many Brazilians impressed by the courage, élan and imagination of the urban guerrillas, they did little, if anything, to build a broader base of support for opposition to the regime. One undeniable accomplishment of some of the kidnappings, however, was the rescue of political activists from prison and possible death at the hands of the regime. Some of those who were rescued would once again become active in Brazilian leftist politics after the military regime began to lose its grip on the country in the 1980s.[5]

While the urban guerillas in particular managed to demonstrate that determined resistance to the regime still lived, none of the guerrilla activities ever succeeded in convincing large numbers of people to enlist, nor did they constitute a serious threat to the stability of the regime. Other groups attempted acts of guerrilla warfare from the countryside, the most significant of which took place deep in the Amazon, in the Araguaia region of the states of Pará and Mato Grosso; this rebellion was based on the *foco* theory popular among some Latin American revolutionaries at the time, which held that a small number of revolutionaries could establish a base in a rural area and gradually build support sufficient to challenge national goverments. The Araguaia guerrillas'

plans relied on a naive belief in their ability to enlist peasant collabora-
tors from a region in which most of the peasants were newly arrived
colonists who were poorly supported by the government or other organizations. While the colonists were frequently full of anger and
grievances, they were also often completely dependent upon ruthless
local political bosses, mine and timber mill owners and wealthy landholders. They possessed little sense of community, had weak social networks and had little basis for collective action.

The guerrillas themselves were mostly young city people, some of
whom had studied in Cuba. Most lacked the toughness of mind and
body needed to undertake the incredible task they had set out to accomplish. The guerrillas' connections in Cuba were unable or unwilling to give any help beyond elementary training for some of the leaders.
It was also unclear how the guerrillas would have translated their local
rebellion into a wider national one, given that the region of their activities was a thinly settled agricultural frontier separated by many hundreds of miles from the nearest significant population centers and by
nearly two thousand miles from the cities of the Southeast—São Paulo,
Belo Horizonte, Rio de Janeiro—the center of Brazilian population,
economy and political control.[6]

The activities of both urban and rural guerrillas met with fierce repression, although the details of what occurred were never revealed
publicly, despite continued efforts by relatives of the *desaparecidos
politicos* (people who disappeared after being seized by authorities). Between the small, fractionalized, underground movement of opposition
and the farcical "official" opposition party, Brazilians had very few ways
to express any ideas, interests or hopes that were not consistent with
those of the regime itself.

THE CHURCH: A REFUGE FOR RESISTANCE

One of the only refuges for independent thought and discussion began
to take shape during the mid-1960s and 1970s.[7] In the 1960s, encouraged by Pope John XXIII, the Roman Catholic Church underwent a period of self-examination, reform and renewal. Latin American bishops
began facing the facts that in many Western Hemisphere countries, the
church was moribund, and that it was often closely associated with the
most reactionary forces in Latin American society. More and more,

young people looked elsewhere for inspiration and comfort: recruitment of priests became ever more difficult. Protestant churches were able to convert Catholics in great numbers, recruiting masses of people long alienated from religion of any kind. Often, it seemed that the church was simply standing in the shadow of dictatorial regimes, quietly offering its support, with little dynamic life of its own.

In Brazil, the Catholic Church faced many difficult challenges. Although more Roman Catholics live in Brazil than in any other country on Earth, the number of people who describe themselves as Catholics reveals neither the health of the church, nor the vitality of the religion. In the sixteenth century, the Portuguese monarchy had obtained a special privilege from the Vatican allowing Portuguese kings to appoint parish priests and church officials directly. The emperors of independent Brazil, who succeeded the colonial regime, maintained the same right until the formation of a republic in 1889. The result was the development of a church that was unusually compromised with secular authority and therefore discredited in the eyes of much of the Brazilian population.

Well into the twentieth century, priests were very often just household dependents of large landowners, and bishops the handmaidens of the collective interests of the same property holders. The crisis of confidence in the church and the lack of a competent priesthood were such severe problems that, in the latter half of the nineteenth century, the church sponsored a movement of lay preachers to spread the faith. One of these, Antônio Conselheiro (discussed in chapter 2), would become the famous leader of a rebellion of the rural poor in Brazil's Northeast.

Indigenous religions, African religions brought over by slaves and even European spiritism—based on visitations of the dead through mediums—competed with surprising success for the spiritual loyalties of Brazilians before Protestantism began its own assault on Brazilian Catholicism.

Throughout the twentieth century, the Brazilian Catholic Church looked for ways to enliven and strengthen its role in national life. The reformism of Pope John XXIII, which flowered in the international assemblages from 1962 to 1965 (known as Vatican II), began to delineate a path the church could travel to reach a new status in Brazilian national life and build new affection among Brazil's people.

Socially minded and ecumenical priests began to organize what they called Christian Ecclesiastical Base Communities (Comunidades Eclesiais de Base or CEBs). For some, the objective was to provide a place where Catholics could come together and celebrate mass without the presence of a priest. For others, CEBs provided a place for Catholics, especially the poor, to reflect on their lives and the meaning of the gospel and to begin to explore ways to live that meaning.

By the time the Brazilian military was consolidating its power in the late 1960s, the term "liberation theology" had begun to be used widely throughout Latin America. Liberation theology offered an interpretation of Christianity that was potentially revolutionary: a call for social justice in the name of Christ. It would lead to meetings of bishops and cardinals who voted that the church adopt what they called a "preferential option for the poor."

CEBs began to be one of the few—and perhaps the most important—places where political discussion could occur outside of families or groups of intimate friends. Although there were still some limits within the CEBs, liberation theology began to push those limits. The concept of a "social gospel" suggested that a greater measure of social equality and justice were the commands of Christian conscience and not necessarily the offspring of communist ideology. The form of the liberation theology message—its language and biblical foundation—and the places where it occurred—CEB meetings in chapels, rectories or church schools—were difficult targets for a conservative military government that had been supported by the church and that made much of its defense of religion against godless communism.

The teachings and actions of the parish priests and a group of bishops sympathetic to the cause of land reform by no means represented the official position of the Roman Catholic Church in Brazil. Throughout the military regime, the Primate of Brazil—the cardinal chosen by the Vatican to head the Brazilian Church—and the upper hierarchy of the church were almost entirely and very publicly dedicated to a position not unlike the one they had promoted for centuries: obedience to secular authority, emphasis on individual salvation in preference to a social gospel and the sanctity of private property, understood as the endorsement of the existing distribution of private property. However, the conservative position of the church as an institution was to an ex-

tent double-edged: it gave support to the military regime and its repressive policies, but it also made it difficult for the regime to question
the authority of the church over its individual priests. No matter how
difficult the internal debates within the church between conservatives
and progressives, progressive priests certainly found these disagreements preferable to prison, torture, exile or murder, any of which they
might have suffered without the institutional protection of the church.
Of course, some priests suffered exile and assassination in spite of the
church's protection. For example, the priest who was the assistant to
Dom Helder e Camara, the progressive bishop of Recife in the Northeast, was hanged from a tree on a heavily traveled road on the outskirts
of the city. Foreign priests fighting on behalf of landless people in the
Amazon were in some cases deported. The balance between the protection afforded by the church and the risks taken by outspoken priests
was a delicate and difficult thing.

Increasingly, rural CEBs and priests began to focus on Brazil's landholding system as the source of injustice that offended Christian sensi-
bilities. The inequality of land ownership had been a major factor in
creating the enormous differences in wealth and welfare in Brazil.[8] Furthermore, a profoundly corrupt and violent political culture was built
on the inequalities of landowning. A rural regime of powerful landowners ruled the countryside and often the nation, with a stingy paternalism in one hand and a gun in the other, for over four hundred years.
Large landowners held life-and-death power over the rural poor, routinely seizing their land. Landowners also dominated local courts and
police, usually ruling over state and national governments, virtually
immune from punishment. Rural property owners often carried out or
ordered assassinations to guarantee their power; far from being punished, they were rewarded with favorable court opinions and protected
by the police from retribution. In the year 2001, more than one landowner proudly told us that the main law in his region was "Law 44,"
the law of the forty-four caliber revolver.

People who gathered in CEB meetings in the 1960s and 1970s read
the Old Testament book of Exodus, seeing in the Jews an oppressed
people who found a road to liberation. They read Jesus' Sermon on the
Mount and its condemnation of injustice, seeing in Christ's attack on
the temple money changers a message of rebellion against capitalist

exploiters. Perhaps just as important, in the CEB meetings, priests sat with parishioners in circles of folding chairs, often with no clerical garb to distinguish them, stimulating discussion rather than engaging in catechism and sermonizing. These priests encouraged people to think of themselves as a community of believers, rather than a flock of sheep led by a pastor.

When Zezinho (pronounced zay-*zeen*-you), a friend of Pacote's, went to his first CEB meeting, he was amazed at the free-ranging discussion. As the meeting broke up, however, Zezinho complained to a companion that the priest who had invited him was not present, and that there was no priest at all at the meeting.

His companion said, "But a priest is among us—that fellow over there in blue jeans; he just isn't wearing his collar."

Zezinho felt even more amazed that a priest had taken part in the discussion as an ordinary member of the group. "For me," he told us, "a priest was someone distant in the pulpit or someone you approached nervously and with reverence, not someone you simply shared ideas with as an equal. The very idea [of a priest participating as an equal] was shocking and forced me to think very deeply about many things."[9]

As shocking as the CEBs could be to some people, their success in Brazil was not surprising. The love of conversation and sociability is strong in Brazil; the CEBs fit comfortably within that tradition. Here in Rio Grande do Sul, the special facilitator of conversation is the *chimarrão*, a large decorated gourd in which *erva mate* is brewed. This is not the small, individual-sized matte gourd of the Argentine *gaucho*, but rather a thing the size of an American football, often requiring two hands for a safe pass from one person to another. As the chimarrão is passed around and as each person takes a sip from the metal-tipped straw, the mild caffeine animates the group, and the shared ritual brings people closer together.

In the uplands of Rio Grande do Sul, the chimarrão sometimes seems like the main preoccupation at social gatherings, even during meetings where arguments over serious matters threaten to boil over; two- and four-liter plastic thermos bottles are filled with hot water and carried about to refill the gourds repeatedly, and somewhere nearby is a stove or fire where pots of hot water are being heated to replenish the thermos. Some people carry specially constructed wooden chimarrão stands with them in their cars or trucks, because the round bottom of the gourd makes it difficult to put it to rest on a flat surface without spilling tea or risking damage to the gourd.

For people here, the chimarrão is the physical expression of a deep unspoken agreement. To refuse to share the hot tea is to break the fundamental code that says that there is equality among members of the group and that unhurried conversation is an obligation required for group membership. Cities, counties and even commercial firms in southern Brazil often use the chimarrão as a logo; in homes it is displayed as though it were a holy statue, like the centerpiece of a domestic altar. In Rio Grande do Sul, the chimarrão could well have been made the symbol for both the form and the intention of the CEBs; later, it would be made the symbol of the state federation of the landless movement that grew partially out of the CEBs.

The chimarrão was not the only tradition that fostered the purpose of organizing people for agrarian reform. One member of Pacote's community reported that he had gone to confession after a lengthy absence. In the confessional box, he was eager to unburden himself of the many sins he had committed. As he went on about his transgressions, the priest interrupted him a little impatiently, "Yes, yes, we will deal with that, but why don't you come to a meeting at the church this week of people who are talking about getting land for themselves?" The man's reaction to this was shock and, for a time, a mixture of discomfort with the priest's having stepped out of his established role and enthusiasm for what he found when he attended the meeting the priest had recommended.

As CEBs flourished, gaining confidence and strength during the 1970s, other sources of critical thought and action were also growing. Within the church, the Catholic student movement increasingly defined itself in terms consistent with liberation theology. Brazilian theologians and students began to explore more openly and explicitly the commonalities among Christianity, Marxism and other forms of socialist thought. Some Catholic universities, such as the Pontifical Catholic University in Rio de Janeiro, gave aid and shelter to neighborhood and union organizers sought by the police. Radical priests, some of them Spaniards and Italians, became prominent figures in struggles over land rights at the remote, ragged edge of agricultural frontiers in the Amazon.

The involvement of the church in these battles led to the formation in the city of Goiânia in 1975 of the national Pastoral Commission on Lands (*Comissão Pastoral das Terras*, or CPT). The CPT would play a key role in the subsequent movement for national agrarian reform.

## THE DICTATORSHIP WEAKENS

In the cities, the violent repression practiced by the government began to reach scandalous levels that tore open the curtain of silence. The death of a widely respected journalist, Vládimir Herzog, while under interrogation on October 25, 1975 in the city of São Paulo, aroused a formerly supine press to the defense of their colleague. One of Brazil's leading daily newspapers, *O Estado de São Paulo*, openly challenged the censorship of the regime for the first time over the Herzog case, making censorship more and more difficult for the regime to enforce. During the standoff with the newspaper's publisher, tens of thousands of people in São Paulo marched in defiance of the police to protest Herzog's murder. Much of the country was stunned and excited to learn that such demonstrations were possible. Open discussion of the government's policies of repression through torture and murder broke out into the open. Once exposed to public view, the issue could not easily be put away.

Open political opposition and internal splits in the regime began to plague the government. Student strikes in 1977 signaled a renewal of a traditional but long-quiescent source of opposition to conservative forces. In 1977, two thousand businessmen meeting in Rio de Janeiro signed a statement in favor of restoring political liberties, and in mid-1978, eight prominent industrialists signed a document calling for social justice through a renewal of democracy. In 1978, fifty thousand autoworkers went on strike to demand significant improvements in wages and working conditions—virtually the only union to do so in nearly fifteen years. General Ernesto Geisel, who became president in 1974, had promised gradual democratization, and it appeared to be happening. But the *distensão*, or loosening up, that he had promised had gone out of the government's control, and Geisel responded with new repressive measures. In the changed political atmosphere, more repression only aroused greater opposition.[10]

Under the military regime, Brazil had experienced very rapid economic growth, tripling the size of its economy in fifteen years. While this growth came at a high social and environmental price and greatly increased the already enormous distance between the rich and the poor, it succeeded in making Brazil the eighth-largest industrial economy in the world (in the 1990s, it moved back and forth between eighth and tenth largest). Central to the growth of Brazilian industry were the foreign-owned automobile factories concentrated in the industrial towns ringing the city of São Paulo, producing close to a million cars per year. When the autoworkers went on strike, the military government's economic strategy of growth on the backs of repressed workers was put at risk. The strikers' defiance led people to begin to question openly the legitimacy of the military regime.[11]

Quickly, the autoworkers' strike became a symbol for poor people's pent-up demands for a greater share of the benefits of Brazil's economic growth. At the same time, the strike represented a symbolic victory for the right to raise a voice in opposition to the military government, as well as the coalition of foreign and domestic businessmen and landowners who supported it. Under the leadership of Luis Inácio da Silva, known as Lula, the auto union strikers won the active support of hundreds of thousands of people, who marched with the strikers and supported them with food and money. (In October, 2002, Lula would be elected president of Brazil.)

Although even critics had been willing to grant the military regime some credit for the rapid economic growth that existed until the mid-1970s, the subsequent economic slowdown began to highlight deep vulnerabilities in the strategy that had produced the regime. The promise of profitable investment based on maximum exploitation of labor and resources ran into severe difficulties and outright contradictions. Without greater expenditures on education, the labor force remained poorly qualified for more advanced production tasks. Without better health care, workers were often absent from work or sick on the job. Changes in international markets hit Brazil especially hard because when workers were paid so poorly they could buy little, which constrained the growth of the domestic market.

Rampant, unregulated resource exploitation led to massive waste of minerals, timber and soils, robbing Brazil of much of its potential productivity. The regime had taken advertisements in American newspapers inviting investors to visit "Brazil, your pollution haven." The promised lack of environmental regulation had led to horrendous environmental nightmares, such as the valley of Cubitão, known as "the Valley of Death," often called the most polluted place on Earth. Brazilians were increasingly concerned and angry about these problems and increasingly resentful of the censorship and repression that made it impossible to discuss the problems openly, much less resolve them.

Economic growth could no longer excuse social repression, which for a time it had seemed to do. President Ernesto Geisel, a general from Rio Grande do Sul, recognized that holding onto power meant forging some compromise with the demands for democracy and permitting a measure of social justice. In the late 1970s, his government constructed a policy of "decompression" and political "opening" (*abertura*), designed to maintain the stability of the regime. Limited as it was, the abertura policy would allow for a variety of organizations and protests that formerly would have been violently crushed.

## The Beginnings of Agrarian Reform in Rio Grande do Sul[12]

Among the movements that had been simmering under the military regime's repressive surface was the movement for indigenous rights. As in the United States, the westward course of European settlement of Brazil had eliminated hundreds of Indian cultures and severely undermined hundreds more over several centuries. The military government's policy of rapid expansion into the Brazilian Amazon region accelerated the process by threatening the lives and cultures of many Indian groups who had enjoyed some degree of isolation from industrial society and Brazilian national culture in the late twentieth century. Many of these groups, often with help from Catholic priests or Catholic religious orders and with inspiration from a rising worldwide movement of indigenous peoples, began to fight against the further incursion of Brazilian settlers.

The indigenous rights movement in the Amazon also gave courage and support to indigenous groups that had been struggling with other Brazilians since the beginning of the colonial era. Among those outside the Amazon were the tribes of the southern states, some of them brought into Jesuit missions in the seventeenth and eighteenth centuries and then left to fend for themselves when the monarchy expelled the Jesuits from Brazil. In the South, the expulsion of the Jesuits touched off an impatient rush by Portuguese and Spanish colonists to seize land and resources.

One of these southern groups were the Kaingang, Guaraní speakers, some of whom lived on a reserve in the highlands of the state of Rio Grande do Sul and along the Paraná River. The tribe had learned a good deal about European culture, for better and for worse, from the Jesuits, who had succeeded in inducing some of the Kaingang into the missions; they learned more when the Jesuits were expelled in the 1760s and expeditions of slave hunters (who operated in spite of a ban on Indian slavery), prospectors and adventurers took advantage of the Jesuit absence to practice a variety of all-too-familiar brutalities on the mission tribes. Through their resistance, the Kaingang gained a reputation as a fierce and independent people. In the twentieth century they nonetheless had allowed and even invited non-Indian settlers to move onto their reserve, charging rent for the land. Some settlers had found it a happy arrangement, and the Kaingang also seemed to be pleased enough to receive cash rents. However, an increasingly large group of non-Indians moved onto the reserve without making any such arrangements with the tribe, paying nothing for the use of the land. A government survey undertaken jointly by various agencies showed that in 1976, 288 families were paying rents under contract, while 682 families had no formal relationship or documentation to justify their presence in the Indian reserve.

From time to time, individual settlers had been expelled from the reserve when the Kaingang had judged that they were violating formal or informal understandings.[13] In the 1970s, an entrepreneurial-minded chieftain named Xangrê was elected to head the tribe. To take advantage of the rich resources of Araucanian pine and other forest trees on the reserve, he established a sawmill. Once the Indians began to commercially exploit the forest for timber, as others had done illegally for years, the Kaingang's accusations that the non-Indian renters were removing and selling trees without bringing them to the Indian mill began to mount. Also, the Indians believed that settlers who came to the mill to buy lumber often paid the mill for a few posts or boards but took away entire pickup loads of lumber. Others remembered that the settlers were beginning to use too many pesticides, poisoning local streams and lakes, killing the fish and birds that were a major part of the Kaingang diet.

One of the former settlers on Indian land, Eleu Shepp, a tall, grizzled man, actively participated in subsequent events and is now an MST-elected representative of his relatively remote community in Sarandí.[14] He remembers the conflicts vividly and believes that it was the misdeeds of the settlers that aroused the hostility of the Kaingang and inflamed the situation. He believed the Indians were justified in their actions, but other settlers felt the accusations laid against them were part of the manipulations of the ambitious new chieftain.

In any case, tensions between settlers and the Kaingang grew. A Catholic Church–based mission group helped the Kaingang force the non-Indians off the reserve. The Brazilian government's Indian agency, FUNAI (the National Indian Foundation, Fundação Nacional do Índio), temporized, attempting to forestall the removals. The Kaingang took matters into their own hands and attacked farms that belonged to the settlers, using bows and arrows, slingshots and a few revolvers and shotguns, burning farm buildings and crops and threatening violence against the families. The expulsion began when the Kaingang burned seven schools run by the settlers. The Kaingang drove all the settlers from the reserve. Some settlers and Indians were hurt in the conflicts.

One group of settlers arrived on a rain-drenched night in the house of Padre Arnildo Fritzen near the church in Ronda Alta. Padre Arnildo had more than official pastoral reasons to be receptive to these settlers. His grandfather had arrived from Germany in Rio Grande do Sul in the late nineteenth century and had managed to acquire land and to ensure that every one of his twelve children received his or her own parcel. The frontier was beginning to close by the mid-twentieth century, however, and to exacerbate the situation greatly, in the mid-1960s agriculture in the region began to shift into the hands of highly capitalized large operators and foreign syndicates, displacing small farm families. Padre Arnildo's generation of the Fritzen family was unable to acquire any land for themselves. Arnildo's father became chronically ill, and the whole family worked in the fields to earn their living, but "everything we earned went to the doctors and the hospitals." With the support of his mother, he entered various seminaries to study for the priesthood, but, as he says, "I was expelled from one after another."

Padre Arnildo remembers that he "always was revolted by the antidemocratic situation" that led to the expulsion of family farmers from the land and by the way *fazendeiros* (a term that can mean rancher, planter, farmer or rural landowner) owned the local hospitals, which they "used to exploit their workers and earn money with which to buy more land." His rebellious attitude had made it doubly hard for the young son of a poor landless family to finish his education as a priest.

On that rainy night, there were nearly fifty people seeking shelter in Padre Arnildo's house, but even in the house they continued to suffer from the cold and damp. Most houses in Rio Grande do Sul have little or no heating or insulation, even though in the highlands temperatures frequently hover not much above freezing. People were huddled together for warmth, many of them crying. Padre Arnildo asked if he could read to them from the Bible.

"I read to them the most critical texts, Exodus, chapters three through seven." It is in these chapters that the Lord commands Moses to lead the Israelites out of bondage in Egypt and assures a hesitant Moses that he will be given the strength and eloquence to be able to do so. When the Pharaoh strikes back against the rebellious Israelites, the Lord begins to send the seven plagues against the Egyptians. It is easy to imagine the power of such passages as this, from Exodus, chapter 3: "And the Lord said: I have surely seen the oppression of my people who are in Egypt, and have heard their cry because of their taskmasters, for I know their sorrows. So I have come down to deliver them out of the hand of the Egyptians, and to bring them up from that land to a good and large land, to a land flowing with milk and honey. . . ." Or, from chapter 5: "Thus says the Lord God of Israel: 'Let my people go, that they may hold a feast to me in the wilderness.'"

Nearly a quarter of a century later, Padre Arnildo recalls, "People took great strength from this [reading]. I also read them the story of David and Goliath. Those are the two essential texts: those chapters of Exodus and the story of David and Goliath."[15]

However, the situation remained unsettled, and the best path of action was unclear. Congregating in improvised camps along the roadside in 1979, angry settlers talked of launching a counterattack on the Indians. The government saw danger in the situation but also opportunity: it was eager to serve its own purposes by sending settlers to the Amazon. The government was not yet ready to actually send them there, however, and the settlers were not eager to go. Seeing the desperation and restlessness of those displaced by the Kaingang action, the government moved some families to a site normally used for animal fairs, near the capital city of Porto Alegre, until further decisions and arrangements could be made. Many of the families felt abandoned and demoralized, with one complaining, "We felt no better than cows left out in the pasture, without even anyone to bring us into the barn at night."[16] After some months of deliberation, the government convinced about half of the settlers driven off the Kaingang reserve to move to government colonization projects in the Amazon in the states of Mato Grosso, Rondônia and Pará.

The other half of the settlers were reluctant to set out on this adventure—as we shall see, they had good reasons for their hesitancy. Instead, some of the people in this group took steps to arm themselves in preparation for a reoccupation of Kaingang land. Before they acted however, local priests and political activists arrived in the camps, asking that people reflect more deeply on their problems.

Among the activists were three men: a professor from the federal university in Porto Alegre, a rural union leader and an agronomist named João Pedro Stédile, who was employed by the state government. At first, the priests, who had already been working with landless people in the region, were suspicious of these men. However, Stédile and the others were eager to work with Padre Arnildo, who was already well known among the settlers: Padre Arnildo had been working with families in the region since 1977 through the Pastoral Commission on Lands (CPT).

As Padre Arnildo had his troubles with church authorities, Stédile was also walking a thin line, doing his job as a state agronomist during his work hours and, during off hours, working to identify land appropriate for expropriation and organizing landless people. On one hand, the state would not have approved of his work as a partisan for the landless, and, on the other, the priests and many of the settlers were suspicious of anyone working for the state. Stédile and Padre Arnildo used a code when talking on the phone: for example, "I'm sending you two boxes of hymnals" meant "I'm sending you two settlers." When Stédile went to the rectory to speak with Padre Arnildo, as a precaution he parked his car, marked with the insignia of the state, in the garage of the padre's residence so that it wouldn't be seen.[17]

The secular activists and priests quickly overcame their suspicions and found that they shared a common understanding of the problem. They began to discuss with the settlers the sources of their chronic need for land and their exclusion from it. The settlers began to see parallels between their own situation and that of the Indians, as both had been systematically pressured to make a living out of less and less land, while wealthy landowners monopolized most of the best acreage. As a local historian of the movement wrote, "The deepening of the contradictions then resulted in the confrontation between two segments of society that were socially, economically and politically marginalized: Indians and landless people. From this began again the fight for agrarian reform and for citizenship."[18]

## THE SETTLERS CONFRONT THE HISTORY OF LAND AND PROPERTY IN BRAZIL[19]

The people displaced from the reserve began to focus their attention on the enormous landholdings in the region and on the way in which these large landholdings reflected Brazil's national history and social problems. It is impossible to understand the depth of the problem the dispossessed families faced without understanding the history of land, land law and land fraud in Brazil. Even more important, without understanding this history, it is difficult to understand how the settlers would design a solution to their problems.

Many large properties had been acquired by means that ranged from dubious to outright illegal. Throughout Brazilian history, professional forgers and audacious amateurs produced a flood of false documents supporting ownership claims. A whole vocabulary had arisen to describe the many aspects of land fraud. One word, *grilagem*, was invented for the technique by which newly made false documents were placed in a closed box with crickets (*grilos*) whose chewing action and elimination would give the documents a look of antiquity. The word *grilagem* came to mean any attempt to acquire land through the use of fraud. In 2001, the Brazilian government used the term to describe its project to identify lands claimed fraudulently. It found that at least ninety-two million hectares, an area 50 percent greater than the total land surface of Central America, had been claimed by various fraudulent means.[20] The state of Mato Grosso, for example, had issued titles to more land than the surface area of the state. In the western part of the state of Bahia, large corporate farmers found that they were impeded in purchasing land by the fact that many preexisting titles were fraudulent, with land claimed by as many as four different "owners," all with supposedly legal documents in hand.[21]

Grilagem is only one kind of land fraud. Another way of acquiring land, especially in the first half of the twentieth century, was to burn the government land office where titles were registered. A famous incident of this sort occurred in southern Bahia in 1912, coincident with the rise to power of a new faction of landowners and export houses who used this method to erase many of the claims held by the older regional elite in a rapidly developing area. After the archives were burned, a bloody battle ensued involving landholding families, their paid gunmen and smallholders. *Queimando o arquivo* ("burning the archives") came to have the double meaning of actually burning papers and of murdering those who had long and stubborn memories. From there, the phrase came to apply more broadly to killing anyone for the sake of eliminating witnesses in court cases.[22]

It was even more common to invalidate land claims of potential smallholders or other rivals through the use of bureaucratic rules and procedures or through use of the opportunities created by the lack of adequate rules and procedures. For example, in the colonial period, landowners used the remarkable expedient of holding title to lands in which no actual boundary limits were specified. In the late eighteenth century, the crown attempted to reform land law by specifying the need for boundary delineation in title documents. As historian Warren Dean wrote, "It had been the practice to omit from the [title] petition all references to boundary and area!" The landowners who were in actual control of local administration resisted the reform, having "not the slightest desire that the state fix their boundaries and legitimize their land claims. They preferred uncertainty, the better to encroach upon public lands and the land of others. Uncertainty led to violence, on a scale that wracked the interior and challenged the authority of the crown . . . the landowners preferred bloodshed to the stability of clear title. . . ."[23]

In the nineteenth century, although the independent government of Brazil, known as the Empire of Brazil, was aware of the dangers of this situation inherited from the colonial era, the parliament did not pass any reforms that would successfully bring order or justice to the system. Indeed, a land law passed in 1850 only tipped the balance further in favor of the powerful and the fraudulent, to the extent that it was observed at all. With the declaration in 1889 of a republic that replaced Brazil's independent imperial government, the federal government passed land law into the hands of the states, and local political machines made up of landholders leaped at the chance to devise methods to increase their ability to grab land and hold it. In a 1976 study of more than thirty thousand land-title applications in the state of Bahia, virtually no land title applications were approved for smallholders; applications languished in the land office until the claim passed into the hands of powerful local landowners or foreign export houses. Even if smallholders could effectively occupy the land, put it to economic use as the law demanded, afford the survey and document fees required and file the application, they almost never succeeded in acquiring title. They lacked the essential metaphorical *pistola*, or pistol, in the usual form of a hired *despachante*, an intermediary who specialized in influence peddling and bureaucratic procedure. Despachantes were usually necessary to push title applications to completion. For those with real power and influence, it was easy to hire despachantes. However, sometimes the needed firepower of a "pistol" that could shoot straight through bureaucratic barriers could be achieved by a simple bribe or threat, without resorting to the despachante's services.[24]

Wherever legal or bureaucratic means failed to smooth the way for powerful landowners, the very real, nonmetaphorical pistol or rifle could do the job. Another rich vocabulary describes the hired gunmen who worked for landowners when the courts could not be enlisted to drive smallholders off the land. Note the number of names for this role listed in a Brazilian dictionary: *jagunço, cabra, cabra-de-peia, cacundeiro, curimbaba, guarda-costas, mumbava, peito-largo, pistoleiro, quarto-paus, sombra, satelite*. Some of these terms, like *guarda-costa*, or bodyguard (literally, back-guard), implied duties not necessarily related to intimidating land claimants, but many a guarda-costa has been assigned such tasks. *Cabra* and *jagunço*, along with the more prosaic *pistoleiro*, are the terms we have heard most often in the Brazilian countryside, where such men are frequent subjects of discussion.[25]

For the displaced people of Rio Grande do Sul, including Pacote and his family, and for the future national landless movement of Brazil, the essential feature of the fight for access to land has been summarized by an American student of Brazil, James Holston. After his study of Brazilian land law, Holston concluded that "[t]he Brazilian legal system aims neither to solve land conflicts justly nor to decide their merits through adjudication." Behind the seemingly hopeless confusion of Brazilian land law is "a set of intentions concerning its construction and application" that promote "extrajudicial" solutions that in turn "inevitably legalize usurpations of one sort or another." Holston defines the norm of the Brazilian land law as "the maintenance of privilege among those who possess extralegal powers to manage politics, bureaucracy and the historical record itself. In this sense, irresolution is an effective, although perverse, means of rule."[26]

The widespread practice of acquiring land in ways that were not strictly legal meant that many land titles were subject to legal challenge. Furthermore, from the beginning of the colonial era, Brazilian governments had tried to deal with the problem of powerful landholders locking up land without contributing to the wealth and prosperity of society—the problem had already been plaguing Portugal on land reconquered from the Moors and was well known to royal administrators. In 1546, the first governor general of Brazil, Tomé de Souza, specified that those receiving land grants should be required to live upon the property and warned the king against granting "more land to one person than he can in your view and according to his own possibilities make use of."[27] He further warned of the lawlessness and arrogance that would surely follow on excessively large land grants.[28] Unfortunately, his warnings were ignored as the king rushed to please his followers and at the same time lock down Portuguese claims to land that England, France, Holland and Spain were beginning to covet. The king's largesse would come to pose virtually insoluble legal, moral and practical problems.

The claims of ownership to vast stretches of land not in production contradicted the essential rationale by which land ownership was legally and morally justified, both in the tradition of the Catholic Church and in the liberal secular theories of ownership that arose in Europe in the seventeenth and eighteenth centuries. From Saint Thomas Aquinas to John Locke, property ownership was justified on the basis that land rightfully belonged to the person who made it productive through his labor. Many Brazilian landowners owned large tracts of land they had not even seen, much less transformed through their labor.

To attempt to discourage such practices, colonial and national governments throughout the Americas, including the United States, adopted property rules that to a greater or lesser degree required "effective use." There are many variations; California water law, for example, uses the principle commonly called "use it or lose it," referring to the loss of water rights for failure to exercise them. If land or resources of the land are not used, someone who had put it into production or showed convincing evidence that he would do so could challenge the title. In nineteenth-century Brazil, legislators and judges also asserted the principle of effective use, partly because there was genuine worry about the waste of Brazil's land by *latifúndio*, landholdings too large to encourage or award effective use and management. In nineteenth-century Brazil, the problem was widely thought to be the principle reason the nation, with all its riches, lagged so far behind the United States, where the more equitable distribution of land in the Midwest was creating a powerhouse of agricultural production and economic development and where the plantation economy of the American South suffered many of the problems that worried Brazil.

The effective-use principle and a whole tradition of legal findings based upon it were reaffirmed in the Land Statute passed by the military government shortly after the 1964 coup. The concept of effective use offered a way to challenge land ownership over much of Brazil's landscape. Unfortunately, while it was meant by some well-intentioned legislators to reduce the prevalence of latifúndio, unscrupulous land officers and judges easily manipulated the legalities, making effective-use clauses more a tool for the creation and maintenance of the problem than for its elimination. The Land Statute would continue to be a

method by which the powerful displaced smallholders, but the contradictions it created in law and practice also opened the way for radical
new possibilities, as we shall see.

Fernando Sodero, one of Brazil's greatest scholars of land law in the
latter half of the twentieth century, came to the conclusion that legalistic interpretations of the land law were futile and, to use Holston's
terms, only promoted "privilege and perverse rule." As a legal scholar,
Sodero could find no just solution in the letter of the law itself and proposed that only enlightened judges using a general philosophical sense
of fairness, along with meticulous and profound examination of the
historical and human circumstances of each case, could reach reasonable settlements of land claims. The law would be of little help.

Sodero's followers in the legal profession took the matter a step further, suggesting that, given the essential illegitimacy of the system, only
a campaign of civil disobedience could resolve particular land disputes
and, more importantly, mount a necessary challenge to the systematic
injustices of the perverse structure of land law. The convoluted confusion and contradictions of land law meant that it was, in essence, a deep
moral wrong. The historical record and personal experience had led
many, perhaps most, Brazilians to have little respect for the specifics of
the laws that protected private property, even when those same people
supported the inviolability of private property in principle. As with the
civil rights movement in the United States, there would prove to be
considerable public sympathy, even among many judges and legislators, for those who broke the law that was known to be a sham for per-
petuating injustice.[29]

The participants and sympathizers with the landless movement that
would become the MST gradually learned through painful practice that
there were three major ways in which title could be legally challenged.
One way was to claim that the land was not, in the Brazilian legal phrase
adopted by the military and the later 1988 Constitution, "serving its
social function"; that is, it was not in effective use. The second way was
to challenge the history of the title to a piece of land, burdened as many
titles were with a scaly encrustation of fraud. The third way was to use
the wider claim that the distribution of property and the law upon
which it was based constituted a grave social injustice, making civil

disobedience not only fair, but also a positive social duty in order to rectify a great historical and continuing wrong.[30]

Given the legal confusion and the essentially political character of the land-reform movement, few situations were clearly or simply amenable to one of these approaches, but instead to some mixture of the three. In practice, counterclaimants to land often shifted between one argument and another, like fencers in a dance of thrust and parry. Purely legalistic arguments on the part of landowners, which asserted the sanctity of private property, invited the landless to use the effective-use principle and the dubious character of many land titles to show that the claim to ownership of the property in question would be difficult to defend in court. Full-blown offensives, in which the original claimants to land confronted the landless as a political movement by using political means and violence, had their own hazards for powerful landholders, often leading to an escalation of claims in which the landless made civil disobedience a challenge not only to particular claims on a given piece of land, but also to an unjust legal, political and economic structure.

None of this was quite so clear to the people who had been evicted from Kaingang land or to other landless folk who had come together to figure out how to deal with their situation. It would prove necessary to puzzle out the intricacies of land law in theory and practice over many years of struggle.

In 1979, the question of how to challenge land claims emerged as a strategic question taking shape in the discussions among the landless. If land law was vague and flexible, so that the powerful might acquire land from the defenseless, how could the poor amass the power that would put rich landowners with dubious titles on the defensive? In the past, poor people who had settled land sometimes were able to receive some form of legally recognized claim, called "possession" (*posse*), which was short of the power of full title. They had nearly always done so with the argument of effective use. However, if the land was good, it invited more powerful landholders to seize it. Often, wealthier landowners deliberately encouraged poor people to deforest land (or, in the South, to plow up prairie ground), leading them to believe that they would receive title; then the more powerful landowners would use legal maneuvers, intimidation or violence to gain the land back once the labor of the poor had been invested in making it productive. For the poor, the legal ambiguities of land ownership meant they were forever at the mercy of the powerful. How would it be possible to acquire land in such a context?

As usual for the cause of the poor, the answer lay in numbers and organization. If the poor could occupy land in sufficient numbers to make their removal a difficult political issue, then perhaps they could turn the tables on Brazil's landowners and the flexible legal tradition the landowners had always used in their own favor. Improved means of communication with sympathizers elsewhere and with the national media, along with the loosening of government censorship, would also potentially allow the occupiers of land to gain supporters from a wider region, perhaps from much of the national population. What would happen if the poor settlers were to create a situation that neither the government nor the landowners could easily dismiss? Would they have to grant the settlers their demands for land?

People involved in thinking about these questions brought a variety of perspectives to the discussion. The Catholic CPT and its clerical and lay workers, who had been turning over this question for some time, had already joined with the landless poor, especially in the Amazon, to challenge the kind of violent land seizures and legal manipulations the system fostered. João Pedro Stédile, an ex-seminarian and the son of a poor farming family in Rio Grande do Sul, had put together his own graduate program in agrarian political economy at the National Autonomous University of Mexico, where he had come into contact with such eminent scholars of rural life as the Mexican Rodolfo Stavenhagen and the Brazilian Theotonio dos Santos. Stédile's experience and education gave him special insight into the way challenges to landownership might be successfully made.[31] Lawyers sympathetic to the movement added their legal expertise. Some people in the Alta Uruguaia region had participated in the land reform struggles in Rio Grande do Sul prior to the military dictatorship's coming to power in 1964; others had experienced frustration trying to work within the compromised politics of the rural labor unions and were looking for fresh approaches. At this moment in 1979, the discussion about how to make claim to land was not simple or naive, but neither was it fully developed nor under the sway of any particular current of political thought.

## SETTLERS TAKE ACTION

As these discussions took place, people still remained uncertain about what to do. Violent repression remained a real danger. Also, most of the people were steeped in conservative religious traditions and had been taught to believe that private property claims were sacred. Some were still doubtful about the critical perspective that encouraged them to see the tenuousness of the wealthy Brazilian property owners' legal and moral claims. Translating the general discussions of the injustices of land distribution in Brazil through parables from the Bible into specific action was not easy for most people. Some, however, were eager for action.

One group of about thirty families acted precipitously, invading a state forest reserve and beginning to clear holdings for farming. The state police reacted quickly and decisively in throwing them off the land. The group had no support from church congregations or priests, nor from any other groups, partly because they had made no effort to organize or to solicit support and partly because they had not properly gauged the generally negative public reaction to cutting down a forest reserve in a state where there was little forest left, and also growing support for environmental conservation.[32]

As people continued to talk about how to deal with their situation, João Pedro Stédile learned a critical fact through his employment with the state. The state government was about to change the legal status of two properties that had been expropriated prior to 1964 for the purposes of a land-reform program that had been subsequently shut down as a result of the military coup. A lumber harvesting company had badly and infamously abused some of the property under questionable legal arrangements and, as had been discussed publicly on many occasions, the two *fazendas*, Brilhante and Macali, were perfect candidates for redistribution to settlers—indeed, the governor had promised to distribute the land among the landless—but Stédile found out that on September 8, the state of Rio Grande do Sul planned to divest themselves of the land without distributing it. Stédile realized that it was essential to occupy the land and demand its distribution under agrarian reform before the state filed its petition to the court. On September 6, he contacted Padre Arnildo, urging him to help organize the occupations before it was too late. Padre Arnildo recalls that the date was important, as well, because Brazilians celebrate September 7 as their Independence Day.

For the next two days, Stédile and Padre Arnildo worked without sleep to bring together the landless people in the area. They were able to assemble forty-three trucks of all sizes and descriptions, because as Padre Arnildo recalled, "everyone in the countryside knows somebody who owns or drives a truck." They were also helped by the fact that, as João Pedro remembers, "The whole situation with Brilhante and Macali was already well known; there was enormous public support already for the idea that these fazendas should be redistributed to the landless." Under bright moonlight and with beautiful weather, on the night of September 7 and the early morning of September 8, the settlers occupied portions of Brilhante and Macali. When the government sent army troops in to drive the occupiers from the land, the occupiers made a critical decision that would echo throughout the movement over the decades to come, determining the critical role of the entire family in the struggle for the land: the women insisted that they would confront the troops along with the children. "They said, 'If you are going to beat our men, you will have to do it by coming over us first,'" Padre Arnildo recalled. Many objected that this would label the people as cowards and would be unfair to the women and children. But the women prevailed, as they would in many other occupations to follow. The troops and their officers hesitated to beat the women and children and found they could not break the lines formed by the settlers. Later, as the dispute lingered on over redistribution, the women surrounded harvesting machines, demanding a portion of the harvest for immediate food needs and promises of land distribution, and finally agreeing with the state governor to end their protest in return for half the soy and corn harvest for themselves and further promises for land distribution. After some considerable jockeying and delay, the fazendas were eventually redistributed to the settlers.

However, the occupation and subsequent division among settlers of Brilhante and Macali still left most of the dispossessed in the area without land. The next step was to be much more daring, because it involved moving onto and demanding land that was claimed—though not without counterclaims deriving from earlier state expropriations in the area—by private landowners. This raised the stakes enormously. Public support was by no means assured, as it had been on Brilhante and Macali.

In one version of what happened next, events were shaped by the individual actions of farm families. In this version of the story, on December 6, 1979, one settler, Adalberto Natálio Vargas, nicknamed Natalino, simply put up a primitive camp at an intersection on Road 324, between Ronda Alta and Passo Fundo. The intersection was next to land whose ownership and use had a long and disputed history. Natalino's friend, Teófilo Wrasser, joined him. At first, they had no explicit demands for land, but were simply insisting that the government act in some way to solve the problems created for them and others by their expulsion from the Kaingang reserve. Slowly, during the following

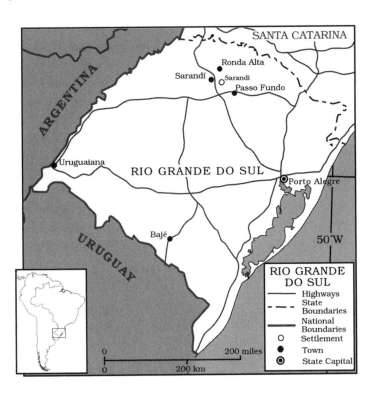

weeks, other landless people set up camp alongside Natalino. A store-keeper who kept a shop at the country crossroads, also named Natal-ino, gave some initial help to the families. The encampment became known as "Encruzilhada Natalino," which, translated literally, meant simply, "Natalino's crossroad," but as time went on it resonated more and more with the ideas of a change of direction, a time for decision and a cross of crucifixion.

Today, Padre Arnildo insists that this tale misrepresents what hap-pened at Encruzilhada Natalino: "No, no, this was very well planned and organized from the beginning—the selection of the place, the or-ganization of the occupation, everything well organized. We knew this would be a major confrontation."

In either case, this particular place was to become one of the most important points of origin for the national landless movement—a fact that was the result of several factors. When one looks at the site now, marked with the modest MST memorial to the beginnings of the move-ment, one would never imagine why the movement would begin here. The landscape might be taken for farmland in a part of Iowa made up of rolling hill country. The crossroads is located in a small valley with a creek and small reservoir, surrounded by corn and soybean fields. There is a scrap of woods. The nearest small town is more than ten miles away. The old store is abandoned, and there is an enormous grain and soy storage facility owned by a transnational firm. On the other side of the road, one of the original MST settlers sells soft drinks out of a wood and tin shack.

It was not the qualities of the place alone, but rather the events oc-curring in the surrounding region that came together in a special way at Encruzilhada Natalino. The events may have been catalyzed by the strong will of Natalino, a man who was little known before or after these events, but for this single telling gesture of taking the first deter-mined step to demand government action. It is clear, though, that Na-talino's catalyst was thrown into a brew ready to react.

Many of those thrown off the land were trying to survive in desper-ate conditions in the small towns or as sharecroppers or agricultural laborers in the region. By the late 1970s, the economic boom of the military government's so-called "economic miracle" had lost steam, and there were few urban job openings. Employers were firing, not hiring, in the cities, and the problem was far from temporary. It was becoming clear that many of the investments encouraged by the military's policies were ill conceived, overly speculative and based on a degree of exploitation of labor and resources that could not be sustained. These investments led to a severe and growing load of public and private debt that further dragged down the economy. Recession and growing unemployment would continue throughout the 1980s (which would become known as Brazil's—and Latin America's—"lost decade"). Seeking work in the city would be an increasingly fruitless strategy for the poor. Urban slums were becoming more numerous and more crime-ridden.

In addition to those thrown off the reserve, many families in the region who had owned or leased land and had never settled in the Indian reserve had sons and daughters looking for land, with little money and less hope of finding credit to buy land. Throughout Brazil's southern states, families had lost farms to well-financed syndicates, many of them based in Japan, Europe or the United States. These companies had been strongly encouraged by subsidies, tax breaks and other forms of government support as part of the military's "modernization" program, which would become infamous in the phrase of a leading Brazilian scholar as *modernização dolorosa* ("sorrowful modernization"). Good land much desired by the syndicates was abundant in the area around Encruzilhada Natalino, and poorer farmers found that banks were far more interested in financing big syndicates than poor farmers.

The displacement of small producers in favor of large companies producing soy and wheat for export set off riots in the early and mid-1970s in Rio de Janeiro and other Brazilian cities, because the small farmers had grown the black beans that were the staple of the Brazilian poor. When urban poor people found black beans unavailable—or much more expensive—in supermarkets, they rioted, sometimes looting what food they could get their hands on. The "black bean riots" became emblematic of a problem endemic in the history of Brazil and other third-world nations: as investors took advantage of opportunities to export food abroad, they displaced the small-scale farmers who produced for local consumption, leading to a persistent paradox of economic growth and declining food availability for the poor. This was not just a problem for farmers, but an equally intense problem for the urban poor.

In addition to the immediate displacements, the southern region had a history of struggles for agrarian reform that dated back at least to the 1950s. During the late 1950s and early 1960s, an organization called MASTER (*Movimento dos Agricultores Sem-Terra*, Movement of Landless Farmers) had militated for agrarian reform in the state of Rio Grande do Sul and was active in the highland plateau surrounding Encruzilhada Natalino. The state of Rio Grande do Sul had an even longer history of agrarian radicalism, based on the disappointed hopes of many people whose families had been lured to southern Brazil by promises of land concessions and then frustrated in a variety of ways. In the years leading up to the military coup of 1964, this tradition of radical thought seemed about to bear fruit.[33]

Encruzilhada Natalino was located in the area of two fazendas that had a complicated history, dating from before the military coup. In 1962, the state government of a rising young politician who was also one of the organizers of MASTER, Leonel Brizola, had expropriated Fazenda Sarandi for the purposes of agrarian reform. Brizola had been encouraged in his political career from a very young age by a wealthy local farmer named Anoni. After the military coup, and before being forced into exile, then-Senator Brizola hid himself on the Anoni property, probably with Anoni's connivance. Like Brilhante and Macali, Fazenda Sarandi and the nearby Fazenda Anoni had been involved in long and inconclusive court battles since the state government expropriated them for redistribution in 1962. A change in government in 1963 stymied the hopes of the landless to receive land on Sarandi, and the military coup in 1964 all but ended them. To complicate matters, part of the land had been grilado, fraudulently claimed, by a timber harvesting corporation during the military regime. The government had also divided up part of Fazenda Sarandi into midsized lots, with most of the land destined for sizable holdings of highly capitalized farmers. A further complication was that some of the land in this area had been expropriated in the mid-1970s in a plan to resettle families displaced by the huge Itaipu hydroelectric project on the Paraná River (and later for a smaller local dam called Passo Fundo), although very little land had actually been turned over to landless families. Thus, on both Sarandi and Anoni, there were complicated claims and counterclaims about state and private ownership of much of the land.[34]

The complex history of the land was notorious, though often some-what confused in the minds of land hungry potential settlers who, throughout the late 1960s and 1970s, saw it as a logical place to begin again with the process of agrarian reform interrupted by the military government. It was well known that land might be available in the area if the right political conditions could be created, but this was no easy matter. In spite of the beginnings of the democratization process and political opening, the people thrown off the Indian land and other land-less folk still faced daunting prospects. This was all too clear in the mis-erable conditions of the improvised camp made of sheets of plastic and cardboard at Encruzilhada Natalino.

What would happen to these poor and largely defenseless people, who demanded land from a government and landholders who had proved themselves ruthless and violent? The answer seemed to come soon enough in the form of military police (in Brazil, a special force controlled by state government), who surrounded the encampment and threatened violent action to displace the squatters, or *acampados*. As discussed earlier, Brazil's past is filled with little-known stories of the violent displacement of poor people by landholders and govern-ments. As in most of Brazil, in Rio Grande do Sul wealthy landowners usually dominated local and state courts and could often enlist local and state police with court orders to remove the poor from land they tried to claim.

If landholders could not obtain court orders, or preferred not to trouble to do so, they could hire gunmen, as we have discussed above. Like the soldiers and police officers, the jagunços (to use the term we have heard used most frequently) were usually recruited from the same mass of poor people they were called upon to displace, torture or mur-der. Jagunços usually had to work at other jobs much of the time, as farmers with hoe and machete or as cowboys with horse, saddle and lasso. They usually spoke the same rural dialects as their victims and shared the same complex mixture of awe, admiration, fear, contempt and hatred for the landlords. (One of the world's great novels, called in English *The Devil to Pay in the Backlands*, by João Guimaraes Rosa, de-scribes in sympathetic but highly ironic terms the lives and terrible moral dilemmas of jagunços.[35]) The one thing that clearly distinguished the jagunços from other rural people was that at some point they were willing to become thugs and murderers, turning against their neighbors for a price. Often, they did their work intermingled with police or military forces, thus relieving the officials in charge of responsibility for men they could claim not to command. At Encruzilhada Natalino, the settlers eventually faced hundreds of men who were mostly official police and soldiers operating under a court order, but with the volatile addition of hired gunmen.

## "DON'T LET THEM DIVIDE YOU, DON'T LET THEM BUY YOU OFF"

In the politically delicate days when the military government's image as omnipotent and unassailable was crumbling, and the government itself had chosen to "decompress" and "open" the political process, the confrontation at Encruzilhada Natalino posed an especially difficult problem for the regime. If it chose to act with sufficient force to crush and disperse the people camped at the crossroads, the government had to worry that there would be substantial bloodshed. With the media becoming bolder in challenging censorship, the incident could become sensational national news. The military government had to face the strong possibility that a bloodbath would fuel a wider movement with ever more intransigent demands.

➤ Stopping short of full-scale confrontation, the government made constant attacks on the encampment, jailing people, administering beatings, stabbing people with bayonets, burning down shacks and threatening people with further violence and death. The attacks were not successful in breaking the spirit of the acampados; on the contrary, they seemed to lead to the further growth of the encampment. Also, each attack on the encampment was followed by waves of demonstrations and an outpouring of material support from organizations in the cities. A few regional and national newspapers eager to test the government's promise of loosening censorship lent editorial encouragement to the urban organizations. At one point, the government had Encruzilhada Natalino surrounded with about twice the number of armed men as there were men in the encampment, and it still was not able to seriously disrupt the encampment.

The people at Encruzilhada Natalino had built a structure of committees to govern the camp and negotiate with the government, a structure that would be used in modified form by hundreds of other encampments over the next two decades and more. They formed a general assembly, with representatives from smaller groups of families, referred to as *nucleos*. Various committees were in charge of food, shelter, health, education and the morale of the camp. A central committee was the executive body in matters that affected the overall organization and future of the camp, answering to the general assembly for its actions. The people in the encampment designed the structure specifically to forbid any single individual from taking unilateral actions or negotiating matters of importance with the government or other outsiders.

In May of 1981, a year and a half after Natalino first camped at the crossroads, the representatives of the camp met several times with INCRA (*Instituto Nacional de Colonização e Reforma Agrária*), the federal agency in charge of colonization and agrarian reform. (INCRA's duties in this era were limited to the resettlement of those displaced by dams and government-sponsored colonization projects in the Amazon and other frontier areas, as there was no genuine agrarian reform taking place.) The committees had studied the Estatuto da Terra (Land Statute) decreed by the military government in 1964, which declared that land not serving its social function to produce goods of economic value and provide employment under proper legal safeguards of workers was subject to agrarian reform. The statute laid out other criteria, including maximum size for landholdings under specified conditions, and conservation criteria—all of this for a reform that had never occurred during the military's long regime. The representatives of the landless at Encruzilhada Natalino made it clear in the May meetings that they wanted land in the state of Rio Grande do Sul, but that they also were not asking for land for free: they were prepared to pay for it under reasonable terms with a government line of credit. "We want to pay for it with our work," they declared. In addition to the intense round of meetings with state and federal officials, which came to no conclusion, the settlers worked to explain their origins and purpose more thoroughly to the local community and to the public in general.

This campaign was designed to counter the wave of accusations coming from the conservative press, politicians and landowner organizations claiming that the encampment was led by outside agitators and not by the landless themselves, that many of the supposed landless in fact owned land already and that many would never work the land they received, but were in the camp simply to gain land for sale before moving on to another encampment.

Locally powerful fazendeiros began to work more aggressively to dismantle the encampment. Among them were the Guerra brothers, owners of a nine thousand–hectare property (about twenty-one thousand acres) near the encampment. In early June, the Guerra foremen threatened to shoot the Rural Electrical Cooperative personnel, who were about to hook the encampment up to the electrical grid. They also threatened to resist by force any attempt to expropriate the Guerra property.

Also in early June, the encampment suffered internal division. Teófilo Wrasser, the friend who had joined with Natalino in the first days, now joined with a local politician and several others to accuse the camp's general assembly and central committee of corruption in the division of food, clothing and money received in support of the movement. They further proposed that the community be divided into two groups: those who had been thrown off the Kaingang reserve and those who had joined later, with the former first in line to receive any land. The general assembly threatened to throw Wrasser and his followers out of the camp if they did not withdraw their accusations, at which point Wrasser and five other families set up another camp several miles down the road, with active help from the police. Some days later, heavily armed men invaded the Natalino camp, treating people roughly and making vague threats. People noted that some of the dissidents who had left accompanied the police. These attacks from outside and divisions within created an atmosphere of crisis in the camp and encouraged its opponents. The encampment had endured for a year and a half, and many were weary. The damp cold and rain of winter greatly aggravated the situation, as people felt under siege while having no shelter other than plastic, cardboard and rough thatch. The ubiquitous mud made every daily task doubly exasperating.

In June 1981, the CPT and other organizations supporting the new agrarian reform movement worked with the committee leadership of the encampment to put on a dramatic show of support on *O Dia do Agricultor* (Farmer's Day), June 25. While the rural union movement (which had always been weaker in Rio Grande do Sul than in some other regions of Brazil, as we shall see) had been weak and unsteady in support of the landless movement, the unions joined with the CPT and a variety of civic organizations to highlight the three themes of crop support prices, health and land reform. Many of the civic organizations had been recently created in the wake of the political abertura. On June 25, Encruzilhada Natalino was able to demonstrate support from more than one hundred organizations throughout the country. Leading up to these demonstrations of solidarity, on June 21, Padre Casaldaliga, a Spanish priest who had been threatened with death and expulsion from the country for his work on behalf of landless people in the Amazon, spoke to the settlers and their visitors. Casaldaliga warned, "Be careful, what I can tell you from my thirteen years of experience in Mato Grosso is that the government and the powerful will try to divide you, be careful. Union among the small people is the strength of the small people. Don't let them divide you, don't let them buy you off."

Dom Vicente Scherer, the conservative archbishop for the state of Rio Grande do Sul, forbade Padre Casaldaliga to say mass in the encampment and launched a verbal attack on him and the CPT. Scherer proclaimed that the landless had no right to ask for land, and the state had no obligation to provide it. He claimed, completely inaccurately, that the CPT was not linked to the National Conference of Bishops (the *Conferência Nacional dos Bispos do Brasil*, CNBB) and enjoyed the support of, at most, one or two bishops. In reply, Dom Balduíno, one of the founders of the CPT, corrected Scherer's mistakes and called the encampment an event as significant and encouraging for the country as the successful autoworkers' strike of 1978 to 1979.

The state government had shown itself unable or unwilling to resolve or diffuse the increasingly heated conflict in the highlands of Rio Grande do Sul. Other encampments had also grown up in Rio Grande do Sul and other states in the South. A sense of crisis was more and more palpable. The spectacle of landless families huddled in the winter rain at Encruzilhada Natalino was becoming a symbol for an increasingly embarrassing national scandal. Far from yielding to pressure, the landless movement threatened to become a genuine national movement for agrarian reform, with a broad base of support in city and countryside. Well into July 1981, INCRA was still attempting to persuade people to leave Rio Grande do Sul for colonization projects in the Amazon, with little success. The national government became increasingly alarmed; it had, after all, come to power in large measure to defeat the movement for agrarian reform nearly twenty years earlier.

At the end of July, the encampment and its supporters hired four buses to carry people to speak to Governor Amaral de Souza, declaring that they were prepared to camp out in the plaza in front of the state capitol building if the governor refused to meet their demands. The police intercepted the buses, preventing the protesters from approaching the area of the capitol, except on foot. Luckily, friendly legislators succeeded in setting up a meeting with the governor, who reiterated previous positions, urging the delegation to accept colonization offers in the Amazon, denying the possibility of settlement in the state. The governor promised immediate relief in the form of limited medical and food assistance to the camp. He also made it clear, as he had done on other occasions, that he assumed the settlers' intransigence was due to political manipulation by outsiders and not due to their own autonomous decisions. At the end of July 1981, with about six hundred families—between twenty-five hundred and three thousand people—camped at the Encruzilhada, it was clear that the state government was not about to solve the problem.

Meanwhile, the federal government decided to use a combination of carrot and stick. They brought in a military "specialist" in such tactics, sending him for an initial visit to the camp in mid-July. Major Sebastião Rodrígues de Moura was a member of the SNI (*Serviço Nacional de Inteligência*), the national intelligence services, dreaded as the agency that planned and often directly implemented the government's repressive measures. He was more widely known by the nickname of "Coronel Curió," a *curió* being a small bird in the Amazon prized for its varied and seductive song. (Although his actual rank at this time was major, to avoid confusion we will refer to him by his better-known nickname, Coronel, or colonel, Curió.) Curió had been in charge of the repression of the guerrilla rebellion in the Araguaia region of the Amazon, where he had practiced a ruthless strategy modeled on his study of the Americans in Vietnam and the British in Malaysia, along with a mixture of traditional Brazilian techniques. If people cooperated in identifying and locating guerrilla fighters, Curió bestowed government money and

projects on towns and villages, establishing semimilitarized colonization projects and settling families who had been cooperative on them—
projects that served a function similar to those the United States
military called "strategic hamlets" in Vietnam. In these projects, Curió's
fabled egotism took the form of encouraging settlers to wear T-shirts
emblazoned with the motto, "Communication, Union, Respect, Ideal-
ization and Organization—CURIO." He had not hesitated to burn out
farms or torture and kill people. Shortly before going to Rio Grande do
Sul in 1981, the government had given him the task of ruling over the
notorious gold diggings at Serra Pelada, a site beset with violent conflicts among miners and mining companies. A few years after his work
in Rio Grande do Sul, he would be convicted of murdering a young
man for stealing oranges from his mansion in Brasilia, but would serve
his brief sentence on probation with no actual jail time. At this writing
in 2003, organizations in Brazil are trying to bring him to trial for the
massacres of civilians he is accused of carrying out in the Araguaia campaign. Meanwhile, he serves as the mayor of Curionápolis, a municipality in the Amazon named after him, and leads a group of miners
claiming exclusive access to Serra Pelada. A leader of the rival miners
group was assassinated in December 2002. In 2001, hardened former
prospectors who gave Curió some begrudging credit for the resolution
of the Serra Pelada conflicts warned us that it would not be wise for us
to try to interview him.

In 1981, at Encruzilhada Natalino, Coronel Curió brought along the
carrot of promised land awaiting the settlers in the Amazon in government-financed colonization projects. The settlement of the Amazon
had been one of the military government's pet projects when it took
power. Since 1970, it had pursued with special dedication the policy of
opening up the Amazon. Admiral Garrástazu Médici, then national
president under the military government, had announced in 1970 that
the Amazon was "a land without people for people without land," portraying the settlement of the Amazon as a kind of land-reform policy
that could be activated through colonization.

Upon his arrival in Rio Grande do Sul, Curió announced that he
would resolve the problems at Encruzilhada Natalino within fifteen
days, after which the encampment would be destroyed. In the encampment, he sealed his promise with a traditional gesture by plucking a

whisker from his moustache. Curió charmed some of the press—and even some of the landless people—by telling jokes and talking freely with the people in the camp. Even some of his enemies admitted that he was "charismatic." Padre Arnildo recalls that he was "very sociable," though he also accuses him of torture and assassination.

Coronel Curió held a festival for the acampados of Encruzilhada Natalino shortly after his arrival in July 1981. He arranged a generous barbecue of the sort appreciated in Brazil's southern states and didn't forget to provide the other essentials: music, dancing, games and treats for the children. Most of the settlers were far too hungry for food and diversion to resist the invitation. They decided that sacrifices should be made when necessary to gain something of value, but when food that they needed was offered, they should take it and continue to demand the rest of what they were due. Though people have different versions of the story, we were told that when Curió passed out food and candy to the children, their parents had instructed them to accept the gifts politely and say, "Thank you, sir, and now can you give our families the land we need?"

Curió had land to offer. It was, he said, a paradise, one he had seen with his own eyes. There was good virgin land, with plenty of water, government-built housing or free housing material ready to use, new roads, timber to use or sell and cheap government agricultural credit to buy seeds, chemicals and machinery. He set up slide and film shows portraying the colonization projects in rosy terms. Some of this land was in the state of Pará, where Curió had won his battle against the guerrillas, some in Acre, some in Bahia and some in Mato Grosso. There would be well-organized communities, schools and clinics. In Bahia, a project was already up and running, constructed to receive people displaced by the building of the huge Sobradinho dam on the São Francisco River. There would be room for more. Curió said the government was willing to oblige the people with their demand for land, but the state government had already done surveys that concluded there was no land available for distribution in Rio Grande do Sul or the other southern states, while in Pará and Mato Grosso there was more than enough room for all. The Coronel would even arrange special bus and airplane trips, in military planes, for people to go see for themselves.

Coronel Curió's song was less seductive than it might have been for

The land of the Sarandí communities in the Alta Uruguaia, the highland plateau in Brazil's southernmost state of Rio Grande do Sul. The soils and subtropical climate here will support a wide variety of crops.

two reasons. The first was that the federal government's own agency, INCRA, had done a survey of land in Rio Grande do Sul and concluded that there were about 800,000 hectares (about two million acres) of land appropriate for agrarian reform in the state, flying directly in the face of the state government surveys that claimed no such land existed. Another survey carried out by the Lutheran Church (a strong presence among the central European settlers in Rio Grande do Sul, where some Lutheran churches still offered services in German) came to a similar conclusion. The acampados were themselves aware of land available for expropriation on Fazenda Anoni, Fazenda Sarandí and other large properties in the area, land whose soil and climate was good for the kind of agriculture they knew how to practice. There were already roads and schools, clinics and communities, perhaps inadequate to the needs of the region, but a beginning nonetheless. It was clear that the state and municipalities could build more as people made the land more productive and taxable. No great forest need be cleared and none of the mythical and very real hazards of the Amazon need be feared in this familiar and gentle temperate landscape.

The second reason to resist the Coronel's siren song was that many people in the region had already been drawn in by the same tune sung by government and private promoters of colonization schemes in Pará and Mato Grosso. They had gone to new settlements there, and while some had found it worthwhile to stay, many others had returned in bitter disillusionment. Many had contracted malaria or dengue fever, unusual diseases in the southern states, but endemic in the Amazon and Mato Grosso. Testimonies of these experiences appeared in Rio Grande do Sul, including the local newspaper, *Zero Hora*, in Passo Fundo.

Some had lost children to disease. Ziderio Biazus returned from Terranova in the Amazonian state of Pará, saying, "I saw things there that I could never have imagined. Many *gaúchos* [people from Rio Grande do Sul; gah-u-*shoe* in Brazilian pronunciation] were dying of malaria, especially children." Floreci de Fátima Oliveira returned from Mato Grosso, having seen a mother lose two children in twenty days to malaria. Rain had cut Floreci's settlement off completely and as a consequence they went ten days with no food. Davi Alves de Moura, one of the settlers expelled from the reserve, went to Terranova, a government colonization project in the Amazon, in 1978. His crops did not produce well, and he found there was little credit available. The family had many health problems and could find no medical help. A young daughter died of typhus. He turned his hand to gold mining in Mato Grosso and then at the notorious Serra Pelada mine in Pará. Discouraged by the conditions there, he returned to work as a day laborer in the colonization project in Mato Grosso, and then returned once again to Pará, where he worked for a military officer who owned a fazenda. After receiving a death threat from the lieutenant, he returned to Mato Grosso, sold the rights to his lot and moved back to Rio Grande do Sul, where he worked with his father. From there, he joined the encampment at Encruzilhada Natalino.[36]

Colonists in the Amazon had often found that once the forest was cut down, the soils of the region eroded quickly and lost their fertility within a few years—they had to keep moving or settle for misery. Even where it was possible to grow a crop for market reliably, the lack of good roads and the great distances from cities made it difficult if not impossible to sell farm products. For these returnees, the difficult conditions for poor rural people in Rio Grande do Sul, even in the encampment at Encruzilhada Natalino, were more tolerable than the challenges of the frontier. They advised their neighbors to stick it out at home.

Whether or not to accept land in the Amazon colonization projects was more than an individual choice. From the landless movement's earliest formative discussions onward, discouraging people from accepting the lure of the Amazon was critical to the movement's strategy. The movement wanted to transform the landholding structure of Brazil, not simply expand the agricultural frontier. Brazil's history was a story of frontiers, and, in each of these frontiers, the initial hopes of the poor for cheap land at the edge of settlement had been largely or completely disappointed, as the wealthy landowners eventually gathered nearly all good land to themselves. No one wished to engage in a long and risky struggle simply for the sake of repeating this story again. After listening to the returnees from the initial Amazon settlements, the people of Encruzilhada Natalino and other encampments adopted the slogan, "land for everyone in his own state," or "agrarian reform in your own state," specifically rejecting the government's opportunistic strategy of diverting agrarian reform movements to serve its own purposes in the Amazon.

In Rio Grande do Sul, Santa Catarina and Paraná, Brazil's three southern states, where slavery and export plantation culture had never taken a strong hold, the land question was unusually complex. In Rio Grande do Sul, huge cattle estates covered much of the south and southwestern portions of the state, leaving much fine farmland in the rest of the state open for colonization. At the end of the nineteenth century and the beginning of the twentieth, the Brazilian government had promoted colonization by Europeans in these states, hoping to create a small farmer culture in imitation of what was seen as the successful frontier settlement by small farmers of the North American Midwest. Relatively progressive Brazilian legislators, convinced of the evils of slavery and the large plantations built on slavery, thought that small-farm culture would be economically more productive, politically more democratic and culturally more egalitarian and robust. For a minority, most of whom had worked for abolition, the relatively unsettled lands of the southern states represented a frontier that could accommodate many of the freed slaves, whose lack of access to land was sure to be a great problem in the decades after abolition in 1888. This would solve an immense social and economic problem and, to an extent, compensate for the moral wrongs done to slaves. For the majority of Brazilian parliamentarians, however, the evils of slavery were identified with the supposed shortcomings of people of African descent, who were at this point the majority of the population. In their eyes, it was necessary to "whiten" Brazil through European immigration. Even many former abolitionists saw the matter in this light—to them, one of the evils of slavery was the growth of the black population. After long debate, the government decided that the fertile subtropical and temperate lands of the South should be used as the incentive to draw white Europeans into making a home in Brazil. Afro-Brazilians coming out of slavery would have to fend for themselves.[37]

Brazilian planters had also been faced with a classic problem of plantation societies. While they tended to favor investing in large-scale export production of tropical luxury crops (primarily coffee, sugar and cacao) for Europe and North America—seeing more profit in selling luxury crops to rich people than food crops to the poor—they often found it difficult to provide sufficient food for their workers and the necessary supportive labor in nearby towns and cities. So strong was the mania for export plantation production that government policy and the rule of planters throughout Brazilian history to the present day made it very difficult for small-scale producers to grow food in zones considered appropriate for export agriculture. Little or no credit was available for local food production, and land was extremely hard to wrest from the planters' monopoly. Plantation owners often went to the extreme of forbidding slaves or, later, free laborers, from growing their own food, for fear that it would reduce their dependence on the plantation or lead to claims to land ownership. As a result, planters often found themselves importing food at great expense. They hoped that if European immigrants could be settled on the temperate soils of the Brazilian South—unattractive for growing tropical export crops—they could potentially solve this problem and thus reduce their own production costs.

However, there were substantial barriers to attracting European settlers. In the last decades of the nineteenth century, during the explosive growth of Brazil's coffee economy in the states of Rio de Janeiro and São Paulo, planters and the national and state governments had recruited Europeans, primarily Italians, to work on the plantations, promising good conditions and the possibility of obtaining land. Ruthless private immigration companies cheated the immigrants on the passage, often failing to provide food and exacting fees for services never delivered. Planters worked immigrant laborers as they worked slaves and saw no reason to change their ways. Few of the immigrants recruited for plantation labor ever acquired land under the agreements made with them before they left Europe. The promises were so routinely violated and the treatment of immigrants so little better than the treatment of slaves that for many years the Italian government actually forbade emigrants to embark for Brazil. The Brazilian government and Brazilian planters earned international notoriety for shamelessly deceiving and exploiting immigrants. When the government then wanted to attract Europeans to settle in the southern states as farmers, it had a mighty mountain of suspicion to overcome.

At the turn of the twentieth century, colonization companies and governments offered the European immigrants a paradise in Brazil's South. There would be good land, roads, railroads, schools and good government. The immigrants were not entirely disappointed. Many did obtain good-quality land, and the life of immigrants in the South was in almost all material respects better than life in the areas dominated by export-plantation agriculture, which comprised the overwhelming share of populated Brazil. These immigrants were more prosperous, more secure, more welcome as participants in local and state government and more respected than the former slaves and plantation dependents further north. As in other small landholding settler cultures undertaken by Europeans on various continents, in the settler South the economy was more diverse and robust than in plantation-dominated regions; both city and countryside were on average more prosperous than most of the rest of Brazil. Immigrants contributed to and enjoyed the results of this success.[38]

Unfortunately, for every immigrant whose expectations were fulfilled, there were others whose lives quickly took on a pattern all too familiar in rural Brazil. Many did not succeed in acquiring or holding onto their own land. Tenant farming or sharecropping began to recreate, as we noted earlier, a pattern of insecurity, poverty and land degradation that mimicked the rest of Brazil, the tenant and sharecropping areas of the southern United States and other similar regions of the Americas. As immigrant farm families grew, even those who had obtained title to land began to see their children and grandchildren slide into poverty and dependency as new land for settlement became scarce. The arrival of the largely foreign-financed soy and wheat syndicates in the 1960s that pushed out family farmers deepened the anger. Some recalled the radical ideas influential among the poor in the turn-of-the-century Europe from which they had come: peasant populism, socialism and anarchism. With egalitarian social philosophies in many of their heads, remembering the promises made to immigrants that had been only partially or temporarily met, these immigrant families became impatient. The taste of justice and prosperity, the experience of being offered privilege, although not always fully realized, filled southern farmers with a fervor for the dignified life of which many other Brazilian rural folk had long since despaired. While overall conditions were certainly better in the South, the special pain of high expectations partially met, but now increasingly gone bad, made Brazil's southern rural poor deeply suspicious of new siren calls for settlement of an expanding frontier in the Amazon. In contrast to most other regions of Brazil, the southern rural radicalism was not simply born of deprivation; it was fueled by disappointed expectations.

It was very easy for these people to see that Coronel Curió was offering a promise of land that was nothing more than a repetition of the deceptions of the past—and worse, because it would carry people into a kind of land, climate and disease environment they knew little of and had good reasons to fear. While government propaganda tried to paint the Amazon in glowing terms, centuries of authentic history mixed with powerful mythmaking largely portrayed the Amazon as a green hell. By the late 1970s, Brazilian magazines and newspapers carried many stories of the suffering and disappointment of Amazon colonists. The real dangers and drawbacks of the region for prospective farmers were much magnified by distortion and exaggeration, and both fact and fiction would soon be further amplified with all the force available to Brazilians and foreigners opposed to colonization of the Amazon because of their concern for the loss of a great world treasure of indigenous cultures, forest wilderness and biodiversity. (These themes are explored further in chapter 3.)

It was also surely less tempting to grasp at Coronel Curió's carrots when the same man quickly began applying the stick. He increased the number of men surrounding the camp, interrogated people roughly, turned back food deliveries and introduced spies and troublemakers into the camp, many of whom were quickly unmasked. Curió's men tried to keep people from gathering firewood for cooking and warmth against the damp, cold of winter. Part of the camp had been set up under trees, and the soldiers were ordered to shoot at limbs so that they would fall on people's plastic tents and on the people themselves.

In the military man's logic, effective, constant harassment involved placing people in a vise between pain and discouragement on one side and a promised paradise on the other. Many people had a different way of seeing the matter: a man who inflicted pain at every turn could hardly be trusted when he offered a faraway Eden. The simple notion of negative and positive reinforcements did not account for people's ability to interpret and understand the manipulator's motives and thus to avoid the trap.

Coronel Curió was up against a much more serious set of problems than he imagined. He failed to appreciate that times were changing in Brazil, and that the changes went far beyond the weakening of the military regime and the political abertura it proclaimed. The determination and creativity of the people living in the difficult conditions of the encampment exemplified just part of the broad political, social and cultural changes that were setting a new context, one for which neither Curió nor the military regime were prepared.

# Life in the Camp
## Hardship and Community

People have very different ways of recalling the time of the encampment. Three of the greatest fears people shared were the violence of the armed men set against them, hunger and disease. Before, during and after Coronel Curió's visits, we were told, people had their ways of fighting back against the armed men surrounding them. The soldiers were, in some ways, subject to many of the difficulties the campers faced. They, too, were camped out in the cold and heat; they also had no good place to wash up. Soldiers went down to the pond for occasional baths, and from across the water, the women of the camp would yell joking insults at the naked men, commenting sarcastically on the soldiers' physiques and making disparaging comments on their manhood, slurs that were accompanied by hysterical laughter. Blatantly burlesque, fake flirtation embarrassed the soldiers, who, when they were not engaged in direct confrontation, often felt sheepish about the pain they were inflicting on people much like themselves.

During direct confrontations, the women and children of the camp often took up the front ranks, making it more difficult for the soldiers to commit acts of violence. As the first line of defense, the women put flowers behind the soldiers' ears and in their rifle barrels. In various instances, women had proved more determined and aggressive than the men in fighting the intrusions of the police and soldiers in the camp. On at least one occasion, a policeman began to cry as he was being ordered to attack the line of women—they talked to him and succeeded in convincing him to quit the police and join the people of the encampment. Another policeman charged with mapping the various encampments popping up around the state became persuaded by his contact with the settlers and also joined the encampment at Encruzilhada Natalino.

One big, awkward, shy man, while standing next to his wife in 2001, told us that one of the changes that happened during the encampment was an alteration in his attitude toward women. "We tend to be sexist here; well, anyway, I have always been sexist. I never trusted the judgment of women. I always thought I knew better than a woman. Better than my wife. But in the camp, it was often the women who saved us, who kept us from being defeated. They were strong! Now that we have been farming for ourselves, well, I have learned to trust my wife's opinion in running the farm, too. I am still kind of sexist, I guess, but I have learned."[39]

Another man, Ne, the fellow recruited in the confession box, remembered that the men often felt helpless. "They would cut us off from the water. Everybody was thirsty, but the babies would be crying for hours from thirst. The women would be crying because the children were crying. The men would be sitting around feeling discouraged and

A characteristic of MST camps is the presence of women and children as well as men; whole families are invested in the process of winning land.

helpless because the women were crying and the men couldn't figure out how to do anything about it."[40]

Some of the people who lived in the encampment remember that they ate well enough—food was shared to a large extent, and some families had the direct support of extended family outside the camp, who managed to send in food as it was needed. Those who had no one on the outside complained more of hunger, recalling times when they went for many days eating only one scant meal a day so that there would be enough for the children. The Placotniks, who were better off than some because they had occasional access to Pacote's grandfather's farm, recall sometimes sharing a single cup of dried rice among two or three families. The women remember the long lines waiting for water—it wasn't worth the interminable wait if you didn't haul five to ten gallons back to the shack, a load between forty and eighty pounds.[41]

Everyone agrees that sanitation was a severe problem. The plastic, crude thatch, cardboard and wood-scrap shacks were densely crowded together. Anir Placotnik recalls that thirteen families were housed in a single long shack. It was not easy to stay clean, to wash dishes and

clothes or to keep living spaces with dirt floors in reasonable order. La-
trines and slit trenches did not always provide adequate sanitary conditions for waste, and safe drinking water was always a problem. People
found it impossible to control plagues of fleas and lice that brought
constant itching and disease. Eye infections were endemic. Typhoid
and dysentery hit children especially hard and were a great heartache
to parents, who, to some extent, worried that they were exposing their
children to these conditions out of choice rather than strict necessity.
Here in the South, general living conditions did not ordinarily expose
any but the very poorest of children to the constant danger of disease
that was common among most rural people in much of Brazil. Some
children died in the camps of diseases they would likely have avoided
outside. The parents might have been able to continue as sharecroppers or landless laborers, as hateful as it was to do so, and they always
had to wonder if accepting a place in the frontier colonization projects
might be the more responsible choice to make for the children.

Volunteer doctors, nurses and public health workers often came to
the camps to help deal with these problems. Everyone remembers their
work and credits them with keeping conditions from getting completely out of control, but the inherent problems of the camp could not
always be solved, and the authorities frequently forbade volunteer medical personnel from entering.

While some people came in groups of friends and acquaintances,
most of the people didn't know each other before arriving at the camp.
The first four or five weeks after people began to gather were especially
difficult, as people had to learn to get along and trust each other, to put
committees and camp rules in place. Although some people were to
become impatient with endless meetings, the camp's committees provided places for people to form friendships and share a sense of common purpose, as well as make rules that would allow the camp to
survive. For example, the camp's central committee strictly forbade alcohol, and those who smuggled it in to drink or sell were immediately
expelled. There were also those who liked to fight and others who
flouted the rules. For example, it was forbidden to cut green wood for
firewood, as it was essential to preserve all available wood supplies by
using only deadwood; those who cut it had to be thrown out of the
camp.

The continued meetings of the CEBs were also helpful in bringing people together. Reflection on biblical texts, as before, provided ways to discuss difficult issues in terms of fundamental values and principles, sometimes cutting through the personal suspicions and animosities that each problem tended to create.

The long, uncomfortable, and worrisome days of the encampment created an environment that was highly susceptible to demoralization. The "fun and animation" committee set up to deal with morale in Encruzilhada Natalino and other contemporaneous encampments would evolve into the *mística* committees operating throughout the landless movement, committees that were almost certainly a revival of the *"animação"* activities practiced in the pre-1964 Catholic youth organizations. Music, dance, special feasts, dancing, skits, poetry reading, juggling and events that might combine all of the above and more were all part of the job of the earlier animação committees and the mística committees of the MST. The committees organized soccer games and invented toys for the children. The acampados discovered that performing song, poetry, dance and skits could lighten the burden and inspire action or simple perseverance in ways that speech making and conversation could not always achieve. Some of these events took place on a daily or weekly schedule, but perhaps the most important were improvised spontaneously, when people were feeling especially discouraged or challenged. People in the animation committees knocked themselves out thinking up interesting and original ways to express the essence of matters at hand, using costume and gesture, chant, lighting effects, candles and arrangements of fruits, vegetables, flowers and grain stalks.

In the rest of Brazil, the universal balm of poor people was the rich tradition of African music and dance modified in various ways by local musical traditions from indigenous and European roots. The samba and its variations worked magic for a people who would laugh and play while singing endless changes on the theme that *"estou fingindo alegria para não chorar,"* the Portuguese equivalent of the American blues line, "I'm just laughing to keep from crying." This tradition would come to shape the movement's mística committees elsewhere in Brazil, but in the South, with more recent European immigrant roots, things were different.

One of the Southern traditions that would take on new life in the movement was *declamação*, which we found to be very much alive in the year 2001. Declamation typically begins after eating and, outside of the necessarily puritan prohibition of the camps, serious drinking. As we experienced it, someone begins to chant the name of a companion, demanding that he declaim—"Sergio, Sergio, Sergio, declamar, declamar, declamar, declamar"—while pounding on tables or clapping hands. Finally, Sergio relents, and after a couple of shy or humorous comments, often making fun of someone or all of his audience, he introduces a poem, explaining its theme or origin. When we saw it in action, Sergio, the young man of thirty or so who led things off had a sardonic way of talking and a slightly nervous, restless air. He introduced a gaúcho poem (the people of Rio Grande do Sul being gaúchos, which also means, in context, "cowboy") well known to all, and began to recite its rhymed couplets: "A man comes riding toward me from the distant horizon. . . ." The recitation was accompanied by dramatic hand and body movements of the kind taught to nineteenth-century actors and was spoken in theatrical voice.

Each person who declaims eventually has to beg off in the face of protest when he has performed as many poems as he knows or wishes to perform. Most of the poems originate in regional literature, and some are well known by all, but there are original poems—we heard one on the absurdities of agronomy training in the university—as well as poems and dramatic set pieces that address political issues. Some are so hilarious that people can't stop laughing, and the declaimer has to stop from time to time in order to be heard above the laughter. Some are sentimental, of the "how wonderful it is to be here among my dear friends" school and some are thinly disguised political campaign speeches. All, however, are greeted with praise and enthusiasm, and each speaker and piece seems to be eagerly anticipated.

Needless to say, the declamation tradition made for rich opportunities for amusement, education and argument within camps like Encruzilhada Natalino. It fit comfortably at camp meetings among well known and original songs accompanied by guitar, accordion, harmonica or violin. Polkas and many of the dances of central and southern Europe went on for hours.

Each day at noon, the settlers held a mass. The mass was kept simple and ecumenical, for among the settlers were many Lutherans and followers of evangelical and Pentecostal sects. The presence of priests in the encampment was a comfort to many. In the late afternoon, people would gather around the cross to discuss the day's events and the problems that faced them.

In the first days of the encampment, they had gathered around a small wooden cross, which had carved into it the command, "Save your soul." As time went on, the families began to feel that this small cross with its message of individual heavenly salvation no longer represented their calvary, which, after all, was more a journey of earthly salvation and of an entire community of people joined together. They fashioned a large, heavy, rustic cross and substituted it for the original. People often attached ribbons or notes or flowers to the cross to memorialize events in the long struggle. Later, they added supports to reinforce the cross, and the supports themselves provided more room for hanging up the shreds of memory. When the first baby in the encampment died of diarrhea, the child's parents hung his diaper from the cross. Over time, many diapers would hang alongside it, reminders of the losses families faced in the encampment.

Although many of the people in the encampment had support from friends and family on the outside, the scorn heaped on them from people in surrounding communities was a continuing problem. "They called us 'vagabonds,' worthless, people who wouldn't work." The wounds of contempt and name-calling are still raw twenty years later for some of the people who lived in the encampment.[42]

Not all the memories of camp are sad. Amazingly enough, one man we talked to said that the camp was "a lot of fun." Everyone speaks of the strong sense of community, of mutual help, of at least occasional high spirits. One woman said, "It was the very best time of our lives." Much more common was the view of Pacote and Anir Placotnik, who said that it was a wonderful experience that they would not trade for anything, because of the sense of community and friendship and shared struggle, but when asked if they would repeat it, replied, "Listen, it was something really tremendous—it made us who we are—but if we knew we were going to repeat it, well, that would be very hard to accept." Pacote and Anir spoke of their memory that "everyone worked together, everyone shared. We sang together, prayed together, made decisions

together and talked together constantly of our hopes for the future."
The idea that the encampment shaped people, transformed them,
"made us who we are," is repeated by many participants.

People in the settlement reached a certain point that may have been
the most critical in their transformation: the point when they realized
that there was no going back. Pacote recalled, "We lost what little we
had when we went to the encampment. We could take little even of
those few things we owned into the new encampment, the only thing
we took was our (wood-burning) cookstove. What little savings we had
were soon gone, because we were earning nothing. We had no house
nor land to return to, no household goods, hardly any clothing, very
few of our tools—everything was lost. And there was no way to go back
and be the same person again to the old neighbors, the friends on the
outside. Everything depended on the future and on the friends we had
made in the encampment. There was no way back."

It was the realization that there was no return that inspired Pacote's
promise. His very religious mother, like many Brazilians, had a fervent
faith in Nossa Senhora da Aparecida. Originally, this faith had its roots
in the same ground that nourished so many poor people's faith in
Aparecida. Unlike that of many other Catholic religious figures, reverence for this saint was based on the faith of poor people, not on the
standards and traditions of white Europeans that had come down from
an august and distant church. Pacote's mother thought of herself as an
Indian and took her faith more from folk tradition than from the formal teachings of the church itself. When Pacote's brother suffered an
automobile accident and was declared dead, she prayed fervently to
Aparecida. The young man began to breathe again and recovered from
the accident. As in every significant event in the family's life, such as
the birth in the encampment of the Placotnik's daughter, their first
child, they gave special thanks to Aparecida.

In the darkest days of the encampment at Encruzilhada Natalino,
knowing that only faith in the future could sustain him and his family
through what would still be a long and difficult path of suffering, Pacote made a promise to Aparecida. He promised that if they got the
land that was the purpose of this journey, he would for the rest of his
life sponsor an annual festival to honor the saint.

Pacote's promise was, in one sense, an example of the most traditional and conservative aspects of Brazilian society. The promise made to a saint is a custom found throughout the Roman Catholic world, but it is an unusually strong and serious matter in Brazil, often associated in Brazilian literature and popular song with the individual's powerlessness in dealing with the frustrations and sufferings of life. One makes a promise to the saint because there is no other action that can take to improve one's chances. For example, the popular songwriter Gilberto Gil of Bahia (appointed minister of culture under the Lula government in 2003) used this tradition ironically in the early 1990s, as many Brazilian poets and novelists have done, to speak of the hunger of a poor woman named Magdalena: Magdalena's crops on her miserable piece of land have failed, so oh well, there is no solution but to go to the chapel, light a candle, make a promise and pray. Said so crudely and to an upbeat samba rhythm, the idea becomes a parody of the conservative litany by which the poor are kept in their place. Amplified over loudspeakers in the streets at carnival, this song joins dozens of similar expressions that simultaneously honor and mock the faith of the poor. The unspoken but clearly recognized dishonor is not to the individuals but to the system that keeps poor people locked in such desperate situations.

However, Pacote's promise, together with his steadfast loyalty to the landless movement, ties this old tradition, formerly linked to powerlessness, to new hopes to be realized through collective political action. Pacote's promise was a private prayer, but Pacote says clearly that he knew then and knows now that its terms would only be met by the success of the landless movement.

# New Thought, New Speech, New Action
## The Grass Roots of Political Change

The state and federal governments found themselves perplexed about how to deal with the expectations of the people encamped at Encruzilhada Natalino. One of the most severe problems was the possibility that the demands of these landless people would generate a large national movement that would once again, as in the early 1960s, challenge the critical interests of Brazil's elites. Encruzilhada Natalino, while one of the first and most significant of the encampments demanding agrarian reform, was not the only one. Many other land occupations had grown up during the same years, especially in the states of the South, but also in other regions of Brazil. As the settlers at Encruzil-hada Natalino joined their voices with those of people in other land oc-cupations, they made up a chorus demanding generalized agrarian reform as well as land for themselves: it was possible to think again of a national agrarian reform movement.

In addition, the landless movement was only one facet of a general deepening and maturing of the political opposition to the military gov-ernment and everything it represented.

Through the long years of the dictatorship, Brazilian political ac-tivists had begun to learn hard but essential lessons: for example, while dramatic actions, such as the kidnapping of ambassadors, had their usefulness in achieving such goals as the release of political prisoners, they did not necessarily lead to political advancements; indeed, they brought deeper repression and set up new barriers to organization. They did not necessarily work as intended to force fence-sitters to more radical stands and actions. Instead, they often horrified and alienated the very people seen as potential recruits. Activists had seen how thor-ough modern methods of political repression could be at eliminating leaders and breaking up underground networks or rendering them in-effective. They had learned that doctrinal purity could be a trap that di-vided and weakened opposition groups, sometimes driving people into extremes of utopian enthusiasm that become self-parodying and self-defeating. In contrast, they had seen in the autoworkers' strikes that, under the right circumstances, it was possible to organize mass actions with a broad and deep social base and public support in spite of repression. A new kind of maturity more firmly rooted in Brazilian ex-perience and less in imported dogma began to characterize the Brazil-ian Left. This new Brazilian opposition became more skilled at using and creating national networks that were relatively open, flexible and legal.[43]

Technological and demographic change and economic growth began to facilitate social movements, including the landless movement, which challenged and eventually played a role in defeating the dictatorship. The most important change that had occurred was the urbanization of

Brazilian society. During the time of the dictatorship, Brazil went from being two-thirds rural to being two-thirds urban, which meant that rather than being under the domination of large landowners in local fiefdoms, most people were now city people with a broader awareness of the world. More and more, the degrading poverty and economic sluggishness of rural Brazil showed itself to be glaringly inconsistent with the nation's spectacular industrial progress—a disgrace that was neither necessary nor excusable. At the same time, people in Brazil's cities became increasingly alarmed by the rapid influx of rural people to the cities, a shift that contributed to massive social problems that posed immediate threats to personal health and well-being, ranging from inadequate sewage disposal to crime. In addition, landowners and planters stood to lose their grip on power in a national economy and government that had become more industrial and urban since the 1930s.

In the early 1980s, most Brazilian households still did not own refrigerators, but the vast majority had televisions or easy access to televisions in public places. Poor people seldom had telephones, but public phones were widespread; institutions such as the Catholic Church not only had phones, but also fax machines and computers. Nearly everyone listened to radio. The mass media were owned by a small handful of people, notably the O Globo network, which commanded the airwaves as few other privately owned media corporations in the world are able to dominate their national markets. Its owner, Roberto Marinho, was considered by many to be the most powerful man in Brazil. In spite of media monopolization and official censorship, however, more news—and more reliable news—got through to the public. Even censored, superficial and sensationalist news programs on television began to create a sense of a nation that Brazilians had not experienced before. For the first time, the vastness and variety of the people and landscape began to take form in most peoples' minds as an image of a nation in which at least to some degree all Brazilians shared a common fate. The expressions of support from scores of national and international organizations for Encruzilhada Natalino and other land reform encampments made it clear that it would be impossible to isolate and quietly destroy individual camps.

Interestingly, political changes wrought by the military dictatorship complemented the growth of communications technology in building a more genuinely national Brazilian identity. When the military came into office, it ran into difficulty controlling cities, *municípios* (counties) and regions formerly under the rule of local political bosses and machines, often led by powerful landowners. In many places, the police were essentially the private armies of local political bosses, with little or no accountability either to the populace or to state or federal authorities. The legal impunity of wealthy landowners and political bosses was an ongoing national scandal and undermined national identity and efficiency in myriad ways. For example, in the early 1970s, there were still municípios in the northeastern state of Bahia where citizens had to buy a postage stamp with the picture of the local political boss on it, as well as a federal stamp, if they wished their letter to leave the município.

This situation made it more difficult for the military regime to achieve both its repressive and its positive goals. Local police and politicians often could not—or would not—carry out the will of the federal government. In response, the military vastly increased the civilian powers of the military and the power of the civilian federal police. Local landowners wanting to monopolize control over land and people of their own regions, even if only to receive payoffs in exchange for granting access to outsiders, often posed an immediate or potential threat to the foreign investors the military regime was so anxious to attract to Brazil. In response, the military government made sure that many local bosses were forced to cooperate with the national government and with its economic plans in ways that they would never have assented to before the dictatorship. In exercising control over many of the local bosses, the military government began to make Brazil more a nation and less a collection of local fiefdoms.

Although carried out by the military regime for deeply conservative reasons, these same political changes also made it easier for progressive movements to survive and grow. As the country emerged from the hardest days of the dictatorship, local political bosses and the national government found it more difficult to isolate or destroy local movements without taking grave political risks. This was a profound change. For example, an operation pitting twenty-thousand federal troops against the guerrillas of Araguaia from 1972 to 1975 was the largest mobilization of troops since the Brazilian expedition to Italy with Allied forces in World War II; yet, until 1979, only one story appeared in the Brazilian press concerning it.[44] In the Alta Uruguaia of Rio Grande do Sul, where Encruzilhada Natalino later came to symbolize a national struggle, one family remembered that previous attempts to occupy land had been dealt with by local landowners who simply bombed the encampments from small private planes, with no regard for casualties. Local news media were pressured to keep quiet about it, and few outside the region ever heard of it. Brazilian history is chock-full of such events that never made it to national awareness, much less historical consciousness.

Contrast these stories with the enormous wave of indignation that rose in response to the assassination in 1988 of the rubber-tapper union leader, Chico Mendes, by landowners; in a previous era, news of such an event would never have made it downriver to the first major city, much less to São Paulo, Rio de Janeiro, New York, London and Tokyo. (See chapter 3 for more on Mendes.) This increase in national awareness and interconnectedness made it easier for progressive movements to create national organizations and gain national support for local initiatives. The Catholic CPT did a good job of linking the local movements and assuring that they got national publicity, demonstrating the amazing power of having a credible source systematically document and publicize crimes and abuses carried out for political reasons. CPT workers, a mixture of Catholic lay people, priests, nuns and monks, also offered assistance to the landless and other poor people's organizations in innumerable creative ways, ranging from taking surveys of what people needed, to providing advice in nutrition and agriculture, to helping build schoolhouses and clinics. One of their most important contributions was their innovative and nonbureaucratic spirit, responding flexibly to circumstances as much as or more than working according to a preconceived plan. They also provided a model for how other groups could do the same. This new connectedness and visibility would influence the government calculus in trying to deal with the settlers: the expressions of support from scores of national and international organizations for Encruzilhada Natalino and other land reform encampments made it clear that it would be impossible to isolate and quietly destroy the camps.

Government officials also found that the traditional practice of identifying key leaders and encouraging them to personally compromise or betray the cause of their followers did not work; nor did intimidation, another classic solution. The highly refined mix of threat and seduction, used so successfully to eliminate or tame other movements, fell flat at Encruzilhada Natalino and other similar encampments.

The CEBs' method of operation, which was rigorously followed by those in the encampment, was to avoid promoting individuals to prominent leadership positions. Also, priests or people not actually living in the camp itself were not allowed to speak for it. People like João Pedro Stédile and Padre Arnildo certainly offered guidance, and these two men sometimes attended negotiations with the government, but they did not represent the encampment nor did they speak for it in negotiations. It was also the policy from the beginning not to allow the leaders of labor unions or political parties to speak for encampments of the landless or the landless movement.

These policies, which were to prove essential to the vitality of the landless movement, represented a convergence of various currents of thought. In order to appreciate how confusing and upsetting it was for politicians and government leaders to try to deal with a movement that refused to play by conventional rules, we have to understand the approaches that some Brazilians had created to deal with poverty and oppression, approaches that would have a global influence.

For the lay and priestly practitioners of liberation theology, a guiding conception was the importance of people learning to speak for themselves and learning to grow through their own experience within a community context. This conception came partly from the observation that poor people often remained passive because they were either actively prevented from speaking on their own behalf or because others, including priests, had been eager to represent themselves as speaking for them. Brazilian plantation and ranching culture had given rise to a particularly strong tradition of paternalism and clientelism (see chapter 2), by which the poor had learned to gain some satisfaction of their needs through submission to and dependence on the landowner. They had also learned to gain favor through asking foremen or owners to serve as godparents to their children, and they used family connections whenever possible. Priests frequently played a key role in these relationships, speaking as mediators in a system in which the poor were dependents who often needed a priest to gain the ear of the influential, and the influential often preferred to speak through the priest. If the Brazilian poor were to learn to be more active on their own behalf, this tradition had to be broken.

This perspective had been greatly sharpened and refined by an educator in the Brazilian Northeast who was to have a profound impact on education around the world. Anir Placotnik likes to wear a T-shirt emblazoned with his name, Paulo Freire, along with a portrait of his bald, bearded, bespectacled face. Anir's children now attend the Paulo Freire Elementary School, the name of which is a common fixture on land reform settlements throughout Brazil. For the Brazilian landless movement, as for many of the world's poor, it is difficult to overstate Freire's importance.[45]

Working with the rural poor for many years before the 1964 coup, primarily in the state of Pernambuco, Paulo Freire discovered that traditional methods of literacy training were largely ineffective. He perceived that this was largely because the traditional classroom tended to reproduce and strengthen relationships of authoritarian dependency, modeled through the classic relationship of teacher to student. Dependency dulled the minds of the students and made them less capable learners. Even where particular lessons made their way through this mental cloud, the model of dependency made it unlikely that the students would actively use newfound skills to define or pursue their needs persistently or creatively. In addition, learning how to behave within the classroom model of authoritarian dependency strengthened the tendency to enter into and accept the norms of authoritarian dependency relationships between tenants or landless workers and their landlords.

Freire developed a variety of techniques to break down the dependent relationship between student and teacher and to encourage critical thinking. Sometimes students were asked to begin by thinking and commenting on situations that were analogous to their own. They might be asked to look at and comment on a picture of a couple of university students drunk on the streets, an exercise that might provoke commentary about how the young people were wasting their privilege and education at the expense of those whose work supported them.

Such commentary could lead to further reflection and anger about the lack of educational opportunities for the poor. In turn, this might lead to a more powerful sense of how important it was to take advantage of education when it was offered. More direct methods involved using a labor or sharecropping contract as the first text in a literacy class, rather than the typical "Dick and Jane" primer. When the students came to be able to read the text, they understood much more clearly the nature of their servitude; at the same time, they understood the importance of being able to read, so that they would not so easily agree in the future to contracts that guaranteed their remaining in poverty. Arithmetic could be taught the same way, beginning with the sums and subtractions that calculated the terms of the students' servitude.

Perhaps Freire's most influential insight was that if people are to become active learners, they must become actors on their own behalf, speak for themselves and learn from experience. His philosophy and methods became closely integrated into the philosophy and methods of the landless movement. The MST adopted his perspective as the foundation for its schools and other educational programs (UNICEF honored the MST with an award for its innovative use of Freire's ideas). His work has had an enormous impact on progressive Brazilian educators in general and on the clergy attracted to liberation theology in particular. Freire's influence has been felt in educational philosophy and practice around the world, even where his name is not known.

## THE DISAPPOINTING PERFORMANCE OF
## LABOR UNIONS AND POLITICAL PARTIES

Further reinforcing the perspective that poor peoples' organizations needed to adopt fresh approaches and strategies was the largely negative experience of the poor with organizations that claimed to speak on their behalf, particularly trade unions and political parties. The Brazilian trade-union structure had been established under the regime of Getúlio Vargas, who led Brazil after a revolutionary coup in 1930, then served as the elected president, falling victim to a bloodless coup in 1944 and holding office again when elected president in 1950 until his suicide in the presidential residence in 1954. Leading Brazil for most of the years between 1930 and 1954, Getúlio Vargas played a role in Brazilian history at least as important as that of Franklin D. Roosevelt in the United States.

A short, avuncular man, Vargas came from a moderately wealthy ranching family in Rio Grande do Sul. In 1930, he took advantage of the weakness of Brazil's ruling clique of coffee planters in the wake of the onset of the Great Depression to stage the short revolutionary war that brought him to power. Many in Brazil were glad to be rid of the narrowly self-interested coffee planters of São Paulo, who had ruled Brazil for several presidential administrations. Vargas was shrewd in learning how to ride the crest of the social movements arising in Brazil and throughout the world in the Depression years, managing these movements to his own advantage. He was famous for tacking a course—first to the left, then to the right, then to the left again, to the right, and to the left again. During the 1930s, he encouraged the Communist Party and then smashed it, encouraged the Integralista Party (the Brazilian fascist party) and then smashed it. His taciturn character and dry wit kept even his closest associates guessing and made for constant speculation on the part of political commentators during his lifetime, speculations that remain alive today in the multiple perspectives among historians on the significance of his regime. One legacy of the Vargas government was the structure of the Brazilian trade union movement.[46]

In the 1930s, Vargas established an official legal structure for trade unions that on one hand gave the unions official legitimacy and importance while, on the other, tied them to a rigid, complex set of bureaucratic rules and creating a strong dependency on the government. While the officially defined role for trade union activity certainly resulted in some important gains for Brazilian urban workers and, at a later date, for rural workers, it also created trade-union bureaucracies that tended to be more responsive to the government than to the needs of union members. Internally, trade union officers became bureaucratic gatekeepers for members, seeking a variety of special benefits available under the Vargas labor law machinery: year-end bonuses, sick leave and disability benefits, severance pay packages and pensions.

None of these was sufficient to lift most workers out of chronic poverty; they were of some help, but mostly they recreated in a new

form the patterns of paternalism so deeply embedded in Brazilian political culture. Rather than expecting the plantation owner to put on a
holiday feast or to provide extra money for a sick child, the unions
began to provide these services through the government or private
companies. Trade unions became at least as much the mediators for the
dispensation of minor privilege as the representative of workers in demanding more solid gains in wages and working conditions.

Vargas pulled the teeth of the labor movement by sharply reducing
its threat to the structure of Brazilian political and economic power.
Any conception of labor unions as leaders in a class struggle with capitalism was nearly completely destroyed by the Vargas scheme, which
was surely one of his intentions.

As dispensers of privilege, rather than leaders in the fight for redistribution of wealth, the Vargas-established unions became permanently
mired in financial corruption and influence-peddling scandals, dis-
crediting themselves with workers and the general public. Though
there were many honorable exceptions among Brazil's trade unions,
union activism became more a vehicle for reaching positions of individual privilege than an opportunity to exercise responsible leadership.
This trend began to change with the autoworkers' strikes in the late
1970s, which gave rise to a "new unionism" that tried, though with
only partial success, to break out of the mold Vargas had shaped.

Although different in philosophy, organization and methodology,
the MST became an alternative to the rural trade unions, and its members consider it essential to maintain these differences and to avoid
falling into traps like those set during the Vargas era. Those who built
the MST were also worried about becoming dependent on political-
party structures that had been built in the Vargas era, structures that
also tended to recreate old patterns of paternalism.

Until Vargas's regime, political parties were little more than small
organizations made up of and representing factions of the Brazilian
elite. Many of these factions represented regional planter groups dependent on a single export commodity, as, for example, when the coffee planters of São Paulo gained ascendance over northeastern sugar
plantation families. Even then the groups were not mutually exclusive,
so that as one elite faction rose to power it always incorporated some
part of the membership and interests of the older clique. Appeals to the

populace as a whole were little more than temporary efforts to organize a real or potential mob as a threat against other elite opponents. With the incorporation of a much broader range of players in the political theater, not the least of which were labor unions, Vargas began to change this tradition.

A more inclusive political life offered new power and influence to workers with permanent industrial jobs and members of the relatively small middle class of tradespeople, professionals, bank clerks and government workers in the more prosperous cities of the South and Southeast. Vargas's Labor Party was usually dominant, but an array of smaller parties came and went. With no coherent base for political power in the labor unions, which were deeply dependent on the government and the Vargas political party, and with no independent, organized social base, politicians who were not themselves straightforward representatives of major elite groups of planters and industrialists had to search for ways to gain attention and influence. They did so largely by launching demagogic attacks on vaguely defined ruling interests and by promising quick and lavish benefits to all. A nearly all-pervasive style of urban populism launched many political careers. Rising populist stars of Brazilian politics were either defeated by those already entrenched or, more commonly, quietly incorporated into the factions of the major elites. Political parties, like labor unions, became political machines dispensing favors and privilege. The Vargas party could dispense privilege through the party itself, through the government and through most of the unions. Political corruption was generalized and often colossal in scale.[47]

In the heated political climate of the late 1950s and early 1960s, this mixture of demagoguery and paternalism threatened for a brief time to spin out of the control of elites, due equally to the excesses generated by the system and by the average person's frustration with it. More radical conceptions of the relationship of citizens to government began to emerge. It was in this atmosphere that Paulo Freire developed his theory and practice of education, that more intransigent and independent peasant and rural worker organizations began to flourish and that agrarian reform was, for the first time, put seriously on the Brazilian political agenda. The military coup of 1964 put an abrupt end to this period of ferment and innovation.[48]

The military substituted a simpler model for the more complex authoritarianism of the old system, which had been often implemented and softened through paternalism and clientelism. As the military regime aged, however, problems that could not be solved purely through authoritarian mandate proliferated. The regime attempted to adjust to new challenges and a more complex political environment, but not without great difficulty.

## CHANGING THE RULES OF ENGAGEMENT

From the beginning, the CEBs, greatly influenced by Freire's thinking, their own independent and growing antiauthoritarian critique and the experience of movements for social change under the military regime, imbued the landless movement with an antiauthoritarian and antipaternalistic perspective. The people camped at Encruzilhada Natalino—and eventually the whole landless movement—came to agree that attacking authoritarianism by creating a new group of professional spokespersons to challenge existing authority would be unsuccessful, for they would themselves become authoritarian and paternalistic in the process of representing the group. This view would be very difficult to adhere to over time, especially when the movement was—and is—under constant surveillance and attack by the dominant system. Issues of the top-down nature of authority and hierarchy have arisen in the movement since the early days (see chapter 4). Nonetheless, the critique of leadership, authority and paternalism remains essential to the movement.

In the first months of the flowering of occupations, including Encruzilhada Natalino, politicians and public officials encountered a raw and uncompromising version of this new approach to politics; Coronel Curió was coming up against it after it had already undergone considerable maturation in the special conditions of the encampment.

Coronel Curió was especially vulnerable to failure in this new political and cultural environment. Curió's supremely self-confident manner, his way of kidding and joking with his adversaries, his superficial generosity in providing feasts and parties and his promises of an imminent paradise to come, combined with his ruthless willingness to threaten, intimidate and punish exemplified the archetype of the successful planter and political boss. This style had been refined over centuries and is still encountered throughout Brazil; for example, planters we have talked to who know their workers are suffering but think that an annual feast makes up for year-round poverty. Regional and national political bosses, who thrive on shamelessly corrupt use of public funds distributed among a coterie of supporters, are another version of the same personality. Curió was playing out a role whose success would hardly have been questioned by anyone in a previous era, especially when it was fully backed by the machinery of a large and powerful militarized government.

Curió and the government did not understand that the landless movement was changing the rules of engagement. People were learning to identify more clearly the seductive and threatening personality of the patron with their poverty and humiliation, rather than with possible protection and safety in a harsh environment. The encouragement and material support, in the form of food and clothing coming from other organizations throughout the nation, helped them understand that the patron was not their only hope. With the encampments negotiating on their own behalf, and with collective and rotating leadership, the traditional strategies of threat and seduction could not work to so easily separate leaders from followers, as it had in previous generations.

After spending four weeks at Encruzilhada Natalino, Curió packed up and left. This was a major victory for the people of the camp, and they took a great deal of courage from it. It was also a bitter personal embarrassment for the arrogant Curió, who had declared that he would solve the problem in fifteen days, stayed for thirty and left with no solution in sight. It was his first significant public failure. To drive home the point, the people of Natalino gave him a going-away gift—a cable woven of straw with sixteen knots in it, representing the sixteen victories he had proclaimed in previous incidents. A seventeenth knot near the end of the cable was cut halfway through, representing his defeat.

Curió had not left without damaging the settlement, however. He had succeeded in scaring or luring away 25 to 30 percent of the six hundred families in the encampment. He had also cut off the deliveries of supplies from church and civic organizations, and these arrangements had to be reorganized. On September 8, the camp hosted a meeting of more than three thousand supporters, who came to show their continuing support and begin the task of reestablishing material assistance.

Curió's departure was a victory for the encampment, but it was not clear that the repression would lighten, nor what other government actions might follow. Shortly after Curió's retreat, contradictory announcements emerged from the national and state governments regarding the possible imprisonment of Padre Arnildo under the National Security Law and the deportation of a Catholic nun, Sister Aurelia; both Arnildo and Aurelia had played important roles in the occupation, and the government believed it could incapacitate the movement by removing them. Neither event occurred, although it would appear that the intervention of the CNBB may have been critical in preventing these actions by the government. Interviewed by the local press, members of the encampment declared, "We are not cloth dolls that do what [the clerics] tell us. . . . How could it be that a priest and nun guarantee the existence of an encampment, when all the agents of federal and state governments were unable to dismantle it?"[49]

Repressive efforts continued by both the government and conservative church authorities. When Curió left, Dom Claudio Colling, the conservative bishop of the diocese of Passo Fundo who had questioned the legitimacy of the encampment from the beginning, forbade Padre Arnildo and Sister Aurelia to continue their work there. However, the two apparently continued to work with the encampment through the offices of the CPT.

The federal INCRA officials and some state officials seemed to indicate that land might be made available to the settlers, but the state government and police stepped up their repressive measures. A delegation from the encampment sent to talk to the governor in Porto Alegre was denied an audience and harassed by the police. Three women in the delegation, one of them pregnant, were assaulted by police officers in Porto Alegre. The delegation returned home without hopeful news. While the state highway police, who were once again in charge of the police barricades, allowed freer passage in and out of the encampment, the atmosphere of threat and hostility increased. Police harassment in the encampment escalated, with a series of arbitrary restrictions that made medical care, food deliveries and normal family life more difficult. Interrogation by police was a constant presence in camp life.

In January of 1982, the police announced that the stop for the bus into town would be moved from Encruzilhada Natalino to a place more

A memorial to the MST victory at Encruzilhada Natalino reminds people of the origins of the many MST land reform communities in the vicinity.

than a mile and a half away. Police officers, however, continued to use the old stop. In February, a group of people from the encampment decided to wait at the old stop. The bus stopped for them, at which point they were attacked by twenty-five police officers, who used guns and tear gas, injuring many people, five of them seriously. Two police officers were injured. The police claimed that the incident had been provoked by the people waiting for the bus, who, they said, had threatened bus passengers.

More delegations visited the capital and attempted to talk to the governor, at one point sitting in on state legislative hearings for several days. Legislators complained about the children crying and the songs sung to the accompaniment of the *gaita*, a small, regional variant of the accordion that was well known as Padre Arnildo's trademark. The landless delegation worked the press for attention and sympathy, replying that the cries of the children were the cries of frustration, and the songs and accordion playing the only way a people denied justice could lift their spirits.

Nationally known leaders helped boost the settlers' morale, assisting them in putting their cause before a national audience. At a forum held at the state university, Luis Inácio da Silva (Lula), leader of the autoworkers' strikes in São Paulo, declared that the fight for agrarian reform was now the most important struggle in Brazil. The support of organizations throughout Brazil placed Encruzilhada Natalino prominently on the national map of Brazil.

The press continued to attack the landless peasant movement, focusing in particular on Padre Arnildo and other church people. Rogério Mendelski, who had written a series of similar columns earlier, accused priests such as Arnildo of being "not at the service of God, but of the four horsemen of the Apocalypse, dressed up like Pharisees." Mendelski proposed that Padre Arnildo suffered from a "Messiah complex." The theme endlessly played by everyone from Mendelski to the state governor, Amaral de Souza, was that the delegations speaking to the government and the press were being manipulated behind the scenes by communist agitators, who cared nothing about the fate of the landless, but were only hoping to foment revolution. Ironically, the people who made these accusations did not listen to the landless themselves, who continued to assert that they were capable of speaking for themselves and that they deeply resented the contemptuous assumption that they did not know their own minds.[50]

## The Church Brokers a Respite

The most serious threat to the prospect of land reform in Rio Grande do Sul, however, was not false accusations, but the lure of colonization projects in other states. As the difficult conditions of the encampment continued to exact a great sacrifice from every family there, the invitation to move to a settlement outside the state, where the federal government promised land, credit, schools, clinics and security, became ever more tempting.

In October, the first large group of people who had been waiting in a camp set up for the purpose by Coronel Curió left for a project in Lucas do Rio Verde in the state of Mato Grosso. As with the colonization projects arranged by Curió to defeat the guerrillas in Araguaia, this project was under strict military supervision. One former member of the central committee of Encruzilhada Natalino was among those who left for Mato Grosso, and his continued support for the project carried a lot of weight with those at Encruzilhada Natalino.

The first reports from those who arrived in Mato Grosso described feelings of "euphoria," and their arrival, as televised by Curió, seemed to augur well for the colonists. While there were doubts about the legitimacy of the title arrangements, the resistance of local land claimants who had come before and the quality of the soil, which required expensive fertilizers to produce a good crop, these questions were outweighed by the seeming potential of the project. After two months, however, some families returned to Rio Grande do Sul, saying the project was too far from all-weather roads, the soil was only productive for those with large lines of credit to buy chemicals and machinery and many of the social services promised had turned out to be illusory. In spite of these reports, however, with the increasing pressures applied to those camped at Encruzilhada Natalino, dozens of the approximately 320 families who remained picked up, week after week, to go to Mato Grosso. Perhaps Curió would win after all.

Then, on February 15, 1982, seven thousand people demonstrated in Ronda Alta, near Encruzilhada Natalino, in explicit support of the landless and of the continued presence of the priests and nuns who had been working with them. At this event, leaders of the encampment announced a breakthrough: the church and other organizations had arranged for the purchase of 108 hectares (about 266 acres) of land as an intermediate encampment until more serious reform could be achieved. This was good land, along the shores of the new Passo Fundo reservoir, easy to irrigate. The people would be able to grow some of their own food and govern their own daily affairs without police interference.

During the following week, the Brazilian bishops held their national meeting in a town in the state of São Paulo, where they called special attention to the problems of the landless in Rio Grande do Sul, particularly those of Encruzilhada Natalino, as well as the problems of people fighting for land in the Amazon. On February 23, the Rio Grande do Sul CPT held in Encruzilhada Natalino its annual event in support of land reform, which they called "*A Romaria da Terra*," the Pilgrimage of the Land. The organizers counted thirty thousand people in attendance. More and more, the fate of the encampment seemed to rely on an increasingly broad social movement incorporating dozens of organizations and tens of thousands of supporters and not solely on the determination of the landless themselves to hold out for their demands.

On March 12, 1982, the people of Encruzilhada Natalino moved to their new patch of land acquired through the church, calling it Nova Ronda Alta. Each family had its own vegetable garden, and a collective community garden was planted. In addition to garden crops, the settlers grew corn, beans, garlic, rice, peanuts and soy. They also had a fine crop of radishes, a load of which they sent to an industrial suburb of Porto Alegre, to the workers who had been the most stolid supporters of the community. The settlers sent another batch to the state secretary of agriculture, to show that they were not lazy, that they just needed land in order to be able to become productive.

Later, some settlers would complain that the priests attempted to impose utopian ideas of cooperation and absolute equality within this settlement, an experience that would strengthen the settlers' resolve to become less dependent on clerics and the church in the future. At the time, however, the new land gave a badly needed breathing space to the movement.[51] Future settlers would continue the practice of growing food in the occupied area as a way of providing sustenance for the duration of the encampment.

# Victory for the Settlers and the Formation of the MST

By 1982, the federal government was officially planning to phase out the dictatorship and restore civilian rule. Civilian elections began to take on new importance as the control of the military loosened.

From the winter months until spring elections in November, those who battled for land reform in the state of Rio Grande do Sul concentrated on the election of a sympathetic governor. People in support of land reform and many of the people in the encampments themselves worked in campaigns for candidates who had supported agrarian reform and promised to continue doing so in office. The candidate of the Left, Jair Soares, won the election, promising to resolve the issue of land distribution to the landless encampments within six months. He kept his promise.

In June 1983, the people of Encruzilhada Natalino won their demands: the 164 families remaining in the encampment received 1,870 hectares (about 4,620 acres) of land. They were given fifteen years to pay back their loans, with a three-year period before payments would begin. The state put together a combination of state-owned and privately claimed land that did not meet the Land Statute's requirement for productive use, its "social function." The land was scattered in different parts of the state, but the largest part was close to the original encampment, on the Sarandí fazenda, which had been expropriated in the brief period of agrarian reform before the military coup in 1964. Some families had been settled there previously, but most of the land had been tied up in litigation. The state settled the lawsuits and made the land available for redistribution.[52]

By the spring of 1983, it was not just the families who had held out at Encruzilhada Natalino who were acquiring land as a result of the landless movement. Many settlements throughout the South of Brazil and in some states to the north were assigned land as a result of similar occupations. By January 1984, the movement was so widespread that it was possible to form a national organization called the Movimento dos Trabalhadores Rurais Sem-Terra, the Landless Workers Movement, known throughout Brazil as the MST. The name was the subject of considerable debate, but in the end, it was decided to adopt the term *sem-terra*, meaning literally "without land." Although the term had negative connotations, it was widely used by the press and in the end expressed the unapologetic recognition of who these people were and what their most pressing need was: land. A year later, the first national congress of the MST met in Curitiba, in the southern state of Paraná, bringing together twelve hundred men and three hundred women as delegates from *assentamentos* (settlements) from twenty-three states.[53]

Formed a year before the official end of the dictatorship, the MST would become an important part of the growth of civil society organizations in a Brazil striving to rebuild democratic institutions and a more democratic national culture. By 2002, the MST had succeeded in acquiring legal ownership for approximately 350,000 families in three thousand settlements; the amount of land going to these families reached about eight million hectares, or twenty million acres, an amount of land about equal to the amount of irrigated agricultural land in the state of California. An additional 61,000 people in 459 encampments were awaiting land.

These figures, which came directly from the MST national office in September 2002, are far lower than those put out by the Brazilian government for the entire process of agrarian reform. The government claims to have distributed twenty million hectares (fifty million acres) to 564,000 families, which includes non-MST settlements. The MST argues persuasively—as do observers not affiliated with the movement—that the government numbers have been inflated to exaggerate how much the Cardoso administration did for agrarian reform. The MST view is that most of the families in non-MST settlements enjoy too little organizational support to have much hope of holding on to the land. In any case, it is very clear that the MST has been the compelling social force that has pushed national agrarian reform forward for the first time in Brazilian history, achieving remarkable progress in promoting alternatives to environmentally destructive agriculture and in education, health and social services.[54]

It was not easy to foresee the successful future of the MST at the first national organizational meeting, held in Paraná in the town of Cascavel in January of 1984, where ninety-two delegates from land occupations throughout Brazil engaged in intense debate about the character and future of the movement. Much of the debate centered on the relationship of the movement with all those organizations—among them the Catholic CPT, lay and clerical organizations from other churches, labor unions and political parties—which had been important in the founding and growth of the movement.

The contributions of the CPT and the Catholic Church were essential in the early history of the movement, and the church remains important to the movement to this day. However, the landless were made up of many religions; in the South, the Lutheran Church and ministers had played an important role, and in much of the rest of the country, evangelical and Pentecostal members had been among the most militant participants and leaders of the movement. There were those in the movement who chafed at the paternalism of some pastors and feared the growth of dependence upon them. Some people rejected the priests as "utopian," feeling that rural people were more practical in their approaches to problems. Others believed that the priests would stifle the movement were its politics to become too radical. Some important participants were either not religious or hostile to religion. The words of several bishops helped resolve the debate, as they urged that the movement would do best if it were independent.[55]

In some areas where successful land occupations and a growing movement for land reform flourished, the rural labor unions also played an important role. There was skepticism about the unions, however, because of their past dependence on the government and political parties, in spite of a "new unionism" that was inspiring some to pursue aggressive organizing. Also, the landless believed that the involvement of the entire family was critical to the success and goals of the movement, while the unions were based on membership by single workers as individuals. The landless also wanted to be open to the diversity of people who had been so important to their success, including "rural workers, peasant families, priests, agronomists, teachers and lawyers," not landless workers alone. In this sense, they wanted to maintain themselves as "a mass movement" rather than an organization on the trade union model.[56]

The new unionism that had started with the autoworkers' strikes in São Paulo had also led to the founding of the Workers' Party, the PT, led by Luis Ignácio da Silva (Lula), later to be elected president of Brazil. The PT had been helpful with several of the occupations, and many felt that both the PT and the MST would be strengthened if they joined forces. But, in the end, a majority of delegates at Cascavel insisted that the movement was unique and needed to remain independent from churches, unions and political parties, although they would continue to seek out and participate in coalitions and alliances with all of these.

The delegates also laid out their four basic goals: (a) to maintain a broadly inclusive movement of the rural poor in order; (b) to achieve agrarian reform; (c) to promote the principle that the land belongs to those who work on it and live from it; and (d) make it possible to have a just, fraternal society and put an end to capitalism. These goals have remained the official guides for the movement to this day.[57]

The growing strength and determination of the movement did not make things easy for new members attempting to acquire land through agrarian reform. It was nearly always a difficult struggle. Hundreds of encampments would have to go through trials just as difficult as those at Encruzilhada Natalino. Well over a thousand rural leaders—and sometimes their entire families—would be assassinated in the process, and thousands more would be beaten or driven from their homes, or would lose all their possessions to fires set by jagunços or police. It is striking, however, and in contradiction to the many press treatments of the MST as a movement that stirs up violence, that those settlements affiliated with the MST have suffered from fewer assassinations than those undertaken independently or in association with other organizations. As individuals and as an organization, the MST and its members would endure a barrage of insults and ridicule from the press, politicians and government. In spite of these and other obstacles, the MST is unquestionably the only organization in Brazilian history to achieve significant positive gains and a measure of land reform for Brazil's rural poor. However, as we shall see, by the beginning of the new millennium, the MST would be facing a combination of challenges as daunting as those faced by the first families trying to grapple with their situation when they first camped at Encruzilhada Natalino.

The biggest challenge remains to make agrarian reform work, that is, to enable the settlers to farm productively and profitably enough to sustain their families over decades on the redistributed land. Many Brazilian skeptics believe this challenge cannot be met, and many agricultural specialists around the world believe that small-scale producers in general are doomed. Others, however, many of them also agricultural experts, believe that small-scale producers can succeed and can even outperform larger producers. A large array of factors will determine who is right: technological developments, government policies, consumer preferences and ecological trends, among others. Our work in Brazil leads us to believe that much of the answer will come from farmers themselves, farmers like José and Anir Placotnik.

# Sarandí
## *The Challenges of Settlement*

On a Saturday morning in January 2000, with the chill of the summer night still in the air, Pacote and Anir sat in their wooden house talking with us about their lives. They are now part of a scattered community of single houses and villages known as Sarandí, though much of the land was carved out of Fazenda Anoni and other lands not part of the old Fazenda Sarandí. After welcoming us to the living room of their solid wooden house and offering us the best chair, they both puttered about, preparing the mate chimarrão. As we talked, they constantly re-filled the big, decorated gourd from a pot on a wood-burning stove painted with flowers and frills in a classic Eastern European style. Their older daughter, born in the Natalino encampment, did her homework, breaking at times to do a little housecleaning and always maintaining an ear toward our conversation. A radio played classical music from the local university FM station. At one point, the conversation was interrupted by a call on the family's cellular phone—cell phones are commonplace among families of modest income in rural areas, because they are much less expensive than having a line run to the house. The wood-plank house, like most in the area, sits alone, except for two modest outbuildings, on the 22.57-hectare plot (about fifty-seven acres) the Placotniks gained from the land distribution in 1983.

Pacote leaned forward on his chair, looking very intently into our eyes. "When we had won the fight for the land, first there was an indescribable happiness. We sang, there was so much happiness, and we couldn't go for a beer—because of the rules of the camp. There was just so much happiness. But then there came a moment that had that *aquela frissão* (hard feeling), when we had to have a lottery to divide up the land. Everybody was nervous, thinking, 'Where is my piece going to be?' We ended up in a group with second priority. That would have meant we would have to move somewhere else, but we didn't want to do that. We said, 'Look, we don't care what it is like, but we want a piece of land here in Sarandí, whatever is left after the first division.' So we got our piece of land here, something no one else wanted.

"It was a rotten place, just an arroyo, with brush and garbage. The whole group from the encampment came to help us clean it up. But now that we had our land, we didn't have even a bucket to hold water. We had lost everything but that stove," recalled Pacote, pointing to the older of two stoves in the room. Anir pointed to the brightly painted one warming the water for the chimarrão, "Now we have the old one and this good, new one, too."

It took a while for things to settle down after the land division. There were conflicts with those who did not get enough land or were forced to move elsewhere in the state. One group of people, who had not been part of the encampment and had no history of reflection or participation in the CEBs, saw that land was about to be made available and quickly created their own encampment and demanded land, too, sometimes attacking those who were in the process of receiving their allotments as a result of the encampment at Natalino. Some local politicians, who had been opposed to the whole idea of agrarian reform, began to promise these people land. Because this was the era when the Reagan administration in the United States was organizing and financing a guerrilla force known as the "contras" to fight the left-wing Sandinista government in Nicaragua, this group also came to be called the contras. Some of the contras were professional thugs, some merely opportunists encouraged by cynical politicians and landowners and some, probably most, simply desperate poor people who suddenly realized that they had missed out by not joining the movement earlier. They launched attacks on people waiting for redistribution of land and on those who were newly settled on their land. This also created serious problems with the public at large, as people began to think, as Pacote puts it, "This landless thing is a beast with seven heads." The contra conflicts continued off and on for nearly three years, until the contras eventually disbanded. The site of their encampment would eventually be turned into the campus of an MST school and research institute.[58]

During the same years as the contra conflicts, another group of families in the area began to join the newly formed organization of the MST. These families were pushing for further expropriations in cooperation with the settlers of Natalino and the MST. The Placotniks' friend, José Armando da Silva, nicknamed Zezinho, was among them.

Zezinho's story exemplifies one version of a theme that has always concerned those who have studied Brazilian rural life and those who have tried to change it. Most large landholdings have dependents of the landowner associated with them who, while subject to some of the poverty and insecurity of other workers on the holding, are, relatively speaking, privileged and protected. It has often been assumed that such people will ordinarily join hands with the owner in disputes with the workers. On the other hand, some theories of rural uprisings suggest that such people may be especially important in leading rural unrest.

Zezinho was the son of one of the *agregados* on the Anoni fazenda. *Agregado* has a variety of meanings in different times and regions of Brazil, but it always has the connotation of people who are dependents of the landowner and who share some sense of identity with him. They usually rent or lease land from the landlord, sometimes as sharecroppers, but they also expect to receive paternalistic favors and, in return, express their loyalty in word and deed. Often, as in Zezinho's family, agregado families are among the conservative allies of the landowner in rural politics. Zezinho's family members were devout Catholics. Zezinho and the other children in the family were able to go to school. But in 1983, Zezinho began to be drawn into the land reform process going on in the area.

Zezinho was the young man mentioned earlier who had been amazed at the priest's participation in the CEB discussion group; it was Padre Arnildo who had invited him to the group but another priest who led it. Zezinho was fascinated by the CEB discussion. As a very serious and studious Catholic teenager, he found that his intimate knowledge of the Bible made it easy and exciting to participate in the discussions. Political activists who had been in hiding during the military regime began to come out in the open and participate actively in the movement, which made it doubly interesting for Zezinho.

Zezinho was amazed at the changes he was experiencing. At the beginning of the conflict over expropriation of the Fazenda Anoni, Zezinho had sided with Anoni and was opposed to the proposal for reform put forward by INCRA. He detested both INCRA and the landless movement. His family had taught that hard work was the key to a good life; Zezinho, like many others, believed that the landless were lazy and worthless.

As he participated in their discussions and began to know those in the movement personally, Zezinho began to change his perspective. Before long, he was being persuaded to work with the landless movement. In the battle for a wider agrarian reform that now involved Fazenda Anoni, Zezinho became a go-between, a person who served as a trusted liaison between the church and the newly formed MST. He also became an essential source of news about what was happening on the fazenda. In the arguments over what was to happen with Fazenda Anoni, he was appointed as a member of a commission to negotiate a solution. Zezinho remembers having to walk ten kilometers (over six miles) to visit a deputy in the state legislative assembly. He still recalls walking with his umbrella in the heavy rain the whole way with only one thought in his head: "Who am I to talk to a deputy?"

The conflicts in these years were at times violent, continuing for nearly six years. When it became apparent that Fazenda Anoni was likely to be expropriated, people camped out all over the property, hoping to nail down land for themselves. Neither Anoni nor INCRA nor the MST was in full control of the situation.

This was at a time of intense activity and learning for Zezinho. In 1989, he was offered land in the southern part of the state. Later, he would become a director of the local school and research institute founded on the land once occupied by the contras, though he maintained his farm in the south and traveled back and forth between the school and his farm. Over the next two years—from 1989 to 1991, Fazenda Anoni was definitively expropriated, the land officially divided, and things began to settle down.

The years of conflict were difficult for everyone, but conflict was not the only problem, as Pacote remembers. "Worse than these conflicts, we fell into the old [production] system that prevailed around here. Plant soy and use a lot of chemicals. The soil degrades rapidly. The profit soon disappeared, and [the application of agro-chemicals] was polluting the pond and creek, destroying the land. We used a lot of Roundup. That doesn't work. I bought five young calves [to begin to shift out of complete dependence on soy]. Now we are going to change, we are going to preserve the soil."

Pacote showed us a map of the family property before taking us on a walking tour. On the map, colored pencils had been used to mark out the areas devoted to erva mate, pasture for the milk cows, a small hay field, corn, black beans, fruit orchards, a two-acre pond with three thousand catfish, carp and perch, a chicken shed and yard and a vegetable garden with tomatoes, squash, cucumbers and peanuts. Later, he showed us the pasture and the fencing materials he was laying out to use in the rotational grazing system promoted by an international movement to improve farm income and preserve soils (the nearby MST-affiliated school was just wrapping up a two-week training course for agronomists on the subject).

"What comes first is what we need to eat, healthy food for the family. Then we are selling our produce in the local ecological market that we have set up each week in Passo Fundo. It sells well, for a good price."

Pacote continued, "We realized that it wasn't just a matter of producing the right crops. We saw how the politicians manage everything." For example, the state and local politicians began to manipulate the federal line of credit available to the settlers, using it to reward loyalty and punish enemies.

At this point in the conversation, an older man dressed in jeans and a bright red vest came in and was welcomed warmly by Anir and Pacote. "The Commander," Antônio Dolina, a man of Polish ancestry, took a quick look at a basket of tomatoes on a countertop and declared, "You don't have the quality of tomatoes I have!"

"Look at him," Pacote said, "he's wearing the red of the Internationale!" The Commander was puffing away on a large cigarette hand-rolled with a cornhusk. Anir explained that Dolina was called the Commander because in the encampment and still, to some extent, people naturally looked to him to give order, to settle conflicts. "Did he have any special office?" we asked. "No," the Commander growled, "I never go for that kind of thing." Anir said, "No, people just respond to him in that way." The Commander's stolid physical build and gruff, self-confident manner made that easy to believe, as did the deep smile wrinkles around his blue eyes that seemed to say he wasn't taking anybody or anything too seriously.

Pacote picked up the theme of politics again. "We had to think about politics. There were hardly any roads here, and nobody in Passo Fundo was going to get them built. Without roads, we couldn't do much." Pacote explained that the settlers began to realize they would have to have a município government in which they would have some influence.

The município of Passo Fundo was too large and had too many entrenched powerful people in it ever to pay any attention to them. In Brazil, as in most of Latin America, outside of some major cities, município governments are roughly equivalent to county government in the United States, but with more authority over the cities within their jurisdiction; essentially, they are city and county government wrapped into one, governing both rural and urban affairs. There is a legal process by which new municípios can be created, or, in Portuguese, "liberated" from the existing ones. The settlers and the MST worked to create a new município. Although most people in the area were reluctant to vote for the landless, the desire for a smaller local município was shared by many, including some businessmen and large-scale landowners. After an intense political campaign, the new município of Pontão was liberated from Passo Fundo.

Pacote was at pains to explain why it would have been impossible to create a new município before the land reform. Like much of rural Brazil, the region had a very low population. It was the land reform that settled several thousand people on a ranch that had previously provided livelihood for only several dozen people, many of them cowboys with no families and with little interest in civic life. The landless who settled in the area constituted the first sizeable electorate. Just as important, this was an electorate that had been awakened to the importance of politics through their own experience. Many were still illiterate, but they began to work with that problem. Pacote, for one, was nearly illiterate—"I never went to school, I learned in the school of the world"—but he could rely on Anir, who learned to read as a child and who has since taught Pacote how to read.

In the first election for councilors and mayor of the new município, one of the conservative wealthy landowners won the mayoral contest and a supportive majority. Pacote won a councilor seat, but he was in the minority. Nonetheless, he found ways to shake things up. For example, the councilors received a per diem when they traveled on município business. The per diem at the time for travel to the state capital was the equivalent of more than seventy dollars. On his first official trip to Porto Alegre, Pacote took the bus, had a good lunch, booked a clean and decent hotel, did his business in the afternoon, went to a movie in the evening, ate the traditional Brazilian light supper, did some business in the morning and returned home. "It was all very agreeable, there was no suffering involved. And it cost a total of $26.50." When he returned, he gave the excess money back to the treasurer. The mayor and other councilors told him that wasn't necessary, that he should just keep what he had not spent. He insisted on returning the money to the município. The other councilors were very angry with him, but Pacote continued to insist. The local newspapers showed up to cover the story. While some treated it as a joke, the ridiculous result of electing a country bumpkin to a responsible office, this was clearly an extraordinary event. In the end, much chagrined, the council felt obliged to vote to cut the per diem allowance to half of what it had been.

Pacote wasn't done with his cost cutting. In Brazil, it is a common practice to allot a thirteenth paycheck at the end of year, which traditionally helps to pay for holiday expenditures or to cover accumulating debts before the New Year. The councilors received such a payment, but Pacote insisted this was wrong. "The thirteenth payment is for workers, for professionals. My profession isn't município councilor. My profession is farmer. Like the others on the council, all of whom have other work that supports them. This was ridiculous!" There was more wry commentary in the press about the mad bumpkin. At the council meeting at which the vote to eliminate the extra payment was to be held, the majority on the council arranged for the presence of extra police officers and police dogs to intimidate people. A big MST crowd showed up and supported the proposal to eliminate the thirteenth payment, and, again, Pacote got his way from the council majority: the council had been shamed into cutting its own pay. With the savings from the councilors' expenditures and pay, the município was able to buy its first ambulance.

One of the classic problems of measuring the success of land reform is that, from the point of view of the beneficiaries, success can still mean a relatively low level of cash income because families are able, like the Placotniks, to produce so much of what they need. The Plactoniks earn about the equivalent of US$500 a month in net cash income, which they consider not bad for a small farmer in Brazil, especially considering they have a house and are able to produce most of the food and many other things the family needs for themselves. This is hard to measure in quantitative terms, but in any case, the family is happy that they were able to buy a television and an old blue Plymouth Valiant. Pacote has decorated the car with a campaign sticker that reads, "Pacote."

Pacote insists on going to council meetings dressed in a simple shirt and jeans, "just as I am today." He refuses to wear a dress shirt and tie, as is customary. "The point is, we are trying to change the whole concept of politics, the relationship people have to the politicians. Not to set one up high and the other down low. You have to think about the meaning of the whole style."

On the day of the next election in October 2000, when the votes were being counted in a local gymnasium, Pacote's supporters knew they had won when they saw a group of fazendeiro wives crying together. Pacote was a councilor again, and this time he was in the majority, with an MST mayor. He would win reelection again in 2002 with a continuing majority of MST councilors and their allies.

Pacote is proud that 90 percent of the people in the município—all the land reform beneficiaries—have potable water, tested regularly by health officials. His children go to school in the well-tended Paulo Freire School down the road. When the students are ready for high school, they ride the rural bus to Ronda Alta. The elementary school is near a cooperative warehouse that doubles as a gymnasium and community center, where people gather to talk and play pool, basketball and the Italian game bocce ball.

Children in Sarandí are nearly all well fed and healthy, although there are health problems in the community, and medical care is a sore point for many. Some health care is available, but its inadequacy was made worse in the 1990s by federal cutbacks demanded by the International Monetary Fund. Padre Arnildo had successfully led a campaign in the 1980s and 1990s to build and run a hospital offering inexpensive care in nearby Ronda Alta, but the hospital burned to the ground in 2000. Padre Arnildo blames the fire on "the local bourgeoisie" who, he says, depend on income from the hospital they own and control in Ronda Alta to finance their political campaigns, as they once used such income to buy land.

MAKING REFORM LAST: INSIDE A LOCAL MST MEETING

For all the improvement in their lives, MST farmers in Sarandí worry a great deal about the future. We got a sense of the range of their concerns when we attended the annual meeting of what are called the "regional coordinators" of the inheritors of the land won at Encruzilhada Natalino, and later, from the Anoni fazenda and other nearby areas. Each of the about sixty delegates represents a small group of farm families. Here, all the problems of making agrarian reform a permanent and positive reality are discussed and debated over a two-day period. At this meeting, we watched these people confront a wide range of very practical problems, and we learned a great deal about their worries and hopes, their values and their political perspectives. The following account of that meeting gives a snapshot of the kind of enthusiasm, opinions, problems and ferment that characterize established agrarian reform settlements throughout Brazil; of course, it also reflects a particular moment in Sarandí's history, as well as the settlement's own character and people.

The settlers of Sarandí organized a credit union and farmers' cooperative that offers credit and marketing assistance and houses a simple grocery and general merchandise store that sells, among other things, seeds, chemicals and tools. The co-op basement provides a meeting place for the community.

In January 2000, the meeting was facilitated by Evander, a short, chunky blond man in his early thirties. As a child, Evander lost one arm below the elbow to a sugarcane mill. One of the people who lived through the land occupation at Natalino, he is cheerful, witty, patient and, above all, incredibly energetic. Hour after hour, he led the group with an enthusiasm that took the edge off the tedious and often discouraging topics under discussion. Throughout the two days of the meeting, Evander urged everyone to remember that if they did not speak up and speak honestly, the meeting could not do its job of improving the lives of the people living in Sarandí. The discussion was mostly very lively and rich in differing perspectives vigorously argued. There was a lot of good-natured kidding, and there were only rare and brief flare-ups of anger.

The regional delegates represented communities within the Sarandí and Anoni complex, with farms and villages as much as forty-five minutes from each other by car, mostly on dirt roads that in rainy weather can become impassable. As in the US Midwest, most of the farms sit on their own plots of land, separated from others. With holdings of about fifty acres per family, however, this implies less isolation than in the Midwest, where farm size is in the hundreds or even thousands of acres. Most houses are within a few minutes' walk from neighbors. In some communities, the houses are all placed together, and most of the farm-work is done collectively.

From the beginning, the MST national leadership favored collective work and, for a time, tried to insist on it. However, on most settlements the majority of people have decided, sooner or later, to farm individu-ally. Some research in MST settlements has found resentment among farm families for what they consider pressure from the national organi-zation to engage in collective work or cooperatives. Some argue that this is still a burning issue. The MST national leadership denies that people were ever penalized over this matter by the MST and maintains that the MST eventually realized that it could not impose such impor-tant family decisions. There is no question that the movement now has laid greater emphasis on marketing, equipment, service and credit co-operatives, while soft-pedaling collective work. The MST also favors settlement in houses that are grouped together (called "*agrovilas*") to favor, in the word of João Pedro Stédile, "sociability." Stédile says that the MST favors cooperation and agrovilas because the organization be-lieves that these are essential to "promote Christian and socialist val-ues." Stédile insists that the only time people have been punished for refusing to engage in collective or cooperative work or settlement has been when INCRA exacted penalties from settlers who failed to meet contractual provisions stipulated by INCRA, provisions requiring par-ticipation in various kinds of cooperation.

People who left collective farm projects to work individually often complain of too many meetings in the collective farms and of the in-ability to make one's decisions quickly and easily. Some, including Pa-cote, insist that the ability to make one's own production decisions is essential to stimulating productivity and innovation. But Pacote and nearly everyone we spoke to throughout Brazilian agrarian reform set-tlements agreed that individual work needs to be complemented by what Pacote terms "semicollective" arrangements, meaning credit, mar-ket and machine co-ops.

In the collective communities, on the other hand, many people speak of the stronger sense of community and security and argue that family income is greater. They also argue, as Maria Edna da Silva of Sarandí does, that collectives are better able to accumulate capital, which, she says, is essential in dealing with the inevitable problems of debt. "The individual builds up debt; the collective also builds up debt, but also accumulates capital that is essential for climbing out of debt in the long run." She cites her small collective's milking barn with refrigerators and cheese processing facilities. The farmers who farm collectively also receive a better credit rate from INCRA, at least partly because of savings to INCRA in administrative costs. Whatever the advantages and disadvantages, most of the farmers at the meeting of regional delegates and most of the people they represent are farming on an individual basis, and Stédile said in early 2003 that more than 70 percent of MST settlers were farming individually.

Many of the key questions debated at this particular meeting at Sarandí had to do with the operation of the marketing cooperative and credit union established by the community. These subjects are bread and butter issues of immediate and obvious importance. Other questions had to do with the MST as a social and political movement that remains important to some degree to everyone present. The annual meeting opened with songs of the movement, with teenaged boys and girls leading the singing and playing guitars. Nearly everyone joined in enthusiastically. When the singing was over, it was not long before the chimarrões of mate begin to circulate, with people coming and going to the stove upstairs to refill the large thermos bottles.

The primary concerns were not surprising. Some people were worried that the members were losing some of their community spirit and political militancy. Eleu Shepp, who had lived through the conflict with the Kaingang while sympathizing with the Indians, complained to us privately that too many people had gotten land without going through the long period of suffering and training that those from Encruzilhada Natalino endured. "They have been handed land on a silver platter and don't know the obligations that come with it," he said. Eleu's concerns permeated the meeting. People commented that once people are assured of having their own land, they sometimes lose concern for others and for the agrarian reform movement. They complained that their fellows don't always attend meetings regularly and often fail to meet the obligation everyone in the MST promises to meet: that every family is to provide moral and material support to other landless families and encampments to expand reform.

People also expressed impatience with the movement leadership at both the local and state levels, complaining that they did not stay in close enough contact, that sometimes they could not be found during what were supposed to be working hours and that they didn't always carry out their duties. But others complained that the leadership, particularly the state leadership, was "always imposing new tasks on the community and regional representatives." Evander pointed out the seeming contradiction: if the leadership has too little contact with the members, how can it be that they are constantly asking for new tasks to be performed? The latter surely implies frequent contact. Not everyone agreed with Evander's observation, and the discussion turned to the nature of leadership, the need of leaders to listen and respond and the need of people in the communities to be more energetic in expressing their concerns to leaders.

People also expressed deep concern about what they saw as the poor participation of young people in community affairs, which led to a broader discussion about the increasing lack of participation by families in the settlement and the prominence of men in the leadership. Sarandí's local governance committee in this year was about equally divided between men and women, but Salete, one of the committee members, expressed her concern that women were not as active as they needed to be. About a third of the regional representatives attending the meeting were women. There was a discussion of the need for the "gender committee," which is responsible for dealing with problems of sexism, to become more effective. When one man asked, "Why do we need a gender committee?" Evander replied impatiently, "Look, we have talked about this at length, we have made a decision about this as a community, we have identified participation of women as a key issue and we have asked the committee to address it. So that is not a matter for further debate. The question before us is how to make the committee more effective."

At another point in the meeting, people were selecting who would go to a special MST course offered in Porto Alegre. Several men and eight women were nominated to go. One of the men appointed argued that if they insisted on the eight women going, he would not be able to go, because his wife had also been nominated and someone had to stay home with the kids. Salete replied, "It is very important that every person be able to make her contribution to the community. We can arrange for others to care for your kids, and I can say that this will work, as I am a very good friend of your wife." The man relented with a shrug.

The large group broke up into smaller groups on two occasions, bringing lists of problems and suggestions for solutions back to the larger group. The upshot of the first day's meeting was a series of resolutions to address the issues raised, with new appointments made to committees and new responsibilities assigned as the group deemed necessary. At one point, Evander asked for a vote on approval of the decisions and asked everyone to raise his or her arm. He demonstrated without thinking by lifting his amputated stub, saw a certain absurdity in it within a split second and said, "Everyone raise a whole arm to vote!" The meeting collapsed in laughter.

The second day's discussion became focused on two clearly defined problems. The first subject taken up was the problem of agricultural credit. The federal government's line of credit for reform beneficiaries had been closed down, making it an immediate and very pressing issue for every family and for the communities. The elimination of credit was universally interpreted both at Sarandí and within the MST as a sign that the federal government under President Fernando Henrique Cardoso was continuing to serve the interests of national and international corporations and big landowners before those of the people of Brazil. There was perhaps a special feeling of bitterness and betrayal in this conclusion, because Cardoso had gained his fame as an internationally respected socialist professor of social sciences, whose many left-wing analyses of Latin America's problems had been carefully read by other professors and by students around the world. He now headed a right-wing coalition government, having saved the Right from electoral defeat at the hands of Lula and the Workers' Party in 1992 and 1996. Cardoso's government had carried forward the Plano Real (an economic recovery plan involving the creation of the new national currency, the *real*), which Cardoso had designed when he served as finance minister in the previous government. The plan had successfully brought an end to runaway inflation, a tremendous relief to most Brazilians, but it also involved enforcing the line of the International Monetary Fund (IMF) and World Bank with little dissent. Many social programs, including health, education and rural credit, suffered in the name of fiscal restraint.

Valdimar de Oliveira, nicknamed Nego, a man who had gone through the trials of Encruzilhada Natalino, spoke at the Sarandí meeting about the credit problem and the debt owed by the credit cooperative that had handled the loans to the farm families. Nego had served on the national directorate of the MST and was treated with a lot of respect. He was a bit overweight, but handsome and self-assured, with an olive complexion and black hair. He quietly explained that if the families could not pay their debts to the cooperative and if the cooperative could not pay its debt to the government, the entire community of Sarandí could collapse. He commented that many families did not seem to realize that government credit was not a gift but a loan that had to be paid on strictly negotiated terms, like any commercial loan. He did not say, although he surely knew it, that some confusion on this point is fairly typical of farmer attitudes toward government credit in many countries.

While the state governor of Rio Grande do Sul was considered friendly to the MST—which promoted him as a presidential candidate of the Workers' Party in 2002—he had been unable up to this point to free up credit that had been approved by the state legislature for agrarian reform beneficiaries. Many of the people at the meeting were furious about this and argued vigorously with Nego. How can it be, they asked, that the governor, supposedly a close ally of the MST, couldn't deliver on a new line of credit the legislature had approved? Nego tried to explain that, while the funds had been approved, they had not been appropriated. The state bureaucracy was doing all it could to tie up the credit, perhaps thinking there were better ways to spend the money or perhaps expressing their hostility toward or lack of interest in agrarian reform. "But he is the governor!" people protested, as Nego tried to explain the limits of executive power in a democracy.

Nego also said that the matter of the debt and the cutting off of the line of credit were simply additional examples of why, in the end, the

MST would have to be part of a coalition of forces to take state power. Without governmental authority, the MST and the poor would always come up short. In the meantime, Nego said, the fact was that the debt was there, and it would have to be paid. Many people did not seem persuaded. Finally, Nego said very forcefully, "Look, you have to understand. This is serious. If the debt is not paid, we lose it all. The state is not going to come through with this credit. We have to face our debt and figure out how we are going to pay it. That's the end of the discussion." The meeting ended up voting for an immediate assessment on each family toward paying off the cooperative's debt. It was far from clear that the amount of the assessment would be sufficient, or that the families would be able to muster it. In the face of these uncertainties the delegates approved a resolution stating that the question of the assessment would have to go back to all the families in the community for further discussion. (Months later, the state government finally resolved the issue in a way that released the settlers of Sarandí from the debt under discussion.)

At the lunch hour, people enjoyed the usual abundant combination of rice, beans, salad and grilled meat. Everyone, including the men and the handful of children who had been brought to the meeting, patiently waited in line to wash their plates and dishes before returning to the meeting. Men were as active in preparing the food and cleaning up as women, if not more so, a significant matter in this culture which local people readily admit is very *machista* or male-oriented.

Before the afternoon discussion started, the mística committee darkened the room, lit candles and asked people to gather at the front of the room around a large mound covered with brown paper, on which the words *organics*, *life* and *survival* had been written. After ten or fifteen minutes of singing, people began to rise out from under the paper to the accompaniment of guitars and song, each person with something in hand: a beautiful squash, a bunch of big radishes, a handful of potatoes, a shaft of wheat, a stalk of corn.

As they rose, they revealed beneath them, laid out on the floor, an amazingly detailed map of Brazil, constructed of garden produce. They stood with their vegetables and grain in front of the vegetable map of Brazil, with the MST flag and a Che Guevara poster on the wall behind

Hoeing weeds on one of the small collective farms in Sarandí.

them. One of the young women recited a poem in praise of Earth and nature. After a moment of quiet, the guitarists broke into the MST hymn, and people sang and clapped loudly. A round of compliments for the ceremony and mística committee came from the regional delegates, and the meeting resumed.

The matter now under discussion was the production model used by the MST farmers in Sarandí. A representative from the statewide MST council, a young agronomist who worked full-time for the technical department and extension services of the MST, led the discussion. He explained that the technical people and committees of MST farmers, including representatives from Sarandí, had been analyzing the production and economic problems of MST settlements in Brazil. The Rio Grande do Sul committee had come to a definitive conclusion, the implications of which would have to be studied, understood and implemented.

According to the agronomist, the situation in Sarandí and other settlements was clear. Even the largest producers in the region were caught in a classic squeeze between the increasing costs of production of corn and soybeans and the decreasing price received for the crops, a squeeze that made it increasingly difficult to make a profit from these crops, which face sharp international competition and are heavily dependent on large investments in chemicals and machinery. Although government policy and subsidies and the excellent Brazilian growing conditions had made Brazil among the top soy and corn producers in the world, government support was dwindling as part of both IMF austerity programs and free-trade agreements that required the national government to reduce its subsidies to agriculture. (It's worth noting that the United States in particular was pushing hard for the elimination of farm subsidies by other countries, only to pass in 2002 the largest package of subsidies to US farmers in history. This provoked a sharp and bitter reaction from the Brazilian government, which thought that by progressively reducing subsidies it had been playing by rules that the US would also respect.)

While larger corporate and entrepreneurial producers might or might not be able to compete, it was clear that small-scale producers like the MST farmers of Sarandí simply could not hope to do so. Already people weren't making enough money to pay their debts. The high capital needs of chemical-based soy and corn farming were not consistent with the small-scale, capital-poor farming that MST members were forced to practice. The sharing of tractors, disks, planting drills, cultivators and harvest machinery through the co-op was a help in reducing costs, but it was not enough.

The agronomist explained that discussions had also begun to focus on making the production model of the MST farmers consistent with the underlying purposes of the MST and agrarian reform. This meant the production decisions had to take into account not simply a profit and loss balance sheet, but a broader set of considerations. First among these was the long-term security of families. The volatile commodity markets and high capital requirements of the old model were inconsistent with long-term security. Families needed to think more about food security, which meant more on-farm production of the food that the family itself required—more self-sufficiency. For their cash needs, people needed to rely on better known and understood local markets, selling as much as possible directly to consumers in regional towns and cities. These were far more reliable and less speculative than the vast international soy and grain markets, controlled by a handful of largely US-based firms.

The agronomist said—as Pacote had told us in nearly identical words—that people had simply fallen into soybean and corn production in imitation of the big operators, assuming that powerful farmers were smart enough to make the best choices and that those choices would be good for any farmer. The MST needed to develop a more critical approach, he argued, recognizing that a production model derived from vast inequalities was probably going to reproduce inequality. Small farmers failed when attempting to compete in a game dominated by the wealthy farmers and corporations.

A second fundamental commitment of the MST was to the earth itself. The MST understood that farm families could not find security on deteriorating land, a problem all too familiar to Brazil's southern farmers, who had seen the devastating consequences of sharecropping, land renting and absentee landlords. In a meeting of the movement's national congress, delegates from the local and regional organizations had approved a very strong statement of commitment to environmental protection. Chemical-dependent soybean and corn production was, as everyone who spoke at the meeting agreed, completely inconsistent with the conservation of soils and wildlife.

Earlier in the meeting, a man of about forty, with ice-blue eyes and light blond hair that contrasted with his deep farmer's tan, had invited us to look at his farm, where, for some years, he had been developing his production model of "agro-ecology." "You have to look at the whole system in its natural context and design with that in mind," Erno Hahn had told us. He spoke of the heavy use of compost, of the production of liquid fertilizers on the farm from plant and animal waste and of planting various intermixed crops to improve utilization of soil nutrients and discourage pests. "We have worked this out over the years, now, with the use of tree crops and herbs integrated in the crop production areas. The whole thing works well. My friends and I are very proud of what we have been able to do with it." Now, Erno lent his quiet words of support and encouragement to the agronomist as he spoke at the meeting.

The agronomist began to talk about the agro-ecology model, which, he said, would mean that every farm family would work out a plan appropriate to their conditions, but always with an eye to minimizing chemical use and with a wide variety of crops planted. He talked of how agro-ecology would mean eliminating dangerous pesticides from the farm and building soils with organic fertilizers, rather than purchased synthetic chemicals. The underlying idea of this model is to use the knowledge of ecological processes to design agricultural production techniques to enhance the health and diversity of the landscape consistent with agricultural productivity. There is no one recipe for how to do this, said the agronomist, which is why each farm needs to develop its own plan appropriate to its place.

Some people, including Erno Hahn and the group of men seated with him, who had been practicing agro-ecology for some time, greeted this discussion with smiles, but kept their own participation to a minimum. Others jumped in with heated questioning and argument. While some people were enthusiastic about pursuing the agro-ecology model, others were very angry at what they saw as an imposition by the leadership on their production decisions. They said that the agro-ecology model was too theoretical, that it required taking risks they couldn't afford.

Evander interrupted to say that two things had been definitively decided by the cooperative board. "The first is that from today on, the cooperative will sell no more poisons [a reference to synthetic pesticides]. They are going off the shelf." Then, introducing a topic that had been only lightly touched upon as of yet, he added, "The second is that anyone found to be growing transgenic soybeans or corn will have their crop confiscated." There were shouts and grumbles of protest. Evander raised his voice. "Growing transgenic crops is still illegal in Brazil, and the MST has a firm position on them. I repeat, we will confiscate the crop."

One man in a baseball cap with an international chemical company logo said, "Evander, you and everyone else knows that in spite of the law, at least 30 percent of the soybeans grown in this region are transgenic. You are not going to stop it, even if it is wrong." Evander repeated that transgenics were illegal, that they were contrary to MST policy, and that they would be confiscated.

Transgenics were and remain a hot issue in Brazil, especially in the corn and soy-producing southern states. In 2001, a legal decision made it acceptable to plant transgenics, but only for research purposes. A large portion of Argentine and North American production uses transgenic crops based on bioengineered seeds using genes from other organisms to give the crops some new characteristic. Transgenic seeds have made some crops more tolerant to herbicides so that more herbicides can be applied without damaging the crop itself. Other seeds have had engineered into them a toxin derived from a bacterium that kills caterpillar pests. Many ecologists and environmentalists have decried these developments as ultimately hazardous to the environment. For example, herbicide-tolerant seeds promote the use of more herbicides, which have negative effects on the environment. Building in the toxic bacteria means the almost certain development of resistance in caterpillars to the bacterium, eventually destroying the effectiveness of the bacterial toxin as a pest-control tool. Furthermore, universal presence of the bacterial toxin in major crops raised the specter of damage to non-pest butterfly and moth species.

Furthermore, many people interested in the economics of small-scale agriculture believe that the patented transgenic seeds will mean an even greater control of farmers by the large chemical companies that produce the seed, capturing for the corporations yet another portion of the value of the farmer's crop and independence.

At the time of the meeting—and still as of this writing—some European countries have banned the importation of transgenic commodities or processed foods containing them because of their worries about food safety, environmental and economic implications. As a result, many North American farmers have lost significant earnings in export sales. This is true even for those who have not planted transgenics, because the grain marketing firms claim it is nearly impossible to guarantee that any batch of grain is uncontaminated by transgenics when they are so widely used.

Although it was clear even from this one meeting that the agro-ecology model and everything it implied would require many more discussions, it was not clear where they would go. Many MST settlements have aggressively developed agro-ecological methods in the fields, while others have lagged behind or even resisted. In some regions, the agro-ecology discussion had not seriously begun by 2001, though overall the movement would like to head in that direction.

What was evident at the 2000 regional coordinators' meeting in Sarandí was that the settlers of Sarandí and Anoni, veterans of Encruzilhada Natalino, had traveled a very long road, moving from the simple demand for land to complex discussions of the implications of farm ecology, state and national agricultural and financial policy, international trade and biotechnology innovations. They knew that the future of their families and their organization would depend on their making good decisions, and they knew that the argument and the uncertainty would go on, as it does for virtually every family trying to make a living from the land anywhere in the world.

After we shared the chimarrão with Pacote and Anir, Pacote took us on a tour of his farm, once a rejected and eroding creekside slope. His six Guernsey and Holstein cows were healthy and were producing enough milk for the family and for sale of milk and cheese at what the settlers called the "ecological fair"—a farmers' market that included products grown in both conventional and organic systems—in Passo Fundo. Pacote had purchased a small commercial milk cooler and milking machine, and he showed us the movable electric fence that he would use for the rotational grazing system and the small hay field he used to supplement the improved grasses he was planting.

At the fence line, he pointed out that the soil on the neighbor's side of the fence was compacted and not very productive. Pacote thought this was a result of excessive herbicide use. He kneeled down from time to time to show us insects that he identified as pests or as beneficials that preyed on pests. He had interplanted corn and squash in one small field. In the woods in the creek bottom, he showed us wild erva mate plants, saying that he was working to encourage a somewhat higher ratio of mate and other useful plants to other wild plants. With this slight manipulation of the woods environment, he planned to make a nice piece of income by harvesting the mate from the forest, figuring he could earn three times more income by harvesting these plants than he could by cutting down the woods and planting the land to pesticide-intensive soybeans.

The farm pond had catfish averaging three to four pounds apiece. The Placotnik vegetable garden and chicken yard uphill from the pond provided nutrients that supported the plants the fish eat, as in ancient and modern Chinese agricultural systems. Anir had primary responsibility for the diverse and productive vegetable garden, which covered about half an acre.

While we were walking on the land, a kind of quail flew up in front of us and Pacote explained that while they were good to eat, he didn't hunt them. "The whole point of keeping the woods in place is to leave places for wild things, which have their own place in the world and should be valued as humans are valued." At two or three points on the walk, Pacote said, "The whole perspective here is agro-ecology." On getting back to his house he proudly showed us some seeds that the University of California at Berkeley agro-ecologist, Miguel Altieri, had left as a gift. Pacote wanted to share them with us until we pointed out that we knew Miguel and could get some seeds directly from him if we needed them. Pacote was a little embarrassed at his own enthusiasm as we said this, and we felt a little sheepish that we had been so crude as to turn down a gift.

Before leaving, we said to Pacote that we intended to write a book about the MST. We asked what he would most want to tell the readers of such a book in the United States. He didn't hesitate: "Agrarian reform works. The conquests we have made here have created a community and put the land to work. Before, Fazenda Anoni had six families and 230 head of cattle. [Pacote's friend Zezinho, who had lived on the ranch before expropriation, said that there were more than thirty families.] It now has 430 families and three thousand head of cattle and has created about one thousand jobs directly related to production from the settlement." Pacote had earlier made the point that local merchants and banks in Ronda Alta, Passo Fundo and other nearby towns often supported the MST because of the greatly increased commercial activity land reform had created. "We have a credit union; we have electricity; we have refrigerators and freezers for our milk production, real production. We are giving value to human beings and to the environment, producing food, good, healthy food.

"The second message is that people elsewhere should work with the excluded. We, the excluded, have shown that we can transform our lives. In much of society the human being is valued less than a puppy, than a dog. We have shown that this can be changed.

"The third message is that the governments of underdeveloped countries do little for their people. Those in rich countries, in the first world, should do more to lend aid to the poor of the third world, that the least they could do is close these factories that make these poisons that are killing us and our land, the agro-toxics."

Pacote began to feel a little at a loss, saying that he realized there were so many things to say, so many messages. "But that is good enough for now."[59]

People on MST settlements meet regularly to discuss community questions; here settlers at Ouro Verde in Pernambuco debate the ever-present problem of debt.

## CHAPTER TWO

# The Land Is Only the First Step

## *Pernambuco and Northeastern Brazil*

I N 1984, WHEN THE MST WAS FOUNDED, there was great optimism about the possibility for real change in Brazil. After twenty-one years of military control, which had steered the economy into crisis, suppressed individual liberties and turned political representation into a farce, people were quick to embrace the hope of democracy. Student groups, trade unions, political parties and new social movements, including the MST, took to the streets, publicly expressing demands that had been frustrated for over two decades.[1]

But turning the promise of the political moment into true, substantive change would prove difficult. Political and economic power was still unevenly distributed, and a minority of the Brazilian population would have disproportionate influence in the new government. At the same time, the rest of the population would have difficulty shedding the scars of political elitism. Nearly five hundred years of patronage politics, wrapped up in intimidation and poverty, would not be overturned with a simple election. The battle over agrarian reform in the new constitution—which lasted for three years (1985–1988)—illustrates how difficult it would be for Brazil's poor to shape the political process, particularly in relation to land distribution. We'll start this chapter with a description of the debate over agrarian reform in the transition to democracy, then move to the Northeast of Brazil to examine the roots of political and economic elitism. The MST has made great strides in organizing the rural poor of the Northeast, but it is there that the movement faces some of its greatest challenges.

## Agrarian Reform and the New Democracy

When the military formally withdrew from the executive office in 1985, the first civilian president elected was Tancredo Neves. Tancredo, as he was called, received an overwhelming majority of votes in the electoral college (480 in his favor and only 180 against, with 26 abstentions). He was much loved by the Brazilian electorate, and activists working among the rural poor were hopeful that he would help smooth the way for agrarian reform. In the months leading up to his inauguration into office, Tancredo appointed a left-leaning intellectual, José Gomes da Silva, as president of INCRA. Tancredo asked Gomes da Silva to prepare a National Plan for Agrarian Reform (PNRA) as a preliminary document to generate popular discussion.[2] Gomes da Silva's PNRA presented an ambitious agenda, including the settlement of 7.1 million families between 1985 and 2000 on over 480 million hectares (approximately 1.2 billion acres) of land. Of the total, 85 percent of the land indicated for expropriation was to be private (roughly 409.5 million hectares) and 15 percent was to be public (71.1 million hectares).

But the PNRA went beyond the simple redistribution of land. The proposal suggested revisions to the customary practice of making land concessions to private businesses and also provided the legal means for the government to deactivate private militias employed by large landowners. It was truly a comprehensive and ambitious plan. The then-president of the Senate, Ulysses Guimarães, commented that "the New Republic's commitment to the establishment of a social reality is being fulfilled principally in this question of land tenure."[3] Unfortunately, the PNRA would not be implemented as it was originally written.

On March 14, 1985, the eve of Tancredo Neves's inauguration, the president-elect suffered severe abdominal pains and was rushed to the hospital. After seven surgeries, Tancredo died from internal infections. The country mourned, and accusations of slipshod medical care and malpractice were thrown about. More importantly for the MST, the task of pushing the PNRA through Congress was left to the much weaker vice president, José Sarney. Sarney did not have an easy time of it. The country was shocked by the loss of its president, and the economy continued to slide ever more deeply into a state of crisis. On the eve of his inauguration, Sarney commented, "I have inherited the greatest political crisis in Brazilian history, the largest foreign debt in the world and the greatest internal debt and inflation we have ever had."[4]

It was not a propitious time for either agrarian reform or the MST as, predictably, the PNRA provoked a vehement backlash. A new organization, the União Democrática Rural (Rural Democratic Union, the UDR), was formed to bring together large landowners and rural business leaders against agrarian reform and in defense of "stability and peace." The UDR was prepared to use any means available—including armed warfare—to destroy organization among the rural poor and maintain its version of peace.[5] The UDR was associated with the more traditional Society in Defense of Tradition, Family and Property (which referred to itself simply as TFP). The TFP and the UDR argued that liberation theology was antithetical to the "Christian tradition of private property, which has been taught for over two thousand years by the Church and put into place by Christian nations."[6]

The two groups raised the specter of communism and revolution in the countryside to scare the government out of its alarmingly progressive ideas. Landlords were prepared to take matters into their own hands if the government did not respond. As one UDR member wrote at the time: "Organized groups, usually full of bloodlust, are invading private property. Here and everywhere, landowners who are tired of appealing uselessly to the authorities in charge have proclaimed themselves forced to defend their rights for themselves."[7] The UDR made little distinction between agrarian reform in Brazil and communism in what was then the Soviet Union.

In 1997, twelve years after the debate over the PNRA, we had the chance to meet with one of the leaders of the UDR, who had been a vocal spokesperson for the organization during the constitutional battles, Roosevelt Roque dos Santos. We telephoned Roosevelt (pronounced hose-e-*vel*-chee) at his office in the Pontal do Paranapanema, a cattle-ranching region of São Paulo that had recently come to national attention because of increasingly violent conflicts between MST members and cattle ranchers. We asked if Roosevelt would meet with us and speak with John Vidal, who was doing a report on the MST for the English daily *The Guardian*.[8]

We were afraid that Roosevelt would be reluctant to meet with us, as his organization was suspected of instigating militia-style violence in defense of cattle ranchers, but he agreed eagerly. Roosevelt is a short man: when we walked into his large office there was as much cowboy hat showing over the top of his desk as person. He jumped up quickly when his secretary announced us and shook our hands vigorously. His secretary left to get all of us coffee, and we sat down in his comfortable couches and translated Vidal's questions about the UDR into Portuguese.

At the mention of the MST, Roosevelt became quite animated. The MST was a menace to Brazilian society, he insisted. He went to his desk and pulled out a picture, which he held out to us as if it were precious. The picture showed a group of people sitting in chairs arranged in front of a man who was clearly an MST activist. He stood facing the group, talking and pointing to a blackboard behind him. Flanking the activist were two portraits: Che Guevara (a hero of the Cuban revolution) stood at attention on one side, Vladimir Lenin (the hero of the Russian revolution) on the other. Roosevelt said the picture proved that the MST's ultimate desire was the same as these revolutionaries': to overthrow the state.

Roosevelt brought out other pieces of evidence: a red booklet on "how to organize the masses," which Roosevelt insisted was originally from Cuba, and police files detailing the offenses that had been committed by different members of the movement, one of which was "false ideology." Though Vidal asked Roosevelt how he had access to such detailed police files, Roosevelt did not answer.

The large room opposite Roosevelt's office was filling up with men, most with wide-brimmed cowboy hats, jeans and boots. Members of the UDR were meeting to discuss new actions in relation to the MST's presence in the Pontal region, and it was time for us to go.

The UDR members meeting with Roosevelt that day had good reason to believe they could influence national politics: their tactics had proven to be very effective in the past. In 1985, the influence of the UDR, in conjunction with that of a wide array of conservative business leaders, essentially defeated the much-anticipated PNRA. On the day the Senate was expected to vote on the PNRA, only twenty senators showed up. Without the thirty-five senators needed to make a quorum, the proposal died.

But the topic of agrarian reform did not totally disappear. It was clear that the call for some sort of land-redistribution project required an official response. Between 1985 and 1988, as part of the national constitutional revision process, politicians, social movement members and trade union activists debated the question of what kind of agrarian reform could be legislated. These were not peaceful years: it is estimated that 181 rural workers and peasants were murdered in 1985, 179 in 1986 and seventeen in the first three months of 1987.[9] During this time, the UDR recruited over 200,000 new members.[10] Under their watchful eyes, the PNRA was redrafted twelve times before a much more modest version than the original was finally ratified; many observers felt that the most conservative part of the 1988 Constitution was the law on agrarian reform.

The version finally agreed upon by the members of Congress provided an exemption from expropriation for productive farms, which ran counter to the original planners' intention of making all farms over six hundred rural "modules" eligible for expropriation. (A module is the amount of land in a particular region that is considered sufficient to sustain a family of four.) The definition of what *productive* meant was left vague enough to cause considerable confusion at the local level. A productive farm was defined in the constitution as one on which 80 percent of the surface was effectively utilized, where ecological and labor standards were respected and where "the use is considered to be of common benefit to land owners and workers."[11] This definition of productivity informs the government's approach to agrarian reform to this day.

José Gomes da Silva resigned from his position as the head of INCRA in protest over the changes imposed on the agrarian reform legislation he had originally drafted. Da Silva argued that without legislating the immediate expropriation of unproductive private land the plan was left without real reform potential. The MST has argued—and many agree— that agrarian reform would never have recovered from this frontal assault by large landowners if the movement itself hadn't continued to promote the idea aggressively.

# The Northeast of Brazil
*Legacies of Poverty and Impunity*

To understand why the idea of a redistributive agrarian reform provoked such opposition among the political elite in Brazil, one has to
understand something about the history of political and economic development in the country, a history that begins—and finds its deepest
roots—in the Northeast.

Well known as both the birthplace of the country and one of the
poorest regions in all of Latin America, the northeastern states occupy
a peculiar place in the Brazilian national consciousness. Although the
Northeast only contains about 30 percent of Brazil's total population,
over half of all the poor people in the country—and two-thirds of the
rural poor—live there. It is Brazil's Plymouth Colony and its Ap-
palachia. It is here that the production of sugarcane began, turning
Brazil into one of the New World's most lucrative colonies and setting
into place the structural bases for inequality and poverty that haunt the
entire country to this day.

At the movement's founding meeting in 1984, MST members recognized that the struggle for land should incorporate the rural poor from
throughout the country, rather than focusing only on the southernmost region. The unequal land tenure that gave rise to Encruzilhada
Natalino and other encampments in Rio Grande do Sul and Santa Catarina existed across Brazil, and the movement knew that in the Northeast they could draw on a rich history of rural resistance. One of the
movement's leaders, João Pedro Stédile, remembered what José de
Souza Martins, Brazil's leading rural sociologist and an advisor to the
Catholic Church, had said at an earlier meeting of the CPT, Comisão
Pastoral da Terra (the Pastoral Land Commission, coordinated by the
Catholic Church). Martins had urged the incipient movement to gain
strength from rural struggles around the country, saying that the MST
would only become a force for change if it were a national movement.

In 1985, the MST held its first national congress, and representa-
tives from twenty-three states attended. Many were activists from the
CPT, the opposition trade union, the Central Único de Trabalhadores
(Central Workers' Union, or CUT) and the newly formed Workers'

Party (the Partido dos Trabalhadores, officially formed in 1980). Then-president of the Workers' Party Lula, who would go on to become the president of Brazil in 2003, also attended the congress.

For three days, the 1,500 people at the congress debated ideological principles and strategies. Their resolutions became the MST's organizational guidelines and were written up in a manifesto to the Brazilian people. At the end of the meeting, the activists pledged to return to their home states and begin mobilizing the local struggle for land within the MST. Over the next ten years, the MST's call for agrarian reform would explode across the country, and the movement would become an important voice for political and social change at the national level.

One MST activist who left his home state in the South of Brazil to work in the Northeast, Jaime Amorim, says the movement was successful in expanding across the country because "we picked an issue that united everyone—the land. The land is the necessity, it is the call that unifies everyone. . . . You offer the workers the opportunity to have land—but [you introduce the idea] of a mass occupation."

Consolidating rural struggles throughout Brazil would constitute one of the MST's greatest strengths, but it would not be easy, nor would the movement succeed everywhere it went. MST activists born and raised in one environment often found it difficult to adapt to the new realities they experienced in other states, and everywhere they went, the MST activists came into contact with people who were already working with the rural poor—particularly local church leaders and trade union members. The young idealists who were the MST's most committed activists would have to learn how to coordinate their activities and expectations with these other social actors, creating a constant tension between organizational flexibility and ideological consistency.

As Dilson Barcello, a longtime MST activist in Santa Catarina said in 1999, shaking his head at the variety of different opinions expressed during a local meeting, "You have to treat diversity with diversity. But how do you do this and maintain a principle, maintain an objective?"

Of all the geographic regions in Brazil, perhaps the most difficult—and significant—for the MST to mobilize has been the Northeast. The production of sugarcane in northeastern Brazil marked the creation of a

very powerful class that controlled large landholdings and exercised almost total power over both the land and the people who worked it.
These powerful landowners were not interested in using the land to
feed themselves; their objective was to get rich. During colonial times,
the Portuguese crown supported this objective, as it had no pressing
need for direct access to the land in Brazil—the population of Portugal
was little more than one million people. The Portuguese rulers were
primarily interested in revenues from export taxes, which filled the
royal coffers and made possible the defense of their far-flung empire.
Producing exports became Brazil's main business. Wealthy consumers
in Europe and later in North America wanted what they could not produce in their own temperate climates: sugar, coffee, cacao, tobacco, cotton and sisal for ropes.

For the first four centuries after "discovery," Brazil depended heavily
on these and other products grown for export. Unfortunately, these
were all products with very unstable markets. Sugar, coffee and cacao
were luxury products whose prices fluctuated rapidly in response to
economic conditions in richer nations. Brazilian producers also faced
fierce competition from other tropical regions. Sisal, cotton and tobacco could either be produced to a degree in nontropical regions or
could be substituted for by other products that were easily available.

Short-term market volatility and long-term trends toward decreasing relative prices have plagued the Northeast for five hundred years.
The severe boom-and-bust cycles created by dependence on these exports generated enormous fortunes during the good times and destroyed the local economy during the bad. The inability of smallholders
to survive these periodic downturns reinforced the domination of large
landholders over the poor. Money was needed to weather the storms,
and, perhaps more important, political influence was needed as large
landholders who racked up high debt levels were able to use their political influence to secure state subsidies and bailouts that kept them
afloat in hard times.

The reliance on export crops with unstable markets was exacerbated
in the Northeast region by the overwhelming tendency to specialize in
single crops (a practice often referred to as "monocropping"). With the
region's fate tied to the markets in a few export crops, the local market
was largely disregarded until the twentieth century, and all the best

resources were devoted to the export economy, rather than to feeding, clothing, housing or educating the local populace. The skills plantation workers needed were minimal, so education was never highly valued or funded. Low levels of education, in turn, discouraged technological innovation and stunted the development of inclusive, democratic institutions. Plantation owners made sure their workers had access to health care services only when it benefited production because it was often cheaper to find new workers than to succor the sick.

The individual and social pains of the population neglected by the plantation monocrop economies resulted in protest and rebellion from time to time, but the landholders always won out. They held the local reins of power and could usually rely on support from outsiders—foreign investors as well as foreign governments—who wanted to maintain abundant supplies of cheap tropical goods. Public institutions such as the police, the courts and the army were all accountable to the landholding elite and not to the public. This legal impunity made it easy for the landholders to practice intimidation and violence against workers and communities, producing massive corruption throughout the political system.

The most widely practiced and effective solution for people trapped by poverty in this region has always been flight. For centuries, escaped slaves, plantation workers and displaced smallholders have sought a better life in the severe and difficult *sertão*, the semiarid interior of the Northeast region, where isolation, weak soils and a brutal climate made prosperity unlikely, but made a degree of independence and security possible.

Unfortunately, most of the sertão itself fell under the rule of powerful rancher and planter families, who ruled as ruthlessly as the coastal planters. When escape to the sertão failed, individuals and whole generations of people went to the cities of the industrializing South. There, some would find a better life, but most would find chronic misery, crime and victimization. At times the migrants from the Northeast were welcomed as cheap labor, but they always suffered discrimination, exploitation, prejudice and, at times, outright efforts to relocate them back in the Northeast. One anthropologist writes: "In the Brazilian imaginary, the expression '*pau-de-arara*' (parrot-perch) is associated with the trucks that . . . transported migrants who had no resources, coming from the Northeast in the direction of cities in the Southeast; their only seat was made out of wooden planks laid across the truck-bed for trips of over 1,500 kilometers that lasted several days. That expression carries with it a strong pejorative connotation in Rio and São Paulo; it is used to this day to socially disqualify someone, stigmatizing them as a 'joe-nobody.'"[12]

Beginning in the twentieth century, and increasingly over the past fifty years, the Brazilian government, along with foreign governments and international development agencies, has identified the Northeast as a political trouble spot and an economic drag on the rest of the Brazilian nation. Many billions of dollars have been sunk into the region in investment subsidies and development programs. Combined with private capital, this money has been applied to grandiose projects, such as erecting dams, carving out irrigation schemes and building impressive industrial facilities in the Northeastern cities. For example, Dow, Shell and other major corporations received massive subsidies to build the Western Hemisphere's largest petrochemical complex on the outskirts of the Northeastern city of Salvador da Bahia.

Although this spending has provided millions of jobs in the Northeast and spurred both rapid urbanization and industrialization, social and political institutions in the countryside have largely remained in the hands of old landholding families. Legally and illegally, the old elites have taken their share of the public and private capital flowing into the region, doing so whether or not they actually used the funds to carry out projects geared toward economic development.

As Warren Dean, the late environmental historian of Latin America, has written, "the exchange of state patrimony for the short-term gain of private interests is a constantly repeated theme in Brazilian history, so ingeniously and variously pursued and so ingrained as to appear the very reason for the existence of the state."[13] For example, money sent to the Northeast to build dams and relieve the suffering inflicted by inequality and periodic droughts has been so famously misspent that it has generated a subeconomy known as *a indústria da seca*, "the drought industry," a term that has become synonymous with corruption and misuse of public funds intended to help the poor. It is one more legacy of the inequalities put into place by colonization and exacerbated by a monocrop economy.

The Northeast of Brazil clearly represents an enormous challenge—as well as a moral obligation of sorts—for anyone interested in promoting social justice and economic development in Brazil. A solution for the poverty and inequality of this region would not only improve conditions in one of the poorest region in Latin America, it would also improve life in all the other regions of the country. However, because of the difficulty of working in the Northeast, the task of building an alternative future will require the perseverance of several generations; this is not a struggle that can be won by simply redistributing land. It requires fundamental changes in political and economic institutions and—perhaps most importantly—changes in the way that people perceive their own situations. As we will see throughout the chapter, the MST has had considerable success in the Northeast, but it is just beginning the struggle to overturn five hundred years of injustice.

### SOWING INEQUALITY (1500–1888)

The Northeast of Brazil stretches out like a camel's hump into the Atlantic Ocean, reaching toward the sub-Saharan region of western Africa. Nine states make up what is generally considered the region, including the small states of Alagoas, Paraíba, Pernambuco, Rio Grande do Norte and Sergipe, as well as the larger states of Bahia, Ceará, Maranhão and Piauí. The entire region is roughly two times the size of Texas and accounts for 18 percent of Brazil's total territory.

The region's landscape is dramatic in its extremes. Driving from the eastern coast inland toward the west along one of the few paved roads (only 9 percent of Brazil's roads are paved, compared to 61 percent in the United States), you might believe you were traveling through three completely different countries. Along the Atlantic coast runs a wide strip of land—as wide as 125 miles in some places—of what used to be tropical rain forest. Much of the forest has been cut down now, and what is still called the *zona da mata* (the forest zone) is mostly covered in sugarcane. Just to the west of the zona da mata lies the transition zone called the *agreste*, which rises up above the coastal strip. Average temperatures are as much as fifteen degrees Celsius (twenty-seven degrees Fahrenheit) lower here than in the rest of the state. This zone is not as fertile as the tropical coast, but it is here that most agricultural goods are produced for consumption in the Northeast.

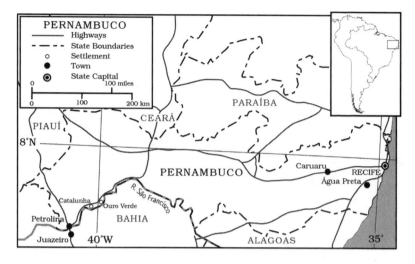

Continuing west through the agreste, one can see subtle changes in the landscape and environment that signal a move from the hills to the semiarid interior. This region of the Northeast is called the sertão, the Portuguese word for desert, though it is not actually a desert, but an area of fairly high average rainfall—it is the variability of the rainfall that is dangerous. A distinctive mixture of thorn forest and cactus vegetation, called *caatinga*, covers the land with a spidery root system adapted to make use of the rain when it is available and to survive years of little or no rain when necessary. This is the most densely populated semiarid region in the world, and the region is infamous for the high number of casualties suffered during its deadly droughts.

When Portuguese ships first landed on the northeastern hump of Brazil in 1500, in a town called Porto Seguro ("safe harbor"), they had no idea what sort of land they had discovered. Pero Álvarez de Cabral was on his way—like Columbus—to India, and he lingered only a few short days in Brazil, just long enough for his scribe to write of the gold he imagined was inside the newly discovered country:

> One of [the indigenous people] saw some white rosary beads; he signaled that he should be given them, and he played with them a lot, and held them to his chest, and afterwards he took them and put them around his arm, and signaled to the land and again to the

beads and the Captain's neck, as if he would give him gold for them. We took this to be his meaning, because this is what we wanted![14]

After Cabral's scribe wrote this message to the Portuguese king, the fleet pulled up anchor and continued heading southeast, hoping to reach India. When the king received word of the potentially rich new land, he did not have the financial resources to develop the colony or even the people to populate it. The "tired, poor, huddled masses yearning to breathe free" who would migrate to the United States in the 1700s and 1800s were not yet willing or able to travel to Brazil. Europe was only just beginning the transition out of feudalism when Cabral landed in the Northeast, and the subsequent population increase had not yet generated an "excess" of people who would look favorably upon the long and dangerous voyage to a foreign land—and the religious persecution that would throw hundreds of thousands of people into British America had not yet gathered force.

Faced with the problem of how to lay effective claim to vast territories in Brazil and the rest of the growing Portuguese empire, the Portuguese monarchy allotted huge territories to powerful nobles and royal favorites.[15] The new colony's known territory was divided into fourteen giant pieces, called captaincies, because they were given over to "captains" who would rule them in the name of the king. Taken together, the captaincies were considerably larger than the thirteen colonies set up in the early days of British America. But, as huge as they were, a mere twelve men (the captains) were given charge of the entire territory (two captains were given two territories each). These men— all of them friends of the crown—were given extraordinarily liberal rights to rule their new property: they were entitled to raise taxes, establish laws, appoint local government officials and distribute land. These rights were all inheritable, although they could not be bought or sold. Theoretically, these land rights could be revoked by the king if a captain proved incapable of making a profit on the land and paying the proper duties to Portugal. In this way, the king set up Portuguese rule in the new colony at little or no expense to himself—and in this way, inequality was introduced into the very core of what would become Brazilian society, economy and politics.

In the early days of the new colony, the most profitable resource was the forest lining the Northeast coast. Portuguese colonists forced the local natives to cut the tall, dense brazilwood trees and carry them to their ships destined for Europe. The trees were named after the *brasis* (in the singular, *brasil*, the source of the country's name), or hot coals, which were the same color as the red dye made from boiling the trees' wood. The red dye was profitable, but the new colony really took off when the first sugarcane stalks were planted.

In the early 1500s, sugar was worth almost as much per pound as gold. Duarte Coelho, the dashing captain of Pernambuco, brought sugarcane plants to his new land in 1537, and, since then, sugarcane has been the dominant crop of northeastern Brazil.[16] The deep red clay soil of the northeastern coast is rich with peatlike humus, making it fertile growing ground for the crop. Sugarcane is also particularly suited for the rolling terrain of the Northeast because the plant's long roots allow it to be planted up and down the hillsides. Between 1580 and 1680, Brazil was the world's largest producer and exporter of sugar. The period was Brazil's golden "century of sugar," and it was not until the 1700s that Dutch production in the Antilles began to challenge the Portuguese colony.

Producing sugarcane in Brazil required significant financial outlays. The high cost of planting and harvesting the plant had to be added to the risky business of transporting it across the Atlantic Ocean. Plantations tended to cover huge tracts of land, as production was only viable if the producer was able to capture economies of scale. All of this meant that sugarcane production in the captaincies was an activity suitable primarily for the very rich. The owners of the sugarcane mills—the *senhores de engenho*—set up plantations as closed societies in which they were the employers, bankers, shopkeepers and father-figures— and the law. *Senhor do engenho* became a title that "demanded to be heard, obeyed and respected."[17]

In the mid-1500s, when the sugarcane mills were gearing up, the most pressing problem was how to provide sufficient labor for the menial but extremely difficult tasks of planting, weeding, harvesting and boiling the cane. Very few independent settlers came over to Brazil in the early years of the colony; those who did were not considered for manual labor on the plantations because, as one colonist in 1690 remarked, "It is not the style for the white people of these parts, or of any other of our colonies, to do more than command their slaves to work and tell them what to do."[18]

Trying to convince people to work in the plantations of their own free will would have been particularly difficult, because the work was physically brutal and the tropical temperatures, combined with high levels of humidity, made the long hours even more grueling. During the harvest months, which could last as long as a year, workers had to cut the cane stalks, gather them into bundles and stack them into carts that they pushed into the central distillation area. Distilling the cane was hot, dangerous work because the primitive technology was rarely safe for people to operate—the workers had to boil the cane stalks in large vats of water, and it was difficult to avoid being burned by the water pouring over the edges of the vats. As one contemporary observer wrote: "A sugar mill is hell, and all the masters of them are damned."[19]

Because of the difficulty of convincing people to work on the plantations, the colonists relied on coercion, turning to the native population as a logical labor source. Pero Vaz de Caminha, the scribe who wrote to the Portuguese king from Cabral's ship in 1500, had been captivated by what he perceived as the innocence of the natives and their strong, healthy bodies.[20] When the Portuguese first encountered the indigenous peoples, verbal communication was difficult, but Pero Álvarez de Cabral thought they communicated through the language of God. On his first trip ashore in Porto Seguro, Cabral brought with him a wooden cross and planted it in the sand to celebrate the Catholic mass on new soil. As the Portuguese sailors held their mass, the Tupi-Guaraní—many of them naked or covered in feathers—crept along the shore to listen to the strange words. They showed little fear, and when the mass was over, they copied the Portuguese by falling to their knees in front of the cross. Cabral's scribe wrote to the king:

> It already seems to the Captain that these people are so innocent that if it were possible to understand them and make ourselves understood, they would soon be Christians. They don't have any sort of faith, as far as we can see. . . . And Cabral believes that our Lord, who gave [the native people] good bodies and good faces, as he does to good people, did not bring Christians to this land without reason.

The possibility that the indigenous peoples had souls and could be converted to Christianity put the planters in a difficult position: they needed labor for their plantations, but the indigenous peoples would not work in the sugarcane mills voluntarily, and it was against church doctrine to enslave people who had souls. In 1570, government legislation also prohibited the enslavement of indigenous peoples, although many planters found ways around the legislation. One such circumvention was to argue that the indigenous peoples were cannibals, and their engagement in this barbarous act made them eligible for slavery. This was in fact not entirely true—only small groups among the indigenous peoples were actually cannibals (not that cannibalism should be an excuse for enslavement)—but the rationale served as a partial excuse for enslavement.

In any event, it turned out that the indigenous peoples made terrible slaves. The people who lived along the northeastern coast had traditionally been nomadic, moving with the weather and following the seasonal movements of flora and fauna from one place to another, and they did not appreciate the long hours or the conditions under which they were expected to labor. Many inconveniently died or ran away. Estimates vary considerably, but one authority calculated that there were approximately 3.5 million indigenous people in Brazil when the Portuguese first landed.[21] Contact with Europeans killed approximately 80 percent of them—mostly because the indigenous peoples did not have the immunity necessary to fight off diseases they had never seen before, such as measles, smallpox, tuberculosis, typhoid, dysentery and influenza.

When it became clear that the indigenous population would not make good slaves, the planters gradually turned to a more reliable source of labor—African slaves. Young African men were considered an ideal labor force because many of them understood the institution of slavery, having seen it practiced in their own regions. Most of the slaves brought to Brazil came from what are today Angola and Mozambique. They were strong enough to withstand the terrible heat and long hours in the mills, and by the late 1500s, African slaves were selling for two and a half times the price of indigenous slaves.[22] African slaves seemed to be an ideal solution to the labor problem, and before slavery was abolished in 1888, Brazil would import over 3.5 million slaves, more than any other country in the Western Hemisphere.

The society set up in northeastern Brazil in the 1500s revolved around the wealthy planters and their slaves. Planters usually lived on their plantations in the *casa grande* (big house), while the slaves lived in long row houses arranged around the casa grande. The few slaves engaged in keeping up the master's house were often treated well enough that Gilberto Freyre, one of Brazil's most well known sociologists, would later deem the country a "racial democracy."

Freyre, from the northeastern state of Pernambuco, examined plantation relations from 1500 to 1888, when Brazil abolished slavery, the last country in the Western Hemisphere to do so.[23] He became famous for his book, *Casa Grande e Senzala (The Masters and the Slaves)*, first published in 1933, which described Brazilian slave masters as often generous and paternalistic toward their slaves. Freyre bemoaned the transition from small sugarcane mills to larger, centralized distilleries in the late 1800s:

> There was, no one can deny, harshness and even brutality in the ways that the whites from the Big House treated their slaves. But the slave owner usually helped the blacks in the slave shacks more than the distillery owner today helps his employees: he would keep on, for example, old or sick blacks, supporting them. . . . The festivities—Saint John's Day, the pastoral days, at the folklore celebrations —frequently created moments of fraternization between the owners and their workers.[24]

Freyre argued that the alleged lack of racism in Brazil—as opposed to the US or Spanish-speaking Latin America—was due to the constant mixing (or miscegenation) between white and black on the plantations. Many young boys had had their first sexual encounters with black nannies and, Freyre argued, grew up with a special affection for the "colored race."

This argument became instantly popular with the academic and social elite in Brazil for two main reasons: Freyre assuaged their national guilt for having relied so heavily on slave labor, and he concluded his argument with an appeal to Brazilian nationalism. Freyre argued that the history of racial miscegenation in Brazil had created an inclusive society without the bitter divisions seen in the United States and Spanish America. (Brazil's recent president, Fernando Henrique Cardoso, turned Freyre's thesis of miscegenation into a crude joke during his 1994 campaign for the presidency, when he remarked that even he had "one foot in the kitchen," meaning that he was the product of a union between an ancestor and an African slave.)

While Freyre did not necessarily believe that Brazilian society was just, he suggested that radical revolutions or social movements based on class or race were inappropriate and could not be expected to succeed in Brazil. He contended that the nation could move toward a better and more democratic society without the price that such movements would inevitably entail. By the 1960s, however, Freyre's argument was being subjected to increasing criticism. Historians were finding more evidence of the cruel treatment that slaves endured in Brazil, while sociological and anthropological accounts of contemporary Brazilian society showed how the injustices of slavery lived on in equally binding relations of poverty, hierarchy and violence. Brazilian racism is different and in some ways more complicated and nuanced than racism in the United States (one recent study lists over a hundred terms commonly used in Brazil for racial identification), but poverty in Brazil is highly correlated with the color of one's skin. As one of the informants in Robin E. Sheriff's excellent study on race and racism in Brazil said, "Slavery has not ended. . . . They used to beat us with the whip, now they beat us with hunger."[25]

Beyond the insular world of the sugarcane plantations, the northeastern interior—the agreste and sertão—was only gradually being explored and settled. Some Portuguese settlers who did not have the capital or connections to operate a sugar plantation found their way to the agreste and became farmers for the growing markets on the coast. The sertão, further inland still, is known today as some of the harshest land in the country. Few people ventured beyond the highlands of the agreste until the late 1600s, when rich gold deposits were rumored to have been found deep in the interior of the country.

The people who populated the sertão were called *sertanejos* (or backlanders)—Brazilian cowboys of sorts, whom people have compared to the ranch hands of the American West (although the gaúchos of southern Brazil are probably a more apt comparison to the American cowboy). Sertanejos were people who—like the caatinga itself—managed to survive extremely harsh conditions, waiting out the droughts until the next rain.

A famous Brazilian novel by Graciliano Ramos, called *Barren Lives*, chronicles how difficult life in the sertão could be when drought hit.[26] The novel follows a family in the sertão who move from their master's cattle ranch to another to avoid dying during a drought. They survive with a stoic, impassive determination, only to have another drought begin. A play based on the book is performed regularly throughout Brazil because it is both a scathing indictment of the poverty of life in the Northeast and a valorization of the human spirit that battles such difficult conditions.

Taken together, the varied geographic regions of the Northeast of Brazil constitute the most impoverished region of the country. A Brazilian geographer well known for his work on hunger in Brazil, Josué de Castro, referred to the Northeast as "600,000 square kilometers of suffering."[27] The cruel social conditions on the plantations and the immense difficulty of surviving in the backlands have generated such miserable conditions that every single indicator of well-being is significantly lower for those who live in the Northeast than for whose who live elsewhere in the country (see figure 2.1[28]).

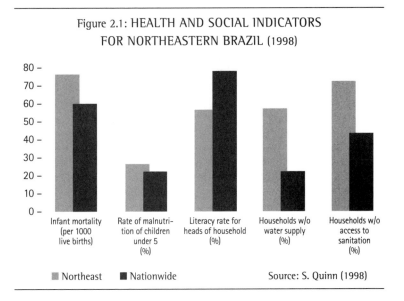

Figure 2.1: HEALTH AND SOCIAL INDICATORS FOR NORTHEASTERN BRAZIL (1998)

Northeast    ■ Nationwide                  Source: S. Quinn (1998)

By the time people in the Northeast reach what Americans would consider a youthful middle age, they look much older than they are. They are victims of diseases that have long been nearly eliminated in the United States. Malaria, cholera, tuberculosis and dengue plague the small towns. Health care is considered a public service, with the government theoretically providing medicines and treatment for free, but the high levels of inequality in the region—as in the country—mean that the best doctors and facilities are reserved for wealthy patients who can afford to pay for private care. The poor who depend on government assistance suffer more and die younger because the government cannot or does not provide adequate funding for health care.

The educational sector in the Northeast is as bad as the health care system. Over 40 percent of the household heads (usually male) in the Northeast are considered illiterate, and that is probably an underestimate. The United Nations estimated that in 2000, 26.1 percent of the youths in the Northeast were illiterate, as compared to 2.7 percent of the youths in the South. Many children are kept out of school to help their parents at home, and even those who do go to school learn little that they can apply in the real world. For example, English is taught in most elementary schools, and children who will never learn how to read Portuguese dutifully practice saying "good morning," "good afternoon" and "good night."

Of all of the difficulties encountered in the Northeast, perhaps the worst is hunger. Hunger is everywhere in the Northeast, and it comes in many different forms. At one end of the spectrum is the quiet hunger that people suffer regularly, the dull, empty feeling of working a long day on insufficient calories. Many people go to bed hungry every night because even working long hours during the day does not assure them of making enough money to feed themselves or their family. It is ironic that people who work so that the rest of the world can sweeten its coffee and cakes cannot afford to buy basic food supplies for themselves—sugarcane is one of many crops that breed hunger.

As one MST activist in the Northeast commented in 1999:

Today, no matter how much you work, you have just enough [to survive]. There are people who work sixteen hours a day [on the sugarcane plantations] and don't have enough to eat. Most of them go to sell their labor without having eaten. In the afternoon, they go to the little plantation shop and get some packages of cornmeal, flour and fish to have something to eat that night. The next day, they are going back to work without anything to eat again.[29]

This sort of hunger is sustainable over the years, although it wears the body out quickly, as people work hard and battle the body's need for an extra piece of bread or a little bit of protein.

At the other end of the continuum is the hunger that overwhelms, the loud, raging hunger of famine, often brought on by the droughts that plague the Northeast, which is prone to extreme weather. Droughts and floods ravage the landscape periodically, taking many lives with them. In 1997, a drought began that lasted until 1999, putting 4.8 million people in critical conditions of food scarcity. The Food and Agricultural Organization of the United Nations warned that those people were in "immediate risk of starvation." Another 5 million people were seriously threatened by the lack of clean water.

A drought is clearly an environmental or "natural" disaster, but social factors exacerbate the situation. Many fewer people would have been affected if they had had some reserves—money in the bank to buy food, a few valuables to sell or relatives who could afford to put them up in a safer region—but when you are already up to your neck in water, the smallest ripple can put you under.

The precarious situation introduced by the drought was aggravated by the endemic corruption that has haunted the region since the Portuguese first arrived in the Northeast. Political scandals accompanying the distribution of federal emergency relief funds happen regularly, generating "the drought industry," in which politicians put money in their pockets instead of into securing water. Food that is intended for drought relief tends to be exchanged for votes, and wells that are dug most often benefit the wealthy who need water to plant, but not to survive. The real tragedy is that the natural environmental conditions of the Northeast may be semiarid, but if properly managed, the region actually has sufficient water for all of the people living there. Beneath the surface is a sea of fresh water that would provide approximately 4,300 cubic meters of water per person. (The United Nations estimates that minimum water requirements per person are 2,000 cubic meters.)

Average annual rainfall in the Northeast is two times that of the rainfall of productive areas in Texas and Arizona. What is lacking is not necessarily water, but the political will to provide the water to those who need it most.

The difficult conditions of the 1998 drought provoked a rash of what were called *saques* (lootings). A saque is the practice of taking goods—usually food—from a store, warehouse or truck, and then distributing them among those who do not have enough. In the months during and following the drought, the MST was one of the most visible organizers of saques in the Northeast. Although such actions are technically illegal, many politicians and religious leaders publicly announced their support for saques in light of the prevalence of hunger in the region. The governor of Pernambuco in 1998, Miguel Arraes, stated that "to confuse saques with assault or a robbery is to treat a very serious social issue with violence."[30] High-ranking members of the Catholic Church have also justified the practice, arguing that "Those who take something that does not belong to them in order to survive do not sin."[31] This comment by the archbishop of João Pessoa was immediately criticized by Brazil's then-president, Fernando Henrique Cardoso, but it did prompt the federal government to expedite the transferal of emergency aid funds to the Northeast.

The vast inequality and poverty in the Northeast seems to validate survival strategies that operate outside legally sanctioned venues. Landless settlers may undertake these acts in the name of the movement, but the saque itself has its history in traditional practices of banditry in the Northeast. Throughout the colonial period and the nineteenth century, one of the most pervasive and persistent threats to the domination of wealthy landowners was banditry. Prudent travelers into the backlands hired gunmen to protect themselves from outlaws.

The most famous of all the bandits was Lampião (pronounced lamp-e-*ow*), an ex-schoolteacher who wore eyeglasses, a symbol of great learning in a region where most of the people could barely sign their own names.[32] Lampião attracted bands of followers who preyed on ranches and plantations from the late 1920s until his capture and execution in 1938. From time to time, Lampião's troops took over entire towns, negotiating for provisions and equipment. Sometimes Lampião would telegraph in advance, advising town officials that if they would provide what he required, there need be no violence.

Lampião had many female companions, but his most constant was a young woman named Maria Bonita. Lampião and Maria Bonita are always portrayed in contemporary photographs, and in the untold millions of iconic copies that still circulate, in the distinctive leather garb and large leather hat, with an upturned brim decorated with stars, of the more flamboyant sertanejo cowboys. Like other bandits, Lampião sometimes hired himself and his gunmen out to landowners who were at war with other landlords or the government. Lampião probably did little or nothing to deserve the reputation of a Robin Hood, distributing loot to the needy, but he won the eternal affection of the poor by merely surviving in flamboyant style, always defiant of the landlords and police who tried to hunt him down.

Banditry is a survival strategy in a context of extreme odds. As an MST activist who organized rural workers in the sugarcane region said, "Because of the way they lived here, violence is the way of surviving in the Northeast. Banditry (*o cangaço*) is nothing more than a frustrated cry from someone who [is] oppressed."

Banditry permeates "legal" politics in the Northeast, as well. *Coronelismo* (or "boss politics," established under the Brazilian monarchy) continues to dominate politics in the region, breeding a culture that lionizes strong, autocratic men. In 1993, Ronaldo Cunha Lima, then-governor of Paraíba, stormed into a popular restaurant and shot the ex-governor of the state, justifying his actions as a defense of his family's honor. The ex-governor had accused Lima's son of using government funds to provide favors for his friends. The papers carried the story for several days, treating it as a delicious scandal. Lima himself was congratulated for being strong enough to take the matter of his family's honor into his own hands. He spent a week in jail and was back at his desk the following Monday.[33]

Although Lima's is an extreme example, connections and intimidation continue to mean as much today as they did in the days of the colonial captaincies. As is the case in Brazil as a whole, hunger, poverty and political corruption in the Northeast cannot be attributed to a lack of resources. The problem here is the incredible inequality and corruption with which the rich resources are divided.

# A History of Resistance
## Quilombos, Canudos and the Peasant Leagues

Despite the conditions of poverty, inequality and political domination in the region, there seem to have been few instances of organized protest among the poor. One explanation is Freyre's thesis that such uprisings were unnecessary because the means to resolve social injustices already existed in the amicable relationship between races and classes. Another explanation, however, has arisen: perhaps people have been resisting in a variety of ways, but their efforts haven't found their way into the official historical record because history tends to be written by the winners. This explanation has become more widely accepted over the past thirty years, as Brazilian academics and scholars of Brazil have uncovered more information about the numerous efforts made by Brazilians throughout the country—and particularly in the Northeast—to resist the circumstances they found themselves in. MST activists and members draw on these histories of resistance to contextualize the contemporary struggle for land.

One such attempt at resistance began on the plantations, among what was previously considered an "obedient" group, well cared for by paternalistic plantation owners: the slaves. In reality, many slaves ran away from the plantations, a sign of the difficult conditions they endured there. These runaway slaves formed fugitive communities called *mocambos* after an African word for "hideout," until the term *quilombo* (meaning hidden—or maroon—communities) came into more popular usage. The deeper historians delve into the historical record, the more quilombos they find, and the more respect they gain for the brave character of these communities.

Perhaps the most famous runaway slave community was Palmares, which brought together escaped slaves in what is now the interior of Alagoas, a state that sits between Pernambuco and Bahia. Palmares was formed some time around 1605 and continued to grow as more escaped slaves heard of the sanctuary. Made up of several different villages, Palmares came to have as many as twenty thousand people living within its reach. The community was governed by a combination of African and European forms of organization. Rule through kingship, village councils and specialized warrior societies came together with legalistic forms of political representation and administration. Palmares was a peaceful community, and peoples' lives there centered more on communal forms of land ownership and production than on revenge for their enslavement. The very existence of Palmares, however, threatened the Portuguese—it was a dangerous precedent in an economy dependent on slave labor—and the people living there came under constant attack from their former masters.

When the Dutch briefly came into power in Pernambuco from 1630 to 1654, they also attempted to reconquer the escaped slaves—to no avail. Starting in 1678, Ganga Zumbi, the king of Palmares, attempted to negotiate a peace with the Portuguese, offering loyalty to the Portuguese crown and promising the return of new fugitive slaves in return for Portuguese recognition and internal autonomy for the kingdom. The Portuguese refused these terms, but still were unable to defeat the people of Palmares, who were, literally, fighting for their lives. After repeated and unsuccessful attacks by regular military forces, the colonial government turned to the use of irregulars, made up of frontiersmen skilled in using guerilla tactics, to conquer Indians and capture slaves. Historian Stuart Schwartz describes the final battle in 1694:

> Two hundred fugitives were killed, five hundred captured, and another two hundred reportedly committed suicide rather than surrender. Zumbi, wounded and in flight, was betrayed, captured, and decapitated. Palmares was no more, but as late as 1746, slaves were still fleeing to the site of Palmares and once again forming into fugitive groups.[34]

In the 1960s and 1970s, government officials exploring remote regions throughout the country, looking for good places to build dams, encountered unmapped villages whose history derived from the old quilombos. As people became aware of the number of quilombos hidden either from sight or from public recognition, a movement developed to establish legal protection for them. In 1988, this recognition was written into the federal constitution, guaranteeing land title to the descendants of quilombos who could prove that they still occupied areas dating back to the original quilombos. The official entity established to oversee this process, the Palmares Cultural Foundation, identified 724 quilombos, although only 33 of them had received title to land by 2001.[35] These "remnant" quilombo communities, as they are called, are now joining together with other social movements and urban allies to fight against the construction of dams, mines and timber operations on their land. The Pastoral Land Commission, the CPT, along with other organizations including the MST, work with the quilombos to help them prove and maintain their rights to land.

Another famous instance of resistance in the Northeast is what has come to be called the War of Canudos (1896–1897), after a settlement built by people who followed iterant lay preacher Antônio Conselheiro (Conselheiro, meaning "counselor," was a name given to Antônio by his followers and picked up by others).[36] Plagued as it was by a scarcity of priests, the Catholic Church encouraged Conselheiro and other lay preachers to travel to remote communities. Conselheiro traveled from town to town, preaching and donating his labor to the construction of chapels or the refurbishing of old churches. He wore a simple tunic and long beard. In his earlier years as a preacher, some found him fanatical and frightening. He preached a harsh moralism and the nearness of the end, the time of judgment. Most people, including relatively prosperous landowners and townsfolk, found him personally kind, gentle and humble. Some even found him charismatic.

Conselheiro lived from alms and slept wherever a place could be found. Gradually, a group of people began to follow him in his wanderings. In the early 1890s, he settled with followers on a hillside in an extremely remote area of northern Bahia, in a place called Canudos. The community established at Canudos was a peaceful one, but—again—its very existence threatened the supremacy of the Brazilian government. Conselheiro angered rural elites by attracting the local labor force, and he angered government officials by disagreeing with their decision to intervene in affairs that were traditionally considered the purview of the Catholic Church, such as sanctioning marriage. The government responded to the existence of Canudos with organized violence, showing how shallow the rhetoric of independence was when compared to the realities of life for Brazil's rural poor in the new republic.[37]

The government sent in armed troops to destroy the community, but they were beaten back three times. The sertanejos of Canudos were poorly armed, but they knew the local environment well. They were able to move silently through the endless stretches of cactus, thorny brush and trees that lined the roadways used by the soldiers, and they picked off their attackers one by one, disappearing in the thickets before they were sighted. The sertanejos knew how to find water and could survive for a long time without it. They were also accustomed to hunger, and they knew how to take the edge off by eating whatever the thorn forest offered: fruits and tubers unknown to townsfolk, as well as lizards, insects and rodents. They were also fiercely dedicated to protecting their families and the community that had brought them some sense of pride and security. The government's fourth offensive was even better outfitted and armed than the previous expeditions, and in this final attempt, Canudos was brutally defeated. But the memory of Conselheiro and his alternative community lives on.

At roughly the same time as the War of Canudos was being waged, labor relations on the sugarcane plantations along the northeastern coast were changing in ways that would eventually give rise to a new form of resistance, the Peasant Leagues.[38] Throughout the second half of the 1800s, Pernambuco plantation owners were slowly replacing their slave labor with free labor. This was not due to humanitarian concerns, but rather a reflection of the high prices that planters could get for their slaves if they sold them to landholders in southern Brazil. Plantation owners found new workers in the families living on the edges of the plantations.[39]

Many of the families who had come to Brazil in the early years with their freedom, but little else, had settled on the outskirts of the plantations when they could not find land elsewhere. These families usually grew subsistence crops and paid rent to the planter in the form of a portion of the crop. In the mid-to-late 1800s, these families were gradually incorporated into the plantation as a regular work force, coming to be called *moradores* (residents) because they were housed on the plantation, much as the slaves had been before 1888. Because they had previously been living on plantation land, the moradores were already tied into the plantation through a series of non-market-driven obligations and rights. The owners simply manipulated these rights in order to engage the moradores directly in sugarcane production.

Daily life for the moradores was not easy, as an observer of the plantation system wrote in 1864:

He cannot be sure of awakening in the same place he lay down
to sleep. He shelters himself in a miserable thatched hut built on
someone else's land and conceded to him as a gift. He does not live
there as long as he behaves himself and pays the price stipulated in
a rental contract, but only as long as he wants to subject himself to
serve as an instrument for lust, for private vengeance, for political
hatreds and rivalries, and to help the landowners fight electoral
battles for a cause not his own.[40]

Depending on the price of sugarcane, plantation owners would sometimes allow moradores to plant subsistence crops around their houses.
Until the mid-1950s, sugar prices were low and land was less valuable,
and plantation owners throughout the Northeast were relatively generous in providing access to land for their workers. Privileged workers
were sometimes given *sítios* (small farms) away from the rest of the
plantation community, where they were allowed to plant fruit trees and
subsistence crops.

After the Second World War, however, sugarcane prices rose, and
production revived throughout the region.[41] Plantation owners in Pernambuco responded to increased prices by expanding and moderniz-
ing production. Moradores were kicked out of the plantations, food
crops were uprooted and sugarcane was planted in every corner. Between 1950 and 1960, the mill owners cut their permanent labor force
in half and centralized production. Moradores who were forced out of
the plantations looked for work *na rua* (in town), but many continued
to work as day laborers for the plantations.

These changing production conditions and labor relations led to the
first large-scale attempts at organization among cane workers. In 1955,
a group of rural sugarcane workers rode together from Galiléia, about
forty miles west of Recife, into the town of Caxanga to talk with a lawyer
named Francisco Julião, who had a reputation for being sympathetic
toward rural workers—even though he was himself the son of a planter.
The rural workers had decided to form an association to protect their
rights, and they needed a lawyer to notarize their documents.

One of the rural workers' primary concerns was the withdrawal of
traditional services provided by the plantation owners. In the case of
the workers from Galiléia, they were particularly upset by the owner's
refusal to pay for a coffin in which to bury a worker who had recently

died. By long custom, the plantation owners were expected to provide a coffin as part of a "fair" working contract.

The workers from Galiléia rode to Caxanga that day with little idea that their association, once formed, would spread throughout the region and challenge the traditional elites of the plantation economy. They convinced Francisco Julião to officiate over the founding of their association, and they asked the owner of their plantation—a man named Oscar Beltrão—to serve as the honorary president. The owner agreed, not expecting that the association would amount to very much. Other plantation owners in the region, however, were horrified. The profitability of the plantations depended on a labor force that was malleable, flexible and weak. Beltrão realized the danger of his position, renounced his position as president and began to demand that the workers disband. His threats had little effect, however, and more of these workers' associations began to form throughout the sugarcane region. The associations were given the name *Ligas Camponesas* (Peasant Leagues) by journalists who depicted the associations as communist.

The official goal of the Peasant Leagues was to promote land redistribution, and their slogan was "Agrarian reform by law or by force." The leagues won a major victory when the government expropriated a plantation in 1959 and distributed the land to the rural workers. This victory contributed to the rise of the associations through the Brazilian Northeast and beyond. By 1964, over 2,000 leagues had been formed in twenty different states.

In addition to the Peasant Leagues, rural unions also greatly expanded their influence in the late 1950s and early 1960s. Supported by the left-leaning governor of Pernambuco, Miguel Arraes, who came into office in 1962, the unions were able to expand rapidly in their position as legal organizations authorized to represent and defend the rural workers. The unions won a major victory in 1963, when federal labor legislation was passed that provided rural workers with the same rights as those that had been granted to urban workers in the 1930s.[42] The rural unions continued to gain strength as they carried out numerous strikes demanding that the legislation be enforced.

Plantation elites, with their allies in the Brazilian military, were alarmed by increasing reports of organizing among the workers on the sugarcane plantations; they were even more worried about the connections between the Communist Party and trade unions in the southern half of the country. In 1960, *The New York Times* ran an article about the rural unrest, painting the Northeast of Brazil in stark terms, describing it as an area with the "making[s] of a revolution." In the context of the escalating Cold War, the US lent its considerable support to the 1964 military coup and the subsequent suppression of worker organization throughout the countryside, working closely with the military government. Presidents Johnson and Nixon both declared the fiercely repressive military regime a model for Latin America.

After the military coup, organization in the rural areas came to a virtual standstill. The trade unions that had started up in the 1950s and 1960s were violently repressed, and also infiltrated by government workers. The Peasant Leagues were broken up, their members intimidated and their leaders exiled. In the late 1980s, however, the history of past resistance represented by Antônio Conselheiro, Zumbi, the famous leader of Palmares, and the Peasant Leagues would provide inspiration for the MST's expansion into the Northeast. Zumbi has become especially important in the growing Black Consciousness movement in Brazil, and the MST's references to him are understood to be a symbol of an antiracist position. Today, throughout Brazil, in thousands of encampments and settlements of the MST, people chant:

> Che, Zumbi, Antônio Conselheiro,
> Na luta por justiça  (In the fight for justice),
> Nós somos companheiros  (We are companions).

Placing Zumbi and Antônio Conselheiro alongside Che Guevara, the hero of the guerilla movements that spread across Latin America in the 1950s and 1960s, emphasizes the MST's belief that its work is only the most recent form of a very long and international struggle for social justice.

# The MST and the Struggle for Land in Pernambuco

One of the most important MST leaders in Pernambuco is Jaime Amorim, a short man with dark, curly hair and an intense energy that infects everyone near him. Jaime was one of the first MST activists to work in the Northeast, and he has assumed the state leadership in Pernambuco since 1992. We spoke to him many times during our time in the Northeast and were able to interview him formally during a statewide MST meeting in 1999.

Jaime was born and raised in the southern state of Santa Catarina. His parents were both Italian, and the family farmed a small piece of land near the state's northern coast, in the municipality of Guaramirim. As Jaime worked on his parent's land, he was active in rural politics. In 1978, he began to participate in the Pastoral de Juventude (Youth Pastoral). He was also a member of the local CEB and worked with the rural union organizing in opposition to the formal unions maintained during the military dictatorship. In 1981, Jaime joined the newly formed Workers' Party, but his most active ties were to the Catholic Church, and, in 1985, he was coordinating the local Catholic Youth Action group in close contact with the Pastoral da Terra, headquartered in the city of Joinville. In 1985, Jaime attended the MST's first national congress as a representative of the Pastoral da Terra. He was inspired by the ideas discussed at the conference and began meeting with local communities along the Santa Catarina coast to talk about the movement and mobilizing for agrarian reform.

In 1986, Jaime was invited to begin organizing movement activities in the Northeast. He worked for the rest of the agricultural season on his parents' land, and, in May 1987, when the harvest had been collected, he left for the state of Bahia. MST leaders from all over the country joined Jaime, coming from Paraíba, Bahia, Santa Catarina and Espírito Santo. The MST's ability to expand out of the South depended on leaders like these, who were willing to travel far from their homes, working long hours in dangerous conditions to spread the movement's message. In the late 1980s, twenty activists from southern Brazil traveled to the Northeast to work for the movement there; only one returned to the South, the others staying on to occupy important leadership positions in different states. These leaders maintained regular contact with the main MST office in São Paulo, and ongoing communication helped them coordinate local initiatives with national ones. Jaime spent two years traveling around the Northeast, working in Bahia, Maranhão, Piauí, Sergipe, Alagoas and Paraíba before he came to Pernambuco.

Although it seemed at odds with the energy and optimism we encountered at the Pernambuco state meeting, Pernambuco was considered one of the most difficult states in the region for the movement to organize in. Because of the immense poverty in its rural areas and its history of radical mobilization, it was also one of the most important.

Jaime talked about the difficulties the MST would confront in organizing the rural poor in the state: "In the Northeast in general, the organizations that worked with the people—unions and political parties—were all killed by the military government. [This was] especially true here in Pernambuco. The Peasant Leagues were totally destroyed, eliminated, nothing lasted—politically or organically—nothing but the fear of the people."

During the military period, the only organizations to continue working in the rural areas were the unions and religious groups. The government allowed certain unions to continue as a way of supervising the rural population and opposing the Peasant Leagues. The rural trade union in Pernambuco, FETAPE (Federação de Trabalhadores na Agricultura de Pernambuco), retained its formal structure and continued to work with rural workers during the military's rule, but its work was much more difficult under the government's watchful eye. Still, FETAPE managed to carry out significant battles, including the bold sugarcane strikes of 1978 and 1979. But Jaime pointed to FETAPE's strength as one of the reasons why it would be difficult for the MST to organize in the state: "There were already strong forces active here, and they worked to impede the organization of the movement." According to Jaime, the rural unions in Pernambuco were against agrarian reform; when we asked him why, he said:

> [The unions] thought that rural workers would not want land,
> that they would only want jobs. So FETAPE carried out strikes and
> struggled for wages and who ended up getting the money? The distillery owners who won subsidies from the government to create
> jobs. And, in reality, they never even created the jobs, and the
> situation just kept getting worse and worse.

The conflict between the MST and FETAPE would become apparent in 1989, when the movement carried out its first occupation in the state. The activists who organized that occupation believed that Pernam-

buco's state governor, Miguel Arraes, would support the landless movement. First elected governor of Pernambuco in the early 1960s, Miguel
Arraes had a reputation as one of the most progressive governors ever
to hold office in the Northeast. In 1963, he helped oversee the passage
of the rural labor statute. Sugarcane workers throughout the rural areas
of Pernambuco remembered Arraes as a politician who had worked to
make life easier on the plantations. As one former plantation worker
said: "Here, things only got better after Miguel Arraes came in [to of-
fice]. He made everything here that was bad easier. There was a lot of
rebellion the year that he came in—mill masters ran, administrators,
everyone ran."

In 1964, Arraes was exiled by the military. Although he was one of
the most popular politicians in the state's history, his plan to improve
working conditions on the plantations, as well as his consorting with
well-known communist leaders, earned him the immense dislike of political elites in the region. But when the dictatorship ended twenty-one
years later, Arraes was elected as the governor of Pernambuco. In 1989,
Jaime and the other MST activists were counting on Arraes to support
the movement's first occupation in Pernambuco. As Jaime said: "We
thought that even if the support [he gave us] wasn't public, he would at
least recognize that it was important for the struggle to go forward."
The occupation was carried out on land owned by the state about thirty
miles south of the state's capital city, Recife. Jaime estimated that the
land, which was part of an industrial complex called SUAPE, covered
approximately twenty thousand hectares, enough to settle hundreds of
families.

One of the people who joined the MST occupation at that time was
Caio Velânço. In 1989, Caio was a sugarcane worker. Ten years later, he
would be known as one of the most active MST leaders in the Pernambuco sugarcane region. His early start in the movement earned him the
nickname "Grandpa," even though he was only twenty-two when he
began as an activist and had no grandchildren. Caio looked younger
than he was—he was one of the few people whose body hid the effects
of working in the sugarcane fields under the hot sun. Only the den-
tures that replaced his missing front teeth were an indication of poor
health care and many hours spent sucking on sugarcane stalks.

Caio was born in the agreste, where his parents were sharecroppers, paying out a portion of their yields in exchange for the right to live on and work three hectares of land. When the landowner switched from agriculture to ranching, the land became more valuable to him as pasture than as a tenant farm, and Caio and his parents were forced to leave. At that time, the sugarcane region of Pernambuco was considered a good place to make money. Leaving his family in the agreste, Caio's father moved to the coast and shortly thereafter he called for his wife and his two-year-old son.

When Caio turned eight, he went to work in the sugarcane fields. Although he was not legally old enough to be employed, it was (and still is) common to find children that young working beside their parents in the fields. Sugarcane plantations have a notoriously poor record of abusing child labor during the harvest season. According to a report prepared by the US Department of Labor, 25 percent of the workers in the Pernambucan zona da mata are between ten and seventeen years old.[43] A survey cited in the report found that 56.7 percent of the children interviewed had experienced some sort of occupational injury, primarily knife cuts to the arms, legs and hands.[44] Some of these injuries were due to the long hours the children keep during the harvest season: "Children must often wake up at 4:00 A.M. and go to work without eating breakfast; they carry candles with them so they can work in the predawn hours. Employers generally do not provide the children with boots or shoes to protect them and most children instead either wear rubber sandals or work barefoot."

On the plantation, Caio planted cane, weeded the long rows and went out with the others when it came time to burn the harvest for the mills. The work was not easy: "I didn't like it. First, because the cane cut us a lot, and there were ants and snakes. And it is very heavy work —weeding cane is work for animals. And you earn very little." Caio and his family lived inside the plantation. They had a small house, but were not allowed to plant anything on the land near where they lived. His family had tried planting a small garden on the land around the house, but the mill owner sent other workers to the house to dig up the garden. Plantation owners were particularly afraid of their workers planting anything "with roots," meaning plants that would last more than one year. The land needed to be kept clear because, when sugar or alcohol prices were high, the cane would be planted right up to the edges of the houses. As Caio said, "When you left your house, when you opened the door, you were already right on top of the cane."

When Caio was twelve, he left home. He moved around regularly, working for plantations in three northeastern states: Paraíba, Pernambuco and Alagoas. When he found a job that paid well, he stayed, and if he heard of one that paid better, he left. This strategy of mobility was common among sugarcane workers, who often chose to express their dislike of a particular plantation by moving on. In an economic system like the sugarcane industry, where wages depended heavily on the discretion of individual planters, conversations with fellow workers about the different plantations constituted an essential source of information. After many years of working on different plantations, Caio found that the pay began to get worse, and so he moved to Mato Grosso do Sul, a state in the center-west of Brazil. He worked on the sugarcane plantations that had recently been set up there, but after two years he decided the less-developed Mato Grosso do Sul was not the place for him, being "covered in woods and fit only for the Indians."

In 1989, Caio was twenty-two and living with his mother in a small town in Pernambuco's sugarcane region. MST leaders knocked on his door one night. They were going from door to door throughout the sugarcane region, talking to people about the movement and setting up group meetings to discuss the importance of agrarian reform in Brazil:

> They talked about how we could free ourselves a little from the situation we were living in . . . and that the only way of changing was to occupy [land]. They said that we had to be strong, though, because there would be some gunmen, some police, and we shouldn't be afraid because the struggle would not be armed; it was a peaceful struggle. So they convinced me, and four hundred other families from all around the town, and we left to find land.

The families left the comfort of their homes late at night on May 9, 1989. They piled into large trucks, fifty people standing in the back of each one. The decision to occupy land was not one that the families made lightly. Violence in the area was so common that they knew they ran the risk of injury or death. The mayor of the largest town in Caio's municipality was known as a bandit who ruled with his own brand of lawlessness, killing those with whom he disagreed and allowing his

An occupation of land in the sugarcane area of Pernambuco, with the typical plastic tents seen in occupations in nearly every state of Brazil in the last two decades.

gang of thugs to roam freely throughout the town. The violence had gotten so bad that Miguel Arraes had stepped in and authorized state troops to disarm the townspeople physically.

The occupation carried out that night met with immediate state censure. The MST leaders had misjudged Miguel Arraes, who did not choose to negotiate, instead sending in two thousand armed police officers to remove the families from their occupation site. Jaime remembered the night bitterly, "We were expelled with more force than has ever been used in this state before. He brought out the cavalry, helicopters, dogs—everything you can imagine." The MST squatters left SUAPE and formed a new encampment in front of the governor's palace. Arraes gave them until midnight to leave or be forcibly removed.

According to Jaime Amorim, it was impossible to negotiate with the governor:

We had been trying to talk to the government, but they just told us that there was already an organization that worked with rural workers, and that was FETAPE. [They said that] any other organization

The MST has won land throughout the Northeast, giving homes and land to settlers like this man, who still plants sugarcane but has also begun to diversify into food crops.

was just here to divide [the rural workers], and Arraes was against division. He thought that FETAPE was strong, and so he was against MST—and he was also against agrarian reform.

During an interview with us in 2000, Raul Jungmann, Brazil's minister of agrarian reform and a former member of one of the country's two main communist parties, suggested that Arraes did not support the MST's actions because he was philosophically committed to a different strategy:

> Arraes and the communists had a vision that you should promote wage labor, because . . . capitalism had already entered the country-side, so what was needed was to take those social rights that had already been won in the city to the countryside. . . . For this reason, Arraes was very much against [agrarian reform] because he thought it was going backwards.

The MST occupiers moved away from the governor's palace and camped out on the side of the highway for two months. The state tried to negotiate a resolution by offering assistance from a public welfare program called *Chapéu de Palha* (Straw Hat). This would have provided people with *cestas básicas* (semiregular food baskets) and some money, but the squatters refused the charity and continued to pressure INCRA to find them land. In July, the families received their first offer of land—from INCRA, the federal agency, not from the state government. INCRA agreed to settle the families in the sertão, on land in the municipality of Cabrobó.

While 120 families from the occupation camp accepted INCRA's offer of land in the sertão, the other families drifted away, discouraged by the violence of the occupation and the lack of results. Jaime went with the families to see the land:

> So, we went there, without really knowing where we were going. . . . The government took us there—it was a totally different thing [than what we were used to]. The government left us some sixty kilometers inside the caatinga. There were no streets, no water— just one well, and the mafia was using it to plant marijuana.

The families from the coastal sugarcane region were accustomed to working in the tropical-humid zone, and the semiarid region presented new difficulties that they were ill prepared to deal with. Caio was one of those who accepted the offer of land; but he lasted only fifteen days there: "What were we going to do in that town? In the desert, without water?" In the end, Caio said, no one stayed in the settlement.

It would take the MST two more years to lay the groundwork for more occupations in Pernambuco. In 1991, the movement carried out another occupation, and the families were expelled two hours later. But on March 19, 1992, the MST had its first victory, and began to consolidate its forces in the sugarcane region, which the movement felt should be a central focus. As Jaime said: "It became a priority for us to go back to the sugarcane region—because we always felt that agrarian reform was the only way out for the sugarcane region." In 1992, Jaime moved permanently to Pernambuco, and the struggle for agrarian reform began to diversify and expand in the state.

## ÁGUA PRETA: ORGANIZING AGRARIAN REFORM IN SUGARCANE COUNTRY

After Caio left the settlement in the desert, he joined the MST as an activist. Several years later, he and his new wife won land on a plantation approximately eighty miles south of Recife. In 1999, Caio was the president of his settlement and one of the most active MST leaders in the sugarcane region of Pernambuco. He had a reputation for being fair and good-hearted, even if he did occasionally linger at the bar longer than his wife would have liked. The settlement where Caio lived sat on the outskirts of a small town called Água Preta, which we visited in 1999 and 2001.

A person can reach Água Preta by driving south of Recife, through the sugarcane zone, passing through a number of small sugarcane towns that were active sites of organizing in the 1960s. Água Preta has always been a sugarcane town and still is today, even though twenty-two of the local plantations have been expropriated and distributed for the purposes of agrarian reform.

As you drive down the two-lane road that connects the sugarcane region to the capital city of Recife, rolling hills covered in lush green meadows of sugarcane undulate before you as far as the eye can see. When the sugarcane harvest begins, the green hills are scarred with even, black rows that spread across the fields like elevation lines on a topographic map. The black rows are the ashes left behind after the sugarcane is set on fire to make cutting the thick stalks easier. Sugarcane workers follow behind the columns of fire and smoke, cutting the sugarcane and arranging it in piles to be picked up by other workers, often small children, who carry the stalks in wheelbarrows to large trucks waiting by the side of the field. During the harvest season, the road that winds through the plantation region is clogged with slow-moving trucks, overflowing with sugarcane stalks. The air hangs heavy with the dust of the fires, and ash-covered men and women can be seen bent at the waist, stolidly hewing their way toward their daily quota of sugarcane.

No matter what season it is, the climate in this region is volatile and hot. Rains are frequent between March and October, sometimes coming down hard enough to generate widespread floods, forcing many people out of their homes and leaving the lingering smell of sewage in the streets of the towns. Average temperatures hover around twenty-four degrees Celsius throughout the year (about seventy-five degrees Fahrenheit), which would be pleasant if you didn't have to work outdoors in the sun.

Along with several other MST activists, Caio works in the area around

Água Preta to organize new occupations, coordinate political activities and assist the settlers who have already won land. None of these things is easy. Organizing new occupations is dangerous because plantation owners are deeply suspicious of people trying to mobilize the sugarcane workers, and even though Brazil is now a democracy, sugarcane elites continue to dominate the rural areas much as they did four hundred years ago, at the height of the colonial sugarcane economy. Wary of possible violence, MST activists try to avoid entering the plantations to do their organizing work. Caio believes that he might not leave the area alive if he were to try to organize inside a plantation. Even worse, the workers themselves might suffer: "If the administrator finds out [that you've been there] and he puts it in the boss's ear, and then the boss calls together the workers and tells them they should not leave [for an occupation] if they ever want to work again."

But there are more serious obstacles to organizing in the sugarcane region than potential violence. For almost five hundred years, the economy, society and politics in the region have been characterized by domination, exploitation and immense poverty. All of these manifest themselves in ways that make it difficult for MST activists to convince even the poorest rural workers that they will be better off if they fight for their own land. Jaime commented on this soberly:

> In the sugarcane region, there has been a very serious cultural,
> economic, social and physical degradation. Imagine the slaves who
> came here from Africa—they were a strong people—they say that
> the average height was very tall! And now 60 percent of the people
> here are unnaturally short. All the values of the people have been
> destroyed. And so this has consequences when you struggle for
> land—because we try . . . to reintegrate people not just economi-
> cally but also with dignity and the beginning of true citizenship.

When MST activists like Caio talk to people in the sugarcane region about agrarian reform, they find that many rural workers are reluctant to occupy a plantation that technically "belongs to someone else." In the South, the small farmers who first joined the MST had a tradition of working on their own land, and they formed the MST as a way of se- curing access to land to maintain those traditions. In the Northeast, however, few people have had any land of their own, as a result they valued land within the context of being employed on the plantation. Access to land meant greater job security than living in town as well as providing space to plant limited subsistence crops, but, in general, Caio and other MST activists found that the rural workers preferred a regular salary over land ownership.[45] As Caio said:

> They are used to a job and when you go to them with an idea about going after land . . . [a person] is going to measure the time [he would spend in an occupation] with the time that he would spend employed, and if he started a job today, in five days he would already have money in his pocket. And so if you go to him and ask if he wants land or a job, he is going to say a job. . . . I say this from experience because we go through it every day.

The rural workers depend on their salaries to buy their groceries at the weekly *feira* (market), an institution in the sugarcane region. Everyone looks forward to the chance to see friends and neighbors while doing their shopping: the excitement begins to build on Friday afternoon, when sellers start hauling in their products from nearby towns and rural areas. People dump bags on the sidewalk, where they plan to spread out their wares the next day. Everything is sold at the feira: different varieties of bananas, yams, live chickens, corn, pencils, marshmallow candies, hair ties, pots, pans and the local rum (*cachaça*, made from sugarcane), and the atmosphere is full of gossip and entertainment. Many of the things sold at the feira cannot be found after it closes up early Saturday afternoon. Little boys run around through the crowds with their wheelbarrows, looking for housewives burdened by their packages. They will carry your shopping as you go and deliver it to your house for about fifty cents.

The market is not just a place where things are exchanged for money; it is also a place for people to exchange important information. The rural workers get the low-down on the working conditions in different plantations from people they meet at the market. The men stand around wooden booths, drinking cachaça as the rest of the market whirls around them, discussing wages, the sugarcane economy, the temperaments of different bosses and so on.

Many of the women we talked to who had won land either on their own or with their husbands also preferred having a regular salary to working on the land for a living. Although there were women who farmed their land happily after receiving it from the government, many others told us that they did not like entering the plantation property because it was so *esquisito* (odd) inside. Most settlement families either lived in the small grouping of houses (called an agrovila—a small rural village) at the edge of the settlement or had a house in town, where the women and children would stay while the husband went back and forth between the settlement land and town. Some of the women had never seen their settlement land.

In spite of this preference for jobs, rural sugarcane workers found it increasingly difficult to find work in the 1990s. In 1989, the federal government withdrew generous subsidies that had propped up sugarcane production in the Northeast since the mid-1970s, subsidies that were part of an attempt to provide an alternative fuel for consumption because two oil crises, in 1973 and 1978 to 1979, had demonstrated the dangers of relying on foreign energy imports. Between 1975 and 1989, the government invested US$10.5 billion into the Alcohol Program (or PROALCOOL). The government specifically targeted the Northeast for substantial PROALCOOL funds because widespread poverty in the region suggested that government assistance was particularly needed. After 1989, when the government began to withdraw these funds, it became clear how heavily the sugarcane industry had come to rely on government support. By the mid-1990s, it was estimated that over 40 percent of all distilleries in the state of Pernambuco were either no longer processing cane or were having serious difficulties doing so.[46] At that time, it was estimated that there were 350,000 unemployed workers in the Pernambuco sugarcane region alone. Some of these unemployed workers joined the MST, because, as one worker said: "There aren't any wages, there aren't any jobs, the only alternative is to fight for land for ourselves; [that way] we can begin to kill our hunger."

As the regional economic slump deepened, the number of day laborers hired without their working papers (called *clandestinos*—clandestine workers) steadily increased. These workers constituted a reserve pool of flexible labor that the plantation bosses could call upon as needed during the harvest. They often ended up working for less money than they were promised, but they could not complain if they wished to be contracted again the following year. As Nataniel, the president of the local rural trade union, said:

> The majority [of the plantation workers in this area] are clandestine.
> Some live in the periphery of the city that sits next to a property
> where they had been legally certified to work. They were obligated
> to leave that property because of oppression or persecution, and
> they ended up as beggars in the city, and they live worse than they
> did on the plantation. They are obligated to leave the house at 4:00
> in the morning, wait for a car in a place for day laborers and many
> times they arrive in the plantation at 6:00 or 7:00 and have to
> [begin hard labor right away].

The severe crisis in sugarcane production, together with the increasingly active presence of agrarian reform interests (particularly MST leaders) in the state and the availability of federal resources for land redistribution, induced the local government to expropriate bankrupt plantations and redistribute the land to former workers and occupants. Throughout the mid-to-late 1990s, temporary squatter encampments were set up across the sugarcane region, and the MST's bright red flag could be seen hanging from improvised flagpoles. Stories about MST occupations and public demonstrations were featured regularly in the state newspapers. Between 1986 and 2001, 2,199 families were settled on twenty-seven former plantation areas in Pernambuco, most of those in the last five years.

José Carlos (known as Zé Carlos) was one rural worker who decided to join the movement and fight for land. Born in Alagoas where his family lived and worked in the sugarcane mills, Zé Carlos began helping his father at work when he was eight years old. When he was old enough, he left and worked on his own in the mills. He was sometimes employed with his legal working papers and sometimes not: "I have always had the same life. I ended up working for other people and earned my bread and the misery was always the same."

Zé Carlos found out about the movement when he was at home, living in the small town of Xexéu, near Água Preta. An activist came and knocked on his door, and when Zé Carlos (who had never heard of the movement) asked what this was all about, the activist said that people were gathering to occupy a mill and see about getting the land divided—"You don't need to bring any food with you, just tools, and we will arrange a ride to take us [to the occupation site]."

The first occupation in which Zé Carlos participated was at a mill called Souza. The occupation was led by the state rural trade union, FETAPE, and over two thousand people went. That occupation resulted in the expropriation of land for four settlements, but there was not enough room for everyone. Those people who had been organized by the MST were not able to get land, and so they occupied other nearby plantations.

Zé Carlos lived in different encampments for over three years before INCRA expropriated the mill near Água Preta and divided the land among the former residents and sem-terra. He was the first person in his family to own a piece of land. He continues to participate in movement activities, such as new occupations and MST demonstrations, because "the way I suffered, other people suffer too but they want to conquer their problems, and they want peace."

Zé Carlos believed that the movement made a positive difference in his life: "Everything [we have] is because of the strength of these men, these men who help us. I can't say that just because we're living here quietly [now] that these men don't help me, because they do." In his first year on the land, Zé Carlos planted about five hundred banana-tree bulbs, four sacks of potatoes and almost a hectare of manioc, beans and corn. He worked alone, with just one young son helping him out in the afternoons after school, but he had big plans: he intended to fence off a portion of the remaining land to raise cattle and he envisioned planting more agricultural crops when he had the time.

Unfortunately, not everyone on the plantations is pleased to see the land expropriated. Some of the moradores who worked on the plantations when they were economically active had continued to live on the land even when the owner stopped planting cane. They hoped that sugarcane would be planted again someday, and, in the meantime, they had their houses, and they scraped together a living with government support (usually in the form of an old-age pension if there was an elderly person in the family), family support and odd jobs. When the MST organized an occupation on a plantation where people were living, tension often existed between the moradores and MST members—

some moradores did not necessarily welcome the chance to become smallholders with title to their own land. As an MST activist in the region said:

> It is difficult to find a resident who doesn't struggle against the presence of [the MST squatters], and there is tension. . . . [The residents] double-cross the [MST members]. When the boss is around, they start saying things behind their backs, but when he leaves, they go to the landless workers and say, "we are your allies." They are afraid. Submission is high—it is, in fact, a dilemma, [the residents] have an internal contradiction. [On one hand, they say] 'I hope the MST people win' and [on the other hand], they treat the MST people badly because they can't see themselves in their shoes.

As one non-morador MST settler said about the moradores: "In the beginning they don't [support the movement], because they think that we messed up their lives, because when they worked for the boss, they had work, every week they had a little income, and after we get there, they don't have this any more."

One of the plantations near Água Preta, called Flora, was expropriated in 1996 and divided among thirty-four moradores, and also among thirteen families who had occupied the plantation with the MST. According to the moradores, INCRA officials had come by the plantation twenty years earlier. At that time, INCRA was considering expropriating the property because the distillery that owned the land was deeply in debt to the government. Nothing ever came of INCRA's inquiries, however, and when the MST occupation camp was set up, the residents were skeptical that anything would be different this time.

The residents had no idea what the MST was or that the people camped out on the plantation land were even part of the movement. When we asked what they thought when they found out the MST was involved with occupying the plantation, most moradores remembered being afraid of or disliking the movement. As one older woman who had lived on the plantation for many years said: "I thought that the sem-terra were only about ransacking cars, coming here like this and invading, fighting with the boss, killing people. . . ."

To complicate matters further, the workers' former boss—called a *rendeiro* (renter) because he was renting the plantation land—fought against the expropriation of the property. He proposed a clever plan that would allow him to keep control: the moradores would all push INCRA for land, and if they were united, they could convince the government that there was not enough room for the MST occupiers. One morador, Sr. Antônio, said that the rendeiro told them that they could get rid of the MST occupiers themselves: "Everyone would get a rifle or whatever they use, and we would set those people [who were camped out] running. And meanwhile, we would divide the land for us, but he would still be the boss, you know?" Although there may have been some moradores who would have liked to see the MST occupiers gone, no one supported the boss's plan. As Sr. Antônio said: "We weren't going to do that because [the sem-terra] have rights too, don't they?"

In the end, the plantation land was expropriated and distributed among forty-seven families. The former moradores were divided in their opinions of the expropriation: some felt that the change was for the worse and were angry with the movement for breaking up their way of life. Sr. Antônio was one of those—even though he was friendly with everyone on the settlement, he found it difficult to reconcile himself to being a small farmer:

> I never thought [the expropriation] was a good idea, you see? I was used to a job where I worked, and every week I received money to do my shopping. . . . I think it's very difficult [to have land here], I haven't gotten used to it. . . . For me, it is a very large difficulty. There are days that I think a lot about how it is that I am going to survive from now on, because the resources that come from INCRA or from the government are not very much, and they take a long time to get here, and we are in a situation that is difficult to survive and so for this I say that I am not yet used to it.

But others welcomed the chance to own a piece of land. On a hot summer day in 1999, we interviewed a morador named Mario, who believed that life had changed for the better when the MST arrived on Flora.

We found Mario in his new house, a large, brick-and-cement structure that was spotless inside but furnished very sparsely, with only a gas stove and a small kitchen table in the main rooms. At seventy-seven, Mario was one of the oldest people on the settlement. He lived in his new house with his wife and three children. The oldest child, a son, had been living in the city of São Paulo when he found out that his father had received land on the settlement. He came back from the city and, by day, worked on his father's land, while at night he taught classes in the town's small high school.

Mario had worked his whole life in the sugarcane fields around Pernambuco. He had come to Flora in 1952, when he was thirty years old. For eleven years, he worked without any legal rights, but on September 26, 1963, his official working papers were processed. Mario described his life working in sugarcane as a difficult one, even though he was luckier than most. He was given a small farm and a house away from the rest of the workers, who all lived at the edge of the plantation in the simple row houses that dot the zona da mata landscape. We walked to the house where he used to live, tucked back in the woods, off the sugarcane fields. The house was relatively large for the region, but made out of clay and sticks and falling in several different places. Mario's living accommodations had clearly taken a turn for the better.

Mario had stayed on Flora through three different bosses. He remembered the first two fondly, saying that they had been good to him, giving him his house and a bit of land and even giving him advice about how to plant around his house. Mario was able to plant manioc, bananas and some vegetables, which meant that he only bought meat, sugar and coffee from the plantation store. But the work was always hard because every person had to cut a certain amount of cane or they would not receive their salary. They had to cut this amount regardless of the quality of the cane or the terrain on which they were working. Often the cane was so poorly planted or the land so hilly that making the quota meant beginning work before the sun came up and ending after it had gone down. Mario worked six long days a week, waking at 3:00 A.M. to get out to the fields on time.

In spite of these conditions, Mario liked his first two bosses; it was only mention of the last boss, the rendeiro who had been farming the land when it was expropriated in 1996, that threw both Mario and his son into a frenzy. This last boss had been very cruel, they said. He never paid the workers their proper benefits and refused to let anyone plant food crops around their house. There were stories, which they relayed grimly, of this boss killing people who had disobeyed him.

Mario found out about the expropriation when he decided to quit work one day and went to the mill office to ask for a proper dismissal and payment of termination benefits. The director of the office told him: "If you want to go away, go, but the distillery isn't sending you away and they also will not give final payments to anyone. I think it's better if you [continue to] work here with your children, because this [expropriation] isn't going to take all that long, no, it's going to get here soon." When Mario heard that he could get the rights to his land, he was happy, saying:

> Even if it was only land, it would still be better than the distillery—
> you suffer as well [on the land] but it's better when it's yours and no
> one will come to take it away. Between then [when we worked for
> the rendeiro] and now, it has gotten a lot better. That was the time
> we took charge, [the rendeiro] had to shut up and I myself thought
> this was very good, so I gave [the MST people] a lot of support.

In the two years since Mario won the right to his land and built his new house, he and his son had put up a brightly painted new fence and planted food crops in the fields around the house. The fence was intended to keep in the cattle that they hoped to buy and to keep out people from the nearby town, who occasionally raided the settlement properties closest to the main road. Mario planted a variety of crops, including corn, sugarcane, manioc and bananas. He also dug out two large fishponds as a way of earning a more regular income.

## THE MST AND THE RURAL UNIONS IN
## THE SUGARCANE REGION

The increasing presence of agrarian reform and the MST in the sugarcane region has exposed some of the tensions between the movement and the local trade unions; at the same time, it has provided new opportunities for collaboration. When the MST first began organizing in the Pernambuco sugarcane region, they were often at odds with the rural unions. MST leaders publicly criticized the unions for being complicit with the plantation industry, and trade union leaders opposed the idea of agrarian reform as a successful option for the region. As one MST leader from Água Preta said: "In seven or eight cities around here, it's the mill owner who controls the unions, so the president of the union does whatever the boss says. So, because of that, it's difficult for the union leader to say to the worker: 'Worker So-and-So, you have the right to this, and that,' because [even though] they could . . . prove it . . . afterwards the boss will order the president killed."

One landless movement activist, Romil, left the union to work with the MST. He was working in health care as a union activist in Mato Grosso do Sul when he "fell in love with the movement. People who work in the union can't help but fall in love with the cause. So, at that time, I left Mato Grosso do Sul because I had a low income and I couldn't support myself. Then I came to the Northeast and joined the MST." We asked Romil what it was about the landless movement that attracted people from the unions, and he said:

> It is the intimate relationship with the people. You can see within the movement all of the people who are excluded from society . . . there are civil servants who lost their jobs, metal workers, people who can't get a job because they are over forty. . . . [As a movement activist,] you work directly with people. So you notice an improvement in their quality of life instead of always reading union contracts and documents. I am not criticizing anything, but [with the union] everything boils down to the topic of raising income, and so our comrades don't engage themselves in the fight for any other category.

But the unions were hurt badly by the sugarcane region's economic crisis—when there aren't any jobs, nobody joins the union and nobody pays the union fees. We spoke with Natanael, the president of the local trade union in Água Preta, in his office one afternoon. A feisty, bullish-looking man, short with square shoulders and a way of speaking rapidly that made everything he said sound urgent, Natanael lamented the decline of the trade unions in the region: "[Some unions that had] a good number of members fifteen or twenty years ago are shutting their doors today; without the means to keep going, they're owing money to their members without any way to either pay them or throw them out."

When the unions realized that the sugarcane industry was in the middle of a crisis that seemed unlikely to end soon, they began to rally their own attempts at agrarian reform. Natanael said: "Yes, we are [organizing occupations]. About three years ago, when workers began to run into real difficulties within the industry, we thought that the only path there was was to begin organizing the workers to occupy land. And these occupations would take place with the very workers who lived in the properties we occupied."

The union's decision to engage in occupations created new difficulties for the MST. We ran into one conflict between the MST and the Federation of Agricultural Workers in Pernambuco (FETAPE) when we visited an MST occupation camp that had been set up the previous day in a plantation near Água Preta. The plantation had not been producing cane for several years, and the pathetic-looking fields were scattered with clumps of sugarcane that continued to grow despite the lack of attention. We rode into the plantation with two MST activists who were bringing food supplies to the occupation camp and checking up on the families.

As we drove into the plantation, we passed the run-down buildings of the former plantation center. The dirt road suddenly became uneven pavement, and we saw children playing alongside the street. One of the MST activists, Antônio, rolled down his window to double-check his directions and called one of the children over to the car. He asked the child where his father was, and the boy pointed toward a man sitting on the front steps of one of the row houses. Antônio got out of the car, walked over to him and told the man about the encampment, explaining that the movement was going to try and get the plantation expropriated. He urged the man to go up to the encampment and check it out—he said that the man should join the movement as well and get a piece of land. The man looked unconvinced, though, and we drove on.

We drove up a steep, grassy hill until the car couldn't make it any further. Everyone got out of the car, and we walked the rest of the way. Just underneath a small overhang at the top of the hill, we came to the encampment. Several tents had been thrown up—there weren't any sturdy trees around, so people had found sticks and made what looked like pup tents, little triangles sitting on the ground. Nine or ten men were standing around a fire, where a pot was boiling. The men had caught a turtle and were boiling it with manioc to make a sort of weak-looking stew.

There were very few women in the encampment, something noticeably different from occupation camps we had seen in the South. The lack of women and children gave the occupation camp a very different feel than in the South, where occupation camps often had a festive air about them. Here, there was little sense of security or comfort.

The men stood tensely around in the gathering dark, with their arms crossed, looking out over the former sugarcane fields. The night before, when they occupied the plantation, there were gunshots. No one knew exactly who had shot at them, but everyone suspected the people who were camped out in the field below the MST site. We looked down the hill in surprise. About a mile away, hard to see in that light, there was a group of tents; when we looked more closely, it was obvious that the tents were part of another occupation camp. A flag was flying; we were told the camp had been set up by the state rural trade union, FETAPE, before the MST's camp. The trade union had been negotiating with the government to turn the plantation over to the workers. MST activists said the movement set up its own camp to try to speed up the expropriation, but FETAPE was skeptical of the MST's intentions, and relations were tense enough between the two organizations that the MST believed they had been attacked by the rival camp.

Disagreements such as this one were not uncommon between the MST and the trade unions in Pernambuco, even though everyone recognized that infighting was not in the workers' best interests. As one rural worker from a different FETAPE encampment said to us while we were visiting the INCRA office in Recife:

> How is this going to end up? Two social movements shouldn't be doing this, a movement ought to seek out the rural workers, not just show up and take something. . . . The problem with these movements is that one always wants to be in front of the others. If you take this encampment here, and pull out the FETAPE leadership and put in MST leadership, the same sem-terra are here . . . the people who suffer with this are the rural workers, the landless. . . .

As the MST and the rural unions increasingly fight for the same goal—agrarian reform—the opportunities for mutual collaboration have become more apparent.

In Água Preta, Natanael insisted that the local trade unions worked —and wanted to continue working—in conjunction with the MST. He said he believed the MST was the only organization that truly possessed the structure and the knowledge to provide food and education for the workers while they lived in the occupation camps. Natanael himself had organized two occupations, but lost them (one of them turned over to the MST) because the union organizers "couldn't keep food in the people's mouths." Without food, Natanael said, people could not continue fighting.

In turn, MST leaders in the sugarcane region were beginning to encourage movement members who had won land to join the local rural workers' union, telling them:

> It's one of our battles to be unionized, to legalize our situation. . . .
> This is all taking a lot of negotiating, but it is important that we be
> legalized. [For example, so-and-so] has a daughter now who just
> had a child, and since he was already registered at the union, he can
> get maternity help for her from the federal government. . . . This is a
> good thing. Also, if anyone needs their retirement pension, like [so-
> and-so] needs one now, we already have the union. For all of these
> reasons, it would be good to have a union to give us assistance.

The more that the MST and the rural unions are able to cooperate in their work, the more likely it is that people living on agrarian reform settlements will be able to maintain a decent quality of life.

## "The Land Is Only the Beginning"
### Facing the Hurdles of Sustainable Reform

Even with all the difficulties of organizing occupations and mobilizing rural workers, the real battles begin when the settlers win access to land. Once their basic subsistence needs have been provided for, the settlers begin to think about improving their positions, and it is then that they run up against the difficulties of farming in a country that does little to support small farmers. Farming is difficult even under ideal conditions, and conditions in the Northeast—as in much of rural Brazil—are far from ideal for small farmers. Perhaps the three main issues the MST has to confront in the sugarcane region are individualism, patronage politics and the pull of sugarcane.

After MST members and moradores have won access to land, the

MST often finds it difficult to convince them to remain active in the movement or in the settlement association. The settlers in the sugar-cane region recognize that the movement was an important advocate for them; one settler said, ""Nothing would function without the movement. If it weren't for protests, the struggle, everyone participating together, then we wouldn't get anything." But if the settlers typically see the movement as a way to gain access to material goods, as soon as they achieve their goal, they also tend to withdraw from the organization and the rest of the group. This tendency to withdraw may be in part a product of life on the plantations, where there are few incentives for cooperation. People rely on their own labor to cut enough cane to earn their weekly salaries, and the workers develop little sense of community among themselves. Romil shook his head in frustration at the movement's inability to penetrate the rural workers' attitude: "They want to breathe in their own freedom. [They say,] 'Now I [have] my piece of land, I am going to take care of my own life. I am not growing cane sugar for anyone else.' They don't have any problem with the MST—they participate in the marches with us—but when it comes to the question of organizing the settlement, then they have this resistance, they just want their little piece of land. Everything the [settler] does is like this: 'I am going to do it like this because it makes money. Dr. So-and-so did it this way, and he made a lot of money.'"

The rural workers' experience with the plantation shapes their perception of land as an independent space where they will be allowed to live as they please. As Romil put it, "First, the people here left slavery and ended up in the [sugarcane region]. Only the white people went to the sertão. The people who stayed in the sugarcane region were the black people who left the *senzalas* (slave houses), and then got into neo-senzalas, which were the shacks the senhores do engenho had for them. . . . Now [they are saying], 'I want my land. I want my space.' . . . Within this space he feels free and he says: 'On these ten hectares, I am the master, I am free. If I don't want to do anything, I will sit on the riverbank and stay there looking at it, but the view is mine.'" Because of this desire for independence, the MST activists find it can be difficult to convince settlers to construct a common living space—the agrovila.

One of the MST's goals across the country is to build agrovilas on the settlements as a way of building solidarity and community among the settlers. Jaime Amorim said that this was exceedingly difficult in the sugarcane region of the Northeast: "You would think that people would want to live together because they were already used to it on the mill, but the tendency is to isolate because of the anger they have—you can't see it—they are so angry at the senhor do engenho. And they just want to be isolated, as far away from everyone else as possible."

Even as the settlers seek independence from one another, they find it difficult to forge new political relationships that are not based on the hierarchical, patronage-style politics of the plantation. Part of the problem lies in the federal government's policy of privileging those people already associated with the expropriated property when distributing the land. On many settlements in the sugarcane region, this policy means that former rendeiros are settled alongside work-crew bosses, plantation administrators and cane cutters, people who had occupied different positions on the plantation. Their subsequent classification as "settlers" does not erase those differences. Former rendeiros, administrators and work-crew bosses tend to have more savings and better political connections than the cane workers. They also tend to be better educated and able to negotiate the new political system of the settlement more easily. As a result, social hierarchies roll over from plantation to settlement. The verb *mandar* (to send, or to order) is expressive of these hierarchical power relations: when one person asks another to do something, the use of the verb *mandar* is an immediate indicator as to the relative status between the two. Someone with more status (or power) within the community can "mandar" another person, but a person with less status has to ask.

It is words like *mandar* that illustrate how subtle power relations tend to be. Even within a community as exploited and marginal as the settlement, there are people who have the status and influence to order others. In the sugarcane settlements, hierarchies are perhaps most visible in the settlers' associations. After a group wins access to land, INCRA obligates them to form an association that meets regularly to discuss and regulate settlement business. The forty-six families on Flora formed an association soon after they had been settled on the land, an association designed to be run by a team of elected officials, including a president, vice-president, treasurer and secretary. Whenever official documents are signed, at least three of the association officials are required to be present. Running the association is occasionally difficult for the settlers, although it is an important political vehicle. Just the act of meeting regularly is something the settlers had rarely done as rural workers. As one former morador said of his experience on the plantation, "In that time, there were no meetings; a meeting was to do forced labor."

Within the associations, however, the interplay between individualism and hierarchy is evident. As Romil, the MST activist, said, "An image has been created of the [settlement] president as someone who can do anything [he wants]. We have this in our culture. Our people believe in the president as the man who runs the country and they don't manage to see that we could create a [different] structure—like a parliament, for example. They say . . . 'the president of the settlement is the one who tells us what to do and he decides for the others what they should do.' The movement has been working with this to try and stop it."

During our interview in 1999, Jaime Amorim supported Romil's observation: "You will see that every president of a settlement association or union leader acts just like the senhor do engenho, the ex-rendeiro. We call it presidencialismo—the president of the association starts to 'mandar.' And this sort of president is what the people are used to." As we'll see, the tradition of "presidentialism" is even more evident outside the settlement—in all the social and political structures the settlers have to interact with—and MST activists can find themselves caught up in traditional politics, because this is the most effective way to get things done.

One example of tension between the movement's beliefs and traditional politics in the Northeast revolves around whether basic resources are all peoples' by right or not. The movement believes that the rural poor of Brazil should be provided with a decent standard of living, because it is their right both as citizens of the Brazilian nation and as human beings. Thus, the movement fights for access to basic services, like electricity, and frames these services in terms of rights, instead of favors or charitable donations. The movement has made considerable progress in broadening the discussion of what it means to be a citizen in Brazil, but even still it is far from overcoming the sort of politics forged on the old plantation, which are deeply embedded in the society and economy of the Northeast. It would be difficult for any organization to operate totally outside these norms—particularly organizations that rely on the state for access to resources.

We saw an example of traditional political business during a late-night meeting held on August 18, 1999, at the mayor's house in Água Preta. The mayor was a cattle rancher, and his family owned a beautiful old farmhouse. The meeting brought together several members of the MST (the regional leader, the local agricultural extension agent, the leader of an encampment built on the edge of town and the president of a nearby settlement) and the mayor on the porch of the old farmhouse, overlooking the cattle stalls and the fields beyond. Everyone sat in straight-backed chairs arranged in a circle around a beautiful wooden table. The mayor's wife brought out small glasses of Coca-Cola with a plate of goat cheese and a fruit spread that is a common sweet in Brazil.

The meeting began after midnight, opening with formal declarations by both the mayor and the local MST leader. Each person elaborated on the strengths and accomplishments of their respective groups, the mayor explaining that he was a champion of education efforts in the sugarcane region and that he supported the MST's efforts to build small farm communities on unproductive plantations, the MST leader listing recent settlements that had been created with the help of the movement and stressing the importance of MST settlers as political constituents. The mayor nodded lightly when the MST representative suggested that he needed the settlers' votes if he wished to keep his political position secure.

After this formal introduction, the MST representatives began to make their requests for assistance, mainly for food supplies for the people living in the encampment at the edge of town. The MST representatives expressed an implicit threat that without government support, the MST occupiers would have to resort to saques—looting supermarkets or trucks. After two hours of discussion, the mayor agreed to send R$100 per week (about US$50 at that time) in food coupons to the encampment. He also agreed to hire a doctor to visit the settlements for two hours every week, to fix a truck on which the movement depended and to fix the leaky roof over the schoolhouse in one of the settlements. The MST representatives left satisfied, having secured some of the most basic services for their members—food, medical attention, transportation and a decent schoolhouse. It was a victory for the encampment and the settlements, even though the MST representatives had had to play the traditional games of personalistic politics.

The MST activists who work in the Northeast are, for the most part, hardworking, incredibly energetic and idealistic young people who would like to make a difference in a region so caught up in poverty and exclusion that any change is a welcome one. But these activists are fighting not only against the legacies of maldevelopment in the Northeast, but also within them. They are not above the people they seek to help; they themselves are embedded in the same social, political, economic and cultural relationships. MST activists are usually slightly better educated than most of the settlers, and they receive assistance for their work from the movement, but they are often torn between their vision for a new way of doing things and a familiarity with the old ways— ways that can bring immediate, needed relief, as the story of the mayor and the MST representatives shows.

We found this tension between old and new embodied in an activist from Água Preta who was working as an agronomist on the local settlements when we were doing research in the area. The town's mayor had nominated him for the post in 1998, and the movement agreed to the selection. Although the government was technically the institution employing the agronomist, the MST paid his salary and set his monthly agenda. When we first arrived in Água Preta in 1999, Antônio (not his real name) appeared to be passionately committed to the movement. He had only been with the movement for a year, having returned from a brief stint working for a large cattle rancher in Bahia. Antônio and his wife, Maria, lived on the settlement in a mud house of about four hundred square feet, which had been partitioned into a very small kitchen, a living room and two small bedrooms.

Antônio worked tirelessly for the movement. He was always up early and in meetings until very late. Every now and then, he would get up before dawn and walk out to the plot of land he had been given when he accepted the position as settlement agronomist. He and Maria had hired a spry elderly man to work their land for them, and they would visit him early in the morning, taking supplies out to the farm and returning laden with whatever was in season at that time.

When Antônio had time, he walked around the settlement, talking with the settlers. He was supposed to provide production advice for 170 settlers unfamiliar with alternative crops, such as bananas and yams. Needless to say, he did not have very much time to visit their plots of land. Most of the time, Antônio was occupied with other business. He had many things to attend to, and he did not feel that the priority for his time was working on the land. There was political work to be done—for the movement and for the local mayor, who had put Antônio into his position as agronomist. There was also administrative work to be done, such as filling out paperwork and gathering signatures to certify the investment loans that the settlers needed for production.

The movement's political work, in addition to the mayor's requests, kept Antônio working, literally, day and night. He would try to dispense as much agronomic knowledge as possible during settlement meetings, but, even then, political messages from the movement took precedence, and it was hard for him to know the details of each person's property as he discussed banana cultivation. Messages from the government were also important, and detailed. Antônio was in charge of ensuring that bank loans were properly distributed, an extremely labor-intensive process. He had to help the settlers plan out their production activities so that they could request the appropriate funds. Then he had to help them fill out their paperwork, not always an easy task when the settlers were hard to round up and most could not fill out the paperwork on their own, as they had difficulty with the technical language. Thirty-two of the forty-seven settlers on one of the settlements where Antônio worked signed their name with an "X," as they could not write out the letters, and so each one had to be legally witnessed, for which a fee of R$26 applied.

After all of this had been done, Antônio had to take the paperwork to the INCRA office in Recife, which always meant several long trips into the city. Antônio may not have spent more time in the city than necessary, but such absences from the settlement deepened the gap between him and the settlers, who sometimes grumbled about not ever seeing their agronomist. For the most part, though, people overlooked Antônio's absence from the settlement because he was well connected to the town's mayor. The two worked well together, with the mayor depending on Antônio to oversee political relations with the settlers and Antônio depending on the mayor to provide the settlement with resources that would have been difficult for the settlers to access otherwise. For example, Antônio received money from the mayor's office to build a pharmacy on the settlement, which he was able to get stocked with basic medicines. He also asked the mayor to provide a tractor so that the families could prepare their land for planting.

All these services were dispensed during personal meetings between Antônio and the mayor, although when Antônio mentioned them during settlement meetings, he stressed that they had been won through the force of the MST. People were grateful for the resources they received and thankful that Antônio had the connections that experience had taught them were necessary to access them. In turn, the settlers would occasionally bring Antônio and his family a treat from their farm—an especially sweet piece of fruit or a handful of manioc, the starchy tuber on which all the settlers relied for nourishment. Soon after we left Água Preta, Antônio left the movement. He had worked faithfully on the mayor's reelection campaign, accompanying him to the settlements in the area and standing with him on the back of large trucks rigged with microphones when he gave speeches. Antônio talked to the settlers about the mayor's support for the movement, ensuring that as many settlers as possible voted for the mayor. When the mayor won reelection, Antônio was asked to begin working full-time in the mayor's office.

Antônio insists that he continues to be committed to the movement's ideals and argues that, although the mayor owns a sizeable amount of land outside of town, he is also committed to expropriating plantations in his município for the purposes of agrarian reform. But without a constant spokesperson for the movement in the settlement, we found little sign of the settlers' previous involvement when we returned a year later.

As Antônio now worked for the mayor, instead of encouraging the settlers to thank the movement when they received medicines for the pharmacy or a new roof for the school, he encouraged them to thank the mayor. The settlers, who were used to seeing state investments as "gifts" or "favors," had little difficulty shifting their allegiance back to the mayor, thanking him for things that, in theory, the movement tries to teach them are their rights as citizens of Brazil. Antônio explains it this way: "The state has that obligation, you know, but in truth it doesn't meet its obligations, and this is even natural for us, we don't even think it's strange."

Mired in the traditions and culture of the same region, Antônio never broke the back of patronage politics; he simply substituted the movement for the old plantation boss, and when he moved to the mayor's office, he substituted the mayor for the movement. In the long term, the MST hopes to overturn this way of doing politics—the paternalistic, hierarchical system where power is in the hands of a few, select people—but reforming this system will be no easy task, in part because the legacies of inequality, poverty and domination are so firmly grounded in everyday practices and ideas.

In addition to the culture of individualism and the reality of patronage politics, the MST activists in the sugarcane region face a third difficulty—the lure of sugarcane production itself. MST production specialists (usually agronomists with some advanced training in agricultural methods and science) put together what are called regional "production lines," which usually focus on four different products in which the settlers are encouraged to specialize. By coordinating these sorts of production decisions, the movement hopes to take advantage of economies of scale, even without establishing production collectives. MST leaders in the Northeast argue that the settlers need to move away from sugarcane if they are to break the cycle of poverty that they—and the region—have been caught up in for so many years. And when the price for sugarcane declines—as it did steadily throughout the 1990s—the settlers tend to listen attentively to the alternative production ideas the MST activists present.

In the Northeast, in 1999, the four production lines were bananas, coconuts, dairy and beans. MST activists argued that if all the settlers in the sugarcane region were able to plant and harvest bananas, they could combine efforts and pay for a truck that would transport their bananas and other produce to urban buyers, who generally paid a much higher price than local buyers. With a large quantity of bananas, the settlers could even hope to negotiate a good price, something very difficult for a single seller to do.

With the exception of beans, the four products chosen for the Northeast were all fairly unusual crops for the settlers. They were chosen strategically: both the MST and INCRA hoped to help the settlers hit niche markets, producing goods that earned a significant profit and had little direct competition in the region. Banana trees were promoted with particular enthusiasm because the MST planned to construct a banana processing factory in the area that would collect bananas from all of the surrounding settlements and make an assortment of banana products, including candy and jams. The movement also considered bananas to be ideal because they required relatively little work once they were planted, although they took an average of three to seven years to produce their first crop.

In theory, promoting bananas made sense. Everyone involved in agrarian reform throughout Brazil agrees that settlers need to diversify their production portfolio and target niche markets for value-added products, like banana candies. But implementing production guidelines throughout a given region can be very difficult. Many of the settlers in Água Preta had land that was not suited for banana trees: the rolling topography of the sugarcane region favors a plant with long roots that can wend their way down into the soil to find water when there is little rain and keep hold when the rains arrive. Banana trees might be able to survive the pressure of the rain, but they do not do well during the dry periods. They need substantial amounts of water to remain healthy and have difficulty surviving on the steep slopes or hilltops where many settlers have land. No one on the settlement had an electric motor to draw up water from one of the small streams that ran through the low areas of the settlement. Still, some of the settlers suggested to us that they were asking for a loan to plant bananas, even when they knew the bananas would never make it on their land.

The difficulties with new products such as bananas led some settlers in the plantation region to plant their old enemy—sugarcane, which was easy for them both because new crops could be planted with the stalks left behind from previous plantings and because the settlers were very familiar with the planting process. As one settler said: "I came [to this mill] young, and with the twenty-some years that I have worked, I have only ever planted sugarcane. Now, I know about planting sugarcane—any type, any quality, I know. Of garden plants, I only know about things like beans and corn that are not difficult to plant."

Most of the settlers admitted that they would prefer not to plant sugar-cane, but saw few other options without better land and more consis-tent funding.

In 2001, even more settlers in the settlement turned to sugarcane. A drought in southern Brazil hurt sugarcane production in the largest cane-growing state, São Paulo, and the distilleries were gearing up again along the coast of northeastern Brazil. When we returned to the region in 2001, the price of sugarcane had risen to almost two times the price in 1999. What had seemed like a dying industry was roaring back into action, sweeping the settlers along with it.

We found that many settlers continued to plant subsistence crops on their plots, and certainly this was an improvement over the days of the plantation, when their daily diets depended on the will of the owner. Some banana trees on the settlement were doing well, but most were suffering from neglect or had been pulled up entirely. The set-tlers, anxious for the chance to make money, turned again to sugarcane production. Many of them had missed the reliable income of wage labor, which put food in their pockets and allowed them to walk through the market with their heads up.

Planting sugarcane to earn money is a strategy that makes sense within the context of the settlers' histories and experiences. Many want to plant sugarcane because they already know how to work with it—they have been planting cane since they were eight or nine years old, and their senses of time and geography are intimately wrapped up in the seasons and the fields. The sugarcane industry is so well established in the area that when the price of sugarcane is up, the distilleries, plan-tations and small towns form an intricate network geared toward pro-cessing cane stalks. Most good roads in the area lead to the distilleries, which own most of the necessary vehicles for transporting agricultural goods from one place to another. It is hard to imagine how the settlers could keep themselves out of this network—it's as though the deep roots of sugarcane plants wrap themselves around the settlers, running along the roads from one house to another and bringing them into the hungry business of producing sweetener for the soft drinks and baked goods enjoyed far away, in the country's capital and beyond.

Leaving the sugarcane industry is further complicated for the set-tlers by the state government's support for sugar production on the settlements. Although the state has argued that agrarian reform can be an alternative to sugarcane production in Pernambuco, there is little real commitment to investing the money into the region that would be necessary for economic development.[47] The entire economic and social structure of the northeastern sugarcane region—including government subsidies and debt pardons—is built around expectations of market protection for producers. Even during periods of generalized crisis, few people suggest that sugarcane production should be entirely abandoned. Instead, in the 1990s, the state government's plans for regional economic diversification included agrarian reform as a means to accomplish three things: occupy land that was inappropriate for sugar production, employ excess labor on a seasonal basis and, at the same time, foster smallholder suppliers of cane for the large distilleries. The government pledged to encourage the modernization of sugarcane through targeted programs that would "free" more labor for small-scale cane production and supply the large-scale distilleries. A 1997 INCRA document stated that agrarian reform in the sugarcane region would ideally allow the settlers to plant part of their land in cane with the rest of the land planted in crops that would provide "above all, for the subsistence of the family in the interharvest period."[48]

MST activists are well aware of the seductive call of sugarcane on the settlements, and they continue to put together proposals for new economic activities that would liberate the settlers from cane production. Without a serious commitment from the state, however, it will continue to be difficult for the MST to help the settlers in the sugarcane region of Pernambuco build alternative economic models. Jaime Amorim expressed a belief that new crops and agricultural activities could eventually replace sugarcane, but that it would take time and energy:

> The Minister brought us this idea of agrarian reform as a way of creating small-scale suppliers of sugarcane—and we didn't accept this idea. We are going to show them that the rural workers—slowly, with organization and technical assistance—can overcome this [dependency on sugarcane]. Because of the diverse topography here you really have to work with a number of different things—cattle, fish, fruit, coffee. And so we are committed to implementing diverse experiences.

# Small-Scale Farmers in a Large-Scale Landscape
## The Challenges of Catalunha and Ouro Verde

At the opposite end of Pernambuco lies the sertão, a region rich in its contrasts to the sugarcane coast. The soil is the same burnished red as that of the coastal region, but instead of rich, green stalks covering rolling hills, the topography is very flat, with horizons spreading out into the distance, broken up only by occasional small, rounded hills that seem to have been placed there intentionally, they jut up so severely. Wiry, short scrubs and trees cover the land—the "white forest" or caatinga, which appears whitish because the air in the area is so dry that it draws the water out of the plants and leaves behind a thin layer of salt, coating the scrubs and small trees in what looks like a white, grayish film. Small green plants that look like fat Ping-Pong paddles, called *palmas*, also litter the ground. They are cultivated to feed cattle, and they are often the food of last resort for people who are affected by the periodic droughts in the region.

Tucked inside this semiarid landscape, in a long, narrow strip covering almost two thousand miles, is some of the most productive and lucrative land in the Northeast. This is the land the spreads out from the banks of the third-largest river in Brazil—the São Francisco River. The river runs directly north from its source in the state of Espírito Santo, and then turns a sharp right and snakes east through Bahia, Pernambuco and Sergipe to the coast. As one drives through the sertão and into the valley of the São Francisco River, the differences between irrigated and nonirrigated land are striking. Depending on the ability of the producer to irrigate, the land along the river is covered in the green and variegated colors of agricultural production. In this region of irregular precipitation, access to the river's water is the difference between life and death.

After visiting the sugarcane area of Pernambuco and seeing agrarian reform in operation there, we decided to take a trip out west. The MST has been working to organize the struggle for land in the São Francisco River Valley region since 1995, and the settlements here represent both important victories and daunting challenges for the movement. This is one of the richest agricultural areas in Pernambuco, but it has been dominated by multinational corporations since the 1960s, when private companies began to invest money into large-scale agricultural production. As economic development expanded in the area, the Brazilian government began to strategically plan the construction of infrastructure geared toward commercial production. The Master Plan for the Development of the São Francisco River Valley (PLANVASF) was completed in 1989, with the aim of providing incentives to both public and private interests who would contribute to regional development through increased agricultural production, power generation, water and sanitation services and environmental protection.

Since the development of the strategic master plan, economic development in the region has taken off. Commercial fruit and vegetable production along the São Francisco River has turned the small towns of Petrolina and Juazeiro, straddling the border between Pernambuco and Bahia, into two of the most important new sites for high-value produce, such as grapes and tomatoes. There has been an influx of capital into the area—particularly foreign direct investment from agribusinesses located in the United States and Japan. Improved refrigeration and transportation technologies have allowed these agribusinesses to take advantage of cheaper production costs and move their growing operations further away from market centers in the developed world. The construction of a well-run international airport in Petrolina has helped to build the region's position in the global fruit market. In the late 1990s, 90 percent of Brazil's mango exports and 30 percent of its grape exports came from the Petrolina-Juazeiro region.

In the mid-1990s, the federal government began to withdraw subsidies from agricultural producers who had relied on government support to prop up their business. Without government funding—or with serious reductions in government funding—agro-industrial companies in the river valley region began to scale back their production. When the model of large-scale development began to show these signs of weakness, the MST began to organize among the rural workers and small farmers in the São Francisco River Valley region. The PLANVASF's weakness represented an opportunity for the MST, but would also generate its own complications for small farm production.

Jaime Amorim described the movement's decision to organize occupations along the riverbanks in this way:

Various agro-industries moved into the region from North America, Argentina and from Brazil itself. They planted tomatoes and different fruits—table grapes, grapes for wine and onions. This industrial pole was based on large landholdings. The [Brazilian] company Etti, for example, had a property that was five thousand hectares—and they only used eight hundred hectares of that! They irrigated eight hundred hectares and planted tomatoes. When the company began to do badly, that was where we held our first occupation. Immediately, when INCRA came out, they evaluated the land and saw that less than 10 percent of the land was being used, and it was expropriated. This pole of irrigated agriculture, which favored many national and multi-national agro-industries, began to fail. . . . The crisis in agriculture brought around the end of that model of production, and we decided to move [into the region]. So, today, we are producing beans, onions, fruits, tomatoes, rice—in a region that was being totally abandoned.

Jaime's assessment of productivity on the MST's settlements in the São Francisco River Valley region was tempered by the recognition that there were real difficulties establishing a healthy, small-farm economy in the region. The settlers were forced to make the difficult decision of either mimicking the large-scale mechanized model of production or trying to implement a new small-scale form of production. While the idea of mimicking the failing agro-industrial companies might seem foolish, it is often the easier route, given that the regional infrastructure is already geared toward capital intensive, highly mechanized forms of production.

The tension between these different models of development was evident when we visited a settlement called Catalunha, which sits along the banks of the São Francisco, about twenty miles away from the center of Petrolina. When it was first expropriated in 1998, Catalunha, named after the property that existed before INCRA expropriated the land, was considered a major achievement for the MST, which occupied the property in 1996 with over two hundred people. Between 1996 and 1998, the number of families living in the encampment swelled to over eight hundred. One MST activist said with pride that the encampment was like a city made up of an endless sea of black, plastic tents, with schools and roads, pharmacies and regular food distribution.

We reserved a car for the 720-kilometer trip from Recife (the bustling capitol city of Pernambuco) to Petrolina, bought the road atlas that is the Brazilian equivalent of the American Automobile Association road maps and began to plan our route. We had already driven 120 kilometers out to the market city of Caruaru, where agricultural produce, handicrafts and cheap electronic goods are all sold in a huge open-air market, so we were familiar with that part of the trip, but we knew that traveling by car in Brazil required caution and thorough preparation. As we plotted our route on the map, we noticed that a red warning was written across the main state highway that connected Caruaru with Petrolina. The warning laid several XXXs along the highway and suggested that travelers should avoid the area after 4:00 P.M. because of the likelihood of assaults along that stretch of road. We were tempted to ignore the warning, but, in the end, decided to fly. (We later asked a settler in one of the areas surrounding the benighted highway whether he believed the warning about assaults. He replied that it had indeed been a serious problem, but it had been taken care of by the federal police who had come into the town and killed all the criminals.)

The Catalunha settlement is close enough to Petrolina for fairly easy access to the local airport and to markets where produce is sold and shipped locally and internationally. The road leading into Catalunha is long and winding; from Petrolina, most of the road is paved, until you enter the settlement's property, where the road is the same red dirt we have seen in other parts of the country. At the entrance of the settlement's central gathering area is a tall, white gate, where a man sits, checking everyone who enters for the proper identification.

The central area does not look like a new settlement. The road is wide and even, with a roundabout in the middle of the street edged with rocks painted white. The white buildings look like they are in need of a paint job, especially the blue trim around the edges of windows and doors, but other than that, they are remarkably solid and in good repair. From the roundabout, the settlement has the look of a pleasant town center on a day when traffic has been rerouted. When we arrived, ten or twelve men were sitting on the roundabout (our car was the only one in sight). These men had met with the settlement's principal agronomist to discuss production matters, and they were hoping he would have time after the paperwork to talk with them individually.

Beyond the settlement's main entrance, however, the living quarters that house almost four thousand people spread out in a disorganized fashion. When we visited in 2001, many families had been living in "temporary" housing—shacks made out of bricks, mud or wood—for almost five years. Because of disagreements over the fairest way to distribute what had been a single property among so many families, the land had only recently been divided into individual lots. The area where most of the families lived—some families had tired of the wait and built houses on property that they staked out within the settlement—still looked like an encampment, with dirt paths for roads and makeshift cooking stoves and bathing areas. The MST was trying to organize everyone into one of several agrovilas that would be located throughout the settlement, but the government funds for constructing the houses were late in arriving, and it was not always easy to convince the settlers to live in common areas.

Before it was expropriated, Catalunha belonged to a construction group called OAS Ltd., headquartered in Bahia. The whole estate covered almost six thousand hectares (or fifteen thousand acres) of privileged land, running alongside the beautiful São Francisco River. The farm was originally set up for grape production but had not been producing anything for two years when the MST decided to launch a massive occupation at Catalunha.[49] An unproductive property with a well-developed infrastructure that could support several hundred families, Catalunha was considered a perfect area for an occupation. Almost a third of Catalunha's area was covered by an elaborate central-pivot irrigation system; central pivots are tall irrigation "spouts" that use powerful pumps to draw water up and spread it out in a circular area as the pivot turns. They use enormous quantities of energy, usually gasoline or diesel fuel. There were twenty-one central pivots on the property, each watering a circle of fifty to eighty hectares.

Jaime Amorim helped to organize the occupation of Catalunha, although he was skeptical about the MST's chances of winning the property because it contained such advanced production technology and because it belonged to a company owned, in part, by the son-in-law of Antônio Carlos Magalhães, better known as ACM, a powerful political figure in the Northeast, whose influence was due in part to his control over energy resources in the region. The semiarid region is plagued by regular droughts and a variability of rainfall that makes existence in the region extremely difficult. But at the margins of the region flows one of the three largest river systems in the country, on which Brazil relies heavily—94 percent of the country's energy is hydroelectric, as compared to 8.3 percent in the US. The need for both water and energy in the semiarid region of the Northeast makes the São Francisco River a valuable commodity, one that is ostensibly public patrimony.

The river's water has been managed by a government-controlled company—Chesf, a regional subsidiary of Eletrobrás—since 1945. Despite being a public company and the "property of the people," Chesf has long been dominated by a handful of people, who are in turn dominated by one person—ACM, the former govenor and senator from Bahia. Although Chesf is headquartered in Recife, Pernambuco, ACM has had considerable power in appointing the leaders of the company—he himself was president in the 1970s—and Chesf maintains a subregional office in Salvador, Bahia.

Over the course of the 1990s and early 2000s, as the Brazilian economy was opening up and becoming increasingly liberalized, there were political pressures to privatize Brazil's public energy sector, including Chesf, the third-largest energy-producing entity in all of Brazil. The International Monetary Fund (IMF) was particularly interested in the privatization of Chesf, because the company was suspected of being associated with crooked politics.

The debate over privatization of Chesf was fierce. Brazil's president during this period, Fernando Henrique Cardoso, had the weight of the IMF behind him, but Chesf had the weight of political strong men in the Northeast behind it, particularly ACM. And ACM was not interested in having the company privatized because, as one official in the *planalto* (the Brazilian version of the White House in the United States) told *O Estado de São Paulo*, a widely read newspaper, "as long as ACM has his tentacles spread out among the different *escalões* [levels] of Eletrobrás, his power will continue to be virtually untouchable."

After considerable political maneuvering on all sides, the federal government gave up trying to privatize Chesf, deciding that any further attempts to privatize the entity would have to be approved by popular plebiscite. It is unlikely that sufficient political strength will be gathered to win such a vote for privatization.

Ultimately, whoever controls the São Francisco River has the power to make the desert bloom; and so under OAS Ltd., Fazenda Catalunha should have been blooming. The company had received approximately US$10 million in subsidized government credit to support grape production, but something had happened: the farm had not been producing at full capacity for several years. The papers reported that the property had stopped production altogether in 1994, and for five years before that had operated with fewer than ten of its central pivots. It would be some time before it became clear to the settlers at Catalunha just why this was the case.

Although Jaime Amorim could not have predicted it, ACM's association with Fazenda Catalunha probably benefited the MST squatters. The occupation camp, created on September 7, 1996, never suffered a violent expulsion, as do most occupation camps. Once the settlers built their black plastic tents, they stayed in them for the two years that it took to negotiate the land's expropriation with funds from INCRA. The relationship between MST and OAS was described in the local papers as "friendly," and MST leaders suggested that OAS benefited from the expropriation of the land. OAS had received considerable state financing for irrigation projects and infrastructure on the land, and given that OAS had not been planting grapes for several years, it may well have been that the company welcomed the R16 million (about US$16 million at the time) it received for the property.

When MST squatters were granted rights to Fazenda Catalunha, they were determined to make the settlement into a model of advanced production methods and economic success. The land was good, the irrigation system as advanced as any in the region and the estate was ideally located to take advantage of new markets opened up by Petrolina's international airport. INCRA officials estimated that the settlers could earn up to four times the national minimum salary within a few years of settling the land.

The problem with Catalunha was that it was set up as a large-scale business, not as an area where small farmers could practice a sustainable mode of farming. The entire infrastructure on Catalunha was built to maximize agricultural production by capturing economies of scale. For example, each of the central pivots on the property covered an area between fifty and eighty hectares in size, and INCRA technicians argued that it would be difficult to break up that area into small plots for individual production. A 1997 INCRA report on the viability of smallholder production in Fazenda Catalunha even suggested that the area be expropriated without the central pivots. There were two potential problems with the central pivot system. The first was that the pivots were geared toward a large enterprise that could manage them as one entity. INCRA technicians believed that turning the pivots over to collective management by the settlers would involve serious administrative difficulties and impede the overall progress of the settlement, which was why they recommended the land be expropriated, but not the pivots.

The second problem, which became increasingly evident as we walked around the property and talked to resident agronomists, was that the central pivot system had exacerbated environmental problems similar to those encountered in the central valleys of both Idaho and California. Irrigation water applied to land over time causes a buildup of salts as the water evaporates and leaves salts in the soil. Salinization occurs more rapidly with fertilizer applications that add additional salts to the soil. If the soil is salty to begin with, as it is in Catalunha, the problem becomes more troublesome. It becomes more difficult yet if, as in Catalunha and much of the American West, the topsoil is underlain by a layer of virtually impermeable soil a few inches or feet below the surface. Then the water that is drawn from below the impermeable layer to the surface cannot drain properly, and the salt builds up even faster. With these perched water tables, as this situation is called, arid lands can begin to suffer from waterlogging as well as salinity. In California's San Joaquin Valley, more than 15 percent of the land has been made unusable in only a few decades due to salinity and waterlogging from irrigation. The same thing is happening in parts of Catalunha, threatening the viability of the whole operation. Sodium and nitrate can have extremely damaging effects on crop production. Scientists now believe that high levels of sodium in the soils are what led to declining agricultural production levels—and eventually the fall of an

Enormous pumps provide irrigation water from the São Francisco River to what is now the MST settlement of Catalunha. It is difficult for the settlers to maintain the equipment and afford the high energy costs, and intensive irrigation has led to accumulating problems with soils.

entire civilization—in the Mesopotamian region of what is today the Middle East.

When we walked into the main housing area of a settlement near Catalunha, we met an older woman sitting in her doorway, shelling corn to make feed for the chickens clucking anxiously around her. We asked her what she thought of the land, whether she was doing well in the new settlement. She replied that the land was no good—it was salty, she said, motioning toward the ground and making a face, as if to say you could taste the salt if you ate a spoonful of the red dirt. Later, a farmer showed us a hole he had dug in his field, revealing salt-laden water sitting just below the surface. The environmental problems associated with Fazenda Catalunha probably explain why production had ceased on the property and why OAS did not protest when MST squatters occupied the area.

In spite of the problems, INCRA expropriated Catalunha in March 1997, the largest single expropriation in the entire Northeast region and, in political terms, a major coup for the movement. The land was distributed among 720 families, the majority of whom were organized by the MST. But the settlers faced several serious challenges. On one hand, the legacy of environmental degradation would have to be overcome. And on the other hand, the existing irrigation infrastructure lent itself to large-scale production practices that would exacerbate the already existing environmental problems and be unsustainable in the long term.

When we visited the property, it was clear that this issue had not yet been resolved. The settlers who showed us around Catalunha were fiercely proud of their high-powered irrigation systems and seemed unconvinced that mechanization might cause problems for sustainable production on the settlement. Even though most of the large irrigation pumps were broken, the young boy who had been left to watch over them took us on a tour of the main irrigation facility, showing off the equipment with visible pride.

The practical difficulties of choosing a production path based on large-scale infrastructure, mechanization and advanced technology are evident in other areas of the São Francisco region. While we were in western Pernambuco, we visited a settlement near Catalunha called Ouro Verde. Before the area was expropriated, the farm had been planted in grapes, and the vines were still standing when the settlement was awarded to a combination of MST occupiers and former farmworkers. The rows of grapes left by the previous owner were still in fairly good shape, and the families divided up the grapes amongst themselves: each family had the right to cultivate and harvest a set number of grapevines. When we visited the settlement, the families were hard at work harvesting the grapes. The fruits were beautiful, big and juicy-looking, seemingly ready to fall off of the vine. And they should have looked beautiful—they had been planted with chemical fertilizers and frequently sprayed with chemical pesticides that are known to be extremely hazardous to people and wildlife. On Ouro Verde, people take somewhat more precautions with pesticides than we have seen on many comparable corporate farms, but still maintain a standard far below what would be necessary to protect human health and the environment. The settlers had brought these production practices over from their former jobs on the farm or on farms in the area. They admired the benefits provided by chemical additions, and it would have been difficult to convince a majority that these production practices would present their own problems down the road.

The high level of chemical and mechanical dependence, especially on Catalunha, where the watershed had already given the former owners difficulty, is associated with large-scale agriculture that is in constant, global danger of degrading local environments and forcing the search for new and still healthy land. If they don't pay attention to appropriate methods of production, MST settlers like those on Catalunha and Ouro Verde risk running their new farms into the ground. If the settlers are to stay on their land for several generations, they will need to find new ways of producing that do not contaminate the water supply or leach the soils of necessary nutrients.

In January 2003, we asked João Pedro Stédile about the problems at Catalunha and Ouro Verde. He agreed that the problems we had identified were quite serious, noting that they were prime examples of two problems that continue to plague the MST. The first problem is that many MST members, leaders and agronomists are still inspired by the chemical- and machine-intensive production techniques introduced to Brazil as part of the global promotion of the Green Revolution. The second is that while the national MST has decided to embrace an agro-

Individual plots dedicated to table grape production provide cash income to settlers at Ouro Verde, but dependence on liberal applications of highly toxic pesticides, the technique the settlers learned from the previous owner of the land, raises serious questions about safety and sustainability.

ecological model that rejects the principles of the Green Revolution, the organization is desperately lacking the trained personnel and facilities to educate people properly regarding the dangers of the Green Revolution approach and the advantages of agro-ecology. Given the difficulties we saw in Catalunha and Ouro Verde, the MST will have to work hard to convince the settlers that they should work on small-scale projects that do not depend on, for example, the mechanized infrastructure left behind by OAS.

As a way of helping smallholders avoid the seductive trap of large-scale agriculture, the MST is committed to working with alternative agricultural products and methods and encouraging cooperative production as a logical way to capture economies of scale with diverse, small-scale producers. As we saw in chapter 1, cooperative ventures can range from a full production collective, where all the land is held in common, to a simple credit cooperative, from which the settlers jointly apply for loans or purchase machinery used by each of the families. If administered properly, such ventures could be very effective on Catalunha, as people could continue to work on their own land while conducting their interactions with the outside market in a more efficient manner.

## Agrarian Reform in the Northeast
### *A Balance Sheet*

*Allow me, dear reader*
*A minute of your attention*
*To speak of an evil that wounds the ground*
*Of my beloved land Brazil*
*A land of excluded and marginalized people*
*A land of poets and working men*
*Where people fight and dream*
*Of patience still unknown*
*But a people who fight for their lives*
*Confronting challenges of pain.*
                —Adauto Nogueira (MST settler in
                      Lagoa Grande, Pernambuco)

At the time of this writing, the MST has been working among the rural poor in northeastern Brazil for approximately twelve years, with mixed results. It would be naive in the extreme to think that the redistribution of land could by itself resolve the problems of poverty, misery and political corruption that are so deeply embedded in the Northeast of Brazil.

The deep structures of Brazilian society could easily make a superficial land reform—land redistribution without structural change—vanish within years or decades. Without profound social transformation, it would be unrealistic to expect smallholders with little capital to remain on the land for long. Even were they able to do so, without improved credit, access to markets, schools, medical and other social services, landownership alone cannot guarantee them equal treatment under the law, equal opportunities to participate as citizens in a democracy or even modest prosperity. Without full citizenship and political power, the poor will not be able to hold on to their gains in their own lifetimes, much less pass such changes on to the next generation. Meaningful agrarian reform is not a simple transfer of ownership of a portion of the nation's land; it must be part of a general restructuring of political power.

The MST has long made it clear that the acquisition of land by landless people is not the sole, or even the most important, goal of the movement. Rather, the MST seeks "a profound transformation of society." As Caio, the "grandfather" of the MST in Pernambuco, said: "While there is still a sem-terra in Pernambuco, in Brazil, the movement will be fighting, it will only stop when there aren't any more landless. And there will always be landless people, so there will always be MST. And when I say MST, I mean agrarian reform in general, with education, training, health—a whole bunch of things." Obviously, providing all these things is no simple task.

The settlements in the Northeast continue to face a number of obstacles, and most have a ways to go before they can be considered viable without considerable government intervention. Perhaps most serious of these are the barriers to production and marketing on the settlements. It is difficult enough for a small farmer to produce on his or her land; it is even harder when that land is hilly—as is the case in the sugarcane region—lacks water or is far from any market. One or more of these factors is often the case with many settlements in the Northeast; for example, one of the settlements we visited near Água Preta was located six kilometers (about four miles) away from town, which was the closest market. These six kilometers included about two kilometers on a good, paved street, four kilometers on an uneven, dirt path that flooded during the rainy season and a broad stretch of river. The settlers had to load up their donkeys with goods to sell at the market and then walk beside them to the river. At the river, they had to get the man who operated the one *jangada* (raft) that regularly crossed the river. The man lived in a house near the water's edge, and, when called, he would come down to the river and pull the raft across to the other side, hand over fist, negotiating a thick rope that had been strung up across the river for that purpose.

Settlers here, as elsewhere, also face difficulties because of inconsistent government policies and aid. In recent years, budget crises at the federal and state levels have resulted in late disbursements of agricultural credit to the settlers. If credit does not arrive on time, it is as good as useless, because the settlers need to coordinate their activities with the weather—and the weather does not wait for elected officials.

The settlers need to produce something and earn money from their efforts, otherwise it is clear that agrarian reform will stop with this generation. The MST and INCRA both encourage the settlers to think about their land as an intergenerational good, but the settlers' children will not stay on the land if something better comes up. One settler said, "I don't think any of [my sons] will stay on the land because, it's like this, when it was time for the harvest, we were going to go cut the cane, there were two sons here with me. But they stopped helping me so they could go and cut cane somewhere else!"

In spite of these difficulties, the settlements in Brazil's Northeast represent a huge victory. Given the region's profound legacies of slavery and exploitation, the fact that settlers can walk around town wearing an MST T-shirt or hat suggests that a new way of thinking about resistance has entered into the local political arena. Perhaps most importantly, each settler's plot of land is his or her own—all settlers are able to make their own decisions and plan their own day, freedoms these people rarely enjoyed before being settled. Even if the settlers continue to plant sugarcane, they do so on their own land, without the heavy hand of an overseer in their immediate presence—although one could argue that the overseer now cracks his whip from the doors of the sugarcane mills. As one former plantation worker said, "At that time [when I worked in the mill], when it was Saturday and I finished my week of work, I was already thinking where was I going to work next week. And, today no! I already am where I am going—I am going to do my work!"

The settlers also have the means to provide their own subsistence, something that was never guaranteed in the days of working for other people. The stability of knowing that at least a bare minimum can be provided—food and a place to sleep—is in itself a tremendous achievement. As one MST leader said:

> We work with the people who are marginalized by the bourgeoisie; they are the . . . thieves, the people who lie around, the idiots. The

movement takes those people and turns them into citizens. The person who was living there in the city, going around making trouble —well, when the movement goes back [to the city] with him in two years, the people who used to not care about him at all, they begin to see him as an authority, where before he lived without a voice in society.

In many ways—including political organization, the basic freedoms of independence and autonomy, and access to a steady diet—the settlers' lives have improved. They continue to plan and organize themselves to fight for a better life. They are not asking to become rich; their goals are almost laughably modest: they want to go to bed at night in their own house without feeling hungry, and they want medicines, some schooling, maybe even a childhood, for their children. Most of all, they want to make a little money to put something away for the next day. They want to put money in the bank, plant crops in the inter-harvest period, send a daughter to work in town because she has a decent education and knows her numbers. They want a bench they can stand on so that if there is a ripple in the pond, the water will lap up against their knees instead of drowning them.

Guedeson, a young MST militante, works on the land reform settlement in southern Pará named after assassinated local MST leader Onalício Barros. More landless leaders have been murdered in this area than in most other parts of Brazil.

## CHAPTER THREE

# Beyond the Lure
# of the Amazon

WE ARRIVED IN SOUTHERN PARÁ in the Amazon during what seemed to us an especially difficult time for the MST settlers and leaders. On the day we arrived in the state, the police threw MST settlers off a large estate called Chão de Estrelas (Starry Ground). The president of the Brazilian national senate, Jáder Barbalho, who claimed to be the legitimate owner of Chão de Estrelas, had obtained a court order to have the landless removed and their leaders charged with incitement of others to commit illegal acts. Some of the leaders of the occupation, who claimed that Barbalho's title to the land was fraudulent, had been thrown in jail immediately, while other state and regional MST leaders were hunted down and tossed in jail over the next several days. The politics of the situation were complicated by the charges of massive corruption lodged against Senator Barbalho by other prominent politicians, state and national prosecutors in Tocantins and the federal attorney general.[1]

A few days after the MST people were thrown off the Chão de Estrelas ranch, private gunmen burned down an encampment organized by a rural labor union on a ranch next to an MST settlement we were to visit; some encampment leaders hid in the woods, hoping to reoccupy the area, while dozens of displaced families showed up searching for jobs and a place to bed down in the nearby town of Parauapebas.[2]

About two weeks later, two gunmen appeared in the town of Marabá, at the door of a local rural union leader who had led occupations and worked with the MST. The union leader was in bed, recovering from a serious bout of malaria. When the man's wife answered the door, the gunmen shot her dead. The men then went into the bedroom, where they shot and killed the rural union leader. The couple's fifteen-year-old son came running down the street toward the house when he heard the shots. As the men left the house, they shot the boy down in the street, killing him, too.

Although much of their leadership was in jail, the MST office was working with the union to demand the police seek out the murderers, which, given past experiences, seemed unlikely. The MST and union leaders were organizing a funeral service that would both honor the man and bring public attention to the need to find and punish the murderers.[3]

It was impressive to see the MST staff and volunteers dealing with all of these challenges with great energy and resourcefulness; nonetheless, the stress showed. People wore worry and fatigue on their faces. Quick meals were being snatched here and there or missed altogether. Money for gas was a problem. Just getting people from one place to another as needed to deal with the situations required a lot of thought and coordination. All of this had to be done while many of the leaders were in jail.

We asked Parazinho, one of the regional officers of the MST, about the situation of the jailed leaders: "What's it like to be in jail in Parauapebas? It must be pretty rough, no?" Parazinho replied, "No, no, it's not bad. The jail here is clean and decent. They won't let you use the television or the computer, but otherwise, it's not bad. The truth is, we sometimes welcome a little time in jail. It's the only chance we have to reflect on what is going on and what we are doing. It's restful." We thought we detected a little envy in Parazinho for those in jail, while he had to be outside running himself ragged.

We felt awkward intruding on the work of people who were so besieged with problems. We apologized to Parazinho, "We know it's hard to have to deal with visitors like us when you have all these other problems. We wish we could have arrived at an easier time."

Parazinho made a dismissive gesture with his hand and shrugged.

"No, it's okay. It is important to have people like you visit and see what is happening here. It's an important part of our work. . . . We are sorry we can't do more to help you."

He paused and looked down thoughtfully for a moment before looking up again and adding, "Besides, you couldn't have come at a better time or a more tranquil time. This is the way it is here. It's normal."

# The Amazon
## What's at Stake? Who Decides?

When the founders of the MST set up their encampments at Encruzilhada Natalino and other sites in Brazil's South in the late 1970s, the government tried to lure them to the Amazon. Most refused, insisting that land redistribution should occur at home. Father Casaldaliga, who had been battling alongside those fighting for their livelihoods in the Amazon since the early 1970s, spoke in person to those camped at Encruzilhada Natalino, assuring them they were right to stay in Rio Grande do Sul and fight for land there. Some ignored his advice and accepted the government's offers of land in the Amazon, and many of these returned home deeply embittered about the experience. Their stories further strengthened the resolve of those who had turned a deaf ear to the call of the Amazon.[4] Those who participated in the first encampments that led to the founding of the MST maintained that the best soils of Brazil were largely outside the Amazon, and that these were more than sufficient to support the rural population, feed the cities and support general economic growth if the land were properly distributed. So why was the MST in the Amazon now?

More than two decades after the government tried to lure the people of the encampments to the Amazon, the MST maintains its initial view that the primary solution to the nation's problems lies outside the Amazon and that Amazon settlement is not the solution for the landless. Nonetheless, events have drawn some MST organizing effort to the Amazon, and the question of where agrarian reform fits in the puzzle of what should be done in the Amazon remains an important one, as we'll see. Conservative forces blame the MST for vast forest destruction, and even some environmentalists who consider themselves friends of the rural poor and of agrarian reform fear the consequences of MST actions in the Amazon. The debate has taken shape in a way that distorts both the MST's actions and the larger issues at stake in the Amazon. Such distortion follows in the tradition of debate established over three decades with respect to the Amazon.

One of the strongest conclusions we have reached from our study and experiences in the Amazon is that the highly charged international debate on the fate of the region fails to capture the complicated reality of what is happening there. For example, controversy rages on the suitability of Amazon soils for settled agriculture, but it is clear that there are not one or two or three answers to the possibilities and dilemmas of Amazon soils, but dozens, dependent upon the enormous variety of soil conditions in a region more than half as large as the contiguous United States. It is simply wrong to believe that the region is so homogeneous that we can make simple statements about the agronomic possibilities there. Nor are there one or two or three major strategies of human adaptation to Amazon conditions—there are myriad conditions and a huge range of culturally established and still-developing strategies of adaptation to these conditions. A Brazilian friend of ours, who is an environmental historian and who grew up in the Amazon, remarks that she hardly recognizes the region under discussion when she hears people arguing about its future—so much of what is interesting and characteristic and important about the region is forgotten or obscured.

This process of vast oversimplification is an understandable, though unfortunate, result of distorted attitudes about the region first promulgated by the Brazilian government in its drive to exploit the region's resources in the 1960s. Since that time, the government and its corporate allies have consistently pursued misguided and, at times, cynical strategies to exploit the Amazon, deceiving people about the potential for massive rural colonization in the region. For decades, the government has systematically glossed over the horrendous human and environmental price that would have to be paid for colonization and the meager returns to most of those whose labor would make the effort possible.

Environmentalists and some scientists have believed that they need to react forcefully to what they rightly see as a tide of misinformation and mistaken policies regarding a region that is without parallel as a reserve of plant and animal species. Beginning in the mid-1970s, however, their concern has all too often been laced with exaggerations or oversimplifications about the extent and pace of devastation. A large percentage of those engaging in both sides of the debate have undermined their own credibility through ignorance or hyperbole, or a fatal combination of the two.

Exaggeration and distortion have consequences. The endemic violence practiced by private landholders, corporations and the government against thousands of poor people was and remains a direct result of the deceptions involved in the arguments of those who favored unbridled development. Many seductive promises made by government officials and business interests were never meant to be honored. Other promises that were made could not possibly have been kept, even had there been the intention to do so. In any case, failure and disappointment have led to conflict and violence in the Amazon.

At times, people promoting colonization in the region have acted as if a culture of violence was a regional advantage—one does not have to worry about legal niceties on the frontier. Although most in the region were quite peaceful, a governor of the state of Amazonas—a man deeply devoted to attracting investors to the region—used to brag about the pistol he kept on the top of his desk and carried on his hip when out and about. But the other side of the debate is not free of violent rhetoric: we recall a world-renowned botanist at an international academic meeting in 1974 declaring loudly and repeatedly that all those government officials and corporate heads who had anything to do with Amazon deforestation "should just be put up against a wall and shot." Obviously, he did not have the same capability to actually carry out his violent wishes as some of his opponents, but his language echoed theirs.

Misinformation has proliferated on both sides of the debate, in part because of the lack of good social and scientific research in the region—for nearly two decades the military dictatorship discouraged independent research and punished dissent from official pronouncements and policies. The problem was complicated by the size and complexity of the region itself.[5] For example, there is so much cloud cover in the Amazon that for a long time it was difficult to obtain aerial and satellite images of the area that were sufficiently consistent in time and coverage to accurately assess the amount and kind of deforestation occurring. It also took a long time to work out how to distinguish primary forest from forest in the process of regrowth. Eventually, better imaging technologies solved these problems. With more experience and research, and with the more open debate Brazil's democratic government now allows, we are beginning to develop a clearer record of what has happened and a clearer view of what may lie ahead.

However, much of the heat generated on both sides of the debate is also a reflection of what is at stake, and with new knowledge we have developed an even greater appreciation of what we stand to lose and gain. Those who argue in favor of development have their eyes fixed on what is far and away the world's largest stock of tropical timber. They are eager to develop the world's most abundant iron ore and bauxite reserves and extraordinary supplies of many other mineral ores, along with hydroelectric supplies potentially many times greater than what is necessary to mine this great wealth. They also see significant agricultural possibilities in the region. The high economic value of these resources is undeniable.

Those in favor of forest protection see a reserve of species incomparably larger in both numbers of species and the size of their populations than anywhere else on Earth. As tropical forest research has proceeded, our estimates of the number of species on Earth have grown from a total of two to three million species to something between ten and twenty million, and possibly as high as forty-eight million. The Amazon is home to the lion's share of the increase. (Most of the species numbers involved in the higher estimates have not actually been individually identified but are instead projected from actual rates of identification that are fed into complex models of speciation and distribution, which attempt to predict how many species are likely to be present in areas not yet fully surveyed.) At various survey sites in many parts of the Amazon, scientists have identified nearly five hundred different species of trees on a single hectare (two-and-a-half acres). A neighboring hectare might have a significantly different set of species. Two thousand species of insects can be found living on a single Amazon tree.

As the Amazon forest burns, hundreds of thousands of species of which we know little or nothing go up in flames, companions in the evolutionary journey who have been traveling with us up to now, but whose identity we will never know. Since one-quarter to one-half of our pharmaceuticals have been developed from tropical forest plants and animals, we can be sure we are losing many useful substances. Probably far more important, with the absence of these vanishing species, we lose the likelihood of achieving a full understanding of evolutionary and ecological processes. Such an understanding might hold the keys to solving immediate problems and to long-term human survival.

It has also become clear from research carried out over the last twenty years that the sheer number of hectares cleared is not a reliable guide to the severity of the ecological damage. The fragmentation of the forest into small pieces creates drastic species loss and slows recovery. Brazilian government legislation beginning in the late 1980s has required from 20 to 80 percent of the forest on any given property to be preserved, depending on the region and local condition. However, even in the rare instances in which it was rigorously enforced, the legislation has not been tuned finely enough to really address the issue of forest fragmentation and its effects on species' reproduction and recovery.

It is not only species that are at stake. The Amazon River carries more than 20 percent of all the river water that flows to the sea over the entire planet. It carries five times as much water as its nearest competitor, the Congo, and twenty times as much as the Mississippi. Except for the spectacularly steep eastern slopes of the Andes, most of the Amazon Basin is fairly flat, so that much of the land is a permanent or seasonal marshland. Outside of the frozen polar regions, half to two-thirds of the fresh water on Earth is present in the Amazon. This vast amount of water is increasingly polluted with arsenic, mercury and other highly toxic substances from mining and smelting. In the 1960s, untreated Amazon River water easily met US standards for drinking water; mining, industry and sewage from millions of the region's new inhabitants have changed that for the foreseeable future.

More than half of the unimaginable quantity of precipitation in the Amazon Basin is generated locally, within the Basin itself. It is becoming increasingly clear that deforestation in the Amazon has large effects on climate both inside and outside the region, due to changing rates of evaporation from the land's surface, evapotranspiration from plants and the changing degree to which the surface of the earth reflects

energy back into the atmosphere. As climate researchers recently remarked, there are few changes in land use more dramatic than the
change from a standing tropical forest to pasture land—anyone who
has stepped from a blazing Amazon pasture into the remarkable cool of
even a patch of forest understands the difference. It seems increasingly
probable that climate at the global scale also will be affected by Amazon deforestation. About one-quarter of the greenhouse gases generated by human activity comes from the burning of tropical forests,
mostly in the Amazon.[6]

There is some good news. With the availability of much more reliable satellite data, scientists have changed their estimates of how much
of the forest has been cut. Original estimates of deforestation have been
reduced from an amount in the range of 25 to 50 percent to something
between 15 and 20 percent. The amount of forest cutting in the past
three decades has nonetheless been stupefying and alarming.[7]

Given what is at stake, it is not surprising that there remains a well-
established set of oppositions between those who want "protection"
and those who want "development," between those who see settlers as
victims and those who see them as destroyers, between those who are
critical of the actions of international financial institutions, multinational corporations and the Brazilian government and those who defend them. These oppositions have their legitimacy. However, the
simplified polemics of the two sides often lead to confusion about the
choices to be made and about who must make the choices. The question of who will prevail in terms of the large questions will certainly be
decided to a considerable extent by large-scale actions, such as those
determined by the policies of the Brazilian government, the World Bank
and Inter-American Development Bank and corporate investors. However, the myriad actions of people in the region, including agricultural
settlers, will also make a difference.[8]

Had government policy regarding the Amazon been consistent with
the MST's views—that landless people should insist on land reform in
their home states—there would have been relatively little settlement.
Companies exploiting timber and minerals would have had to rely on
recruiting labor independently, rather than on hiring failed settlers.
Concern over environmental devastation in the Amazon would now be
much less urgent.

But that's not what happened, and after three decades of active government and corporate policy favoring Amazon development, new responses are required. Millions of people have now been lured to the Amazon and are trying to make some sort of living there. So while the MST still argues that redistribution within agricultural regions outside the Amazon is the best policy for poor rural people, for Brazilian development and for the Amazon forest, the movement's success in the rest of the country and intensity of land conflicts in the region have led to MST involvement in some parts of the Amazon, making it necessary for the movement to work out some vision of what it should do in the Amazon context.

Do MST strategies and tactics make sense in the Amazon? We wanted to see for ourselves, which is why we found ourselves in the state of Pará in 2001, the region of the Amazon where the movement is most active.

## The Transformation of the Amazon

When he told us we could not have come at a better time, Parazinho was right: it would be difficult to define what is normal in the southern part of Pará without talking about conflict and violence. For the past thirty-five years and more, the region has been forcefully and dramatically transformed. The change began in 1958 under the Kubitschek national government, with highway construction into the Amazon. There was no paved road access to southern Pará, however, until the early 1970s. Then, for the first time, the state capital of Belém, near the mouth of the Amazon, was linked by road to the Northeast and the industrialized Southeast. Other major projects followed in quick succession.[9]

With major financial assistance from the World Bank and the Inter-American Development Bank, the government built an enormous dam, called Tucuruí, on the Tocantins River and other dams on neighboring rivers. These dams supply electricity to run huge mining and smelting projects that were opened in the late 1970s and 1980s. Some of these facilities were part of the Grande Carajás project, which includes one of the world's largest iron mines, one of the world's largest copper mines and an enormous manganese mine. The government and the mining company (which was a state-owned firm at the time) built a

Trucks carrying loads of more than twenty tons bring iron ore out of one of the mines at Carajás—this particular section of the mining complex is dedicated exclusively to producing iron to be exported to China.

railroad that cut nearly ramrod straight through almost eight hundred miles of forest to the Atlantic coastal port city of São Luis in the state of Maranhão. Bauxite mines in the area provide ore to the world's largest aluminum smelter, a couple of hours by boat from Belém on the Amazon River. Only thirty miles or so from the iron mine is Serra Pelada, a huge gold strike mined with infamously primitive techniques that generated legendary levels of violence until the mine's closure in 1988.[10]

Most of this activity meant pushing indigenous people off land they had managed to hold on to over more than four centuries of Portuguese and Brazilian occupation. Some tribes had succeeded in avoiding much contact with Europeans throughout all this time, defending large roadless and forested territories against most intrusions. In the 1970s, some indigenous groups in the Amazon, such as the Kayapó, sought out new means of defense in the form of urban alliances in Brazil and help from European and North American groups. These alliances sometimes succeeded in pressuring the government to mark out large reserves providing a significant measure of protection from miners, timber companies, ranchers and settlers. In general, however, the story was much more bleak. Once the powerful wave of immigration began in the late 1960s, most Indians were either forcibly removed from the land or fell prey to diseases that the new immigrants introduced into their territories. Alcoholism took a terrible toll. Many Indians languished in a miserable solitary existence, similar to others among Brazil's rural landless people whose communities were shattered by the impact of the new projects and settlers.[11]

In the centuries before the mass immigration of the 1960s and 1970s, many indigenous people had intermarried over the years with *caboclo* (an imprecise term used largely for poor northeasterners in whom characteristics of mixed European and indigenous heritages predominate) and black immigrants who had trickled over the centuries into the region from the coast and the Northeast. In rural areas, and even in and around major cities, these people had often adopted the life of *ribeirinhos*, river folk of diverse origins, who lived in wooden houses with thatch or tin roofs, built on long stilts or rafts to provide protection against annual flooding. Many of the ribeirinhos were descended from people who had come to the region in a previous wave of immigration during the height of the Amazon rubber boom in the late nineteenth and early twentieth centuries. Their communities combined centuries-old indigenous ways with new adaptations. The river people had worked out ways of surviving that involved some combination of farming small agricultural plots, planting valuable coconut and acaí palms and other trees that provided saleable products, rubber tapping, fishing and gathering wild products from the forests. They traded for iron tools, cooking utensils, other basic necessities and the occasional small luxury at riverside trading posts and with itinerant merchants who visited them in boats and canoes.

For the ribeirinhos and their like, the new wave of immigration that began in the late 1960s presented both opportunities and challenges. Some of them prospered from new employment and trading opportunities, but many suffered from the pressure put on wild game and fisheries and the destruction of the forests. Others were swept away from their homes by dam and colonization projects. Many of the displaced headed farther up the tributaries or to the growing cities of the region.[12]

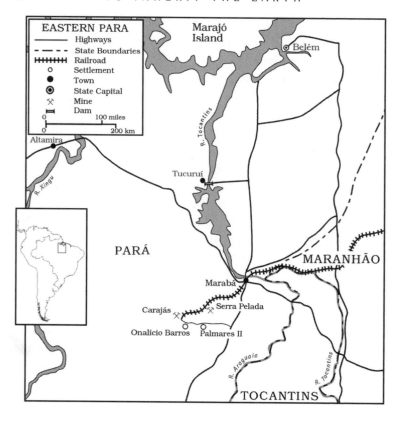

Some of the colonists lured to the region in the 1960s and subsequent decades came directly to plots of land made available to them by the government. In Pará, most came from the Northeast. Some came first to work on construction of the roads. They received better wages than anything available back home and were attracted by the promise of land at the end of the job. Part of the lure in some projects was the food provided to road workers. Hunters contracted by the government combed the forests for game and supplied an unusual but often satisfying array of meat. At the end of the construction projects, the men would seek out land identified by the government for colonization, or land that was up for grabs in fluid situations in which land ownership was poorly defined and defended.

Some property claims in the region dated back a century or more and were associated with the exploitation of rubber and other products of the standing forest. The state of Pará, governed by the barons of the rubber trade, had passed legislation to recognize such holdings as legitimate, arguing with considerable justification that they met the standards of effective use appropriate to the Amazon. An important legal distinction was to establish the principle that effective use could occur without cutting down the forest, since the predominant use of the land—rubber and nut gathering—depends on a relatively undisturbed forest. It makes sense to define "effective use" differently here than in other parts of Brazil. However, most of these claims proved difficult for the traditional landholders to defend in the face of the military government's determined colonization efforts and a tradition of Brazilian law that favored property claims based on forest clearing as the only valid demonstration of effective use of the land. Much of the land in Pará and elsewhere in the Amazon that had been claimed as rubber or nut gathering properties was legally defined by the federal government as public property open to settlement and homesteading under Brazilian law.[13]

As they settled and made claims to the Amazonian land, new settlers in the region did their best to bring families from back home or form new ones with partners found in the region. The forest itself was often their main capital. When the families had cut down the forest, buyers from timber companies came to purchase the trees that were of interest to them. The lumber was sent to build the scaffolding, and sometimes the framework, needed to erect the high-rise buildings going up at a dizzying rate in the cities of Brazil's more prosperous southeastern region. Lumber was also exported to the United States, Europe and Japan—one enormous pulp mill was actually constructed in Japan and floated around Cape Horn and up the Amazon River. Much of the wood was consumed in the Amazon itself, going to make charcoal to fuel the iron smelter at Carajás—about a quarter of all the destruction of the Amazon forest is chalked up to providing charcoal to smelters. The proportion is much higher for the southern portion of the state of Pará.[14]

The diversity of tree species in the Amazon made acquisition of timber from cleared agricultural plots much more attractive than independent clearing by the timber company. While the forest was composed of several hundred species in most locales, the timber companies had developed markets for only twenty to thirty species. When we visited the Amazon in 1979, at a time of intense timber cutting, mill owners we spoke to could market only twenty to twenty-two species familiar to buyers. These marketable species were hard to identify and extract from the standing forest; it was much easier to identify and extract the saleable logs once they were lying on the ground in a plot cleared by the settlers. In 1979, we found that, for valuable hardwoods such as mahogany, the price paid to settlers was around 3 percent of its retail price in the United States. Most of the wood, of little interest to the company timber cruiser, went up in flames. The settlers, especially ones who keep moving on, are a major economic asset to timber companies.[15]

Colonists in official programs during the military dictatorship were allotted land under terms that gave them use rights for ten years (this practice is still in effect at the time of this writing in 2003). Legally, colonists could not sell their land. Only after ten years had passed could they apply for purchase of title that would allow legal sale of the land. They could not mortgage land they did not own, so they were forced to rely almost exclusively on income from timber sales or on politically fickle, corrupt and poorly administered government credit programs for planting and subsistence expenditures until harvest. Of those who lasted the full ten years on their original plot, few ever managed to make it through the bureaucratic barriers to acquiring permanent title to their land. Entrepreneurs in the business of putting together large cattle ranches grabbed up much of this land through seizure of abandoned land or through illegal sales—illegal because no right to sell the land existed under the terms of the colonization grant. The entrepreneurs and land speculators commonly used intimidation and violence in acquiring land. Ranching operations put together by these people, in spite of their shady titles, were usually subsidized by federal programs meant to encourage the opening of the frontier in general and beef production in particular.[16]

The colonists found that the cleared forest ground presented unfamiliar problems. This was not the sertão of the Northeast. Amazon soils had not been adequately understood or even properly identified by the government officials planning the colonization efforts. The enormous body of traditional agronomic knowledge developed by indigenous people over millennia was largely ignored, and in any case it proved difficult to translate this knowledge into terms useful to immigrants to the region who were determined to duplicate types of agriculture with which they were familiar. The lack of markets for unfamiliar products and the prejudices of credit institutions also penalized innovation and adaptation to local conditions.

Even in the twenty-first century, Amazon soil science remains in its infancy. Certainly, in the 1970s, neither government extension agents nor the settlers from the Northeast knew very much about what the soils would support, for how long or under what kind of treatment. Some soil was so heavily mineralized, particularly with aluminum, that it was toxic to many crops. Much of the soil was nutrient poor; almost all the nutrients were contained in the forest itself, which, when left undisturbed, quickly recycled leaf-litter nutrients back into live plant tissue. When the forest was cleared and burned, torrential rains washed away many of the nutrients and eroded unprotected fields at some-times catastrophic speed. Crops also faced intense predation from combinations of insects, birds, rodents and other animals largely unknown to the colonists. An awesome variety of weedy plants adapted to Amazon conditions competed for water and nutrients with crops planted in cleared fields. Fungal diseases that could wipe out entire fields in a few days proliferated easily under the hot, moist conditions.[17]

## INDIGENOUS STRATEGIES

The new immigrants would have been at least somewhat better off if they had understood more about the techniques that had been used by indigenous people and the ribeirinhos of the Amazon. Broadly speaking, indigenous agriculture in the Amazon had been based on one of two strategies, or a combination of the two, that avoided or minimized the problems defeating the new immigrants. On upland ground, Indians cut out small clearings, burned the forest debris after removing the largest or most useful logs and planted diverse food crops that had become adapted to Amazon conditions over centuries, if not two or three millennia. The Indians used digging sticks rather than plows, which minimized soil disturbance. The larger forest debris that resisted burning was left scattered across the soil, where it tended to slow erosion. The Indian farmers, men and women according to the customs of the particular group, watched carefully for signs of declining fertility in the fields. Declining yields was one indicator of reduction in fertility, but a dangerous one on which to rely, because a field with noticeable declines in productivity in one year would be disastrously deficient in the next and might take too long to recover when left fallow. Prior to noticeable drops in fertility, traditional farmers also identified the presence of certain invasive plants and insects, which signaled that a plot needed to be abandoned in favor of a new clearing. With the opening of a new field, the old one was abandoned until the forest had substantially regrown—it did so easily because the soil had not been driven to complete exhaustion and the field was surrounded by forest that provided natural reseeding and vegetative regrowth.[18]

The second strategy of indigenous survival relied on the annual delivery of sediments on land called *várzea* that flooded every year, a reliable event on 3 to 7 percent of the enormous extent of the Amazon basin. These flooded várzea soils, properly managed, are extremely fertile and productive over centuries, if not indefinitely. In some places, flooding is too intense for tree growth, but the várzea soils support what are generally the most diverse and lush parts of the forest: flooded forests tend to be critical reproduction and nursery sites for fish and animals.[19] Many kinds of knowledge are essential to successful agricultural exploitation of várzea, including good judgment about when to plant in relation to the arrival of the floods, knowledge of pest species of plants, insects and animals and management of water to avoid waterlogging. Curiously, management of drought conditions can be critical too, because the system is adapted to lots of water and must be able to make the transition to relative water shortage when drought occurs.[20]

It was important to indigenous people and later to ribeirinhos that they never relied on annual crops for all their food and that they supplemented their diet with fishing, hunting and gathering in the wild forest. There is also evidence of small orchard plantings dating back centuries, and we know that the ribeirinhos today rely on tree-crop plantings. Excessive reliance on annual field crops was likely to guarantee that pressures on the soils would fairly rapidly overwhelm their productive capacity. For many groups, annual agriculture was a secondary activity that supplemented other ways of acquiring food and income.

Indigenous systems of survival in the midst of the forest allowed cultures to flourish in the Amazon for thousands of years with relatively little damage to the diversity and resiliency of the forest. An increasing number of archeologists and anthropologists now believe that as many as six million people—some venture as many as fifteen—may have lived in great long villages stretched along the Amazon and its tributaries. If true, it is striking that the aboriginal population may have equaled or exceeded the number of people who live in the Amazon today. It is at least a very good bet that the number of people who made a living from the natural environment in the Amazon—hunting, gathering and agriculture—exceeded the number who do so today. The majority of modern Amazon residents are urban and make their living from employment that has little relationship to the productivity of Amazonian agriculture.[21]

In any case, it is certain that the arrival of Europeans decimated most indigenous cultures with old-world diseases beginning in the sixteenth century. Europeans also broke the backs of many indigenous survival systems by quickly devastating the most easily exploited food production systems, including turtle farming at the edge of rivers and the harvest of easily found fish species, such as the enormous and extraordinarily delicious *pirarucu*. Fleeing the destructive, slave-hunting, pestilential Europeans, many, if not most, Amazon Indians sought isolation away from the main streams. In doing so, they were forced to live in much less productive and less forgiving environments, away from the fisheries, várzea soils and easy transport offered by the large rivers. Many lived in circumstances permanently impoverished relative to the past. When settlers arrived, much of the traditional knowledge that had once made a decent life in the Amazon possible had already disappeared with the death or displacement of those who had learned it through centuries of culturally transmitted experience.[22]

## SMALL-SCALE COLONISTS TRY TO SURVIVE

When the desperately poor northeastern immigrants arrived in the Amazon in the 1970s, they had little or none of the adaptive knowledge necessary to survive in the forest environment. Government and corporate agronomists encouraged colonists to proceed as though the Amazon were little different from the fields of home. Site selection for farms was often ill informed, if not simply haphazard or arbitrary. Proximity to roads was a logical criterion for farm-site selection in the view of those who thought in terms of market access, but the roads did not always pass through the most favorable agricultural land. The agronomists pushed chemical pesticides and fertilizers as the best way to solve many of the problems the immigrants encountered, but the chemicals were very expensive for credit-starved colonists, and when used, they often created ecological problems that undermined the conditions for successful long-term agriculture. For example, sporadic, ill-informed and inconsistent use of pesticides quite likely intensified the buildup of pesticide-resistant species. Pesticides also decimated many species that had kept actual or potential crop pests under control, setting the scene for massive crop failures by releasing the pest species from predator pressure.[23]

Agronomists and government policy makers also often encouraged settlers to rely very heavily on export crops, particularly cacao. While this sometimes made a certain ecological sense—because cacao is native to the Amazon and can even be successfully farmed under a standing canopy of large forest trees—the smallholders' excessive economic reliance on cacao and other export crops was fatally flawed because the prices of crops in international trade were and remain notoriously volatile. For small farmers, cacao was more viable as a supplementary crop in the context of overall crop diversity, which usually promotes wild species diversity as well. Only farmers with large amounts of capital or credit could afford to rely heavily on volatile export crops, because only the wealthy could outlast the frequent dramatic downturns in price.

The colonists found it extremely difficult to remain on the land they cleared. Declining soil fertility, soil erosion and crop-pest outbreaks forced many to abandon their plots of land. Others fell prey to malaria, dengue fever, yellow fever, gastrointestinal diseases, intestinal and skin parasites, skin diseases, tuberculosis and a variety of other diseases that flourish among poor folk in the Amazon. Those who still had the strength to move on abandoned the land they had cleared, often opening a new clearing to which they were even less likely to have or ever obtain legitimate ownership rights. They cleared their next and subsequent pieces of ground under the burden of accumulating debt. With no prospect of an ownership claim to the land, it was less likely that they would qualify for the inadequate if somewhat helpful government services open to first-time colonists. Their chances of success declined each time they moved across the landscape.[24]

Behind the colonists came the big-time ranchers and speculators. Some of these were large multinational corporations, and others were established and experienced large-scale ranching firms. Some were nothing more than unscrupulous entrepreneurs with little capital but an aggressive determination to succeed through whatever combination of hard work, fraud, violence and milking of government subsidies should prove necessary. The various scandals regarding the misuse of government development funds made it fairly clear that many firms were put together simply to take advantage of the sometimes lavish and deeply corrupt expenditure of government money. For example, Jáder Barbalho, the deposed and imprisoned head of the national senate, used his position as head of SUDAM, the regional development agency for the Amazon, to disperse millions of dollars to old business associates and to a company headed by his wife dedicated to the production of frog legs.[25]

In some cases the ranch operations simply took over the land when it was abandoned, threw a fence around it, and defied counterclaimants until some form of title could be arranged by fair means or foul. In the case of acquisition of official colonization land, it was extremely difficult to produce a convincing legal title because few colonists had ever obtained anything more than the form of ownership that forbade sale or transfer of the land to a second party. Whatever the legal niceties or lack thereof, ranch land rapidly expanded into the vacuum left by failed small-scale colonists. Little beef was exported from the Amazon—this was not the Central American rain forest hamburger that became notorious for being served by North American fast-food chains—but the swelling urban populations within the Amazon provided a growing market. Some ranches were profitable through intensive management, including the use of chemical fertilizers and herbicides to favor the best grasses, but few large landholders were interested in investing the attention and capital that such close management required. Unless intensively managed, a relative rarity in the Amazon, the ranch land supported few cattle per unit of land area. The operation could be made to pay when enormous properties could be assembled and with the help of tax breaks and a 50 percent subsidy to ranching that came courtesy of the Brazilian government until the late 1980s. Some of those accumulating land probably did so in the belief that it represented an effective hedge against the runaway inflation then endemic in the Brazilian economy, though in retrospect this may not have been a good bet.[26]

As colonists and other small farmers gave way to ranchers, those displaced became workers building dams, roads and electrical lines. Many were returning to the kind of work that had brought them to the Amazon in the first place. They got jobs in the iron, bauxite, gold and manganese mines. They worked in sawmills or cutting timber or driving trucks. Many became *garimpeiros*, gold prospectors working on their own account but controlled and exploited by private firms who sold them supplies and bought their ore. In some regions where garimpeiros were numerous, they were governed by criminals who organized private armies composed of scores of well-armed men. Many other settlers became largely unemployed wanderers and slum dwellers in towns and cities, looking for whatever chance opportunity came to hand. Many would be forced again and again to return to cutting out plots at the forest edge, no matter how discouraging the long-term prospects for such activity.

Some analysts of the Amazon colonization effort have concluded that those in charge of government policy never seriously thought that small-scale farming would succeed in the Amazon or that colonists would be able to build permanent livelihoods. Others have concluded that most of the policies of the government were designed primarily with national security concerns in mind, attracting economic activity to the area as a means of gaining stronger national control over the vast territory of the Amazon, with relatively little concern for net economic growth. In either of these interpretations, the promise of land was simply a lure to capture labor to fell the timber, clear the land for ranching, build the dams and roads and work the mines. A relatively small number of corporations and a somewhat bigger group of large landholders gained great wealth, while the men and women who did the work of building the empire of natural resource extraction were not able to establish homesteads. The employment that some of them found as an alternative was mostly poorly paid and even less stable than the volatile

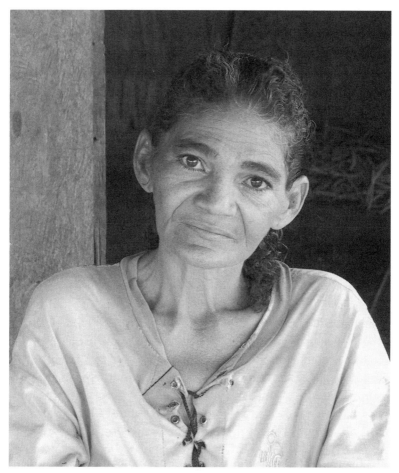

A woman from the backlands sertão region of the state of Pernambuco who now lives in Assentamento Onalício Barros with her sons. She is one of many poor northeasterners originally drawn to the Amazon by government colonization and road building programs.

international commodity markets in which the resources were sold. Whether or not it was the policy makers' intention to exploit the desire of poor people for farmland by enlisting their energies for exploitation of the region's timber and minerals, that was the result. In the process, thousands of square miles of the world's most diverse rain forest vanished from the face of the earth.[27]

The majority of Brazilians were no better off as a consequence. The income earned went mostly to an elite sector of Brazilian investors and professionals and to foreign investors. The resources did less to build the economy of Brazil than those of rich nations. In the Amazon, the exploitation of the desperate desire for land among Brazil's landless remained a vast machine for devouring forests, just as it had been in the destruction of the nation's Atlantic coast rain forest.

## DEFORESTATION FEEDS ON FAILURE

Glauco is an agronomist who now works for the MST. He was born and grew up in the southern Amazon state of Rondônia, far from the state of Pará where he now works. He had worked for private companies, and then for the CPT, the Catholic group that was originally organized in the Amazon to support small-scale farmers struggling to gain land and make a living. In July 2001, we agreed to drive with Glauco in his tiny car from Belém to our study area around Marabá and Parauapebas in southeastern Pará. Contrary to the initial plan to drive the ten hours during daylight, circumstances put us on the car ferry out of Belém in a raging thunderstorm in the late afternoon, and we arrived in Marabá at 2:30 the following morning.

Overworked, sleepy-eyed and slow-speaking at the best of times, Glauco fought against drowsiness as he drove through the night, navigating thousands of gaping potholes, broken bridge planks and pieces of road largely washed away or under repair. Sandy soils and torrential rains are relentless enemies of Amazon roadways. The traffic on the road was made up mostly of lumber trucks carrying a few enormous logs; in some cases a single, huge tree trunk was all the largest of truck trailers could hold. The lumber trucks travel at night to avoid direct confrontation with forest officials, who might question the legality of the logging. Whatever the legality of their work, it has to be admitted that the truck drivers, while pushing as fast as they can to arrive at the mills, are courteous guides to the few hapless souls who travel by car at night, employing an elaborate code of headlight and turn-light signals to warn of danger. We probably owe our lives to them.

As he drove, Glauco had a long time to explain his work. He had been engaged for several years in a study for the CPT that sought to answer in detail the question of why smallholders were unable to stay on their land. Slumped down in the bucket seat of the car, pulling the steering wheel hard to left and right to avoid potholes and obstacles, Glauco described what he saw as the typical would-be settlers' attempt to establish a farmstead, a story that in its general terms is confirmed by many other studies of the issue. Although the story shares many elements with the fate of official government-sponsored colonists, Glauco's analysis is based on the kind of spontaneous colonist who now greatly outnumbers those involved in officially sponsored settlements.

Glauco's story went like this: "As he looks for a place to settle, he will be approached by an agent of the timber company. The agent offers a deal. 'We will get you into a piece of good land. You won't be able to survive without a road, that's the key. With a good road you can get your crops out to market and get in and out of town as you need. Everything along the existing roads is taken. But don't worry, that's why we are here. We take you to the land. You clear it. We will build a road to take out the timber—that's how you know we will actually build the road, because we get nothing out of the deal unless we can get the timber out. We buy the timber from you and that gives you the capital you need to build a home, plant your crops and get through the first year.'"

Glauco emphasized that the amount the company is offering for the timber is usually more than the man has ever seen at once in his life, to him a small fortune, even though it is a small price for the timber and not as much money as the man will really need before he can establish a successful farm. "But he doesn't realize that at the time. The deal seems like a dream.

"So the man cuts down the timber, the company builds the road, and they usually will pay him what they promised they would to haul out the wood. It looks good so far. But the road is little more than a bulldozer cut through the land that can't last long in the rains. Soon, it is impassable. Now he is isolated on his own land. If he has a family, they can't get health care, the kids can't get to school. Growing the crops presents all sorts of problems he hadn't anticipated. What he grows he can't get to market. He is desperate."

Glauco paused for a time in thought, then continued. "Now here is where you have to understand something about how these people think. It's simple enough, though. They say to themselves, 'I'm poor, but there are many rich men making a killing around here. How do they do it? They run cattle. I have to get myself some cattle, and then I can make it.'

"So, the poor guy spends whatever money is left from the timber company, gets a loan if he can and buys some cattle. He doesn't have enough land or capital to support many. The land usually supports fewer head than he thinks it can; he may lose a lot learning that lesson alone. He doesn't know how to work the government subsidies and tax breaks. In any case, the number of cattle on his plot just don't provide enough income to survive. In the end, he sells out to a large operator, most of the land around him now having been cleared by others like himself."

Glauco picked up energy as he talked. "The only ones who survive are those who resist trying to become like the big guys. A guy who will make it works out ways to grow enough subsistence crops for himself, which typically really isn't all that difficult in spite of the problems. Then he has got to figure out how to produce a bit of a cash crop that is sustainable under these conditions. No one here makes it without a little cash, but he can't go for too much. He is going to have to work hard, his family is going to have work hard. Just slowly getting a decent kind of living, no luxury, but a home, a life, a place he can stay. We found in our study that this is possible, that it can work. But it isn't always easy to convince people of this. That's a big part of our job now. . . .

"Of course those of us in the movement think these families are not going to succeed in the long run as individualists. They will have to be able defend their land from intruders. They will need to cooperate at least in marketing and in setting up the credit arrangements they need. If they succeed, there will be many who want to see them brought down, to free up the land and the labor. Most of all, they need a movement to protect themselves against that. There are many individualists who came to the region because that is the way they thought, as individualists who would find their own land here. We have to change that mentality."

In this respect, the original vision of Amazon colonization promoted by the government was in partial agreement with Glauco's view. No one who had thought about it much, including the government, imagined that settlers would survive in the Amazon as lonely individuals.

The colonies designed by INCRA beginning in the late 1960s were supposed to comprise communities supported by marketing and credit cooperatives. However, the government discouraged organization —sometimes violently—that would challenge government policy or influential economic interests. INCRA itself was shot through with corruption and incompetence. In short, the government model of collectivity was a paternalistic one in which the patron, INCRA, was unreliable and frequently dishonest—an old story in Brazil. The end result was to discourage collective organization and action rather than foster it.[28]

Glauco's view of the matter touches on one of the most important questions about the landless movement, especially in the Amazon. To many people in Brazil and abroad, the landless movement represents a threat to the forest, for the obvious reason that there are a lot of landless people and that one of the main ways to get land is to clear forest; forested land is less likely than cleared ground to have prior claimants. Traditionally, Brazilian land law has favored forest clearance, because clearance shows effective economic use of the land, thereby endorsing ownership. When a central thrust of government policy was to promote economic development and the occupation of national territory the bias toward deforestation was deliberate. Now, Brazilian law was reformed in 1998 in this respect in order to discourage deforestation, though the effective use principle is still valid outside of forested areas. In forest land the principle still lives on both as an influential informal tradition in peoples' minds and in some court decisions that fail to recognize—or simply deny the significance of—recent reforms. Given the remaining vitality of the tradition and given that landless people can be seen in many Amazon regions chewing away at the forest edge, many people conclude that the landless and the landless movement that represents them are to blame for deforestation.

This perspective blames the direct agents of destruction for the results of a process that compels their actions. It is those who manipulate the poverty and powerlessness of the landless that are to blame for the relentlessness of forest destruction. Were people able to establish permanent homesteads on suitable land, some of the Amazon forest would still have been sacrificed to the process. However, most of the vast territories sacrificed to the ax and chainsaw are clearly the result not of poor peoples' establishment of homesteads but of their *failure* to establish homesteads and their constant need to move on.[29]

The failure of settlers to gain permanent homesteads is not in the interest of settlers. But it is in the interest of timber companies, mining companies, construction firms and those who believe that national policy should be driven by the most rapid possible resource exploitation. Were settlers able to actually permanently settle on their land, it would be necessary for these companies to pay much higher wages to attract workers to the difficult and dangerous tasks of felling timber and mining the earth. Resource extraction would slow in direct response to landless peoples' ability to gain a measure of independence from the extractive economy, and the fruits of that economy would also be more widely distributed.

In short, it is the people who direct the process, rather than those caught up in it, who are to blame for the unceasing deforestation of the Amazon. Many poor people in the region are quite aware of this and have dedicated themselves to changing the situation for themselves and for society. They want exit from the process that destroys their hopes for a decent life as cruelly as it destroys the Amazon forest. The hope and fear involved in this commitment are easy to observe in MST settlements in the region.

# Visiting MST Settlements
# and the Carajás Mine

The rapidly growing town of Marabá sits on the banks of the Tocantins River, not far above the upper end of the huge reservoir behind the Tucuruí hydroelectric dam. It is also a stopping point and crossroads on the Belém-Brasília highway and a station on the railway built to take iron ore to the coast at São Luis do Maranhão. Marabá is a lively town that sprawls across the denuded landscape, in three hastily thrown up suburbs that lack a central city to orient them to any shared sense of urban place. Marabá is obviously flush with money spent on big pickups and SUVs and in noisy restaurants and nightclubs. At the same time, it is awash in the peculiarly restless kind of poverty associated with geographical and social displacement. The elegantly designed bus station, for example, has for its counterpoint the ragged and occasionally barefoot families and solo travelers staring helplessly at pastries and sweets that they can't afford, while keeping close track of the cardboard boxes and cheap nylon bags that may hold all they own. This kind of poverty is not unique to Marabá, but is endemic to those parts of the Amazon opened to development in recent decades. Like many boomtowns, Marabá is a big advertisement for the main chance, and a living diorama that illustrates how unlikely it is that you are going to be the one who wins it.

In Marabá, we arranged to visit MST settlements near the town of Parauapebas, on the road that goes to the Carajás iron mine and the Serra Pelada gold mine. Because the security of the people in the settlements and of the movement itself is a constant preoccupation of local MST leaders, the MST office in Marabá has no sign indicating that the MST is housed there; rather the discreet small plaque beside the door indicates that it is the headquarters of the rural cooperatives set up by MST settlements. We arrived there in the morning, and after some pleasant but guarded conversation with people meeting in the office, we were advised to go enjoy the sites of Marabá, eat lunch and buy the hammocks we would need for sleeping in the settlements if we were cleared to do so. Although we had contacted the Marabá office by email, no one remembered receiving it. Returning several hours later, we found we had been vetted by email through the national MST office. We were now treated much more warmly and put into the hands of Guedeson, who would guide us to the settlements.

Guedeson, a handsome, athletic-looking young man with skin the color of dark mahogany and an electric smile, wore a white cap, sparkling clean trousers and shirt and a pair of flip-flops, the most common footwear of Brazilian rural people. From the MST offices, we went to a shaded plaza to find a taxi-van that would take us to Parauapebas, about a two-hour trip. As we waited, we shared a drink called *guaraná*, which was prepared in a blender at a small stand. The drink as prepared here is incomparably richer and more delicious than the caffeine-loaded guaraná soft drink so popular throughout Brazil, more like a tasty milkshake than like soda pop. Guedeson laughed when he realized that when we said we had tasted guaraná, we meant the commercial soft drink. "No, this is a completely different thing," he said. The fruit from which the drink is made is one of the many wonderful-tasting forest products popular in the Amazon. Most have not been successfully marketed outside of it, though many efforts have been made to do so by people anxious to put greater economic value on natural forest products.

The van could hold about fourteen people, depending on how hard everyone squeezed in. We sat with Guedeson in the seats farthest to the back, where each of hundreds of bad bumps was transmitted immediately to the spinal cord with a hard snap. As we rode, Guedeson was able to say who owned or claimed most of the properties along the road, and he knew a good deal of detail about each of a dozen or so settlements and encampments made by settlers affiliated with the MST or, more commonly, with other rural union organizations. He also pointed out various properties that the MST had its eye on for future occupations. He transmitted all of this information in a combination of whispers and hand signals to avoid being overheard by others in the van. The condition of the road and our anxious spinal cords made note-taking impossible.

As we neared Parauapebas, we passed a monument to those killed in the massacre of El Dorado dos Carajás. In 1996, MST settlers had marched along this asphalt highway to bring attention to land conflicts in the region. They were attacked by a column of well-armed military police dressed in protective gear, who killed nineteen of the marchers and injured many more. A video taken by an observer, although jerky and of poor quality, confirmed the testimony of the marchers that they had been brutally and needlessly attacked. There was no evidence of any provocation. The shocking video of men, women and children running to escape the bullets being fired at them played repeatedly on national television networks. The El Dorado dos Carajás massacre, coming as it did at a time of heightened conflict between the national government and the MST, sharply turned national public opinion in favor of landless people throughout Brazil and in support of the work of the MST in particular. Some scholars believe that the event did more than anything else to win sympathy for the movement; it is undeniable that the number of expropriations made in favor of the landless went sharply up in the three years following the El Dorado dos Carajás incident. The massacre thus represents both tragic loss and bittersweet victory to the local and national movement of landless people. The steady toll of assassinations of rural landless leaders throughout Brazil over a fifteen-year period had resulted in at least a thousand well-documented deaths prior to the incident, but these deaths had never succeeded in seriously arousing the national conscience as El Dorado dos Carajás did.[30]

The bitterness of the loss remains because of the slow and faltering work of the justice system. An initial court judgment relieving the police of all blame was overturned, but it took years of legal work and political pressure to pursue the case and bring it to trial a second time. In 2002, two of the responsible officers were sentenced to significant prison terms, but the question of culpability among higher military and political officials remained a burning issue for the MST and others who value human rights in Brazil.

The first monument erected to the memory of those who died at El Dorado dos Carajás was a grand steel affair designed by Brazil's most famous architect, the leftist Oscar Niemeyer, who designed the main buildings of the national capital, Brasília. An unidentified gang attacked this sculpture in the night, dismantling it and carrying off most of the pieces. In response, local people decided to put up their own monument. In place of the grand conception of Niemeyer, they erected nineteen great, partially burned trunks of forest trees, ranging from twenty to thirty feet high, in a rough semicircle where people had fallen. Such trunks dot the landscape for hundreds of miles around, usually solitary reminders of the forest devastation. The nineteen trunks brought together at the massacre site along the road created an unforgettable symbol of the tragically linked loss of human life and natural beauty. The monument also links the death of at least nineteen dreams for a better life and renewal in crisis of a movement that now inspires many new dreams. As we passed the monument in the late afternoon, conversation quieted in the van and heads turned toward the massive trunks. No one said a word.

Not much further down the road, we passed the town of Curionápolis, county seat of the município named after the notorious military man and intelligence officer who had attempted to put an end to the settlement at Encruzilhada Natalino (see chapter 1). Coronel Curió now lives in the município named after him and serves as its mayor. A side road takes off from Curionápolis to the gold mines at Serra Pelada, now closed, where Curió had been brought in by the government to resolve ongoing violent conflict. He had better luck at Serra Pelada than at Sarandí, and at the time of our visit the government was contemplating reopening the Serra Pelada diggings under the supervision of a consortium of large corporations. However, as the date approached for the reopening of the mine, a group of garimpeiros led by Curió was insisting on its exclusive access to the mine while another group of garimpeiros asserted that they too should have access. The leader of the second group was assassinated by unknown assailants in December 2003. While speaking of Curió, Guedeson once more spoke in a whisper with his head down between the seats.

Further down the road, Parauapebas presents itself as another (though smaller) bustling boomtown. Wide streets and relatively new storefronts give it an open and pleasant feel. The proliferation of busy shops and a lively street market flush with clothing and electronic gadgets of every kind make it clear that there is a good deal of money about. There are also sprawling slums with open sewers and stagnant water that fuel the spectacular rates of malaria and dengue fever in the area. Near the market are a series of open-air bars where muscular men, mostly in big cowboy hats and fancy high-heeled boots, sit, usually one to a table. They stare at passersby through mirrored sunglasses as they pour beer into small glasses from the one-liter bottles nestled in Styrofoam thermos containers. Some carry automatic pistols openly on their belts; others have telltale bulges in their trousers or jean jackets.

Parauapebas, a town of roughly forty thousand inhabitants, has had roughly one murder a week since 1989. According to the Workers' Party candidate for mayor, only three people have ever been officially accused of any of these murders since 1989, only two have been brought to trial and only one convicted. Whatever the precise accuracy of these figures, the area has been well documented by the Catholic CPT as one of the two most violent areas in Brazil (the other is the Amazonian state of Acre), particularly with regard to land conflicts. Not surprisingly, most people seemed to give the men in sunglasses and boots a wide berth and to pointedly avoid looking at them.[31]

A SMALL NEW SETTLEMENT:
ASSENTAMENTO ONALÍCIO BARROS

We bought some groceries and arranged with a big man with a large potbelly to take us by taxi to the settlement where Guedeson lives, Assentamento Onalício Barros. As we barreled down gravel and dirt roads, the talkative taxi driver, given only a little encouragement to express his opinion, declared that the people in the landless movement are lazy good-for-nothings who simply live to steal from those who work and invest. He said he felt sorry for them in a way, but couldn't sympathize with what they do to get land and had no faith in their ability to succeed. He was eager to promote his own business wherever possible though: he left Guedeson and us with multicolored business cards and declared himself ready to serve at any time.

We arrived at Assentamento Onalício Barros in the last light of the day. The sixty-eight families of the settlement had spread their houses along two broad dirt streets that intersect each other at right angles. At the time of our visit in summer of 2001, the settlers had been in legal possession of the land for three years, after occupying the land for more than two years before that. Since taking legal possession, most families had built houses made of wood planks. Some houses were made of daub and wattle, adobe mud spread across a network of sticks. All had spacious yards. Most of the yards spoke of pride and meticulous attention, planted with manioc, garden vegetables and carefully kept flowerbeds, but a few were rather barren and a little forlorn. Children wandered where they wished, as vehicles and other dangers were rare in the settlement. Each family had an agricultural plot of twenty hectares outside the village, within easy walking distance of the houses. The settlement owned a tractor and some basic tractor-drawn farm implements.

The settlement as a whole managed a sizable stretch of pasture for which the agrarian reform agency had provided some breeding stock. A small, attractive ranch house with a long covered porch, predating the settlement, sits overlooking the pastureland about twenty minutes' walk from the main settlement. Some settlers would prefer to live in this well-built house, but most would rather live in the settlement, near their friends and companions. The settlers decided that living in the ranch house is to be rotated among those who want to live there and who are willing and able to take primary responsibility for daily vigilance over the cattle. At the time of our visit, a widow and her three children lived in the ranch house.

There is no doubt that the land of Onalício Barros was originally cut out of the lush Amazon forest. On two sides of the settlement, magnificent forest remains. The very carefully protected forest preserve surrounding the mining project of Grande Carajás covers the ridge that defines the horizon on the north side of the settlement. Within the settlement itself, great solitary forest trees were scattered about, most of them dead from the burning of the surrounding vegetation. Some of these old giants survived. Nearly all the clearing preceded the occupation and settlement of the land by the MST; the land had been claimed by previous settlers and by the rancher who succeeded them, who still had extensive holdings in neighboring pastures and forest patches. At one point, Guedeson told us ominously that the rancher was simply waiting to see the settlement fail so that he could reoccupy the pastures and once again assert an ownership claim, having already been paid for the land by the government in the expropriation leading to the founding of Assentamento Onalício Barros. When successful, this strategy can prove very profitable to ranchers. Land is acquired by dubious means, worked for a time, sold to the government for agrarian reform and then reclaimed if the settlement fails. The failure rate among non-MST settlements is hard to document, but it is certainly fairly high.

The gravel road leading to the settlement was fairly well constructed and maintained by Amazon standards, where downpours sometimes take out long stretches of even major asphalt highways. It is the policy of the MST in Pará to establish settlements only where good roads are already in place—to do otherwise would guarantee the economic failure of the settlement. It is also policy, less rigorously observed, to occupy land that has already been cleared. Violations of the latter policy do occur, but do not make a major dent on existing forest, since forest clearing is already fairly thorough wherever decent roads exist.

In the center of the settlement is a monument to the two leaders who were assassinated in the course of the struggle to gain the land. One of these leaders was Onalício Barros, known to all his followers and admirers as "Fusquinho." Guedeson told us how, in the difficult days when they were first occupying the land, Fusquinho had inspired everyone in the settlement. "He always had a joke or a funny saying or something to cheer people up. He was a poet, he wrote poetry, he spoke like a poet, spontaneously. He always kept people going. He never seemed discouraged. He was always making people think of the future they could have." Guedeson told of how Fusquinho had a wife and three children and how he spoke of the fight for land in terms of the fight for the future of the settlers' families. "But he never let worry for his family keep him from fighting. He was always out in front."

"It's hard to explain all that Fusquinho meant to us, to me," Guedeson continued. "Just in the way he was, he taught us so many things. Just about how to be, how to live, how to think. It's not easy to put your finger on it. It was the way he was that was always teaching something. But he wasn't an educated person. He couldn't read very well. He relied on his wife to read for him. What he had to teach wasn't something he had learned in school. No, it was about what he had learned from life."

Guedeson explained that Fusquinho had a speech impediment or, as Guedeson called it, "a funny way of speaking." This often resulted in his saying things that sounded strange to people, but they treasured the fractured form in which Fusquinho had said them. For example, he frequently said, "É impostante lutar!" ("It is impostant to fight!"), instead of the proper "É importante lutar!" ("It is important to fight!"). Later, we were to see poorly reproduced black-and-white posters in Parauapebas with a photo of Fusquinho and his wife and child, and the phrase, "É impostante lutar!" (Obviously, even the most politically radical people in southern Pará have not yet heard of the form of "political correctness" that meticulously warns against using words that might be taken as insulting to particular people or groups.) Though Guedeson did not mention it, Fusquinho had attracted national notice when he went to Brasília to plead for the expropriation of the Rio Branco fazenda, on which the assentamento named after him would be founded.[32]

Guedeson witnessed Fusquinho's assassination. It happened on a day when privately contracted gunmen attacked the encampment in an unsuccessful attempt to permanently remove the settlers from the area. According to Guedeson, at one point in the confrontation between settlers and the hired band of jagunços, two gunmen walked up to

Fusquinho and another of the leaders and shot them with pistols at point-blank range. Although his companion died quickly after being shot, Fusquinho did not. Guedeson helped take him to a shack to hide him from the gunmen and try to treat his wounds. Guedeson remembers his own hands and pants soaked in blood. Looking at his hands as though they still dripped in blood, he recalled, "It was horrible—how can I tell you, the way it was?" There was no medical help available. Fusquinho died in two or three hours.

Guedeson said that no one had ever been apprehended or charged with the crime, even though settlers occasionally laid eyes on the two men they had seen commit the murders. As far as the settlers could tell, the police had taken no interest in pursuing the killers. The relationship of the assentamento with the surrounding villages was not particularly cordial—many of those who lived in the villages worked for the rancher who claimed the land prior to the MST occupation or engaged in trade with the ranch or its employees. Three years after the assentamento's official founding, things were becoming more relaxed and friendly, though the killers still enjoyed a friendly reception among at least some families in Parauapebas and the surrounding small towns.

Guedeson explained the importance of the monument to the two fallen leaders—two large stones set on buried vertical tree trunks—and laughed a little, remembering how hard it had been to bury the trunks and set the heavy stones on top of them. "We don't want anyone to ever forget them."

In the dying light of the day of our arrival in Assentamento Onalício Barros, we still had time to walk to an encampment that had been cleared of settlers the day before. The encampment was under the leadership of one of the old rural worker's unions in Pará that had in recent years occupied land in hundreds of locations throughout the state. The day before our arrival, private gunmen had driven out the settlers after giving them an hour to gather up their belongings. The gunmen had then burned the houses the settlers had erected and cleared the ground of nearly every trace of the occupation. When we saw the site at dusk, we saw a few supporting poles of the burned houses and smelled the sweet, pungent smell of the ashes, still in the air. In one of those melodramatic touches in life that seem too eloquent to be true, a large plastic doll missing one arm lay among the ashes at the entrance to the settlement.

Two days before this photo was taken, this acampamento bordering Assentamento Onalício Barros was burned to the ground and its inhabitants thrown off the land.

As we walked back to Assentamento Onalício Barros, a small Toyota car with five men and a visible rifle passed us slowly on the dirt road. The men looked us over carefully. Guedeson judged them to be jagunços keeping an eye out for settlers who might be attempting to return to the burned-out site. We were to see the men in the same car several times over the next few days.

I asked Guedeson if the people of Onalício Barros would be offering aid or support to the displaced people from the encampment. A newspaper story I had seen that morning reported that they were desperately wandering the streets of Parauapebas, looking for places to stay. Some, including some of the leaders, were said to be hiding in the woods not far from the encampment from which they had been removed. Guedeson's answers to my questions about support for these people from the settlers in Assentamento Onalício Barros were obviously meant to be evasive.

The next day shed some light on his evasive approach. We were in a little store that sold a small selection of groceries—eggs, soft drinks, a few canned goods, packaged treats, cigarettes, and locally produced liquor—when a short, wiry, middle-aged man entered in an obvious state of agitation. After some mumbled remarks that we did not understand, he began to make a sustained and angry set of declarations: "We won't be driven out! They can't do this to us! We have every right to be here and we are not going to let anybody drive us away! I tell you, I don't care what they try, we will be back. They say they will kill me. I don't care what they say! They aren't scaring us away. Let them try to find me. And if they do, they can kill me. I'm ready. They won't stop this settlement!"

Guedeson barely responded to any of this. Instead, he began to assume a look of studied boredom and apathy. The man began to ask explicitly for support. "We need a little help. The people who care about the poor are not going to desert us. The people who care about the poor will always help us. I don't care if some people don't care."

Guedeson's expressions began to seem downright aggressively indifferent. He toyed with his necklace, which held a wooden cross. He stared at the ceiling.

The man continued, "I have put up with this shit as long as I am going to put up with it. Those who say they are our friends and don't support us, fine, I can live with that. But the union is not going to abandon us like some people do. Some people say they are with us, but they aren't. Some organizations don't mean what they say. But the union, they are with us, they are with us one hundred percent and they are going to stay with us. They have made that clear. We are in this for the long term. They know it and they are behind us, the organization is behind us one hundred percent. If people don't want to lend a hand, we have the support to go on. No one is going to defeat us."

Guedeson began to balance the cross on the tip of his nose as he continued to stare at the ceiling. The couple who ran the store looked from face to face, apparently trying to read what was going on, but they also did not respond to the man's entreaties except with faintly embarrassed smiles and an occasional mumbled word of sympathy. For perhaps twenty minutes he went on, ever more agitated and obviously frustrated by Guedeson's indifference. Eventually, the man left the store, even more upset than when he had come in. When he was gone, no one picked up the conversation where it had ended, and no one commented on it. We left the store with Guedeson after some small talk about moonshine liquor. Guedeson did not respond to our questions about what had gone on in the store. It was, at least for the moment, a forbidden topic.

Later in the day, revisiting the site of the burned-out encampment, we pushed on Guedeson to discuss the encounter in the store. "We take it he was one of the leaders of the encampment. Will he get any support from your settlement?"

Guedeson began to talk with uncharacteristic speed and force. "This guy knows our position. He knows where we stand. We debated all this with him for a long period of time. It was all very clear, very clear. Yes, sooner or later, we will give them some support, but he can't expect it that way, like he was saying."

We asked for clarification. Guedeson explained that the site of the burned-out encampment was the site of the original encampment that led to Onalício Barros, and many of the people who had been forced to flee the encampment were originally part of the MST encampment. However, the MST leadership in the original camp began to realize, Guedeson said, that they had bitten off more than they could chew and decided that it would not be possible to gain as much land as they had intended, nor defend the site on which they were camped. Prudence demanded that they retreat to a more defensible site. This decision led to a split in the encampment. Those who refused to accept the decision split from the MST and sought out support from one of the older rural unions, which had begun to be active in land occupations. According to Guedeson, when the breakaway group decided to join the union and defend the original encampment, the other settlers and the MST leadership made it clear that they were on their own.

"It was just bad tactical judgment on their part. They couldn't see that they were unable to stand where they were. We were not going to be pushed into exposing ourselves to something we couldn't defend. So they knew, and they knew it well, and they still know it perfectly well, that they have no right to call on us for support." After a pause, he added, "Oh, they'll get some support from us sooner or later, but we can't let them think they can just call on us to do what they knew we had refused to do." After a little more discussion, in which we expressed some understanding for the MST position, Guedeson added with a sly expression, "And you can see it, in the end, this is going to be good for us. They [the union-affiliated settlers who had been removed] can't defend it, and sooner or later we are going to have the strength to retake it for ourselves. This is a big mistake on their part."

This was an interesting episode in the long and complex relationship between the MST and the old rural unions, a relationship with complications at the local, regional, state and national levels. The old rural unions were part of the corporatist structure of labor unions established during the 1930s, under the dictator Getúlio Vargas, as discussed in chapter 1. The rural unions in Pará had begun to break out of the corporatist model and had become much more active in recent years.

One of the statewide leaders of the rural labor confederation in Pará was quite frank in praising the MST for having reenergized rural politics. When we interviewed him in the federation office in the state capital of Belém, he pointed out that while the MST had only fifteen active assentamentos in the state of Pará, the two main union federations had more than five hundred between them, and there were perhaps two hundred or more assentamentos that were unaffiliated with any major organization. When the MST began its work in Pará in 1992, there were already scores of land occupations going on. Union militancy in the countryside was strong and had deep roots in the past. Nonetheless, the union leader stressed, some of the occupations and settlements would not have existed—and none of them would have had much meaning—without the MST:

> It was the MST that pushed the agrarian reform issue at the national
> level. They made it an issue. . . . Then, even at the state level, it was
> the MST that took the lead and opened the issue up for the rest of
> us. Without the MST, the assentamentos we do have would be
> meaningless, they would not be defensible, and they would get
> nothing in support from the government. They [the MST] are the
> ones who have known all along, and still know, how to keep the
> matter alive.[33]

The vice-director of the federal agrarian reform agency for the state of Pará made much the same point to us. "Of course, it is the MST that has put dynamism, energy, into this issue. Without them, there would be no agrarian reform in the state of Pará. The number of assentamentos is not as important as the ability to keep an issue on the political agenda. Only the MST has been able to do that from the beginning. Only the MST continues to do it."[34]

From the perspective of those thrown out of the union-backed encampment adjoining the MST Assentamento Onalício Barros, all of this may have been difficult to understand or appreciate. They were dismayed by the challenge of being dispersed. For them, as for much of the press, the public and many politicians, the landless movement is a single thing, and organizational distinctions can be blurred or lost altogether. The frustrated leader of the encampment, pleading for help, certainly understood the distinctions at one level, but at another was expecting the distinctions to be forgotten in times of crisis. MST leaders and even base-level political organizers, such as Guedeson, are much more aware of the way the MST differs from other rural organizations. Disciplined decision making and trained leadership are key to this difference.

Guedeson's story gives some insight into the unusual clarity and discipline of the MST leadership. The selection and training of leaders is one of the hallmarks of MST strategy, and Guedeson's experience is one of many versions of how the movement identifies and trains leaders. He was eager to tell us his story.

"I grew up in São Luis do Maranhão [the port city and capital of the state of Maranhão, the end point of the railroad that brings minerals there from the Carajás project]. My parents were poor, but not that poor. That is, my father had a job, as a security guard, we had a house, we never went without food. But poor. My father and mother were religious people, not evangelicals or anything, but good people who wanted us to be good and who worried about us, they took care of us. I don't know why, but when I was about twelve or so, I began to be an alienated youth."

Taken aback by the fancy phrase, which we were not sure we had understood correctly, we asked, "What does that mean?"

"You know, an alienated youth, drinking alcohol, taking drugs, running around with bad elements, cutting school, committing small crimes, like trying to steal money from tourists on the street." He paused and shook his head, "I was so lucky, I never did anything really serious and never got caught, just so lucky that I didn't."

He continued, "My parents became very worried about me. They tried to discipline me, but really there was nothing they could do. I didn't pay attention to them. It just got worse. Then, my father decided something had to be done. His brother, my uncle, was out here in southern Pará, and he decided that he should get me out of the city and live with my uncle. We came out here together. When we got here, my uncle was encamped with the group that would become Assentamento Onalício Barros. My father and I had no idea what this was about. He had never heard of a land occupation, and he had never heard of the MST. He said, 'We are going to find out about this.' He stayed two days, and we had long conversations with people in the encampment and found out what it was about."

"At the end of two days, my father sat me down for a long conversation." Guedeson struck his forehead in recalling the impact of the conversation. "It was a beautiful conversation, really beautiful what my father did. He said, 'Look, son, you are now sixteen years old. You are a man. What happens to you now is in your hands, yours and God's. Only you can decide what you are going to do, what will become of you. I have to return to my job. I am going to leave you here with your uncle. Now, I don't know much about this landless thing, this movement, but from what I can understand it seems like a very beautiful thing. Something for the poor, really something for the poor to make a new start. But you will have to decide. You can stay here with your uncle or not. You can become part of this movement, or not. You are a man. This is in your hands. And God's.'

"Well, that is the main part of what he said. Really, it's hard to tell you all, it was a beautiful conversation, it lasted for about three hours, I think. I understood my father as I had never before understood him, and what he wanted for me. The next day he left to go back to São Luis.

"So, I stayed. In the encampment, well, life was really hard and scary. But I'm not sure why, I just took to it. It made sense to me. Soon, I was becoming a kind of leader among the young people. Then, the movement, they identified me and asked if I wanted to make a serious commitment to the movement. They had to explain what they meant. Anyway, I said, yes, and they arranged to send me to the school in Rio Grande do Sul where the MST trains militants. I was one of the few blacks at that time being trained for leadership."

What Guedeson did not say, was that with much of the MST's original leadership coming from Brazil's southern regions, where Afro-Brazilians are a small minority, and with forms of racism still very much alive throughout Brazil, the MST has had difficulty recruiting black leadership, though it is officially committed to doing so.

"You go there for two months. It is something. Well, really something. You would have to understand it, see it, to know. You get there and they tell you that you are going to have to put things together somehow. They don't tell you how. You are expecting to go to a school and just go to classes and live in the dormitories and that's it. But no, you have to work it all out from the start. They tell you that you are going to have to organize the food and the dormitories and figure out how to make things work. You have to discuss and decide what you need to know. This was so different. I didn't understand, none of us understood, and then we began to understand. It was like an encampment, how you had to organize everything and get people to cooperate. It wasn't just set up for you, a school, no, it was something that was there, yes, but they, you, we, had to create, had to organize, had to decide this and that. And it was just the most fantastic experience you can imagine.

"When I came back, I participated again with the encampment. We had our confrontations with the jagunços and the police. There were the murders. It was very hard, well, you know that, how hard it was, I already told you that. But it was another school, another learning place. You learn so much. The learning doesn't stop. Now I work for the MST and the assentamento; there is so much to do."

With a slightly self-deprecating laugh, but also with pride that emerged out of the laugh into the point he was making, he said, "Now, I am a farmer. Here [pointing to his plantings of manioc and vegetables] I am a farmer. I am here to stay. This is my life, such as you see it."

"THE LAND IS GOOD": LIFE IN ASSENTAMENTO
ONALÍCIO BARROS

Most of the inhabitants of the assentamento, like Guedeson, came from the state of Maranhão, as do most of the rural people in this area of the state of Pará. Some come from the poor states of the Northeast, such as Piauí, Pernambuco and Ceará. Unlike Guedeson, most of them come from rural areas. Maranhão is traditionally one of the poorest of the Brazilian states, but with its own particular kind of poverty and rural traditions. The backlands of Maranhão are settled largely with the descendants of slaves originally brought to Brazil to work plantations. The very unsuitability of much of Maranhão's land for the major plantation export crops and a lack of interest by most planters left niches that could be exploited for subsistence by poor folk. In some parts of Maranhão, escaped or freed slaves, indigenous people and poor whites were able to establish a degree of independence through their exploitation of the unique possibilities of the Maranhão landscape. Most notable of these is the babaçu palm, which yields a valuable fruit; poor people managed in the nineteenth and much of the twentieth century to gain a degree of control over babaçu production. This control in turn established the basis for a relatively independent rural culture of people, who were very poor in possessions but relatively secure and able to provide for their basic needs reliably. In the latter half of the twentieth century, the combination of population growth and the increasing ability of entrepreneurs, many of them outsiders, to wrest control of babaçu production and marketing led to a deepening crisis of rural life in Maranhão. The crisis fed emigration to Pará and other Amazonian states. Conflict over land has a long tradition within rural Maranhão itself, and in recent years it has become particularly intense.[35]

Rural Maranhenses are known as independent-minded, tough and combative. Although relatively little systematic study has been done of their methods, it is also clear that many Maranhenses are savvy farmers, who know a good deal about the agro-ecology of land and forests. In Assentamento Onalício Barros, there were real distinctions between what some knew about farming in this particular environment and what others knew. While everyone we spoke to agreed that it is not difficult to feed a family from the plots they have acquired through land reform, some are clearly more knowledgeable, able and industrious than others.

Friends of Guedeson, Robinson and his wife, make a good example of successful producers. Robinson is a young Afro-Brazilian man, tall, handsome and powerfully built. His wife is short and small, but never stops working at some task or other and successfully involves the young children in cheerfully helping her. At our visit, the living room of their house was piled high with sixty-kilo sacks of rice, representing about half of the previous year's harvest. They exchanged or sold some of the rice they grew. They also fished regularly and successfully. The plot around their house was planted with a variety of fruit-producing vines and trees, some of them domesticated from the surrounding forest. Also in the yard was an impressive garden yielding tomatoes, *xuxu* (known in the US by its Mexican name, chayote) and other vegetables. Some of the plantings had been trained into a cooling arbor that made the yard an attractive retreat from the sun. Robinson and his wife seldom seemed to sit still, always engaged in some task, even while their neighbors took extended afternoon naps.

Robinson's family preferred to live in the agrovila, the cluster of houses and buildings laid out along the two streets where most people had their primary residence. Some families had built crude shelters they could use while tending their crops. Some seldom lived in the agrovila, preferring to spend their time in houses they had constructed on their agricultural land.

For example, one couple we met preferred to live most of the time in the simple thatched house they had constructed on their plot of land rather than in the settlement. The husband of the pair, an Afro-Maranhense like Robinson, is considerably older than his wife. He is a small, grizzled fellow with a crippling limp from a sawmill accident. We required frequent help from Guedeson to understand his strong rural accent, but his difficulty in getting around had not kept him from having a thriving farm. The family lot was chock-full of beans and vegetable crops that were interplanted, or mixed in the same field, a practice used by many organic and agro-ecological farmers around the world in order to control pests and improve crop nutrition. Many of the plant varieties were unfamiliar to us and to Guedeson, but we were assured they were good to eat.

The couple were engaged in shelling beans when we visited them the first time; there were several different types of beans, none of which were familiar to us. Many other family plots were fallow at this time of the year, but here production was year-round and prolific. Our guide was familiar with most of the wild plants we asked about and was prepared to explain why he had left them in his plot, even though they did not yield food. One was said to be "good for the soil." Another was prized because "the birds like them." At one point, Guedeson referred to the man as "my teacher," and it was obvious that this elderly Maranhense was operating at a level of knowledge and understanding of the environment and its possibilities that most in the settlement probably did not possess.

In spite of the clear differences in farming practices among families, few people in the settlement were concerned about shortages of food. One morning, we saw a farmer pull out an enormous manioc whose circle of tubers was more than six feet in diameter, with the larger tubers six inches or so thick. Holding up the tubers for admiration, he declared, "They say this land is no good! But look here! The land is good!" Everyone was eating a variety of fruits, vegetables, beans and some meat to complement the starchy manioc, native to the Amazon, that is the traditional staple. We saw no obvious signs of malnutrition among adults or children, with the exception of elderly people, whose small stature and delicate frames may have indicated a lifetime of occasional or frequent deprivation. Nor were people concerned about housing—they were content with the simple houses they had been able to construct with the help of government credit, and they thought it was easy enough to expand the house if necessary, using materials readily available to them.

Concern instead focused on other matters. Almost everyone worried about the need for electricity, a health clinic, bus transportation to town and a school. Utility poles and lines had been erected in the settlement, but connection to supply lines only a few kilometers away remained a matter of broken promises. The region as a whole was awash in hydroelectric power from large dams constructed to provide power to the Carajás mines and processing facilities. Getting even a tiny fraction of that power to land reform settlements, however, has proved an iffy proposition.

Settlers in Onalício Barros realize that the few hundred people in their settlement probably cannot justify a fully supplied clinic or a doctor on site. They do think, however, that it would be appropriate to have a basic clinic and a nurse or, as an absolute minimum, a social worker trained in first aid and able to judge when people should be taken to a hospital in Parauapebas. They have repeatedly been promised some such accommodation by INCRA and by the município, but at the time of our visit it had not materialized.

The município had been providing three-times-a-day bus service, but during our visit it suspended this service, claiming budget shortages. Within a day of suspension, the service was restored, but with the warning that it might be suspended again at any time. The bus itself takes nearly an hour to get to town—walking is not a realistic option and there are no car owners in the settlement.

The settlers desperately wanted a school, especially for the smaller children. During our visit, the children were taking the bus to another school, but frequent interruption of the bus service, whether for budget reasons or because of torrential rains, made it difficult for the children to keep up or maintain their interest in schools. Again, the settlers understood that the agrarian reform agency had promised to resolve this problem but had failed to do so.

The settlers were also much disgruntled about the inability of the federal agrarian reform agency, INCRA, to come through on its promises for production credit. In the last season, for example, the credits that had been programmed by the government came in more than three months late. Farmers all over the world rely on public or private production credit to pay the costs of planting and cultivating a crop, depending on the harvest to pay off the loan. In less-developed countries, in particular, these credits are often available to most farmers only through government rural credit programs. INCRA's late payments of the production credits have been a continuing problem throughout Brazil. If credits don't come on time, then little can be planted, and there is not much opportunity to earn any money. In Onalício Barros, many had suffered severely from the delays and were now so disillusioned that they felt they could no longer rely on credits, whether they were promised or not. This year, it did not appear that any credit would even be promised.

Some in the settlement believe that the failure to come through with promises regarding such matters as health, education, transportation, utilities and credit is a deliberate attempt to sabotage the settlement and agrarian reform in general. One man in particular to whom we spoke was deeply convinced of this.

Although many agrarian reform houses are often built of ceramic brick, they are also frequently built from traditional, locally available materials like these houses in Assenta-mento Onalício Barros, one made of planks, the other of thatch.

We frequently spent the evenings in Onalício Barros in the well-constructed plank house of Wilson, one of the settlement's elected leaders and a friend of Guedeson's. Most people know Wilson by his nickname, Pitibu, or Piti, pronounced in Portuguese like "peachie" in English. A green-eyed caboclo from the poor backlands of Pernambuco, Piti came to the Amazon to prospect for gold as an independent garimpeiro. In addition to being a leader of the settlement, Piti is the poet and troubadour of the community. He is also a fine cook. In his house, we ate the tastiest *feijoada*—a kind of bean stew that is often considered the Brazilian national dish—that we had tasted anywhere. After eating, Piti would expertly play the guitar, sing and recite poetry. He had learned some of the songs and poetry from tapes or publications distributed by the national MST; others he had learned at regional or statewide meetings. Some of the songs he liked to perform are famous throughout Brazil, many of them from the days of the strongly politicized popular song movement, Musica Popular Brasileira (MPB), which began in the early 1960s, when poverty, landlessness and agrarian reform became major themes elaborated by popular singers on the radio every day. In our opinion, some of the most subtle, poetic and beautiful songs he sang Piti had composed himself.

Piti's songs—and his long political and philosophical discussions—often focused on the issue of commitment. When we asked what he thought of the future of the settlement, he replied forcefully.

"I can't really say very much about the future, but I can tell you one thing with absolute confidence. That is that most of the people you see here now will be gone."

We asked why he thought so.

"Because they are going to get sick of what goes on here. They won't stay."

"You mean because they won't be able to feed themselves?"

He answered a bit impatiently, "No, that's not the issue. We can eat from what we have here, that's not much of a problem for anybody. The problem is everything else. No schools, no health care, no services, everything promised that people want and aren't going to get. Here we sit tonight in the dark. These are just the normal services that government provides in other small towns as a matter of course. Why not here?"

"So what are the people going to do?"

"What they always do. They will try to sell their plots, though that's illegal. They will try to find work in town or in the mines or lumber mills. Lots of them are already working in the city, that's why you see so few people around here. [It had struck us that we did not seem to see as many people about as one would expect from the size of the settlement.] They will wander around. Some will even end up in new land occupations when they can't find work. Some have already been through this cycle before, just hoping for something better."

"Why won't the settlement work to eventually get the things people need?"

With increasing impatience, Piti said, "Because the government doesn't want us to succeed, don't you see that? The whole plan is to set us up for failure. Promise a lot, come up with things late or not at all, get people to abandon the settlements. That way the government succeeds in its own plan to say, 'Look, see, we tried agrarian reform and it didn't work. We did our best and people just abandoned the land. So, let's move on. Agrarian reform has proven a failure and we aren't going to try it again.' That is the plan, and everything they do is consistent with it."

We asked how many people he thought would still remain in the settlement five or ten years from now.

"It's hard to say, but I can tell you this. Of the sixty-eight families here now, after ten years I will be able to count on my fingers how many have stayed. Not more than that. But I can also tell you something else. I am going to be here, and I am not going to leave under any circumstances. Some of us who are the ones who will stay have already discussed this. We have analyzed the government's strategy very carefully, and we are clear that they are relying on the failure of these settlements. We have also thought about our response to this strategy, and we have formed our own strategy. What I can tell you is this: we are going to stay and there will be nothing, including guns, that will remove us. I will live here and die here, and I can promise you that."

"Why are you so determined to stay?"

"I don't know. Politically, it's necessary. But personally, as my own decision, that's a little hard to say. It's just that I've been through too much. Too much shit. I'm sick of it, and I'm going to make a stand, and there will be some others who are prepared to stick it out with me. The truth is, I like it here. I like the land; I like being out here in the countryside." He gestured toward the horizon. "I can't stand to go to town and all that shit. That way of living as a poor person in the city. What will happen in the end? Can't say. But I'm making a stand and I'm making it here."

## A TRIP TO THE MINES AT CARAJÁS

Before setting off to visit a larger, more established settlement, we were able to arrange a visit to the mines at Carajás, less than an hour's bus ride from Parauapebas. It is not easy to visit the mine without advance arrangements: security is tight and the government and mining company are anxious to protect the carefully nurtured international image they have promoted. We arranged our visit through the MST connection with the local PT, or Workers' Party, and the affiliated union of mine workers. The connection between the mine and the settlers in the region has always been significant and, as we were to see, is becoming more significant with the passage of time.[36]

The Grande Carajás project, which includes various mines, hydroelectric dams, a railroad to the coast and other facilities, was built and is still owned by the Companhia Vale do Rio Doce (CVRD). The CVRD was a company under majority government ownership until 1998 when it was privatized amid heated debate and protest. Initially, the CVRD was intended to be an instrument of government policy and a tool for making Brazil less dependent on the decisions of foreign corporations and governments. It was largely responsible for building the Brazilian iron and steel industry and, as a consequence, played a major role in setting the pace and character of the industrial development that had done so much to make Brazil the eighth-largest economy in the world. Grande Carajás was first and foremost intended to promote profitable economic enterprise and national economic development, but it was also conceived of as a response to domestic and foreign criticism of the transformation of the Amazon.

The mine itself was to involve little deforestation. The extraordinary richness of the mineral deposits made this easier. The story has it that the ore deposit was discovered because a helicopter doing geological mapping encountered mechanical trouble and needed a place to land.

In the midst of what was still a vast forest extending to the horizon in all directions, the pilot spotted a barren ridgetop, on which he was able to land. Among some desertlike scrub, a geologist picked up a stone and realized that it was very heavy and composed mostly of iron. The soil was too mineralized to support anything but light scrub vegetation. The ore deposit proved to average nearly 75 percent iron, an exceptionally rich find.

The mine itself was elaborately planned for low impact. Small operations that might have attempted to exploit marginal deposits further into the forest were forbidden by the CVRD. The mine would get its energy from hydroelectric dams to be built in the region. The iron would be exported on the railroad to be built from the mine to São Luis do Maranhão, and settlement along the rail line would be forbidden. The mine would be an enclave in an area already devoid of forest, and its operations would be strictly designed to minimize forest disturbance. Furthermore, the company would rigorously protect a large reserve of forest around the project from any deforestation; the mine was promoted as nothing less than a nature reserve.

Workers would be housed in an attractive model town the company would build near the mine. They would be offered job security and a package of schools, clubs, swimming pools and health clinics. All "very First World," as Brazilians often say with varying levels of knowing irony. The workers would have little incentive to leave the mine to carve out farms in the forest.

Strictly speaking, much of this scheme was carried out as planned. However, some elements of the mine's operation were more damaging than the company admitted. The smelting of the iron ore required huge amounts of charcoal that was produced outside the Carajás reserve, but in the adjoining region; as mentioned earlier, this has accounted for a large portion of the deforestation in the region. The brutal, smoky work of making charcoal from felled trees was performed by poor folk, many of them children. The charcoal makers remain today among the most infamously exploited and shortest-lived workers in Brazil. The dams built to provide energy were poorly planned in a number of respects, causing significant damage to local rivers: the companies failed to remove trees and other vegetation before flooding them with the water of the reservoirs. The result was that the reservoirs became a rich, organic brew, producing toxic substances that killed fish, endangered local villagers and rapidly corroded the hydroelectric turbines. The attempt to prohibit settlement along the rail line to Maranhão proved largely impossible to enforce, and the line became another widening slash of forest clearing.

For a time, life in the model worker town looked like paradise to Brazilian workers and still does to some. The houses are spacious, cheerful and well-built, and the services promised were delivered. However, with the privatization of the mine, the initial, privileged cohort of workers has been supplemented by and partially replaced with temporary workers, who lived in Parauapebas and other nearby towns and enjoy none of the benefits of the model town. Visitors who are flown into the Carajás airport see the town. They are likely to miss or fail to understand the significance of the long line of dreary olive-drab buses that we saw taking exhausted, raggedly clothed and ill-paid workers between the mine and humble homes outside Carajás. The ready availability of these workers is dragging down the wage concessions that the older workers had hoped to win from the company. According to the miners' union officials, workers in the model town who complain too much about the situation are fired; on dismissal they must immediately leave their homes in the model town. A company truck and crew arrives to move them out.

When we visited the mine, the forest reserve surrounding it appeared to be in excellent condition; Guedeson treated his first view of it in my company with the excitement and awe of someone from New York City visiting Yellowstone, although he can see the reserve from his home in Assentamento Onalício Barros a few miles away. He is usually excluded from entering the reserve. A decently kept zoo displays the spectacular local animals, including the huge harpy eagle and the large Amazon wildcat, the onça. From the bus into Parauapebas, we were lucky enough to observe some of the more impressive birds and smaller animals in the wild, some of which Guedeson had never heard of, much less seen.

The mine complex itself is enormous beyond belief. At the time of our visit in 2001, CVRD was about to open the world's largest copper mine nearby. One of the world's largest manganese mines was already in operation as part of the complex. We visited a newly opened area

dedicated exclusively to mining iron for export to China. Trucks carrying twenty-seven-ton loads left the mine for the smelter at the rate of
about one per minute, stirring up great clouds of iron-red dust. The
company was working on a contract to ship iron to China in the same
ships that would bring Chinese coal to São Luis do Maranhão for ship-
ment to the mine, an arrangement that might succeed in saving some
forest from destruction.

The relationship between the Carajás project and agricultural settlements in its shadow is complex and changing. What is clear, however,
is that present trends will mean more and more settlers will be seeking
jobs in the mine as it expands, and more and more mine workers who
are periodically laid off will be looking for land. The newer cohort of
workers are given little job security by the privatized CVRD. It will be
difficult to stabilize the situation on the land without stabilizing the situation of the mine workers. Will the government and company want
to do this, or will they welcome the existence of a floating reserve army
of workers in the region chewing on the forest edge when not employed
in the mine? Present developments are more consistent with the second hypothesis.

A LARGER, OLDER SETTLEMENT: PALMARES II

The small settlement of Onalício Barros seemed to us far more precarious than other, better established and larger settlements in the region.
We took a bus from Parauapebas to Palmares II, an MST assentamento
of about six thousand people who by 2001 had been in official possession of the land for six years, after several years of encampment. Palmares I, a similar community a few kilometers from Palmares II, had
also been founded by the MST, but had switched its affiliation to one of
the rural unions.

The first sight we had of Palmares II was the top of a Ferris wheel.
We were surprised to find that a small traveling amusement park was
visiting the settlement for a couple of weeks. It was the first sign that
Palmares II was quite different from Assentamento Onalício Barros.

The ceramic brick houses of Palmares II are laid out on a standard
grid of wide dirt streets. On entering the town, one sees the white
stucco wall that surrounds the cooperative warehouse and the attractive, sprawling school building. The headquarters of the settlement's

production and marketing cooperative association are across the street in a small, tile-and-brick building with the flags of the association and the MST flying from above the door. The street is lined with small stores, cafes and bars. Although Palmares II, as we shall see, has its share of problems, few rural towns in the Northeast or Amazon regions of Brazil present a more orderly or prosperous-looking face to visitors.

We stayed with the production association's coordinator, who shares his house with a young woman companion. By coincidence, the house sits next to the office of the association. Glayason (not to be confused with Guedeson) is a slender man in his late twenties. He is shy with visitors and became talkative only after we had spent a few days with him.

Glayason, like the vast majority of the men in the settlement, was a garimpeiro, a gold prospector and miner, before joining the MST.[37] Also like most of the people in the community, he grew up in the peasant culture of rural Maranhão and was drawn to the Amazon by the news of gold strikes. Once he became comfortable with us, he told us his personal story.

"Like practically everybody else here, maybe 85 percent, I was a garimpeiro. From the age of twelve, when I came out here. It was an incredible life, hard to even imagine now. As soon as a strike was established, the woods would be full of men trying to get rich. Then, in those days [the late 1980s and early 1990s], it would soon all be under the control of a group, a gang, that would build its own private army. These private armies might have scores of men, heavily armed with modern automatic weapons. They took control of everything that touched on the miner's life. Bars, alcohol, drugs, provisions, prostitution. See, the big thing was to control alcohol and prostitution. You can imagine, here were young men hundreds of kilometers from home for months or years at a time with no women available to them except prostitutes. Working like crazy. Exhausted. A lot of violence. I never carried a gun, but almost everyone else did. Anything could happen. The work is horrible. Where I was, it was half in the water of the streams all day, moving tons of rock and gravel by hand, you dream you are going to drown, if not in water, then in gravel and sand." He explained that the miners worked to "get their bamboo," a section of large bamboo several inches in length, a fairly standard volume, which when filled with gold was considered enough to support a man in luxury for life. "You think about nothing but getting your bamboo and women."

Glayason continued in his quiet voice, "I saw many a man make his bamboo, but I never saw one leave the area with it. Goes to a bar, gets drunk in celebration, thinks of women, spends on prostitutes, pretty soon, he is out on the street again and you see him back in the morning moving rock. He's broke. The guys who control the prostitution, the booze—the gunmen—they've got it all. It's a well-worked-out system, perfected."

Glayason explained that this system began to weaken, partly as a result of lower gold prices and partly as a result of the Brazilian government's increasing concern about the social chaos and negative publicity for Brazil. Glayason did not mention that there was also an international campaign to stop this kind of mining because of its heavy use of arsenic, cyanide and other highly toxic materials that were killing the life of major and minor streams throughout large sections of the northeastern Amazon basin, and in some areas continue to do so. Whether this helped to motivate the Brazilian government in partially cleaning up the industry is difficult to say. The government is moving to open up the gold industry again in what appears to be a concerted attempt to bring more of the operations and profits under the direct control of large Brazilian and international mining firms. In any case, in the 1990s garimpeiros were finding themselves under increasing government prohibitions and receiving prices that didn't compensate the effort. Some goldfields were completely shut down by the government, and the Brazilian military and police for the most part broke up the private armies associated with gold mining.

The decline of the *garimpo* (gold mining) operations created a difficult social and political situation. Here were tens of thousands of men who had no place to turn. They had left home because there was little for them there—there would be even less for them on their return. The initial decades of Amazon colonization were fizzling out in disgrace, as potential settlers as well as the general public in Brazil began to recognize the deep and tragic deceptions involved in the previous patterns of colonization. The official colonization efforts were largely over. Many of the early colonists were engaged in bitter, often violent, struggles to retain or acquire land. At this time, the mega-projects like Grande Carajás that had absorbed large numbers of laborers in the construction of dams, highways, railroads and processing facilities were laying workers off, not hiring new ones. As we have seen, the privatization of the state-owned or para-state corporations, most notably the Companhia do Vale do Rio Doce, would certainly lead to both the dismissal of many workers and declining wages and worsening conditions for those newly contracted. What would happen to the former garimpeiros, not to mention the many other landless and unemployed?

Paradoxically, this "frontier" region, reliant on the exploitation of the soils, minerals and timber of the Amazon, was becoming more urbanized than the rest of Brazil. Cattle ranches and other rural enterprises failed to provide labor for the new immigrants, and huge dams, mines, smelters and mills caused older cities to grow and new ones to arise out of the forest. The restlessness of the poor would not necessarily be conveniently scattered across an unimaginably vast Amazon landscape; rather, it was increasingly and potentially explosively concentrated in the region's mushrooming cities and towns.

# Where the MST Stands in the Amazon, and Who Stands with It

The national MST began its work in Pará during this crisis. The MST cannot be blamed for or credited with creating the widespread conflicts over land in the Amazon, nor can it be blamed for the overwhelming forest destruction, in which it played no role at all. The movement arrived in the region in 1989 and only had a significant presence from the mid-1990s, after three decades of rapid deforestation and intense and violent conflict had already taken place. Not only is the movement a recent arrival in the Amazon, it carefully limits its organizing efforts to areas already beset by the problems of migration and deforestation.

If anything, the MST should be credited with beginning to provide some vision of an answer to the problems of the region. The MST did not argue for government policies that would open up new roads or frontiers to colonization. Instead, it maintained that much of the land already deforested provided little social or economic benefit because it was locked up in cattle ranches with extensive grazing, low productivity and employment of a small number of low-paid workers. Much of the land was completely unproductive, held by claimants for largely speculative purposes. Most of this land was held without legal title. (As mentioned in chapter 1, the Brazilian government has identified ninety-two million hectares of fraudulently held land, an area one-and-one-half times bigger than all of Central America, and most if it is in the Amazon.)

While some of this land, perhaps most of it, was unsuitable for agricultural production, a portion was potentially productive if proper credit and technical support were provided to smallholders for more intensive production. It was also absolutely essential, the MST argued, that these smallholders form their own independent organizations as the foundation for production and marketing cooperatives. These organizations would have to be politically mobilized to aggressively and insistently pressure government to provide supportive policies and resources. The organizations would have to be capable of forming and utilizing alliances with urban organizations at the local and national levels—without such alliances, the large landlords and corporations controlling ranching and extractive enterprises would always succeed in isolating and defeating smallholder interests in the countryside. Most critical of all, the creation of smallholder agriculture in the Amazon would have to be part of a national agrarian reform, for only a national reform would provide sufficient incentive for most Brazilian rural people to stay where they were in traditional agricultural regions rather than pursuing dreams of land or gold in the Amazon.

The coherence of this political vision, combined with the militancy and discipline of the national MST, makes sense to many both inside and outside the Amazon. It makes sense to many agrarian reform officials, who are long since weary of the traditional colonization approach they have been administering with disappointing results for decades. Many policy makers in the federal government are also attracted by the strategy suggested by the MST.

Many of the discouraged settlers, garimpeiros, miners and mill workers had to be willing to grasp hold of the MST strategy and put their lives on the line to make it succeed. It would not be easy to understand why or how they did so without realizing that the MST was building on a base of political organizing and consciousness that had been constructed over the decades. The work of the Catholic CPT and other church-based organizations was clearly very important in preparing the ground for the MST. The CPT had led and defended smallholders in their battles with land speculators, ranchers and corporations, even during the most repressive days of the dictatorship in the mid-1970s. They knew the territory and the players and were willing to share this knowledge with the MST. They had helped to build a base of experienced rural leaders developed through the largely church-based organizations. In both Onalício Barros and Palmares II, the offices of treasurer, secretary and other positions of trust and confidence were held by people in their fifties and sixties who described themselves as "long-time church activists," while the more active organizing roles of president and militant organizers were held mostly by younger people recruited and trained by the MST. This was expressive of what had occurred: a foundation of experience and trust in the church organizations allowed the construction of a more politically sophisticated, militant and disciplined organization on top of it.[38]

Beyond the individuals who had been seasoned in the struggles of church-based groups, the CPT, although separate from and sometimes critical of the MST, continues to offer support in many forms. It provides reasonably credible documentation on the nature and levels of rural violence and publicizes this information internationally. It provides a quiet but effective living network of individuals who do everything from organizing food deliveries to people in land occupations to providing temporary medical services to helping get people out of jail.

## THE RUBBER TAPPERS

The ground was prepared for the MST in the Amazon by secular organizations as well. The most important of these by far was and remains the Rubber Tappers' Union (O Conselho Nacional de Seringueiros, CNS), centered far from the state of Pará in the Amazonian state of Acre, but with affiliates in Pará. Its founder, Chico Mendes, had worked with the rubber tappers, rural unionists and national and international environmental organizations to put together an alternative vision for the use and settlement of the Amazon forest. Mendes had been educated in a socialist vision of society by Euclides Fernandes Tavora, a politician who had been prominent in the Vargas days until forced during Vargas's fascist period in the late 1930s to take refuge in the forest of the state of Acre. Mendes worked, as did thousands of others, gathering rubber and other products from wild trees in the Amazon forest.

Large-scale production of rubber on plantations had never proven successful in Brazil. Brazilian natural rubber production, as well as brazil nut production, were dependent on the ecological character of the standing forest that ensured natural pest control and, in the case of brazil nuts, pollination. Rubber tapping required workers to develop and follow trails in the forest connecting widely dispersed trees, gathering the sap and transforming it into large masses sold to intermediaries who worked the trade from boats along many thousands of miles of Amazon rivers and creeks.[39]

The difficult, dangerous and poorly paid work of the rubber tapper nonetheless provided a livelihood for tens of thousands of people for whom the likely alternatives were less promising. The difficulties of the rubber tapper's livelihood were mitigated by the opportunities of the ribeirinho life that most of them adopted: small agricultural plots, fishing, hunting, gathering of brazil nuts and other wild forest products, cultivation of small plantations of palm trees and craft manufacture using easily available local materials. This way of life had always been seen in Brazil as the epitome of isolation, poverty, ill health and social marginalization. The rubber tappers began to define it more positively in the 1980s, especially as they were increasingly deprived of their livelihood by the timber companies, cattle ranchers, officially sponsored colonists and spontaneous migrants, all of whom were devastating the forest along the course of newly built roads.

Government programs meant to control the amount, location and purposes of deforestation had utterly failed, even when programs of protection were designed in consultation with large international conservation organizations, including the World Wildlife Fund. In the midst of this crisis, Thomas Lovejoy, a renowned scientist and World Wildlife Fund official, confessed to us over an informal lunch in the late 1980s that he had been appalled by what happened, although he had himself been involved in crafting the Polonoroeste Project, in which, in his words, "everything was planned perfectly."

The massive Polonoroeste Project in the southern Amazon region was a social and environmental catastrophe that epitomized not only the headlong rapaciousness of forest devastation, but the complete bankruptcy of ideas of environmental protection put forward by the World Bank, the Brazilian government and conservation organizations involved in planning and financing forest "development." Tens of thousands of settlers, many of them fleeing the dispossession in southern states caused by by the rapid growth of wheat and soy syndicates, had flowed into the region. Few of them had been able to establish viable farms, and most were forced to keep cutting further into the forest, where they came into frequent conflict with indigenous people. The assumption that the Brazilian government had the ability and intention to enforce the plan to avoid these consequences was fatally flawed. Overwhelming social forces—the desperation of settlers and the impunity of ranch and timber firms that routinely violated the law—were storming into the region.[40]

Rubber tappers began to organize to oppose forest destruction. On at least forty-five occasions, they physically confronted timber company employees and ranchers over forest destruction. Increasingly, they more actively identified their own economic survival with the survival of the forest. They confronted poor migrants to the region, but went beyond confrontation to discuss the issue with them, in some cases convincing them that they too had little future in simply clearing the forest and planting crops before moving on. The migrants might have a more promising future, the tappers argued, by adapting a more diversified and complex livelihood that depended on leaving much of the forest undamaged. Sometimes rubber tappers also stood alongside indigenous people to block forest cutting.

Local and international environmental groups began to make common cause with the rubber tappers. The rubber tappers solved a major political problem for the environmental groups, who feared being driven into a corner where they were being portrayed as representing the interests of an effete international elite in opposition to the interests of poor people and nations in the process of development. A few environmental groups shared the analysis that the MST would also develop: that the primary reason for migration of poor people was monopolization of the best agricultural land outside the Amazon in the hands of the wealthy, but very few environmental groups had aggressively or successfully put this view forward in Brazil or internationally. However, many groups had been working for years on ways to define the high economic value, particularly to the poor, of the standing forest. The rubber tappers carried this argument a quantum leap forward. Here were poor people who had already demonstrated a way of life built on the resources of the forest, a way of life integrated with the larger national economy in a way that rapidly collapsing indigenous cultures were not. The rubber tappers had also been able to build solidarity with many of the indigenous groups and, for the first time, were able to present a picture of shared interests in forest preservation between indigenous and nonindigenous people.

The international environmental organizations, aided by rock stars like Sting and movie celebrities, publicized the plight and vision of the rubber tappers and highlighted their leader, Chico Mendes. Mendes had been repeatedly threatened with assassination; the UDR, the national organization of far-right-wing ranchers, made it clear that it would welcome Mendes's death. There developed a kind of international watch on Mendes's life, dramatizing as it did the fate of the Amazon forest. In spite of the glare of international publicity, in 1988 he was murdered in cold blood. His well-known murderers, members of a local ranching family with strong connections to the UDR, went free for an extended period of time before being convicted, escaping from prison, being recaptured and again escaping in an all-too-familiar burlesque of the justice system in rural Brazil. Mendes has assumed the character of a kind of secular martyred saint in many Brazilian circles, his face appearing on millions of T-shirts and even in national television advertisements by multinational corporations.

Environmentalists and rubber tappers used public opinion, galvanized as never before by Mendes's death, to pressure for government adoption of a scheme for Amazon forest protection based on "extractive reserves," vast areas legally designated and protected for rubber tapping and other extractive activities consistent with preserving most of the standing forest. The degree to which these reserves correspond to the desires of the rubber tappers, the degree to which they provide for reasonable livelihood for Amazonian poor people and the degree to which they are succeeding in reducing the rates of deforestation are matters for continuing heated debate.

What is clear, however, is that the struggle of the rubber tappers, along with that of indigenous people, educated the Brazilian and international public to Amazonian conditions, particularly to the cynically manipulated claims that the Amazon was being "developed" on behalf of the poor. The rubber tappers' union also provided a much-publicized model for aggressive organization and creative political action by the poor that was strongly influential throughout the Amazon and Brazil.

The MST and the rubber tappers' union maintain an official alliance and have often worked together successfully. They have had only relatively minor and local clashes, and in the long run will surely be seen as complementary movements. Both movements have been able to maintain an effective and mostly amicable alliance with movements of indigenous people, although clashes between indigenous people and organized settlers demanding land reform have occurred. These alliances have been extremely important in redefining the politics of the Amazon, removing the false dichotomy of "cowboys and Indians" that portrayed the primary conflict in the Amazon as poor frontiersmen in conflict with local and indigenous folk or that pictured poor migrants moving into an empty frontier. Instead, the conflict has been increasingly redefined as the struggle of locals and migrants against corporate and large-scale agricultural interests seeking to exploit the poor in order to capture Amazonian resources.

When the MST began to build a significant presence in the Amazon in the 1990s, this redefinition of the conflict was increasingly persuasive to all involved. The rural unions, which are relatively militant in Pará as compared to other regions, worked closely with the MST in the early years and still maintain mostly cordial relations with the movement. The older unions, the church-based organization, the indigenous rights movement, and the new rubber tappers' union had made it clear that poor people could organize successfully, and a network of supportive and experienced organizations and individuals was in place. The MST did not begin the struggle in the Amazon by any stretch of the imagination; rather, its contribution was to energize and organize it more effectively. Essential to this was the MST's success in placing the Amazon land conflicts in the context of a national battle for agrarian reform.

## THE GARIMPEIROS

The garimpeiros who settled Palmares II and other agrarian reform communities surely had no trouble understanding the meaning of systematic exploitation. They were accustomed to the most difficult conditions, and they were facing severe challenges in finding a livelihood as the mining fizzled out. The great majority of them had grown up doing farmwork and were familiar with crops, animals and soils. Some, though by no means all, may have hated salaried farm labor and sharecropping but idealized independent farming as the best way to live and vainly had hoped that gold mining would provide the money to buy land and the capital to make this possible. Certainly, they were tough people who were not easily intimidated.

What the MST brought to such people was a much more disciplined political organization aimed at land reform than had been operating in the region. The MST quickly worked out a regional version of its well tested strategies, tactics and alliances. The MST's kind of rigorous organization made the difference between the countless land battles that usually fizzled out into defeat or demoralization and the new ability to organize real communities enjoying legal possession of the land and a good chance of survival. Nothing could better symbolize this than the remarkable transformation of the garimpeiros of Palmares II, rough and highly individualistic gold prospectors, into farmers living in a well-organized and reasonably peaceful community. As we heard the tales of land occupation, encampment, violent confrontation with gunmen and local authorities and subsequent acquisition of the land and settlement into a community, the stories seemed more or less familiar from what we knew elsewhere. The levels of violent opposition, as epitomized by the massacre of nineteen settlers at El Dorado dos Carajás, were higher, but this was not surprising given the history of the region. A striking new question that arose was how the garimpeiros could tranform themselves into members of a cooperative community.

Raimundo Nonato dos Santos (among rural Maranhenses, the flowery name Raimundo Nonato, honoring a hero of the Maranhense rural poor, seemed to us more common than Jim Smith in the United States) gave us the most convincing account of how it happened. Raimundo Nonato is the treasurer and historian of the community. He is a man in his late fifties, tall, lean, physically tough, with a wonderfully warm, welcoming smile and the gentle manner of a saint. He grew up in rural Maranhão, but poverty and landlessness sent him to the Amazon, where he eventually ended up as a garimpeiro. Like Glayason, he had lived for a time under the control of a private army in the mining camps. Raimundo Nonato is also a devout Catholic and longtime participant in CEBs. He kept records of the formation and maintenance of Palmares II neatly organized in large plastic folders and was happy to go over them with us.

We asked, "Was it difficult for the garimpeiros to work together and settle down peacefully?"

Raimundo Nonato reacted by drawing himself up straight in his chair, smiling broadly and saying, "Yes, you have certainly put your finger on a problem."

"So what did you do to deal with this?"

Shaking his head a little, he replied, "What we needed was nothing less than"—and he said the next phrase with emphasis as though it were carefully chosen and much considered—"a complete revolution in social behavior." (We had heard the same phrase used by Glayason.)

"How was it possible to accomplish this?"

"You see, it was a very long, complicated process. Hard to explain."

"Was it a matter of establishing clear rules and penalties?"

"No, you see that would have to come later. No, with these men, you have to see that they would do what they liked. You couldn't control them that way, you couldn't teach them that way. They are fearless, they can leave, they don't fear punishment. You see, what you had to do was to get them to come to see that they needed to change in order to work together. Now, sometimes, they could see that because sometimes garimpeiros had to work together in teams in the mining work. Some understood something about this from that experience. But in general, well, it was a whole process of talking and building an understanding of what was needed. Why violent and individualistic behavior would destroy the effort. A lot of discussions, often far into the night. This, that, working it all through to the point that they develop their own understanding. So that they see it themselves. Punishments, no that isn't much good. Well, it is a kind of moral education, but very specific, very practical."

"Was there any outside help for this? Was it all something you did yourselves?"

"The MST helped. They had the organization, people who were good at it. But the church was a big help. The whole process that was worked out in the CEBs. That was very important. I had a lot of experience with that. Because, you see, people have to come to see these things for themselves, they have to understand it deeply, very deeply, for themselves."

"And this worked for Palmares II?"

He seemed a little surprised by the question. "Look around you. This is a community. A peaceful community. There is some crime, but not much. Here there are families, wives, children. There are young people. Living together, working together. Yes, as you can see, it works."

## Making a Life on Palmares II

Though it certainly had its problems, Palmares II did seem to be working. Everyone we spoke to, even those who were otherwise unhappy, agreed that producing enough food for the family was easy. We often joined families for meals with no prior notice. The families were eating an abundance of beans, rice, potatoes, vegetables and fruit. In most cases, families also ate a combination of meat, milk and cheese, sometimes far more than many Americans would consider healthy. On other occasions, meat was present only in very small quantities, providing flavor to bean dishes or vegetable stews, and cheese was offered sparingly, clearly being thought of as something of a luxury. Many families had a milk cow or two, some had small herds that were their main assets. The economic questions being thought about by community members individually and collectively centered not on subsistence but on cash earnings—families average about US$250 per month, nearly two times the legal minimum wage for a single wage earner, but less than the average wage of officially registered urban workers in Pará, who of course have to pay for their food, housing and other items that the farm families do not. As one man commented about the cash earnings, "It's just enough to buy all the little things you need—it's not enough to save."

Many families had televisions, inexpensive stereo sets with small collections of tapes or CDs and electric fans. Virtually all had refrigerators and propane stoves. Everyone had a collection of cheap plastic-and-wood furniture, and most houses were cheerfully decorated with houseplants and a colorful array of postcards, plastic flowers, bright calendars and, often, locally produced oil paintings of forest and lake scenes or religious images. Though these living conditions would be the envy of most of Brazil's poor, in Palmares II cash is scarce, which can become a serious problem when medical or other emergencies arise.

The price of medicines is a universal concern. Parasites and the mosquito-borne diseases malaria, yellow fever and dengue are nearly ubiquitous in the rural Amazon. Respiratory diseases, including tuberculosis, are also problems here, as in much of rural Brazil. As is common in small towns in the rural Amazon, local people and MST leaders said that approximately half of the population of Palmares II had contracted malaria at some time in their lives. Some live with it as a recurring problem, and some have more than one form. We found that at the covered stop for the bus into town one of the most frequent topics of conversation was dealing with bouts of malaria; many people favored home remedies over purchased medicines, arguing that they were at least as effective against the symptoms of malaria, were more gentle on the body and, of course, were cheaper. Fortunately, everyone in the settlement has been vaccinated against yellow fever, but dengue fever, for which medical science has not been able to produce a vaccination, is a constant and very serious problem. Palmares has a *posto de saúde*, a health clinic, which formerly enjoyed the services of a medical doctor and was later staffed only by a nurse who headed the clinic once the doctor left. People are proud that the children of the community exhibit general good health, but parasites, malaria, dengue and the economic costs of medicine are all serious issues.

However, the most serious economic problem is the lack of agricultural capital and credit, because that is the primary reason families cannot readily solve their other cash needs.[41] As in every other settlement we visited, in Palmares II the late delivery of government credit was a constant complaint. Late credit makes planting and raising crops very difficult at best, and, at worst, it makes any kind of sensible planning of production decisions nearly impossible. Government credit is a perennial story of "too little, too late." At the turn of the twenty-first century, the Brazilian government was slashing production credit to small-scale producers and to land reform communities, making it virtually unavailable. The government argued that this was in response to budget shortfalls and pressure from the International Monetary Fund and in conformance with free-trade agreements being negotiated through the Mercosul free trade area of southern South America and the World Trade Organization (WTO).

However, the rhetoric of free trade was directly contradicted by the many subsidies to large-scale agriculture that remained in place both in Brazil and among its trade partners. In 2002, for example, the US Congress passed a farm bill that gave immense subsidies to American farmers—with the overwhelming share going to the largest producers—completely violating WTO promises for a more level international playing field for farmers. The credit problem was so serious at the national level in Brazil that many knowledgeable observers pronounced Brazilian agrarian reform to be at a dead standstill and perhaps at the edge of disastrous generalized failure. Nonetheless, in Palmares II, as in thousands of land reform communities, people are finding ways to make do.

The farm plots we visited were strung out along a web of dirt roads that basically parallel the Carajás mining ore railroad that goes to São Luis do Maranhão. Visiting the plots, we crossed the rail line repeatedly, sometimes having to wait for the great, long trains of cars loaded with ore that pass about every hour. This rail line is notorious for opening the way for ranchers and settlers to clear great swaths, hundreds of miles long, through the forest. Considering that, it is obvious that Palmares II does not represent a new wave of forest clearance, and we were surprised by how much forest is left along the route or within a kilometer either side of it in the area of Palmares II.

Some farm families in Palmares II were receiving credit through commercial channels. For example, Raimundo Pereira Galvão farms seventy-five hectares of land in Palmares II. Here, he cultivates between fifteen and twenty varieties of tree and vine crops, depending on weather and market conditions, among them cashew, limes, lemons, passion fruit, cherries, plums, *dendê* (a palm from which a cooking oil is derived), acaí (a palm producing a flavoring for ice cream and other sweets), guava, mangoes, papayas, oranges, grapefruit and pepper. Many of these crops had been planted with the assistance of credit and technical advice from private marketing firms. These firms financed a fifty-horsepower pump to take irrigation water from a local stream (in spite of heavy rainfall, sandy soils and the trees' high evapotranspiration rates can lead to rapid drought damage to trees) and provided Raimundo with nursery transplant trees for many of his orchard crops.

The firms also give pest control advice. Raimundo considers it unfortunate that he depends on frequent sprayings to control the ants that attack most of his crops. (Ants make up as much as 20 percent of the total weight of all animal life in the Amazon forest.) The ant-control chemicals he uses, also used in the United States and around the world, are very toxic to humans and other animals. On the advice of the marketing company agronomists, he tries to control the toxicity by using a highly diluted spray (which may or may not be advisable as a means of minimizing overall toxicity, as the dilute spray may require more applications and may be encouraging pesticide resistance among the ants). Acutely aware of the dangers, he is one of the few of hundreds of farmers we have observed throughout Latin America applying pesticides who rigorously uses a proper face mask, rubber gloves and other precautions. He worries about harming his family with the sprays, but considers that he has no choice.

Raimundo also cultivates subsistence crops for the family, including sweet manioc, rice and beans. His plots are cut out of a secondary forest, and he regrets that he will have to take about half the twenty hectares of remaining forest area for planting, "because I don't have the resources to afford to leave it." His intention is to increase his already remarkable reliance on permanent plantings of trees, bushes and vines, rather than on annual crops, because he considers them more dependable under Amazonian conditions. Many of his orchards and annual crops are planted in mixtures, to take advantage of the nutrient maximization and pest control that interplanting promotes.

When we arrived, Raimundo was processing sweet manioc (*macaxeira*) with a homemade gasoline-powered mill, both for family consumption and sale, and his wife was cooking bread in a homemade clay oven. Raimundo interrupted his work to take us on a tour of the farm. A fifty-year-old man only a little over five feet tall, his ambling walk

Raimundo Pereira Galvão, an MST farmer on Palmares II, and his daughter. His main efforts are spent planting and caring for more than fifteen types of tree and bush crops, some of which he markets through commercial firms, which provide him with investment funds.

was nearly a jogging speed for us, and we had difficulty keeping up in the blistering sun and sweltering humidity, even though he was somewhat slowed in his pace because he pulled up and slashed at weeds with his machete as he walked. We commented on how hard he had to work to keep up this sizable and complex farm with very little machinery. He replied with a smile, "This doesn't tire me at all. I've been doing it since I was a little boy. It's every day of my life like this, there is nothing tiring about it."

Raimundo was also enormously proud of his eleven-year-old daughter, who accompanied us on the tour of the farm. She was going to school, making good grades, and "has never once received a reprimand of any kind at school." He has hopes that she will be able to continue her schooling and perhaps go to a university and study for a professional career. Father and daughter beamed at each other as they discussed her future. He made a point of the fact that he keeps her and his wife far from the fields when he is spraying pesticides.

A nearby farmer, known as Ceará because he comes from that north-eastern state, also is planting a variety of permanent tree, bush and vine crops. His crops are considerably less diverse than Raimundo's, and he does little interplanting. His production is supported by commercial firms that provide him with credit in return for exclusive marketing contracts. He has invested considerable money in heavy posts and wiring to support his *pimento de reino* (pepper) plantation and in machines for mowing and milk production. Ceará, an amiable man, turns severe and scornful when he introduces the theme of the waste of credit by many of his neighbors: "You have to invest! You don't just take the credit and spend it getting through the year. Invest! It's the future that counts, and that takes investment. Some of these people around here . . . well!"

The family's country house, though made of poles and straw with a dirt floor, is sparkling clean, as is everything in it. Everything, from calendars to magazine pictures to old vinyl phonograph records, has been hung from the walls to make for a bright and cheerful place. Like Raimundo and most of the other more successful farmers we visited, Ceará and, by his account, his family, prefer to spend most of their time in their improvised house in the countryside rather than in the more solid, government-financed houses in the town of Palmares II. "You waste too much time going back and forth every day, and, besides, we like it here—it's clean, healthy, beautiful. Here we are a real family."

Raimundo and Ceará are looking to the future of their investments to make their farms prosper and to open up new opportunities for their families. They are entrepreneurial, and they do not hesitate to take on contracts with outside financial interests to achieve their goals. They both attribute their opportunities to the success of the MST and the occupation of the land, but they are also counting on success as commercial farmers.

In contrast, some settlers are more content to build a life as subsistence producers. For example, Celino Cardozo da Silva lives with members of his large extended family, dividing his time between city and countryside. Celino is a white-haired fifty-seven-year-old man with burnished brown skin and a nearly constant gold-tooth smile. He credits his wife, Mariana, with having brought the family through many hard times, because "she has always been good at mixing it up in the market," while he confesses he has never been successful at any thing but farming itself, "the only thing I have ever known." Mariana was too shy to agree to talk to us when we met her in the house in town and, it appeared, perhaps too busy as well.

Celino is from Maranhão and has worked *na roça*, in agriculture, all his life. "I know nothing else." He says that before he joined the MST occupation leading to the expropriation of Palmares II, he had no land and "was just wandering around, trying this and that and really just lost in the world, not knowing what to do." He commented that "for me, a person with a little more advanced age, it [the MST] is a marvelous thing; before [the MST] it was always hard for us. I only know fieldwork, this movement gave me everything. . . . I thank God first, and then the MST." Like many at Palmares II, Celino had worked on ranches as a day laborer, but he had never been involved in gold prospecting or mining. He was grateful to be able to spend most of his time in the countryside, working alongside family members, including a number of children who said they were feeling a little bored on the farm because school was out for the summer.

The farm itself had none of the neat organization of Raimundo and Ceará's farms. There was an even greater variety of crops. Many were planted in areas of still-standing forest, and in places it was difficult to perceive what was forest and what were deliberate plantings. This is often the case with the plantings of indigenous or traditional agriculturalists in tropical forests. There were no straight lines, and moving from crop to crop required taking circuitous paths whose logic and very existence were far more apparent to Celino than to us.

When we arrived one day to visit the farm, a group of family members were all working at peeling and cutting up macaxeira. To make manioc flour, Celino's son-in-law put the pieces through a mill run by hand with a converted bicycle chain and gears. Celino stopped his work with the macaxeira to give us a tour. He pointed out the many kinds of fruit trees. He had planted two kinds of bananas in orderly rows. One variety was doing very well and another was clearly failing; Celino had concluded that the failing variety was not suitable for the area. Papaya,

Celino Cardoza da Silva and his family work together to cut up macaxeira on their plot; Celino's wife works in town marketing the family's products. Celino observes that "there is always a need, there is always hunger somewhere," and grows a wide variety of crops with a strong emphasis on subsistence and security.

*maracuja* and other fruit crops were doing very well. Some overripe papayas were rotting on the tree, as "we have too many to use and they are flooding the market." He showed us a new planting of cacao trees, and when we commented that the price of cacao was always volatile and had been very low for years, he responded, "That's all right. If there is a market, we will sell, if not, we will use some of it, and some of it will find its place."

We asked what he meant by "find its place."

"Well, food always finds it place. Remember those papaya I showed you that were rotting on the tree? My grandson likes to throw rocks at them and knock them down. I say to him, 'No, don't do that. Leave it alone. Something will eat it. Birds will need it. There is always a need, there is always hunger somewhere.' Same with the cacao. If it is the birds or animals that eat it, okay, fine, that's all part of having a farm, there is always a need somewhere."

Clearly, Celino is not interested in financial accounting. The informal balance sheet of the family's farm was hard to figure out. The several pigs, kept in a pen, were skinny, listless and apparently suffering badly from the heat. Some of the maize was in good shape, and some had been badly damaged by pests. How were the pigs and the corn to be balanced against the flourishing manioc, potatoes, maracuja, papayas, coconut palms, pineapples and citrus fruits? The family itself seemed strikingly well-fed and there seemed no worry whatsoever about the prospect of hunger. They found it highly amusing to watch our pleasure at such delights as drinking freshly prepared maracuja juice, which was incredibly delicious, and eating fresh pineapple ripened before picking; for them these pleasures were unremarkable. They were very clean and clearly health-conscious; for example, before preparing our maracuja, Celino's tall, eleven-year-old granddaughter washed her hands in the style of a conscientious surgeon, soaping, scrubbing and rinsing up beyond the elbow.

This appeared to be an agriculture of ample self-sufficiency. There were no credit or marketing contracts. There was little capital investment on the farm, except for transplant sets and buildings made by hand from available materials and equipment made from spare parts. Flexibility, diversity and a degree of coexistence with forest creatures were more prominent principles guiding the farm than profit or loss, although Celino's wife spent some of her time marketing produce. The farm supported a modern house in town with stereo, refrigerator and television. Even the farmhouse had an electric line that ran a refrigerator. Celino's farm, not so different from that of traditional ribeirinhos, seemed to be more characteristic of Palmares II than did the entrepreneurial model of Raimundo and Ceará.

All the farms we observed had several characteristics in common. All had a mix of subsistence and cash crops. All relied on a diversity of crops. All were emphasizing and consciously moving toward a maximum of permanent plantings that protected soils from erosion and exhaustion—trees, bushes and vines—rather than annuals. All still had forest on the property, though it was not clear how long it might last.

All used, to a greater or lesser degree, the interplanting of crops to minimize pest damage and maximize utilization of available nutrients and water. Although all were using some highly toxic pesticides, all were also making use of homemade composts, manure and some nonchemical pest control strategies. In general, then, all these farm families seemed to be at least partially carrying out the kind of agro-ecological vision that ecologists and ecologically minded agricultural scientists argue has a chance of making it possible to live permanently on the land in a tropical forest environment. The news of the MST's recent commitment to agro-ecology did not appear to have reached most of the people in Palmares II, whose agro-ecological practices were more grounded in observation and practice than in outside advice.

A relative of Celino, Trindade, had brought us by motorcycle to visit the farm. Trindade is a former garimpeiro who lives with two of his old garimpeiro workmates in town, one of whom visibly continues to suffer from a serious pesticide poisoning incident years before. They all told us how much happier they were in Palmares II, where they made a decent living from farming and didn't face the terrible dangers of collapsing excavations, violence and virulent disease that had plagued them in the minefields. Trindade's friends were delighted with their stereo and small collection of pop music CDs. Trindade, while good-natured and unassuming, is among the leaders in the community and thinks seriously about it. He seemed to be a little concerned about what we had made of Celino's farm and more generally about what he worried was our excessive focus on production issues. Walking back to the motorcycle, he said, "You do understand, don't you, that the land is just a beginning? It is not all about the land. It is about a whole transformation that we have to accomplish. The land is just a door we must walk through. Nothing more than a door."

Trindade and other residents of Palmares II are concerned about the long-term viability of both the individual farms and the community. They worry about all of the following: the prevalence of malaria and dengue, the lack of production credit, competition from larger producers, keeping younger people on the farms and in the community after they have been educated in the community's school, the financial viability of the marketing and credit cooperative and the condition of the roads. They also worry that if the price of gold were to rise significantly, some settlers might abandon the community for the garimpo and some might even dig up their own agricultural plots, as it was known that the sandy soils of the area contained an amount of gold that might be considered profitable to mine at the right price. Some settlers were already trying to sell the lots they had received. The leaders of the community were determined to do everything possible to stop this illegal practice, because it undermined the practical gains made by the community and, just as importantly, discredited the whole idea of agrarian reform in a way that many critics relished publicizing.

To catalog these and other concerns of people in Palmares II and other communities, however, does not in any way adequately express the quality of their dreams and what they believe is at stake. As Trindade said, the land is just a door, and the task is an entire transformation. Part of that transformation is captured in peoples' intense interest in education, formal and informal, for children and for adults.

As in every settlement we visited, people in Palmares II believed strongly that educating the children was not only vital to the community, but also an important end in itself; for many it is the most important goal of the movement. If the children receive a good education, then it is all worth it. If they do not, then everything else is shadowed in failure.

The national MST has followed a complex strategy with regard to the development of schools in the settlements. It has insisted that education is the proper role of government and that the movement should not have to assume the financial burden. It has relentlessly pressured national, state and municipal governments to provide financing for the schools and for teacher training. It has solicited the help of universities in developing training programs for teachers to serve in agrarian reform communities. It has also sought out like-minded university professors to teach and administer the teaching training—not such a difficult task in a country where the innovative educational ideas of Paulo Freire have been so influential on intellectuals of every sort. In addition, the MST has provided special training programs to supplement the university programs, and these have been strongly influential on the lives of the teachers and their students.

As a result of all of these efforts, MST communities tend to have markedly better schools than other comparable rural communities, not only by quantitative measures, but, more importantly, by qualitative ones. The MST also has a national high school in Veranópolis, Rio Grande do Sul, where future farmers and leaders of the MST can pursue various paths of study. They work at making craft items for sale and on building projects undertaken by the MST in order to support the high school and to build a national agrarian university near São Paulo.

Francisca Maria Ferreira Souza is a fourth-grade teacher in Palmares II. She is proud of the new school building and, most of all, proud of the powerful educational philosophy that guides the school. She comes from Maranhão and had not dreamed of being a teacher; as a young woman she had gone to Marabá looking for a job and ended up selling things on the street. A neighbor invited her to talk about getting land, and she eventually joined a land occupation in 1995. In Palmares II, she lives with her parents and three children because she is separated from her husband. She was chosen by her community for a three-and-a-half year teacher-training program. The last part of the course was given in Rio Grande do Sul, where she joined students from all over the country.

Francisca was greatly inspired by trading experiences with other teachers from agrarian reform settlements throughout Brazil. "The most important thing is the opportunity to trade experiences and live with people from all over the country. To get deeply into discussions about all those experiences. It was an incredible time; there is no way I could explain to you how powerful it is. How it changes you forever. It creates greater love for this movement because of the way our kind of education is different from others.

"The essential thing is this: we defend the idea of an education of opening up [abertura]. Traditional education is to educate employees. We think differently: it is to educate a person to be free and to fight for his rights and for a better society."

She explained that, in order to teach at the school, an applicant had to compete in a process run by the municipality according to statewide standards. Some of the MST applicants did not yet have sufficient qualifications. This made for a difficult situation, because the MST-trained teachers were not a majority in her school. Most of the teachers commuted in from Parauapebas. "They are trying to teach from the book, while we are trying to teach the students to think, to research, to analyze."

We were pleased to be speaking to Francisca, because it had proven a little difficult to interview women in MST communities in the state of Pará. As we suggested earlier, sexism is seen as a major problem within the movement, and each MST community is supposed to have a special working committee on "the gender question." Particularly in the Amazon, we saw only a handful of women in leadership positions, and this was the case in Palmares II. At the national level, 40 percent of the national directorate is made up of women who are elected from their states to serve there, but no one denies that sexism and "machismo" remain major problems in the movement, as in the larger society.

In January 2003, João Pedro Stédile said that gender equality was the area in which the movement had been most frustrated in making significant progress at the settlement level, as well as at the level of winning supportive government policies. He said that the MST would like to see all land titles and loans made out exclusively to the wife in married couples, because it was well known that wives were more stable and responsible and more likely to invest. None of these proposals had gone anywhere under the Cardoso government, but Stédile hoped the new Lula administration might adopt them.

We asked Francisca how she felt as a woman in the movement. She answered with head high, defiantly, "As a fighter (*lutadora*)!" Then she bowed her head toward the table as tears of frustration came to her eyes. When she recovered her composure, she said, "We don't have a problem with the organization; there are spaces opened for us. There are no spaces in the movement that are not open to women; the movement has opened these spaces to construct a better society." She pointed out that there are both a man and a woman on the MST flag, with the woman in front, in order to demonstrate that "we are all equal."

We asked, "And do you feel equal in the movement?"

More tears flowed. "We are trying. The human being is slow to change, but we are not satisfied to say this because it is also just an excuse—we have to change things."

Glayason, the coordinator of the production association, worries about how people cling to old patterns of behavior in other ways. Because we were staying in his house, we were able to observe for ourselves that people came to his door night and day, while he was eating and while he was trying to sleep, asking him to resolve problems for them. They often came dressed in their Sunday-best clothes, with the whole family and babes in arms, to try to move him to sympathy, just as they might have done with the overseer or owner of a ranch or plantation. We were surprised to be witnessing something that looked like classic paternalism and clientelism in an MST community. The most obvious difference was that it was clear that Glayason took no pleasure in building or maintaining this kind of relationship with people and, in fact, was actively trying to discourage it. We were struck by how badly this kind of constant special pleading was wearing Glayason down, and we asked him about it.

Glayason seemed grateful that we had noticed the problem and was eager to discuss it. "One of the most frustrating things is that people are usually coming for help with small problems that they could resolve for themselves, except for their lack of initiative." He talked about how the people's dependency on him or others in the organization fails to develop their sense of independence. The problem is well recognized at the national level, Glayason said, and there is a major attempt to develop new principles and methods of social work and agricultural extension. He said that it was the tendency toward recreating dependency relationships that led the leadership of Palmares II to change the title of the head of the production association from "president" to "coordinator," but he had to admit that it didn't seem to help much. Glayason said that one of the worst aspects of the problem was that it discouraged others from wanting to serve in leadership positions. Glayason said it was all "driving him crazy."

Other attitudes lived on in Palmares II that, like sexism and paternalistic dependency, had the potential to undermine it. There was an intense battle going on with regard to whether the community should maintain its affiliation with the MST. Some people argued that the 2 percent contribution from income that the MST asked for was not well spent on the community's behalf. They maintained that affiliation with one of the rural unions might serve the community better, although it seemed fairly obvious that Palmares I, which had made this very move from MST to union affiliation, was languishing because of its relative lack of political effectiveness in the municipality.

We also discovered that among those making this argument were a group of Protestant fundamentalists, who told us that they were quietly trying "to teach people what the Bible teaches us—that to go on the land of another without his permission is a sin" and that, therefore, the whole strategy of the MST is sinful. Evangelical and Pentecostal Christian sects have experienced rapid growth in Brazil in recent decades. They are especially successful in the Amazon. In most MST communities, the Protestant, Catholic and secular people work without notable conflict, and there are many *evangélicos* who are militant and effective leaders. Here in Palmares II, however, there is a clear emergence of critical political differences based on religious ideas. It is not clear how important these differences may prove to be in the long run.

## The Dialectic of Amazonian Development

Is it possible to establish stable communities in already developed regions of the Amazon? Will agrarian reform outside the region be capable of stemming the tide of migrants who move into the Amazon out of desperation? The answers to these questions will not only depend on the political and economic decisions of the elites. It will also depend on how successful Francisca is at educating her fourth graders in "how to be free and fight for [their] rights and a better society." It will depend on how successful Glayason and other community leaders prove to be in encouraging people to avoid the traps of paternalistic dependency. It will depend on whether the mix of commercial, entrepreneurial farming and subsistence farming that is developing can succeed in supporting the life of a community. It will depend on how well the people of these communities can adapt their survival strategies to the nature of the Amazon environment with its enormous challenges to crop production and human health.

The progressive deforestation of the Amazon is based on the moving wave of failed settlers, who believe they have no alternative but to cut more timber for the mills, mine more minerals for the companies and exploit yet another piece of ground before moving on. Corporations and ranch owners are well adapted to build their success on the foundation of this highly exploitable failure.

The fate of the forest and of Brazil's poor, as well as Brazilian society, will depend strongly on the intelligence and adaptability that Brazilians bring to the problem, and on their creativity not just in bringing victory to one side or another in terms of the present lineup of forces, but in shaping new possibilities and solutions.

There is little that will stand in the way of the wave of devastation except the success of those who are making their stand in place, both in the Amazon and outside of it. Their ability to make this stand will depend on the transformation of the larger society and of the people themselves. Again and again, the people of the MST have tried to make this point to us, fully aware of the shortcomings in themselves and in their communities. They did not want to be judged by those shortcomings alone, nor even by their present accomplishments, but by what Francisca saw as "the opening," what Trindade saw as "the door," what Glayason and Raimundo described as "the revolution in social behavior" and what Guedeson tried to explain to us out of a sense of frustration on a moonlit night in Assentamento Onalício Barros.

Guedeson said to us, "I'm still not sure you get it."

"Get what?"

"Get what is really important about this movement."

"What is it we don't understand?"

"Well," he replied, "it is what happens when you come into this movement. That's what it is. Take me for instance. Before, I hardly knew where I was, I was so ignorant. Now I have learned so much! My head is exploding with what I have learned and with all the things I want to know! I want to know everything there is to know, and I know I can't do it all in a lifetime. But I want to know it all! My head is just exploding with ideas and information.

"Take, as an example," he continued, "the dialectic. How could I, that little street criminal, have ever known about the dialectic without this movement? Now I know about the dialectic."

We replied rather stuffily, "Well, the dialectic is a concept you are bound to learn about in a movement of this sort."

"No, no, no, you still don't get it! It is not the dialectic itself—that was just an example. Look here, you just used the word *concept*. Concept! Concept! Now I know what a concept is when you use the word. Before I would have had no idea what you were talking about. Concept, now I know what a concept is, and I know that there are many, many concepts about many things. That's it. Do you see?"

Guedeson's point is critical. The mad confrontation between devastation and a futile attempt to simply "protect" the forest cannot have a happy result for people or the forest. It will take economic policy changes, creative politics, adaptive agricultural practice, community organization, cultural change and scientific understanding to adapt the needs of Brazilian society to a surviving, healthy forest. What Paulo Freire called *conscientização*, the awakening of consciousness, is surely the most important single thing in such an adaptive process. Guedeson has got that right.

But it is not just the consciousness of those in Palmares II and Onalício Barros that counts here, nor of all the MST members in Brazil. In recent decades, humanity has had its consciousness awakened to its legitimate interest in the destiny of Brazil's forests, important as they are to all of us. During all those decades, indigenous people, rubber tappers, Catholic lay and clerical activists and, more recently, the MST, have brought home a powerful message: the primary destroyers of the forest are not the poor, but those who exploit the poor, resorting to violence when they see fit in nearly complete legal impunity. This is an old problem in Brazil. It was the same process that felled and burned nearly all of Brazil's Atlantic coast rain forest over four and a half centuries. But the MST, along with its predecessors and allies, has shown that poor people can fight back against this process. The movement's members have made impressive progress against terribly powerful forces thrown against them and have built stable communities where it had seemed impossible to do so. They will need help from many quarters to build on those successes.

The man who owned the traveling amusement park with its Ferris wheel provided a worthwhile reflection on what Palmares II meant for Brazil. He is a powerfully built barrel-chested man with a surprisingly gentle manner. He had grown up in a very poor Afro-Brazilian family in Maranhão and told us how he felt he should leave home when, at the age of about eleven, he found he had grown too large to get into and out of the family's tiny house reliably without bumping his head or damaging the door frame. He was a talented storyteller and conversationalist, able to talk entertainingly on almost any subject. He was politically well informed about national and international events. Many of his stories had a subtle undercurrent of self-criticism of himself as a boss that was clearly meant as a kind of general social criticism.

He had, for example, thought carefully about the relative advantages of owning an amusement park and a circus: in a circus, for example, one absolutely had to feed the animals every day, but the people you hired to do the work in an amusement park, he said slyly and with self-mockery, "Well, you know they will go hungry if they have to."

We asked him what he thought of the MST. He began his reply by telling us how difficult municipal officials had made it for him to get the permit to bring his "park" to an MST settlement. "Usually it's sign the form, pay the fee, and it's already done. But no, you wouldn't believe the days of delay and trickery they pulled to try to keep me out of here."

Interesting, we agreed, but what did he think of the MST and agrarian reform?

"Look, what on God's Earth is wrong with these people having a chance at building a life, a community? I think about it this way. Forty years ago, everyone in Brazil but the rich and the generals knew that Brazil needed an agrarian reform. It was the only thing that would bring this country around to use its land rationally, economically. And the only way to reach the poor. No, we threw that chance away and went through years of dictatorship instead. What if Brazil had had its reform starting then? Where would these people be now? Where would Brazil be now? What kind of a country we would have been able to construct! Instead, we have all this crap, this violence, this waste. Now it is time. We shouldn't waste another forty years."

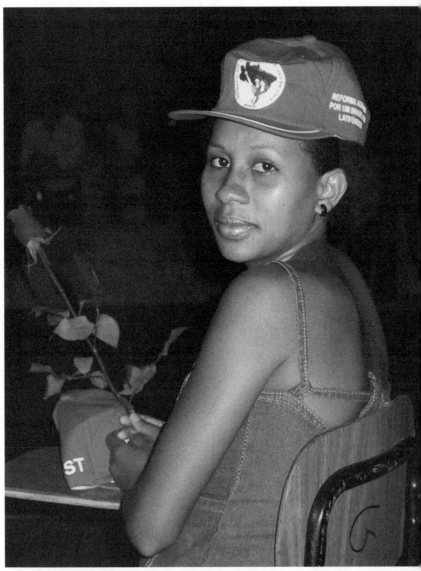

The MST has been successful at greatly improving education for the formerly landless settlers, successfully demanding that the government provide resources for education and setting up programs with public universities to train teachers. Here, a young teacher holds a rose she has received at the inauguration of a teacher training program at the Federal University of Pará in Belém.

## CHAPTER FOUR

# Assessing the MST

I N REACHING THIS CHAPTER, we have talked to hundreds of people about the MST and have observed hundreds of MST settlers' lives. We have journeyed a great deal in three of Brazil's major regions and have thought about the stories most important to each and about what the movement means in those regions, in Brazil and in the world. In this chapter, we try to address some of the most pressing questions about the MST, although these questions usually have no simple answers, and our perspectives are necessarily influenced by the particularity of what we have seen and by our positions as academics from the United States.

The list of questions that comes out of the first three chapters in this book is considerable. How are MST settlers doing, both in absolute economic terms and relative to how they fared before joining a settlement? How does the story of the MST compare to stories of agrarian reform in other nations? How is the movement shaping both Brazil's national development as a whole and its peoples' hopes that it will become a more prosperous and happier place? What might agrarian reform mean for the future of Brazil's lands and forests? What does the MST experience contribute to the ability of people to become more effective citizens in a democratic society? What of the relationship of the MST to other movements for social change in Brazil? How might the governments and peoples of other nations affect the future of the

MST and of agrarian reform in Brazil? Do people outside of Brazil have a role to play in the ongoing story of the MST?

## Is Life Better on the Settlements?

In talking to MST members from the southernmost state of Rio Grande do Sul to the northern state of Pará in the Amazon, it seemed clear to us that these people were better off than they had been before they joined the movement. However, many complications and uncertainties attend this assessment, and unresolved problems make it difficult to definitively evaluate the settlers' prospects for the future.

We saw that people who had been suffering extreme poverty before joining the MST were now eating better, living in decent houses for the first time in their lives and sleeping without the constant fear of crime and violence that had characterized life outside the settlement. Most had more ready access to health care. Most of the children were attending school, in schools that were often more lively and animated than the demoralized classrooms of the poor, with which we were all too familiar. Many adults had started down the difficult path of achieving literacy late in life or were systematically improving their knowledge and skills. Most people felt, usually for the first time, that they were positively involved in a community that worked to their benefit. Many were becoming active participants not only in shaping events in their own agrarian reform community, but also in their municipality and, in some cases, in their state, region and nation. Most people felt that they were participating in something that was good for themselves, their children and the land itself.

In sum, in every settlement we visited, people were enjoying a level of comfort, security, nutrition, education, health care and sense of community participation that is remarkable among the Brazilian rural poor. The people on the settlements who told us that they were as well off or better before the reform were usually those who had enjoyed favored positions—supervisors, accountants, foremen—on properties that had been expropriated.

A more typical response—and a fairly typical situation—was that of a middle-aged man in a settlement started by the MST in the cacao-growing area of southern Bahia. When we asked if life was better in the settlement, he said he was now much happier. Like many people in the area, he worked on cacao plantations at times and at other times exercised additional skills; in his case, he was a watch and small appliance repairman, but there was seldom enough such work to make a living. He seemed to think that we might not be impressed with the mud-and-stick houses and the experimental farming we saw in the community, so he phrased his view as a kind of argument, "But you would have to know what life is like in the slums of the little towns around here. Here I can go to bed when I want, early in the evening, and sleep soundly without worrying about what will happen while I am sleeping. Here, I eat good food, breathe clean air and drink clean water." He also noted that his children were in school and that they had a health clinic in the settlement staffed by a nurse. (A doctor had visited the clinic, but his services were terminated as the federal government met an IMF mandate to cut social spending.)

Since the late 1980s, when agrarian reform returned to the political agenda, there have been numerous attempts to go beyond impressionistic analyses and quantify the "success" or "failure" of reform. Some of these studies have been overwhelmingly pessimistic, and, for various reasons, these are the studies most often covered in the local and national press. In 1998, *Veja*, Brazil's rather conservative version of *Time* or *Newsweek*, ran a story titled "The Defects of the Settlements," summarizing the results of a 1998 study from the Food and Agricultural Organization of the United Nations (FAO).[1] The FAO study analyzed ten settlements it considered "successful" and ten that were considered "unsuccessful" in terms of average income generated per family in order to determine what led to positive income generation and what hindered it. The FAO study described the ten "unsuccessful" settlements as victims of poor soil quality, bad environmental conditions and poor access to local markets. One of the settlements was forty-two kilometers (about twenty-five miles) away from the nearest urban center, and the *Veja* journalists commented with a combination of sympathy and disbelief: "It's frightening that there are still people who live in such places."

According to the article, even the ten "successful" settlements in the study did not provide much cause for celebration, because even though people living in these settlements had more than enough to eat, they were still experiencing serious production difficulties. One of the main problems brought up in the FAO study was the lack of investment re-sources, like credit, but the *Veja* article suggested that the sem-terra were too inexperienced even to take advantage of the resources they had been given. José Rainha, one of the MST's most visible leaders in the state of São Paulo, was quoted as having said that running the set-tlement's flour mills was "more difficult than we thought it would be." Overall, the *Veja* article used the FAO report to emphasize the impossi-bility of agrarian reform—even an MST-led agrarian reform—as a pos-itive solution to poverty and inequality in the country. The article concluded that "from the purely economic point of view, agrarian re-form is a bad business, and turning a 'sem-terra' into a farmer is more expensive than it seems."

A different study that offered an equally pessimistic view of eco-nomic viability and agrarian reform was conducted by the Brazilian government in 1998, in an attempt to find out whether or not settlers around the country were likely to pay back their loans.[2] Antônio Már-cio Buainain and Hildo Meirelles de Souza Filho interviewed 1,035 set-tlers in nine different states and concluded that although government loans had contributed positively to production and quality of life on the settlements, the only state where the settlers seemed capable of re-paying their debts was the southern state of Santa Catarina. The settle-ments in the eight other states were evaluated as having little chance of repaying their loans in the time allotted.

Other studies, however, have been much more optimistic. One of the earliest and most comprehensive studies of agrarian reform in Brazil was undertaken by the FAO and published in 1992.[3] The study exam-ined living conditions on forty-four representative settlements in the diverse geographical regions of the country and concluded that the av-erage income was approximately 3.7 times the minimum salary in Brazil (see table 4.1). This was generally equal to or above the average income of households living in the areas surrounding the settlements.

Another comprehensive study was conducted in 1996 by a non-governmental organization called Vox Populi (Latin for "voice of the people").[4] The researchers from Vox Populi interviewed 720 settlers on 113 different settlements spread throughout the five regions of Brazil. Although the study is not well known, its findings were generally very positive. The total number of households that were found to have an

Table 4.1: AVERAGE INCOME ON THE SETTLEMENTS (1992)

| Region | Settlement Family Income (in minimum wages*) |
|--------|:---:|
| Brazil | 3.70 |
| North | 4.18 |
| Northeast | 2.33 |
| Center-West | 3.85 |
| Southeast | 4.13 |
| South | 5.62 |

*Where the minimum wage is equal to 1. Source: FAO (1992).

annual income of less than R$1,000 (approximately US$1,000 at that time) was only 18 percent, while the total number of households that were found to have an annual income over R$2,000 was 48 percent. One thing that this study emphasized was just how different these figures were by region. Only 21 percent of households in the Northeast boasted an annual income over R$3,000, as compared to 51 percent of households in the Southeast.

One of the few studies that has taken the settlers' "starting point" into consideration was the government study of the settlers' ability to repay their investment loans. While the overall conclusions of the study were negative, the numbers presented indicated that most of the settlers throughout the country were dramatically better off than they had been (see table 4.2; *patrimony* refers to household wealth, including assets and income).

After our work in Brazil, where we visited many settlements and spoke to a variety of people involved in agrarian reform (including MST settlers, MST leaders, government officials, large farmers and more), we do not agree with either the studies that are strongly pessimistic or the studies that are unqualifiedly optimistic. We have seen how complicated the situation is in rural Brazil, and any study that tries to simplify this situation is more than likely motivated by political concerns. As one scholar who has worked on agrarian issues for many years noted: "In the economic analyses, there is often an implicit political viewpoint, given that the analyses are undertaken in order to prove

Table 4.2: VARIATION IN HOUSEHOLD WEALTH ON AGRARIAN REFORM SETTLEMENTS

| State | Initial Household Patrimony (R$) | End Household Patrimony (R$) | Variation In Household Patrimony (%) |
|---|---|---|---|
| Amazonas | 373 | 1,010 | 171 |
| Rondônia | 77 | 415 | 443 |
| Bahia | 184 | 550 | 199 |
| Sergipe | 96 | 782 | 717 |
| Mato Grosso do Sul | 182 | 2,092 | 1,048 |
| São Paulo | 272 | 999 | 267 |
| Paraná | 291 | 962 | 231 |
| Santa Catarina | 95 | 1,320 | 348 |
| Rio Grande do Sul | 214 | 1,673 | 683 |

*Source: Buainain and de Souza Filho (1998).*

either the weakness or the success of a 'politics of agrarian reform settlements' and, by extension, the possibilities of a politics of agrarian reform."[5] The studies that we agree with most, then, are the ones that recognize how complicated the situation is, studies that tend to emphasize that the record of agrarian reform—and agrarian reform settlements—in Brazil is very much mixed.

First of all, collecting statistical information about agrarian reform is notoriously difficult. For example, the first-ever National Agrarian Reform Census, commissioned by INCRA and conducted in 1996, was supposed to provide a definitive statistical portrait of the 1,711 agrarian reform settlements in existence at that time throughout the country.[6] But most scholars in Brazil have viewed the census with extreme skepticism, because the research teams were given very little time to gather their information, and some had to battle difficult weather conditions while they collected the numbers. In this age of Internet connections and cellular phones, it continues to be very difficult to collect information from settlements in rural Brazil. One of the settlements we studied for our research was located a mere sixteen kilometers (9.6 miles) away from the center of town, but it took about an hour to drive to the first house on the settlement because the road was so full of rocks and holes that going over fifteen kilometers an hour made our car shake and rattle ominously. It would have taken a full day just to visit everyone on that one settlement—a good indication of the amount of time needed to travel to every settlement in the country.

But even if the statistical information that various academics, NGOs and government officials have gathered about the settlements were totally reliable, there would still be problems understanding exactly what the numbers are telling us. People have been arguing about the meanings behind statistics in the countryside since European scholars began analyzing the Russian agricultural censuses in the late 1800s and early 1900s. One scholar, Alexander Chayanov, was sent to Siberia and eventually executed in part because his interpretation of the statistics was so at odds with the official interpretation.[7]

An example of the limitations of statistical measurement is presented by the Placotnik family from chapter 1. They report a net cash income of US$500 per month, a respectable income by Brazilian standards. As mentioned previously, however, this figure does not reflect the facts that the family is able to produce virtually all of its own food, has a solid, comfortable house with no mortgage payment due, sends its children to a good, free school nearby, has access to health services, drinks potable water, burns firewood for cooking and heating that is available on the land itself and possesses an old car, a television and a working cell phone. Like farmers all over the world, Pacote is able to account many of his costs as business expenses, even those that, like his cell phone and the fishpond and forested area on his land, provide considerable personal satisfaction.

On one hand, the Placotniks' gross income stretches much further than would the average city family's, because so much of what they consume does not have to be paid for in cash. On the other hand, the family is exposed to the risks of markets, weather and pests, as are nearly all farmers, so their average net income may not reflect the troubles encountered in difficult years. It would be nothing short of amazing if the Placotniks did not experience years in which they were not able to make their loan payments, as do farmers all over the world, including large corporate farms. On balance, though, it is no surprise that Pacote says firmly, "Agrarian reform works."

Though the houses of MST settlers vary widely in style, size and construction, they are almost always far better than those the settlers lived in before. They are usually built with the help of government credits. This one is in Sarandí, in Rio Grande do Sul; see also the photos of plank and thatch houses in the Amazon, in chapter 3.

As we noted in chapter 1, even in the Placotniks' settlement the families exhibit substantial differences in living conditions. Few own any kind of car, as the Placotniks do. Although some on the settlement have more impressive houses than the Placotniks, many of the houses are smaller or not so well built. Some families report very little recent net cash income, though this is not so unusual in agricultural households, where varying conditions often mean that lean years are balanced against the fatter ones. However, one of the leaders of the settlement admitted after close questioning that "there were some tendencies toward the re-creation of class structures" among Sarandí settlers. He added that although these divisions still seemed modest, they were beginning to be the focus of considerable concern and attention on the part of the movement. In any case, despite these differences, it is clear that people on MST settlements in the prosperous South are nearly universally much better off than before the reform.

In the other parts of Brazil we visited, the evidence is more ambiguous. Net cash incomes were clearly lower than in the South, although hunger was still rarely a problem. On only one settlement—out of approximately twenty-five—did we hear anyone complain that there were sometimes food shortages. The durable goods owned by families were less numerous and less expensive than those owned by settlers in the South: they typically included a refrigerator and a television. Most settlers also had a radio, a cassette player or a CD player. The majority of settlers in the South and Amazon regions had one or more small electric or gas motors, used for such tasks as processing crops or powering wells, but this was much rarer in the Northeast. Everyone owns a variety of hand tools for agricultural tasks. In most of the settlements we visited, farmers had shared access to tractors and machinery for planting, cultivating and harvesting. Private cars were a great rarity among settlers, but many owned bicycles. Some owned motorcycles, horses or mules, and others were able to rent them when needed. Most reached their fields daily by walking or by some form of collective transport, either buses or flatbed trucks contracted by the community for the purpose.

Given that the evidence is so far from complete and short of definitive, generalizations about the economic success of agrarian reform or MST settlements in Brazil need to be treated cautiously. Certainly the evidence of our own observations and other people's work has revealed that some individuals have not succeeded and have chosen or felt forced to abandon their land and settlement. As we have seen, there are those who are deeply devoted to the MST and agrarian reform who worry that land reform beneficiaries will abandon the land in their frustration with the lack of credit and basic social services in some settlements. Many economic ventures and cooperative organizations in settlements across the nation have failed to live up to expectations or have failed altogether. In the areas dominated by the old plantation economies and culture, we have seen that some land reform beneficiaries are not altogether convinced that land is the solution to their problems, falling quickly into producing for the monocrop economy when prices are high, yearning for a salary and the occasional beneficence of a good patron.

We have also seen that some settlements are starved for capital, and some, such as Catalunha in the sertão of Pernambuco, may be burdened with capital equipment of which they cannot make good use. Again, as in Catalunha, some have received land that superficially looks valuable, but is plagued with problems that had led prior owners to invite expropriation for agrarian reform so that they could recover all or part of a bad investment. In southern Bahia, families are receiving land that formerly well-to-do landowners are readily giving up to expropriation for agrarian reform, because the regional agricultural economy is in collapse. Whether there are good economic alternatives available to the land reform beneficiaries in this situation is not yet clear, though very interesting agro-ecological experiments by settlers in cooperation with international conservation organizations are offering hope.[8]

An INCRA land reform official in Pará confirmed what many others had told us: many relatively wealthy people with extensive land claims are happy to sell them to the government for purposes of land reform both because their claim to title is dubious and because they are pessimistic about the land's economic prospects. When asked what a landowner in the state of Pará would have to do if he wished to sell his land for the purposes of agrarian reform, the INCRA official said, "Wait." He went on to explain that sooner or later, someone would claim any piece of land not vigorously guarded. The official believed that many claimants to large holdings were just waiting for the settlers to make a claim and for the government to then make an offer through expropriation proceedings. Again, the question is whether once settled on this land, people will be able to make good use of it. So far, our experience would say that the landless have had sufficient interest in improving their own lot and that they have been able to do better with the land than the large landowners who came before. Only time, further development of the agrarian reform process and a great deal more research will be able to answer this question definitively.

Security on the land is far more than an economic question. Battles for the land during occupations, as we have seen, are often ferocious, and they sometimes flare up even after the land is expropriated and settlers have received title. In other cases, some people have felt pushed around or threatened by MST leaders; some of these have abandoned their communities as a consequence. Most people we spoke to, however, strongly expressed a sense of security that grew out of being members in a militant movement that has been able to successfully stand up to the government.

Even in the initial struggles for land, MST settlements have apparently produced fewer violent deaths due to landowner or police repression than have settlements that show up spontaneously or that are led by other movements, probably because they tend to be better organized and better led. Nonetheless, inside and outside the MST, there have been hundreds of deaths and many more people injured or traumatized throughout the country as a result of the struggle over land.

It is evident that there are some serious problems on many agrarian reform settlements. That said, we do believe that the overall record from MST settlements throughout the country is positive. The problems on the settlements need to be viewed in relation to where the settlers were before they joined the MST and received land. From our observations, most people in the MST have transformed their lives in a very positive direction, but life remains complicated. A slender young man in the Amazon settlement of Palmares II spoke to us about a dilemma that many must feel. Deeply involved in the politics of his community and serving on the MST committee for the promotion of education, he was seeking out the coordinator of the settlement's production cooperative for advice and protection against some people who had threatened him over factional disputes in the community. He was visibly frightened, and when we asked him about this, he replied, "Yes, I am frightened. It is very tough and scary living in a settlement like this. It is much tougher and scarier living outside of the MST, but it can be scary inside, too. There is no real safety in either place. There is no safety anywhere in Brazil."

His words reminded us that the struggle for agrarian reform is indeed a constant and daunting one. Nothing about it is easy. The gains are hard won and can never be taken for granted. The losses are very often the logical consequences of hostility or lack of cooperation from those outside the agrarian reform movement. Many of the most important gains of agrarian reform, such as the experience of helping forge the future of one's community, are intangible. In our view, these gains will only be fully realized in the future, when those involved in or sympathetic with agrarian reform transform Brazilian society into one open to social change and rooted in equality.

For all of these reasons, nothing in the presently available statistics on agricultural production, health, nutrition, education and the survival of settlements can answer the most important questions about the potential of agrarian reform and the MST's role in it. The different interpretations of MST settlements—whether of success or failure—have a lot to do with the kinds of questions people ask. If we ask questions that look from the outside in, or from the top down, then we will probably see very little positive change on the ground. If one looks at the MST's formation from the outside, for example, the numbers seem insignificant next to the towering figures of rural poverty in the Brazilian countryside. And if one looks at the settlements from the top down, then the fields of carefully planted corn and beans look pitifully small next to those of the large-scale mechanized farmer down the road. The settlers seem to be at the mercy of implacable political and economic structures—whether they offer constraints or opportunities. But if we ask questions that start from the bottom and go up, or start from the inside and work their way out, then the numbers matter less and the difference the changes make in people's lives seems greater.

## "Agrarian Reform Light"
### Assessing the Government's Approach

Any evaluation of agrarian reform in Brazil also has to take into account the fact that the movement has made the progress it has with very little support from the state. In fact, the inconsistency of the government's positions, programs and pronouncements is perhaps the one thing that makes it most difficult to evaluate the progress of agrarian reform. For example, although apparently very generous, government expropriations and agricultural support funds seem intended more to staunch a social wound than to implement an enduring and successful agrarian reform.

The recent Cardoso administration (1995–2002) should receive some credit for promoting positive economic and social reforms in Brazil. While constantly quarreling with the MST and other citizens' groups, the administration usually, although not always, recognized the importance of maintaining a dialog with the MST. The administration also initiated some creative programs for positive change, such as the Comunidade Solidária, which was sponsored by the president's wife, Dr. Ruth Cardoso, an internationally respected anthropologist. Comunidade Solidária attempts to build partnerships between nongovernmental organizations and the government in order to increase the effectiveness of public assistance to the poor. In addition recent studies indicate that the administration significantly increased the government's ability to efficiently collect taxes on rural properties, for the first time in Brazilian history collecting an amount reasonably approaching what the law requires. If true, this is in itself a major step. If nothing else, Cardoso's administration, simply by staying in office through its two terms, renewed hope that elected regimes in the post-military period can endure without disastrous economic or political crises.

The raw facts remain, however, that MST leaders and settlers have been continually threatened by hostile landowners and that the government has offered no protection against what have even amounted to mass executions of landless squatters. Local, state and sometimes the national governments have tried frequently to repress the process of agrarian reform, often with direct violence or more indirectly, by allowing local elites to commit violent acts without adequate punishment.

It is not difficult to find people critical of the government's agrarian reform efforts. All one has to do is talk to officials in the government's own agrarian reform agencies. In 1992, the head of federal agrarian reform efforts in the state of Bahia told us straightforwardly, "The purpose of the agrarian reform agency [INCRA] is to keep agrarian reform from happening." He explained that the government's strategy was to allow just enough agrarian reform in major trouble spots to keep the movement from spreading or taking on regional or national significance. The government's agrarian reform programs were just a pressure relief valve to forestall genuine or generalized reform.

In 2001, the vice-director of INCRA for the state of Pará said, "What you are seeing here is not real agrarian reform. It is just what you might call 'agrarian reform light' (as in Pepsi Light)." As we noted earlier, he argued that only with a left-wing government in Brazil would it be possible to move toward real agrarian reform. He remarked that the present efforts were "merely cosmetic."

These views have certainly been confirmed by the actions of the federal government. A 1996 document on former president Fernando Cardoso's official web site, entitled "Agrarian Reform: Everyone's Responsibility,"[9] makes a forceful argument for the necessity of agrarian reform in Brazil. It lays out strategies and methods for achieving reform, many of which seem to be in line with the MST's goals. In spite of the rhetoric, the Cardoso government promised much but delivered little or, as we have noted in various examples in previous chapters, delivered too little too late. The document argues quite rightly that the mandate of agrarian reform cannot be that of a single governmental administration, but will have to be the job of an entire generation. But this does not explain why new expropriations and titling for agrarian reform came to a virtual standstill toward the end of Cardoso's presidency, while credit and other programs deemed necessary by the government itself to support agrarian reform were sharply cut back or eliminated. With such policies, agrarian reform may be defeated by the government in far less than a generation.

Those evaluating the current state of agrarian reform frequently assume that the Brazilian government has acted of its own volition to implement the programs necessary to carry it out. This is clearly not the case. What has happened instead is that a social movement has forced the first steps of an incomplete reform while the government has played a complicated and demoralizing game, crippling rather than fostering any real societal commitment to reform.

Many of the studies we cited earlier in this chapter point to the government and government agricultural policies as the main obstacles to economic success in the settlements. In general, economic policies in Brazil have favored industrial development over agricultural development. Within agriculture, they have favored export agriculture over domestic food production and large-scale producers over small. While raw agriculture crops now account for only 11 percent of all marketed goods and services produced in Brazil, agricultural products make up 37 percent of export earnings. These export earnings are important to a nation such as Brazil that needs to earn hard currencies to make payments on a heavy foreign debt load. The recent liberalization of the economy cheapened agricultural goods in the hopes that increased exports of key crops would provide what is referred to as a "green anchor" for the rest of the economy and for the stabilization of the currency. These policies benefited some large farmers who produce for the export market, but hurt those smaller producers who sold most of their goods on the domestic market. These smaller farmers include the settlers who have benefited from land reform.[10]

The focus on large-scale export agriculture accounts for an apparent paradox in the statistical picture of Brazilian land reform. While the government proudly announces that it has settled hundreds of thousands of families in its agrarian reform program, the overall distribution of land has become less rather than more equitable. That is because government policies favoring large producers have resulted in large farmers and corporations continuing to take over the land of small-holders throughout Brazil while also opening up new land to agriculture. Most of the new land opened up over the past twenty years is in the states of Goiás, Mato Grosso and Mato Grosso do Sul, where the fields displace not the Amazon forest, but a neighboring biologically rich and unique area called the *cerrado*, a kind of dry forest and savanna supporting hundreds of species found nowhere else. Expressive of what is happening is the fact that the state of Mato Grosso produced two thousand metric tons of soybeans in 1991, but by the year 2000 was growing around seventy thousand tons, almost all of it coming from large, mechanized farms of the sort Brazilian government policy favors. The soy is not destined to feed the hungry in Brazil, but to feed livestock for Europeans and Japanese—North Americans already produce a surplus of soy, competing with Brazilian producers. Other big corporate farms in the same frontier regions produce the world's largest supply of orange juice concentrate, again not primarily for Brazilians, but mostly for export to foreign markets.

In the countryside, Brazil is moving in two directions at once. While begrudgingly and very partially acceding to a cosmetic "agrarian reform light" in response to social movements, primarily the MST, the government puts the full weight of its trade policy, tax policy and structure of subsidies behind the most rapid possible development of highly mechanized, chemically dependent, large-scale corporate agriculture. In many areas, these new corporate farms also require the development of large new irrigation and transportation facilities built at government expense. While proclaiming its virtue in settling rural poor people in land reform communities, the government pursues policies whose overall effect makes it extraordinarily difficult for smallholders of all kinds to survive and easy for corporate investors to sink millions into expanding impersonally managed agricultural operations of the sort termed "factories in the field" in the western United States.

One way the government has justified this seemingly contradictory policy is by saying that agricultural policy is one thing, social policy another. From this perspective, agrarian reform is not about agriculture and the agricultural economy; it is a social policy to distribute benefits to the needy and as such it has little or nothing to do with the economic needs of the nation.[11] Agrarian reform is assumed to be neutral or negative in agricultural production terms. One of its main benefits is simply to keep people out of the cities, where they are often seen as an intractable social problem. In this way of thinking, it may be easier and safer to accommodate the poor and marginalized in the countryside where they do not require sewage and water systems and other urban infrastructure and where those who are dissatisfied will pose less of a political threat.

Seen as social policy, agrarian reform has been compared to other social initiatives of most Brazilian administrations in the 1980s and 1990s. These include the extension of mediocre pensions and some other social benefits to agricultural workers who were previously uncovered. However, these social programs still extend benefits only to workers who were officially "registered," a requirement that excludes many urban workers and an even higher percentage of those in the countryside. Certainly, good things have come out of the extension of pension benefits to a portion of rural people. Many rural women were made eligible for pensions for the first time. Studies have shown that these pensions have not only benefited individual women and families, but, because women are often good savers and ready entrepreneurs, they have sometimes joined together, combining portions of their old age pensions to help their families or community buy such essential items as trucks to take crops to market.

Another program, *bolsa escola* (school scholarship), provides around fifteen dollars a month to the families of students who stay in school. Bolsa escola, a school lunch program and other ideas were taken up in 2001 by the Cardoso administration after the opposition Workers' Party had proven the program's success in states and municipalities under its control. Some see these programs as joined with the very modest agrarian reform to improve the lives of the rural poor in significant ways. Surely, they add a small measure of justice to the lives of the rural poor and can be of real assistance as a complement to serious agrarian reform.

A variety of welfare payments without serious land reform, however, is no real solution. There are few who deny that, without continuing access to land and a level of support to small farmers at least equal to that enjoyed by corporate farmers, a simple pension-and-benefit economy in the countryside will fall far short of providing the foundations for healthy families and communities. People and communities must have viable livelihoods, not simply a source of inadequate income.

For the Brazilian government, agricultural policy at the beginning of the twenty-first century is about increasing exports. Brazil produces far more food than necessary to feed its population, though for tens of millions of Brazilians unequal income and lack of access to land mean that hunger remains a serious problem. The federal government, in conjunction with the FAO, estimates that approximately forty-four million people suffer from chronic hunger. Brazil's agricultural exports—coffee, sugar, poultry, cacao, orange juice concentrate and soy and corn destined for livestock in rich nations—do more to create than to satisfy hunger in Brazil. Those producing these exports are mostly wealthy farmers or large corporations paying marginal or starvation wages and monopolizing the best production resources, including land, water and government subsidies. Poor farmers are left with little chance to compete successfully. What we see is the mechanized, chemical-dependent, state supported modern form of the radical inequalities of the old plantation economy.[12]

This federal focus on increasing export earnings is quite similar to the policy perspective of those in charge of agriculture in the US government. They share the view with their Brazilian counterparts that the problem of agriculture is not about feeding the hungry, it is about profits and the national balance of trade. The potential for profitable agricultural expansion lies not in feeding the hungry but in better serving the markets of those with plenty of money to spend.

# Land Reform Around the World
## *The Legacies of US Policy and Influence*

It is at this juncture that the argument regarding agrarian reform in Brazil comes home to North America and Europe. We raise questions in this book that are as basic and troubling to North Americans as they are to Brazilians. Can a healthy society be built on the foundations of social policy that accepts or encourages consigning a large portion of the population to permanent social exclusion? In the countryside, is it acceptable or desirable to have our food produced by impersonal corporations with no particular loyalty to or interest in any particular piece of land or people except as they are, respectively, "production sites," "labor force" and "markets"? Is it reasonable to use as a model for the agricultural development of other countries the experience of the United States? The US likes to think of itself as the world's breadbasket and yet fails to adequately feed about 10 percent of its own population. Is it reasonable to emulate US agriculture, when it depends on the use of a fifth of all the world's pesticides, massive taxpayer subsidies to large growers, the application of fertilizers to the point of creating very serious water quality problems in the nation's major rivers and lakes, scandalously high rates of soil erosion and feedlots for cattle and pigs that create far more serious water pollution problems in many Midwestern states than the sewage from human populations?

With some justification, Brazilians frequently respond to criticisms of their own society and social policies by pointing out the powerful contradictions between the wealth of rich nations and the poverty and environmental damage that are routinely accepted as inevitable in those same nations, overflowing with material abundance. Are Brazilians doing nothing more nor less than following our lead? Are their leaders simply adhering to what is called "the Washington consensus" about what nations should be doing, responding to the US idea of what is right?[13]

Brazilian presidents operate under powerful pressures from abroad. The United States, for example, has influenced policy in Brazil through governmental agencies and institutions, including those that provided money, training and equipment to the Brazilian military and police as they suppressed agrarian reform and other social change movements during the entire period of the military dictatorship. More recently, US institutions, such as the Export-Import Bank, and multinational institutions largely allied with US purposes, such as the International Monetary Fund, have pressured the Brazilian government to minimize social expenditures and promote economic policies favorable to international investors.

In the summer of 2002, for example, when Lula, the Workers' Party's four-time candidate for president (and, this time, the winner) showed strongly in Brazilian polls, Wall Street firms downgraded Brazil's "risk rating," causing a rush of funds out of the country. US financiers and government officials, including the US secretary of the treasury, Paul O'Neill, made disparaging public comments on the state of the Brazilian economy and the Brazilian government. Financial soothsayers began to predict a severe economic crisis in Brazil, and, indeed, the

Brazilian currency began to lose value, and other economic indicators started to look ominous. The International Monetary Fund, which was playing hardball in negotiations with the neighboring Argentine government awash in economic catastrophe, implied that Brazil would face similarly difficult attitudes were it to adopt policies considered unorthodox by the IMF. Reassurances from all the presidential candidates that they would play by Washington's rules to at least some degree helped avert a severe crisis for the time being, though considerable damage to Brazil's economy was still done. Such confrontations are numerous in Brazilian history. So, some Brazilians who might consider economic or political alternatives feel that they have no choice but to cooperate with the US lead—which means proceeding without the potential distractions posed by agrarian reform.

In the United States, many people assume that large-scale industrialized agriculture is not only a good thing but an absolutely inevitable consequence of inalterable economic forces. This assumption ignores much of the reality of modern agriculture, both in the US and abroad. While it is true that in the United States there has been a steady march toward large-scale industrialized agriculture, this fact alone does not prove that the trend is desirable or inevitable. Large farms have received an overwhelming share of government resources even in countries where agrarian reform played a key role in strengthening the agricultural sector. Many economically successful nations have undergone relatively recent land reforms. Among these are Italy, Germany, Japan, South Korea and Taiwan. In these countries, the United States government insisted on or strongly supported land reform as part of post–World War II reconstruction.[14] The US did so for several reasons. First, US policy makers believed in the dramatic success of their country's own small farm culture, which had successfully turned the nation into the world's breadbasket. The degree to which that small farm culture was even then beginning to yield to large-scale industrial agriculture was not then appreciated, nor were the implications of the change. The triumphant US also believed that fascism and militarism in Japan and Germany were partly the consequence of the concentration of land and political power in the hands of reactionary large landholders. At the time, it was a belief widely held by those who had studied the question that smallholder agriculture, as Thomas Jefferson had argued, was a basic foundation for democracy and that cultures characterized by large landholdings encouraged authoritarian and militaristic government. In addition, the US feared that angry peasant movements calling for land reform might cause the triumph of communist movements and the fall of friendly governments, as was happening in China.

The depth and thoroughness of land reform varied in the nations that pursued it under US sponsorship or encouragement, but economic historians generally agree that the land reforms were successful in underwriting the amazingly rapid economic growth and industrialization of these nations, all under regimes that remained close and essential allies of the United States.[15] In most of these nations, there has been some tendency toward the reconcentration of land, but all of them maintain lively and economically successful small farm economies. Compared to the degree of concentration of land in the United States and Brazil, these countries are still strikingly small-farm cultures.

In some of the most successful reform movements, left-wing social movements played a major part. For example, it is interesting to see how impassioned well-to-do North Americans are about rural life in Italy, particularly in regions like Tuscany and Emilia-Romagna, where communist and socialist farmers' movements forced through land reform programs in the post-WWII era, all with the assent of the US, which was otherwise propping up conservative Italian governments. France, an agricultural powerhouse, maintains a large and vital small farm sector that until recently it fought vigorously to protect against destruction by international agribusiness corporations pushing liberalized trade. Americans, glorying in the food and wine grown mostly by small farmers in Europe, seldom seem to have any idea why European markets are so overflowing with exceptionally high-quality food, a large share of it—and generally the best of it—produced locally. Certainly, few of them realize that in Tuscany, for example, the bounty has to do with successful movements of militant tenant farmers in Italy's so-called "Red Zones," so named because socialist and communist movements were and remain strong in both the city and countryside. While small-scale agriculture is supported by subsidies in Europe, as larger-scale agriculture is supported by massive subsidies in the United States, European governments have done so not simply to cement electoral alliances, but also because urban and rural people alike endorse the value of lively rural culture, excellent food and social equity.

In China, which accounts for almost all of the last decade's global reduction of the numbers of hungry people, "capitalist" or "market" reforms have greatly increased local food availability. What is less obvious to some people now is that these reforms are being laid over one of the undeniable accomplishments of the Chinese Communist Revolution: a relatively equal distribution of land and the destruction of the stranglehold of rural landlords over the poor. This feat, combined with market incentives, has very successfully enlisted the energies of hundreds of millions of farm families producing extraordinarily high yields of a great variety of crops. As inequities in the control of land grow in China as a consequence of market reforms and as the progressive effects of environmental degradation set in, it will be interesting to see whether hunger rises again among a displaced rural population.

Of course, the record of land reform in many other nations has not been so encouraging. Mexico implemented a massive land reform program, but haltingly and through several decades of contradictory policy directions. The reform roughly followed the mandate of the Mexican Revolution and the constitution adopted in 1917 under the influence of the primarily peasant-based movements of Emiliano Zapata and Pancho Villa. Most of the reform actually occurred in the 1930s. Outside of the period from 1936 to 1940, however, the main thrust of Mexican government policy was toward rapid promotion of large-scale capital-intensive agriculture, for which most of the best land was reserved. But successive Mexican governments were obliged by the alignment of political forces and by certain other policy goals to grudgingly support a continuing agrarian reform sector. Approximately half of the country's land was divided up among rural communities. The communities, called *ejidos*, allotted plots of land to community members. Neither the ejido nor its members could sell their land, though by tradition the right to cultivate individual plots was often passed down among families. A small portion of the ejidos chose to work their land collectively.

Overall, the performance of the land reform sector of Mexican agriculture was distinctly disappointing, although there were many successful ejido communities and individual *ejiditarios*, or ejido members. Because the land could not be sold, it could not be mortgaged, and so ejiditarios could not borrow significant sums in the private credit market. They had been reliant on a corrupt and unreliable system of government credit, which dried up during fiscal crises and policy shifts beginning in the 1970s. By the 1990s, credit-starved ejidos were desperate for change, and many Mexican and US investors were anxious to be able to buy land freely in Mexico. As part of the lead-up to the signing of NAFTA (the North American Free Trade Agreement) in 1994, Article 27 of the 1917 Constitution was amended in such a way as to undo many of the essential elements of the land reform program. Ejido land could now be bought, sold and mortgaged under certain conditions.

On January 1, 1994, the day Mexico joined NAFTA, promising to liberalize its agricultural sector, peasants revolted in the southern region of the country, forming a new movement that grabbed international attention and came to be known as the Zapatistas.[16] Those who revolted had many concerns, including violent attack and displacement by local landlords and politicians and the abandonment of agrarian reform at the national level. Limited as they were to small plots of largely mountainous land, they also worried about the prospect that smallholder corn production in Mexico would be wiped out by the influx of corn grown by capital-intensive farmers with excellent soil and massive subsidies in the United States.

In the 1950s and 1960s, agrarian reforms were attempted in other Latin American countries.[17] They were part of the general turn toward populist and left-of-center administrations in the region. Between 1963 and 1973, the Chilean government distributed land to approximately 20 percent of the farm families in the country. The United States government supported the initial phases of the reform under a Christian Democratic administration. When Socialist Salvador Allende came to power in Chile, the Nixon administration swore to topple the regime and used many of the difficulties inevitably encountered in agrarian reform processes to help it do so. By 1973, before Allende was murdered and his regime replaced by a military government under US sponsorship, seventy-six thousand rural workers had access to land in large agricultural cooperatives. After the 1973 military coup, under US tutelage, General Augusto Pinochet's dictatorship mostly dismantled the reform, opened the agricultural economy up wide to foreign investors, and turned production toward a concentration on export markets, particularly the US. The Chilean table grapes available throughout US supermarkets in the Northern Hemisphere's winter are a tangible result of this history that affects virtually all US consumers, though they may not be aware of the historical processes that placed the grapes before them.

In 1979, the newly victorious Sandinista government in Nicaragua distributed land as part of its socialist political agenda. Over half of the farm families in the country received access to land. The United States government, under Ronald Reagan, openly opposed the Sandinista regime and financed the brutal Contra War that sapped the regime of money and support, and the Sandinistas were voted out of office. Again, the land reform was largely dismantled.

The United States government organized a coup d'etat in Guatemala in 1954, after the government of Jacobo Arbenz began a land-reform program by moving to expropriate the land of the US-held United Fruit Company, which dominated the national economy. The land reform was quickly undone. In subsequent years, in Guatemala and El Salvador, guerrilla armies fought for land reform while the governments offered their own watered down versions in an attempt to reduce popular support for the rebels. In Guatemala, 200,000 people died in the decades of warfare in the wake of the 1954 CIA-planned coup. In El Salvador, limited land redistribution has been an important part of the recent return to peace after many years of civil war.

Costa Rica, the only Central American country that has been comparatively prosperous, democratic and politically stable, enjoys the high productivity and democratizing tendencies of a strong smallholder agriculture. A revolution led by ranchers and farmers in 1948 instituted land reform measures to strengthen the smallholder sector. Smallholders prospered in Costa Rica because only a small portion of the country was suitable for large-scale plantation agriculture—the nation's prosperity had grown out of the view of earlier international investors that the nation was too poor to be of much interest.

In Peru in the 1970s, an ambitious but top-down land reform was declared by a military government hostile to the United States. Unfortunately, Peru's military leaders were also hostile to or suspicious of independent peasant organizations and did little to respond to peasant wishes and initiatives. The reform was conceived and implemented within a narrowly military conception of order and control. When the government fell, the reform languished and died, leaving deep disillusionment.

The dolorous history of Latin American land reform has many

causes. The attitude and policies of the United States government and corporations have been a critical factor. The wave of progressive politics that brought agrarian reform in the Western Hemisphere was resisted by the United States, which decided that while reform was good for certain countries, it smelled too much like communism in its own backyard, plus it directly threatened the interests of US investors and their allies. The US often installed and consistently supported military coups and governments that halted or reversed the reforms.

The most profound changes in world agriculture in the last half-century are strongly associated with those forces hostile to agrarian reform. The story is far too long and complex to tell here, but, in brief, the Green Revolution that combined plant breeding with a package of chemical inputs to offer dramatic production gains was originally conceived as an alternative to agrarian reforms. In 1941, conservative Mexican politicians teamed up with the Rockefeller Foundation and the US Department of Agriculture under Henry Wallace to begin a program of agricultural research, originally centered in Mexico, that would lead world agriculture in the direction of greatly increased dependence on synthetic petrochemicals, irrigation and machinery. A publicist working in the Rockefeller Foundation, noting discouragement among researchers because they thought governments were insufficiently supportive of the research, coined the term "Green Revolution" to contrast this work with the "red revolution" identified with land reform initiatives. Thus, dramatic improvements in crop yields were ever more clearly identified as an alternative to redistribution of land—not, as might have been the case, as a program conceived of and engineered to support small-scale beneficiaries of land reform. But then, the technology developed would have had to be quite different—less capital-intensive—as would, obviously, the politics. The Green Revolution's political character was consistent with US foreign policy in Latin America—a politics of protecting the interests of large landowners and investors. The Green Revolution's technology and biases have now become intricately woven into the politics of land reform in Brazil.

So, while agrarian reform has been quite successful in many nations, the record of land reform in Latin America has not been so encouraging. We have seen that over the last sixty years the United States government has played a complex role in the story of agrarian reform, insisting on its implementation in some places and reacting violently to prevent or destroy it in others. The US has been peculiarly hostile to serious land reform programs in Latin America. However, if we take a more global perspective that includes Europe and Asia, then the story of land reform and small-scale agriculture is far from one of universal failure. Land reform is neither essentially capitalist nor essentially communist. It is not just for poor countries, and, where it has succeeded, it is not a social welfare program, but a vital part of economic growth strategies.

## Avoiding the Dependency Trap

From the nineteenth century onward, many economists have argued that agrarian reform is important not only to the rural poor, but also important—if not essential—to national economic development. The fundamental insight behind this argument is that national economies cannot grow beyond a limited point without a strong domestic market for the goods investors wish to produce and sell. As discussed in chapter 2, Brazil is a perfect example of a country that has spent most of its history directed toward providing goods for foreign markets where consumers had more money to pay for them. As long as this remained the focus of public policy and private investor choice, there was little incentive for providing for the welfare of Brazilians themselves. There was, in fact, an incentive to keep wages low in order to reduce production costs. Agricultural export products required low skill levels to produce, so there was no incentive to educate the local populace. Taxes were kept to a minimum because social expenditures on health and education were viewed as adding to the costs of the products sold abroad, and there was sufficient low-skill labor available to make investment in the health and well-being of the populace economically unnecessary.

The Achilles' heel of such an economy is its dependency on foreign markets, foreign marketing concerns and the policies of foreign governments, dependencies that sap a country's unity and resilience. The local population becomes increasingly alienated from government and society because it becomes obvious that these are structured to serve foreign investors and consumers in preference to improving the lot of the majority of local people. Local elites become, to a large degree, intermediaries in an international system of economy and rule. As governments began to understand the problems of dependency more clearly and as social movements began to demand change, some governments (including Brazil's) moved cautiously in the mid-twentieth century to build local markets, encouraging farms and industries whose production was directed at meeting the needs of local populations and beginning, if hesitantly, to attend to the health and education needs of local people.

They met considerable resistance in these efforts from the governments and investors of richer nations, especially the United States, who wanted to maintain control of the labor and resources of the dependent economy for their own purposes. Arguing that only increased export earnings could provide enough capital for national development, the richer nations have concentrated their main efforts on keeping dependent nations producing for international markets. (Ironically, it was this dependency trap that was the focus of President Cardoso's internationally admired scholarly work before he became a politician on the national scene and began to pursue policies that strengthen dependency.[18] Not surprisingly, he became a favorite of the United States government once he changed his tune.)

One of the primary ways to escape the dependency trap is to develop local markets. In turn, one of the most effective ways to develop local markets is through reasonably equitable distribution of land. If agricultural enterprises consist of an owner, a few modestly paid managers and a host of miserably compensated sharecroppers, tenants and landless laborers, only a few people in rural areas can enter the market to purchase goods beyond bare necessities. If landowners own as much land as they have in Brazil, they can live well without using and managing their land carefully. If they exhaust the land, it is easy to acquire more or put previously unused land into production. With modern chemical-based farming, they may alternatively choose to concentrate synthetic inputs on a progressively smaller land surface, increasing harvests while ignoring destructive processes on relatively less productive land. Through the process that creates and maintains inequitable ownership, land itself is wasted and mistreated, reducing the actual and potential productivity of the economy.

In contrast, small-scale producers, especially if they perceive that their future depends on the piece of land in their possession, have a strong incentive to use the land fully and in a way that will maintain its productivity over time. In 2001, a joint INCRA/FAO study showed that small-scale farming in Brazil is significantly more efficient in the use of credit and land than larger-scale operations. Small-scale family operations "represent . . . 82.5 percent of the farm establishments, occupy 30.5 percent of the total area [in agricultural production] and are responsible for 37.9 percent of gross value of agricultural and livestock production, [while] receiving only 25.3 percent of the financing destined to agriculture." The study also noted that the crops produced by small-scale family operations supply a disproportionate share of the basic food crops required to feed the Brazilian people, as opposed to export and luxury crops.[19]

In using the land more fully and managing it more carefully, small-scale producers require many goods to be sold to them by local merchants and are far more likely to buy from local suppliers than from large bulk wholesalers. They and their families will want and be able to acquire more than bare necessities, and so consumer markets will grow. As they wish to add value to the products they sell, they will be interested in building more processing facilities for locally produced farm goods. As the production and management requirements of the farm become more complex, farmers and their families will need more skills and want better education—and will become more willing to finance it. They will be more interested in and better able to provide for the health of themselves and their families. All of these things contribute to the growth of the overall economy and the improvement of its productive capacity. They are also the foundations for healthy local communities.

This "virtuous circle" of economic growth and improving human welfare, in turn, accounts for the fact that in many agrarian reform areas of Brazil, local merchants and politicians have begun to reconsider their previous loyalties to the most powerful local landlords and have started to support agrarian reform. More producers and more investment on the land mean an expanding local economy, more sales for local merchants, and altogether new economic opportunities. It is also in this growing alliance of interests between independent farmers and merchants that some see agrarian reform, for better or worse, as an essentially conservative initiative.

Analysis of the United States' economy into the mid-twentieth century and those of the post–World War II nations of Europe and Asia that pursued land reform indicates that relatively equitable distribution of land was key to the overall growth of these economies. It is in the colonial and post-colonial economies, where land distribution has long been strikingly inequitable, that it has been so very difficult to establish this virtuous circle.

In the United States, the virtuous circle leading to economic growth occurred during the nineteenth and early twentieth centuries and has given way over the last fifty years to rapidly developing inequities in land ownership. Thousands of rural communities have literally vanished in the process of consolidation. Many believe, as do we, that the land itself is suffering from the machines, chemicals and management philosophies that have come with large-scale agriculture. In any case, it would be impossible to imagine the United States developing as it did without several generations in which small farming was a way of life for the majority of the population and the springboard for US economic growth.

It is certainly true that the growth of nonfarm production and technological development in all economies complicates the picture. But wherever land is a fundamental national resource, its equitable distribution and rational use are keys to healthy national development. So, while land reform is admittedly not important in the tiny trading, financial center and high-tech industrial nation of Singapore, it is essential in land-rich Brazil.

## Agrarian Reform, Legal Impunity and the Future of Land and Forests

The political character and consequences of land reform are clearly very complicated. In Brazil, however, one thing has always been clear, from the time when Tomé de Souza warned the Portuguese king about the arrogance and lawlessness of large landowners, to the present era of the murder of Chico Mendes and the El Dorado dos Carajás massacre: the legal impunity of large landowners is a fundamental political and economic problem for Brazil. So long as owners of vast stretches of land maintain political power over the national, state and local courts and governments, the nation cannot be fairly nor well governed. Nor can the land and forests of Brazil be protected or used wisely.

We have written here that powerful people in Brazil have carried out innumerable murders, beatings and campaigns of terror against the landless. As noted, these routinely take place with no appropriate control or punishment from the government or no control at all. Sometimes the government itself commits blatant acts of injustice in land conflicts. We have also noted examples, from among the literally hundreds available, of the endemic problems of corruption associated with the inequities of landownership. The injustices and corruption arising from Brazil's landownership patterns are so serious as to call into question the legitimacy of the state and the social order itself in Brazil.

This situation has powerful consequences for both the people and the landscape of Brazil. In 1992, we were witness to one expressive example of the government's failures around land use matters. While doing research in southern Bahia, we were pleased to learn that the Brazilian government had made it illegal to cut timber in any of the remaining remnants of primary or old-growth forest. This was critical to conservation efforts, because the Atlantic coast rain forest of Brazil has been reduced to well below 10 percent of its original extent—estimates are that 3 to 8 percent is left—and yet it remains one of the most species-rich places on Earth. The International Union for the Conservation of Nature considers the area to be one of the important sites in the world for emergency efforts to preserve biodiversity. While prohibiting logging of primary forests, Brazilian law also required that before anyone could log secondary forest, IBAMA, the conservation and environmental department, had to approve logging plans. We had visited regional IBAMA offices and been shown the stack of such plans awaiting approval—none had yet been approved. IBAMA officials confirmed that with no secondary logging approved and all primary, old-growth logging forbidden, it was illegal to do any logging in the region at that time.

Unfortunately, the reality was that, in March 1992, there were three logging mills operating in public view. We frequently encountered logging trucks on regional roads. The sound of chain saws was commonplace in the woods. In March, José Lutzenberger, the Brazilian minister of environment and national head of IBAMA, attended a closed-doors meeting of the World Bank. The discussion concerned the upcoming Rio '92 Conference on Global Development and Environment, the brainchild of Lutzenberger himself. The World Bank told Lutzenberger that they were prepared to offer US$50 million for forest conservation to Brazil as a highlight that could be announced at the conference in June. Lutzenberger dramatically and forcefully declined the offer, declaring that such funds would only be used for further devastation of Brazil's forests because he was unable to gain control of his own department—IBAMA was, in his words, "controlled 100 percent as a branch of the international timber companies" and "nothing but a den of thieves." Needless to say, he was soon dismissed from his post as environment minister. As if to confirm his viewpoint, during the same week in southern Bahia, a fourth lumber mill was opened in a public ceremony involving proud speeches by local landowners and politicians—yet another mill opened in an area where logging was illegal.

This incident is only one of innumerable examples of the progressive degradation of the Brazilian environment in defiance of the law. Historians of Brazil have shown how the Atlantic coast rain forest, some of Brazil's richest agricultural soils, the Amazon rain forest and Brazil's extraordinarily rich wildlife have been devastated over centuries by landlords, government officials and local and foreign companies operating in defiance of Brazil's long-run economic interests. It must be remarked that similar destruction has occurred in the history of the United States (recall, for example, the Dust Bowl of the Great Plains in the 1930s and the near complete devastation in the nineteenth century of eastern hardwood forests) and of many other nations. But in Brazil it has been particularly difficult for the government or the larger population to gain a measure of control because of the extraordinary legal impunity of powerful landowners. Recent research by José Pádua has shown how this process was intimately tied up with the practice of slavery and latifúndio until slavery's abolition in 1888; Pádua's research also shows that some enlightened government officials have vainly fought against this process for a very long time, beginning with Portuguese colonial officials as far back as the middle of the eighteenth century.

We saw in chapters 1 and 2 how environmental destruction has been linked to landownership patterns and the impunity of the large landowners. In chapter 3, we saw how this process continues today, linked to mining and timber companies, in the Amazon. Many encouraging government and some private initiatives in recent years have brought some hope to those interested in forest conservation. However, nearly every effort is partly or completely frustrated by the legal impunity of the powerful firms and individuals involved in resource extraction on one hand and, on the other, the desperation of the poor who do environmental damage for lack of any alternative way of making a living. Even more serious, as we have seen, is when the power of the rich deliberately exploits the desperation of the poor. Writing of the severe difficulties encountered by the environmental movement in Brazil in attempting to address these problems, Warren Dean summarized the situation thus:

> The contradiction that afflicted the movement was, after all, generic in Brazilian society—the chasm that stretched between those few who owned most of the country's forests and felt little responsibility for preserving them and the mass of the citizenry, desperately in need of relief from a social system that had denied them land, education and justice.

## AGRO-ECOLOGY ON THE SETTLEMENTS:
## A POSSIBLE ALTERNATIVE?

The most important environmental question to ask of the MST is whether it can significantly contribute to resolving the contradiction Warren Dean describes above. Can it reduce the chasm that separates those who own the nation's resources and "the mass of the citizenry," who have been denied "land, education and justice?" In chapter 1, we saw that some local MST farmers and the national MST were determined to promote a new agro-ecological vision of agricultural production. This is partly a response to the difficulty that small producers have—in Brazil as in many other nations—in competing with the capital-intensive large-scale producers of major commodities favored by government subsidies and trade and tax policies. The idea of adopting an agro-ecology model also arose out of small farmers' need to build a greater degree of self-sufficiency and reduce their dependency on national and international markets. In these markets, ruinous price fluctuations are common, and any ability to accurately predict and control these fluctuations has shifted more and more to a handful of large international marketing firms. In these international markets, farmers typically recover less than 20 percent of the retail value of the product—Kansas and Rio Grande do Sul wheat farmers get about eleven cents on each dollar that the consumer spends for bread. Wheat farmers using capital-intensive technologies can take advantage of economies of scale—diversity on modern wheat farms has virtually been eliminated—and so the farm lives or dies on that eleven cents. In contrast, the cheese made by Sarandí women and the fruits and vegetables raised by the family return 100 percent of the retail price to the family when sold in the local "ecological fair," and the family is not dependent on the price received for a single kind of product. As an economic matter, the MST sees it as essential that small farmers get out of trying to win in a game in which they are ever more severely handicapped and get into a game where they can win.

An agro-ecological approach would be based on serving local markets with a diversity of high-value products and capturing most of the value by eliminating middlemen through farmers' markets and on-farm processing. Such an approach would also protect and enhance the productive quality of the soil and the farm environment, ensuring long-term economic stability. However, the movement's shift to an agro-ecological vision is also inspired by a growing realization that small farmers attempting to compete with large-scale capital- and chemical-intensive producers are caught in an environmental trap intimately linked to their economic dilemma.

Large-scale farming corporations are constituted as profit-making enterprises. The farm has nothing to do with the farmer's need for a home or a community or a sense of place. It is quite possible for the corporate farmer to look at land as an expendable resource because of his ability to acquire new land. The old logic of plantation agriculture that we discussed earlier is easily transformed into the modern logic of chemical-dependent agriculture. Land can be regarded as something that can be amortized, like a piece of equipment. Its declining productivity over time can be anticipated and roughly calculated; so long as the profits taken during the period of decline can be made to pay the cost of acquiring new land in the future, the corporation or large-scale individual holder can regard declining land productivity over time as a perfectly acceptable cost.

MST farmers sell organic products alongside other organic producers in a cooperative farmers' market in Porto Alegre, capital of the state of Rio Grande do Sul.

Short-term high productivity can be profitable even if excessive chemical fertilizer and pesticide use destroys soil quality, if excessive irrigation leads to salinity, if indiscriminate use of pesticides encourages pest resistance, if pesticides cause secondary pest outbreaks due to elimination of pests' predators and if heavy machinery compacts the soil, making it resistant to water, nutrient and root penetration. These problems are all endemic in modern agriculture, particularly those areas dominated by large-scale corporate production. They can all be absorbed as simple production costs by corporations able and willing to roam the world in search of new and more productive land.

Corporations or investors also often extract maximum short-term profits from the land in order to reinvest in activities that have nothing to do with agriculture. For example, the Mexican head of a large vegetable producers' association told us he knew that the land he had invested in would no longer be suited for intensive production soon; for that reason, he was investing all his profits in an electronics factory in Tucson.

This perspective makes sense to large-scale investors in Brazil, because, for those with wealth and influence, new land can be acquired relatively easily. It is easy partly because frontier expansion is encouraged by government policy and government investment in new roads and other infrastructure. It is also relatively easy to acquire new land because of the impunity with which the powerful can use fraud and intimidation to seize land from smallholders. These two factors are why the history of Brazil is the history of careless use of land by the wealthy.

The situation is quite different for a smallholder settled on a given piece of land—especially when that farmer has acquired title to the land through an arduous land reform process that would be difficult if not impossible for him or her to repeat. New legislation in Brazil forbids recipients of land acquired through agrarian reform from acquiring another such plot after abandoning or selling the original land, under most circumstances. This is quite reasonably aimed at discouraging an agrarian reform version of the venerable but socially and environmentally destructive *indústria de posse* (land-title factory), by which some people over the centuries have attempted to establish a claim to land merely to sell their interest cheap to someone else. The combined effect of the new legislation and the difficulty of acquiring land in the first place means that small farmers must regard the piece of land they receive as their foundation for all future livelihood and as the inheritance they will leave their children.

The extent to which smallholders identify their land and its quality with their destiny and fortune is strongly influenced by the degree to which their ownership of the land is stabilized and reasonably assured. Other factors being equal, an agrarian reform that succeeds in stabilizing land ownership on a reasonably equitable basis is one that should encourage land conservation.

Of course, the smallholder needs more support than simply title to the land. If agricultural credit is not available on reasonable terms and the farmer doesn't earn enough cash to pay annual production loans, the pattern of land ownership will fall apart: landowners will lose their farms to moneylenders, as they have throughout the United States. Also, great environmental damage is done by farmers around the world who desperately push their land to pay off loans contracted under ruinous assumptions. The health of the land depends on stable land ownership and sustainable economic strategies. A workable reform movement must in turn be built on stable farms, whose land is of high and enduring quality. Production must be diverse and of high value. Farmers must capture a large share of the final value of every-thing they produce. Otherwise, those who have fought for and bene-fited from the reform will simply lose the land to others or to environmental degradation.

This logic is making itself felt in Brazilian land reform settlements and in the thinking of the national movement, and it is within these terms that the MST has encouraged many agro-ecological initiatives on small farms throughout Brazil. We discussed some of these in earlier chapters, and saw that some settlers were out ahead of the national movement while others were skeptical about agro-ecology or were re-sisting it.

When we revisited Sarandí in early 2003, Pacote gave us the good news that his fishpond has produced so prodigiously that he has added two new reservoirs to his farm. His first harvest of fish brought in more than two thousand kilos, including one monster fish of thirty-nine kilos. The Placotniks were proud that they sold the fish for about half what their neighbors did, but they also slyly admitted that they partly priced the fish low so that everyone would come to them the next time for fish. "Everyone is asking us, 'When are you going to have more fish?' We are going to have a reliable market."

The harvest of wild mate from the forest on the land had also been very profitable. The rotational grazing had resulted in a dramatic im-provement in the cows' health—"before, they often got mastitis and died; now, never." They explained that now the cows never sleep in the same place two nights in a row, and thus insects and diseases do not tend to build up. They observed a marked improvement in the quality of milk and cheese and were being given higher prices for the milk products by buyers. In short, Pacote and Anir consider that the diversi-fied and more complex production strategies of an agro-ecology ap-proach are paying off for them handsomely.

Others at Sarandí have a less optimistic view of agro-ecology. One of the settlements leaders told us that while everyone agreed with the goal and the overall concept, many people had been forced to slow down and take a step or two backward in trying to implement agro-ecological approaches. He remarked that it was easy to conceive of agro-ecology but difficult to implement. In particular, he said that re-gional soils were all suffering from decades of abuse and that achieving the high soil quality that the agro-ecology approach demanded meant investing in the soil at the expense of high production for a period of years. "Very few people have figured out how to afford that."

In response, people in the same settlement said that this leader's pessimistic view was typical "of the great distance between leaders and the base." In particular, they said, the leaders knew that they were to promote the agro-ecology idea and they did so, but that most did not practice it themselves. This was true, these settlers said, even when people not in leadership positions were having good success with non-chemical, diversified approaches.

When told of these contrasting views, João Pedro Stédile agreed that there was a serious problem. He said that it was true that it was very difficult to convince much of the older leadership that the agro-ecology approach was needed and that many of the movement's technical people "are still trapped in the Green Revolution way of thinking." Adoption of the agro-ecology model is a great step forward in his view and ours, but there are many problems to be met in its overall implementation.

We saw how settlers in the old northeastern sugar plantation region were adopting a more diverse agriculture than they were accustomed to, although this change has been fragile and tenuous. In the Amazon, we observed farmers in the process of working out ways to adapt to the special conditions of the region—some of their efforts were clearly consistent with an agro-ecological approach, although they had not yet been introduced to the language or formal concepts of agro-ecology. They were simply using their own observations to intelligently adapt to circumstance, as the farmers who have made human survival possible have been doing for millennia. However, the Amazon farmers have shown themselves open to new ideas, and their present experiments may well come to be recognized as pioneering efforts in practical agro-ecology.

Zezinho, or José Armando da Silva, whom we met in chapter 1, made the interesting observation that sometimes good things can come out of sharp breaks with local traditions. Although he works at the MST-affiliated school in Sarandí on the high plateaus of Alta Uruguaia in Rio Grande do Sul, he farms in the southern part of the state, in a lowland area previously devoted almost exclusively to extensive cattle ranching.

His community of Bagé specializes in organic production of agricultural seeds, contracting with European seed companies. The community
also produces organic market and subsistence crops. The production
of the seeds is a sensitive and complicated affair that was rejected by
MST farmers in other parts of the state, who were already wedded to
the kinds of agriculture practiced in their regions. In Bagé, the MST
settlers were ready to try the new experiment because they were bringing few preconceptions to the matter; they knew that the extensive
cattle ranching previously characteristic of the region wouldn't work
and were casting about for the best transition ideas available. Zezinho
reports that because of the success of the experiment, the cash income
and living standards in Bagé are above those in the fairly prosperous
settlements of the Alta Uruguaia.

In other cases, the revival of old traditions has proved adaptable to a
modern agro-ecological vision. Throughout Brazil, various communities have come to specialize in the production of medicinal herbs highly
prized by local populations. Merchants sell them in markets everywhere in Brazil because many Brazilians, for better or worse, are not
wedded to modern medicine, either because of its relative cost or because they are less skeptical of the remedies recommended by grand-
mother than those sold by Bayer and Squibb. These medicinal plants
are strongly linked to African and indigenous cultural traditions, as
well as to the rich pharmacopeias of traditional European peasantries.
Some medicines can be grown in intensive agricultural systems, and
because many contain fungal or insect toxins, they are often effective
in reducing pest damage to crops with which they are interplanted.
Others can be gathered from the wild forest or, more commonly, from
the disturbed and secondary forests found near many Brazilian agricultural fields. They are adaptable to complex land use designs that incorporate surviving or regenerating forest with agricultural production
and have been used for centuries by the Brazilian poor in such fashion.
As José Lutzenberger has observed, much of agro-ecology depends on
memory and not on invention.

This rich mixture of memory and invention, tradition and innovation, production and conservation, can be found on MST and other
land-reform settlements in the southern part of the state of Bahia, where
we carried out a research project in 1992.[20] The idea was to use the

knowledge of land ownership patterns, power relationships and land law in the region's cacao economy that we had gained during prior research to help guide ongoing forest conservation efforts. As we noted above, this area had been identified as a key global "hot spot" for biodiversity conservation. We found that many conservation efforts were languishing because they were being carried out with little attempt to confront local legal, social and economic realities—not an uncommon finding among researchers working on international conservation.

The encouraging finding, however, was that some people in the region were beginning to explore the possibilities of conservation projects that would allow the continued production of cacao as well as a more diverse production. These investigations were being carried out on land reform settlements. Cacao, the source of chocolate, is a tree native not to the Atlantic coast rain forest of southern Bahia, but to the Amazon and to Meso-American rain forests. It is a short tree, about twenty-five feet high at maturity, which naturally grows under the much higher canopy of the rainforest. Some southern Bahian planters, mostly very wealthy holders of large fazendas, had resisted the advice of agronomists who, from the early twentieth century on, had advised complete forest destruction to eliminate the cacao trees' competition for water, light and nutrients. Instead, these stubborn fazendeiros had allowed some of the forest to stay in place or to regrow to form a canopy over the cacao trees.

(The Brazilian biologist Cristina Alves has found that these *cabruca* plantations, with their mix of cacao and remaining or regenerated forest, preserved a very high percentage of the biodiversity of the remaining remnants of primary forest and provided corridors for species to move about and reproduce successfully between forest remnants. In particular, Alves demonstrated that the golden-headed lion tamarin, a much-prized and highly endangered monkey, depended heavily on cabruca forest. Happily, once biologists began to look in cabruca stands, they found that the monkey was not quite so endangered as they had thought.)

Since the 1990s, other farmers have begun to see that with the collapse of the cacao economy due to overproduction and newly arrived cacao diseases, no one would be able to survive economically without moving wholly or partly out of cacao. While the worst of the fazendeiros converted the rich forests and plantations to cattle or sugar production—both short-term and ecologically devastating choices—some people had begun to explore the possibilities of diversifying production with cabruca cacao plantations.

Some of the most interesting experiments along these lines were initiated by land reform settlers who were aware that cacao could no longer provide a living—more than 50 percent of cacao workers had become permanently unemployed—and who were distressed that their only other option was a short-term exploitation of annual crops in cleared forest. They had begun to experiment with planting a wide variety of perennial crops in cleared forest and in remaining forest: fruit trees, palms, the fiber-producing piassava used for roofing, pepper, pineapple and other crops. Some fazendeiros began to experiment along similar lines. This work would eventually be supported by international chocolate corporations concerned about the collapse of cacao production and by international conservation organizations, and it would link up with work by researchers and farmers in Central America and Mexico, many of them exploring the same approach to incorporating cacao and coffee planting.[21]

In the Pontal do Paranapanema in the state of São Paulo, another effort to save remnants of the Atlantic coast rain forest (and another species of tamarin monkey) produced an alliance between conservationists and MST settlers. The Pontal was one of the most outrageous examples of land fraud in Brazil. Wealthy speculators and shady ranching operators arrived in the 1950s to claim land. They sometimes "proved" their title claims by hastily erecting farm buildings made to look ancient, complete with falsely out-of-style decorations and furniture, to impress land officials with the idea that the farm was long-established. They wreaked complete havoc on the local forest, and their violent exploitation of the people they hired to clear the land led to the "Grass War," in which laborers and prior settlers tried to establish their own land claims. Violent confrontations and repression foreshadowed those endured by subsequent movements for agrarian reform. (This region remains an area of intense MST activity and planter violence. In September, 2002, José Rainha, a prominent MST leader, was jailed for his activities.)

In the 1980s, during the exciting opening up of Brazilian life at the end of the dictatorship, a successful young Brazilian pharmaceutical executive from a venerable political family in Minas Gerais made a personal decision that would lead to hopeful developments in the Pontal. Cláudio Valladares-Pádua decided he wanted to be biologist and not a businessman. He asked his wife, Suzana, an interior designer, if she "would prefer a husband who's rich and miserable or one who's poor and happy."[22]

Cláudio would go on to earn a doctorate in biology at the University of Florida at Gainesville. He returned to Brazil and the Pontal to initiate an attempt to save some of the Atlantic coast rain forest. Founding a nonprofit called Instituto de Pesquisas Ecológicas (IPE, the Institute for Ecological Research—an *ipe* is a valuable and beloved tropical tree), Cláudio and Suzana began their work in 1992, in a forest remnant called Morro do Diabo in the Pontal do Paranapanema. Within three years, MST settlers began to move into the area. Cláudio 's first reaction was despair—like many other conservationists, he regarded the landless as anathema to forest conservation—and he and Suzana believed they might have to abandon the project. They persevered, however, and found it easier than they thought over the years to engage the settlers and the MST in productive conversation. They began to realize that they could all work together for common goals.[23]

The settlers and the MST were anxious to prove that they were not the enemies of the forest. They knew that the soils and ecological health and productivity of the region had been devastated by the landowners who had moved into the area in the 1950s. At the same time, they needed wood for cooking and building, and they were accustomed to hunting wherever forest was to be found. At Cláudio and Suzana's suggestion, they undertook to establish *abraços verdes*, green embraces, around forest remnants by planting trees and shrubs. With help from the São Paulo Forestry Institute, Cláudio and Suzana obtained plantings and training in agro-forestry for the settlers. They also planted corridors of trees and animal-friendly crops between forest remnants. The settlers achieved their goals of gaining a sustainable supply of wood and protecting soils from rampant erosion while better protecting the tamarin and other forest species.

Although there is good reason to be optimistic about and supportive of all of these efforts in the direction of a truly sustainable agriculture, a strong word of caution must be spoken. Agro-ecology does not work miracles. Farmers undertaking agro-ecological methods must still compete with other producers. If other farm operations—specifically large producers—are able to do so, they will drive the agro-ecological farmers out of business. To a degree, they legitimately will seek to reduce their costs through better management and technologies. Unfortunately, however, in the Brazilian context as it remains today, they will have other, less legitimate, tools at their disposal. The playing field is not level. There are commanding heights of economic and political power and a lowland plain for the poor.

The strategy of large farming corporations and of individuals with large landholdings will continue to be composed of the following familiar elements:

- Keep pressing government to reduce or eliminate credit or any other form of subsidy to smallholders.
- Work to maintain and expand the government support given for frontier expansion of large holdings, for trade deals favoring large-scale commodity producers and for subsidized credit to large producers.
- Continue to press for government and multilateral development banks to finance new irrigation schemes, electrical production and distribution and road-building programs in frontier regions, even where it makes at best only short-term economic sense.
- Reduce production costs and increase profits through lavish use of chemicals and other production strategies that are damaging to land but profitable in the short run.
- Use political influence to avoid environmental regulation.
- Maintain starvation wages for agricultural workers by union-busting, corrupting of rural union leaders, influencing government policy and, basic to all of these, by ensuring that most of the landless never succeed in getting land for themselves.
- Continue to pressure, intimidate and defraud smallholders at every opportunity to drive them off their land and acquire it at a low cost.
- Maintain a legal and political environment that continues to facilitate the acquisition of new land through both frontier expansion and displacement of small producers.

This is a simple, tried-and-true strategy of maximum exploitation of land and labor using force, intimidation, undue influence over government and the ill-constructed and ill-enforced legal system.

Variations on this basic strategy have worked for the more powerful planters, ranchers and agribusiness enterprises for nearly five hundred years. There are thousands of more responsible and honorable Brazilian large-scale producers who do not and will not participate in such a strategy, but participation is not required by all to make the strategy work effectively against the poor and in favor of the most aggressive and irresponsible. So long as the rural oligarchies of the Brazilian regions, in concert with national and international corporations, maintain their control of Brazilian agriculture and rural life, smallholders cannot be secure in their ownership of land, their income or their physical safety. Under such conditions, neither an agro-ecology approach nor any other will provide fertile soil for the growth of a small-farm agriculture and a more equitable society.

That is why the environmental battle for the productivity, diversity and beauty of the Brazilian landscape is an essentially political battle. This conclusion is completely consistent with the MST's approach to the question. As noted in various contexts earlier, the MST has always argued that land distribution and the establishment of smallholders on the land are insufficient in themselves. Even former president Fernando Cardoso's document on agrarian reform insists that broad political changes—and specifically the end to the impunity of large landholders—are essential to a successful agrarian reform program. Neither agro-ecological production on land reform settlements, nor Brazil's forests, can stand up against rapacious and powerful people and corporations routinely operating in disregard of the law.

A large share of Brazilian politicians become themselves the owners of extensive estates as they rise to power. The MST carried out occupations of a Cardoso estate to call attention to the compromises made by Cardoso and his administration with the politics of latifundia. Recall that they also occupied the estates of the political boss of the state of Pará, Jáder Barbalho, helping to force his resignation as leader of the national senate, and they have occupied the estates of the enormously powerful Bahian politician, Antônio Carlos Magalhães, who was also toppled as Senate president for similar reasons. For many Brazilians, the occupations of these fazendas seemed to prove in an outrageous way that the MST was not interested so much in agrarian reform as in a broader political program. What this misses is that the MST has always argued, and quite reasonably so, that agrarian reform is absolutely inseparable from a program of sweeping political change. Drawing public attention to the way prominent national politicians tie themselves into rural oligarchies and the politics of systematic corruption is an impeccably appropriate way to make the point.

We saw how the first landless people to carry out land occupations as part of the movement that would become the MST had to fight against the constant lure of the faraway Amazon frontier, dangled by Coronel Curiô and the government. Many people wondered why the MST was not willing to settle for new farms of much larger size that the government was more than happy to hand out to all comers. Why the stubborn insistence on staying in place, the obstinate, rude challenges to present claimants to land in the neighborhood, rather than the apparently easier and less troublesome choice of accepting what was freely offered on the frontier? Didn't this also prove that the point was more political than agricultural, more about challenging those in power than about establishing independent homesteads?

Again, those who raise such questions show that they are naive about both agriculture and politics. They fail to understand that the frontier land being offered was often inappropriate for agriculture and human settlement and was in many ways a trap, part of a larger scheme to draw labor for the exploitation of timber and minerals. But even where the land was good, or where the government honestly believed it to be so, it was being offered in a newer version of an old process with which the rural poor had become all too familiar. This was a process in which opening new agricultural land always required enlisting the energy and hope of the poor, but in which the takeover by land barons always followed in the wake of frontier development, converting the frontiersmen into peons, tenants and sharecroppers on someone else's land. It is essential for both the causes of the landless and of the forest that this process be stopped. In order to stop it, the political relationships that make the process run have to be disrupted and reconstructed on new terms. Changing these relationships would represent a sea change in Brazilian politics.

This is the unfinished task of the MST, and it is an essential political task that cannot be carried out either without the MST, or by the MST alone. Brazilian politicians from the nineteenth-century abolitionist Rui Barbosa to President Getúlio Vargas to President Fernando Henrique Cardoso, not to mention the country's socialist and communist parties, have complained bitterly about the stranglehold that powerful, reactionary landlords have on the national government and the disastrous influence they have on government policy. Rural landlords continue to be powerful even though Brazil is not predominantly an agricultural nation and is among the world's top ten industrial economies.[24] They relentlessly obstruct or defy reasonable taxation. They succeed in building legislative coalitions to pass subsidy programs that only serve to increase their wealth and influence at the expense of smallholders and urban taxpayers and are economically counterproductive for the country. They resist judicial reforms that might put an end to their impunity and introduce a greater degree of predictability and rationality, which would better serve other investors as well as the public. They are able to do this because they are embedded in family, business and patronage networks that have been five hundred years in the making and because rural areas are overrepresented in the national legislature. In turn, through the patronage, corruption and intimidation they exercise in their personal fiefdoms, they are often able to deliver blocks of votes from rural areas with a unanimity and reliability that city political bosses can only dream about.

We mentioned earlier the murder carried out in public by a prominent rural politician; we could mention others as well, such as the father of former president Fernando Collor, who murdered a legislator on the floor of his state's senate, but was found not guilty because he had meant to kill someone else—something like innocence by reason of bad aim. "Very folkloric," as the Brazilians say, but in the end, no joke for the Brazilian political system and the task of building a decent society.

The systematic perversity of the land law, the legal impunity of landlords and the disproportionate power and influence of the rural oligarchies join with urban and rural corruption and crime in a way that calls into question the very legitimacy of government in Brazil. It is a problem that eats away at the thousands of efforts by Brazilians of all kinds and classes to improve life for themselves and their fellow citizens and protect the nation's resources and natural beauty. When any honest effort can be destroyed in defiance of logic and law, it becomes very difficult for citizens to continue to work in a public-spirited way. At this writing, outrageous scandals in the North American corporate and political worlds remind us that this is not uniquely a Brazilian problem. In the context of the discussion of Brazilian agrarian reform, however, we can say that one of the keys to giving Brazilians greater faith in their society is to reduce the influence of the rural oligarchy and break the arrogant impunity with which the worst of landlords rule many areas of the Brazilian countryside. The marvelously hopeful irony is that it is the poorest and most despised Brazilians who, through the MST, have begun to mount a serious challenge to a problem that no one else has been able to approach.

## The MST and Revolution

People have argued that the MST is an antidemocratic movement because it ultimately pursues a revolutionary goal—to overthrow the state and institute a socialist system. Remember Roosevelt Roque dos Santos from chapter 2, the head of the UDR who held up pictures of MST activists lecturing in front of life-sized portraits of Che Guevera and Vladimir Lenin? Dos Santos believed these pictures proved that the MST had a revolutionary purpose and should be treated as a violent threat to national order. And accusations of radical intent appear regularly in media coverage of the movement. An editorial written in the Sunday, April 7, 2002, edition of the *Estado de São Paulo*, a major national newspaper, warned in its headline: "MST Documents Show: The Objective Is to Overthrow Capitalism." What followed was a vulgar interpretation of several MST documents, including the "educational philosophy document" and a historical booklet.

It is absolutely true that the MST takes the idea of revolution very seriously, and the movement's belief that true reform can only happen in Brazil with radical, comprehensive change has considerable support in history and in theory. Scholars, including, most prominently, Barrington Moore, Jr., have argued that a revolutionary break with the past may have been necessary for the modern transition from authoritarian

The MST views itself as part of a worldwide revolutionary struggle, as the banner at this movement meeting illustrates.

feudal monarchies to democratic capitalism.[25] Moore attributed the differences between England and Germany to a more decisive break with the past in England, which led to a much earlier (and, some would argue, more complete) transition to parliamentary democracy and market capitalism. This belief in the developmental power of a break with the past is part of the reason why José de Souza Martins, one of the most important intellectuals working on the question of agrarian reform in Brazil, argues that the MST is not a backward, primitive movement, but a forward-looking movement geared toward progressive change. Caio Prado, Jr., one of Brazil's most influential historians, has argued that the greatest injustices—and therefore, the greatest potential for revolutionary change (which he saw as both inevitable and necessary)—were to be found in the Brazilian countryside.[26]

But what kind of revolution does the MST support? Are they simply interested in a clean break with an unjust past, or are they interested in overthrowing the current state in order to implement a new socialist government? Certainly in the early days of the movement, revolutionary language and actions promoting radical state transformation were highly visible. The first declarations agreed upon during the national congress in 1985 included the intention to expropriate all large farms, implement collective production on new settlements and devise a set of laws to change the country's political system. In an interview with Ilse Scherer-Warren, professor of sociology at the Federal University of Santa Catarina, João Pedro Stédile said that whoever was with the movement in the beginning was automatically against what he called "a bourgeois state . . . invested with class interest."[27] MST members pitted themselves against the state because they distrusted the facile transition from military dictatorship to democracy. The military leaders who controlled politics from 1964 to 1982 were still very much in power during the transition, and many Brazilians worried that the new republic would be democratic in name only.

Belief in the necessity of revolutionary change motivated the movement's choice of symbols, language and goals. The movement's classic symbol is its flag, bright red with a green map of Brazil in the center. Laid over the map are pictures of a man and woman, who represent the landless throughout the country. The man holds a machete high over his head, and the message is clear: agrarian reform by any means necessary. The design at the center of the flag is seen in MST settlements and offices throughout the country, on caps, T-shirts and posters. Other movement symbols are equally revolutionary: the movement's anthem is a stirring call to arms ("come, let us fight, with our fists raised, our homeland will lift us up . . . tomorrow belongs to the workers") and the slogans woven through official movement discourse are meant to inspire dedication to a revolutionary cause.

The MST's ideology is also heavily influenced by revolutionary authors, most notably Karl Marx and Vladimir Lenin, who offer a political and economic analysis of capitalism that MST leaders have used to help explain the dynamics underlying the ongoing exploitation of the poor in Brazil. According to Karl Marx, profit in a capitalist economy comes from exploitation of the working class. An internal MST document agrees, quoting Karl Marx: "All progress in capitalist agriculture is progress in the art of exploitation, whether of the worker or of the soil." Participation in the MST is seen as an expression of a class for itself: "We aren't fighting against one land-grabber, we are fighting against a class, the land-owning elite."[28] Young activists who join up with the MST's cause spend anywhere from a couple of weeks to several months or even a year in "formation classes" where these works are part of a range of readings that are discussed and debated as a key part of the activist development process.

The Marxist part of the movement's ideology was also supported by other leaders from the Brazilian Left, some of whom played a role in shaping movement ideology in the early years. It is not known to what extent other groups influenced MST leaders, but the Communist Party of Brazil (PCdoB) and the Brazilian Communist Party (PCB) have both supported the MST as the vehicle for overseeing the official agrarian reform process.[29] Individual activists, like Clôdomir Santos de Moraes, were also extremely influential. A sociologist, Moraes was one of the main intellectuals behind the MST's early collective production policies. The production collectives initially supported by the movement were an indication of their revolutionary ideology: settlements where land and labor were held in common were conceived of as socialist islands within Brazilian capitalism. They were a key element in the creation of a "new man and woman," who would help to develop a "new society" on the settlements. As the settlements gathered force, they would set free the forces for a new society in all of Brazil.

This vision of a new society is laid out clearly in the early editions of the movement's newspaper, *O Jornal Sem Terra* (*The Landless Newspaper*). Ademar Bogo, one of the movement's first and most influential activists, wrote several columns about the sort of personalities that would be considered acceptable in this new society. MST members are warned against personal vices, which were "reflexes of a subideology generated by the private ownership of the means of production."[30] The vices range from individualism ("the individualist is the type of opportunist who only believes in the individual and always puts himself above the organization") to spontaneity ("the spontaneous person resists planning") and immobility ("the immobilist is a type of opportunist who deliberately doesn't involve himself with anything"). MST activists were encouraged to promote discussion so that people would "know the vices [in order] to overcome them."

In order to explain what might be difficult concepts, present information and motivate people, MST activists employ what is called mística (mysticism). Mística comes out of the Christian traditions of liberation theology and is intended to "reduce the distance between the present and the future, helping us to anticipate the good things that are coming."[31] Communicating through theater, song and dance, mística inspires faith in the strength of the MST and facilitates discussion of mundane but difficult issues, such as the organization of production. The main methods of mística are movement songs; "words of order," such as "Agrarian Reform, this is our struggle!" that are chanted in unison; theatrical presentations; and symbolic representations of *A Luta* (the struggle), such as the movement's hymn and flag. According to the movement, "the more that the masses attach themselves to their symbols, leaders and the organization, the more they fight, the more they mobilize and the more they organize themselves."[32] The principal messages portrayed during the mysticism are humility, honesty, conviction, perseverance, sacrifice, gratitude, responsibility and discipline.

These messages are presented at the open and close of most meetings, assemblies and demonstrations held by the movement. For example, during the 1998 year-end MST meeting in Santa Catarina, politicians, local civil leaders, farmers and urban employees sat together in a large auditorium as several young children led a procession down the center aisle to a stage in the front of the room, where they laid their offerings: ears of corn, a spade, fruit and long green beans. The offerings were set on top of a map of Brazil that had been drawn on the floor using tree branches, leaves and flowers. As the last offering was made, the MST's red, green and white flag was raised and everybody stood, shouting "Viva Reforma Agraria!" This popular theater has been repeated countless times all over Brazil. The content changes, but the message is always the same: members of the MST are united in their efforts to create a new, just society in Brazil.

One question commonly asked of the MST is whether movement members envision their revolution to be a violent one. Revolutions are often equated with violence, and reactionary observers have been quick to accuse the MST of planning or supporting armed warfare. The accusations are somewhat ironic, however, given that almost all of the violence MST members experience is practiced on them, not by them. MST members do defend themselves when set upon by armed police, military or private gunmen, but the movement's policy is that only tools used in agriculture—pruning hooks, machetes, hoes, shovels, pitchforks—be used. MST activists argue that given the overwhelming monopoly on violence held by the state and elite landlords, it would be suicidal for the movement to respond in kind or to take actions that would escalate the level of violence. In all of the occupations carried out by the movement (over 230,000), there have been only occasional accusations that someone in the occupation camp had a rifle or pistol, and their use is certainly not condoned by MST members in general. This contrasts sharply with hundreds of proven cases of shootings, beatings and torture practiced against MST settlers, including men, women and children. To the extent that the MST is a revolutionary organization, it has pursued its aims through occupations, demonstrations and political argument and alliance and not through any campaign or training for armed revolution.

From the beginning, MST's revolutionary ideology has been tempered by three things: an eclectic infusion of alternative radical ideologies; conservative resistance from the grass roots; and the changing nature of the movement as it expands throughout the country. As the MST has grown, members and activists alike have filtered out ideas that have been shown not to work, and new ideas have been incorporated that reflect both the movement's experiences and the changing membership base. Today, the MST's ideology includes elements of liberation theology, Maoism and Pãolo Freire's educational philosophy, as well as ideas from progressive national thinkers such as Milton Santos, Florestan Fernandes and Emir Sader. International intellectuals and activists have also contributed to a new ideology. Gandhi's struggle for national liberation in India inspires movement members; Franz Fanon's discussion of the death of culture through colonization appeals to people who feel their own culture is threatened by capitalism; Noam Chomsky's defense of alternative ideologies in the face of a globalizing neoliberalism supports the idea that the MST's struggles are inherently international. MST leaders and members have read, chewed over and attempted to incorporate all these ideas in some fashion. There is still an emphasis on the language of class struggle and revolution, but the MST's methodology and ideology recognizes that many different groups do not fit within the traditionally dualistic structure of workers and employers. And the movement recognizes that any solution to the problem of landlessness in Brazil will be unique to the Brazilian context.

The somewhat conservative nature of the movement's grassroots base has also pushed the MST's ideology in new directions, particularly as it has expanded outside of the South. On one hand, MST members engage in radical acts simply by joining the movement—they experience a sort of revolution in their personal and collective experience. This is, ultimately, the creation of the new society that we have seen emerging through the pages of this book. On the other hand, it seems that the minority of the MST's grassroots members (those not involved in leadership or activism) are interested in generating a true socialist revolution that would overthrow the government—but it's hard to tell. Most of the settlers we visited in the different areas of the country were interested in doing better for their families, having more money to buy a new piece of machinery or a new pair of shoes. But just doing these things, things that we might take for granted, should be seen as revolutionary given where most of these people were coming from. Some of the settlers we talked to even asked timidly if we knew whether the MST was planning revolutionary activities. These settlers had joined the movement in order to win land and wondered aloud if they were involuntarily engaged in an attempt to overthrow the state. These misapprehensions are the product of overwhelmingly sensationalistic and negative media coverage, and they are indicative of the distrust the settlers have for talk of revolution.

The third reason why the MST's ideology has become less stridently revolutionary over time is because the movement's expansion has necessitated a professionalization that is almost inherently conservative.[33] As the MST has grown from four hundred members to over one million, it has had to fulfill the tasks of a professional organization. This means developing increasingly bureaucratic means of coordination. Each settlement has its own leadership arrangement, as does each microregion, each state, each geographic macroregion (comprising several states) and the country as a whole. The MST's belief in the value of participatory democracy means that hundreds of local decisions have to be communicated on a regular basis to the relevant people at each level. And, in return, a whole sophisticated array of electronic and human networks has to be maintained in order to disseminate information and assure feedback between and across organizational levels. The MST's bureaucracy is constantly expanding in order to accommoda new members, and this is cumbersome even though the moven tries to maintain as much flexibility in its system as possible. The increasing professionalization has meant the formalization of certain movement activities, such as financing and media representation. Movement activists need to be paid for their work, and so the movement needs to move a considerable amount of money around every month. Brazilian sociologist Zander Navarro believes that the movement's need to finance its ambitious activities has essentially turned part of the organization into a bank, an observation he uses to criticize the movement.

Perhaps the real reason why the need for steady income exerts a conservative influence on the movement is that one of the movement's primary sources of funding has been the Brazilian government. As would the members of any organization, the settlers pay a sort of movement membership fee out of the government credit they receive; so not only do the settlers rely on government programs to produce on the land, but the movement itself depends on that money for its own books. The government contributes other sources of money as well, particularly through agricultural programs such as one called Lumiar (which was cut in 2001). Lumiar paid for agricultural extension agents on the settlements, and the MST was allowed to contract all agents for settlements affiliated with the movement. Another important source of funding is international charity, such as Christian Aid in England. It could be argued that the goals of these organizations are at odds with socialist revolution and that this has a conservative effect on the movement, but there is no evidence to that effect, and the MST has always strictly maintained its distance from the goals of its funders.

The MST has also tempered its revolutionary rhetoric as it has made its way from the countryside into the cities. In the early days of the movement, *Jornal Sem Terra* issues were full of discussions about the new society, but in later issues the content became much more general. Discussions of the new man and woman were replaced by pictures from a "mini-Olympics" held on one of the settlements and by recipes for dishes that could be made with food grown on a small farm. This change in style reflects the influence of MST settlers and also coincides with the movement's decision to move into the cities and appeal to as wide a base as possible. Appeals for socialism or revolution have been substituted with appeals to national sovereignty, anti-imperialism and social justice—all worthy goals and certainly revolutionary in the context of Brazilian society and politics.

In fact, far from being dangerous for Brazilian democracy, one could argue that the sort of revolution the MST supports is exactly what Brazilian democracy needs in order to become truly democratic.

## The Creation of Citizenship and the Fight Against "Politics as Usual"

The question "Is the MST helping democracy?" may seem like an odd one. Brazil is a democratic country already, and some people would argue that in occupying land, the MST is in fact subverting the democratic process. Despite the movement's claim that the federal constitution legitimates their actions with the mandate that land has a "social responsibility" to be productive, the aggressive act of entering land in the middle of the night and setting up camp does not seem like a strategy that the writers of the constitution would have had in mind. Critics of the MST argue that the movement ought to utilize recognized, democratic, political channels in order to make its claims on the government. Osmar Dias, a senator from the southern state of Paraná, responded to an MST demonstration in 1997 with "We cannot continue to live with the subversion of order. If we want a democratic regime, we need to have, as a principle, order in democracy. Every time that order is subverted, we are attacking, destroying democracy."[34] Large farmers also regularly exhort the MST to work within the framework of the Brazilian political system. As one cattle farmer from the southern state of Santa Catarina said: "They need to fight, you know. But, I don't agree with the way they fight. Invading the land, asking the government to expropriate and the government doing it! . . . You could do it another way, register everyone, and then when the government knows that there are ten million unproductive hectares, it gives that to them!"

But the MST argues—as do many other organized social movements—that the constitution is little more than words on paper, because it is not backed up a guarantee of universal citizenship rights and is unresponsive to collective demands for change. As Father Beto, a well-known activist for social justice in Brazil, said:

Elected by the people, the government fears basing itself on the people. This is a formal democracy, a salon democracy that doesn't like the smell of the people, as General Figueiredo confessed, that keeps only one foot in the kitchen, with the other one, and its body and soul, in the carpeted corridors of those who have not even the slightest sensitivity to the growth of poverty and the abysmal inequality of income that characterizes the Brazilian nation.

Brazil made the transition from military dictatorship to formal democracy at a time when several other countries in South America—including Argentina, Bolivia, Chile, Ecuador and Uruguay—were also moving toward democracy. Several Central American countries would follow suit, as well, after lengthy civil wars, including El Salvador, Nicaragua and Guatemala. No one doubted these would be difficult transitions, but there was considerable optimism about the possibilities for economic, political and social change now that legitimate democratic regimes would be accountable to their constituencies.

In Brazil, civil and political groups that had begun to organize quietly in the late 1970s, during the military's abertura period, came together openly in the 1980s, taking to the streets in 1982 to demand direct presidential elections. Trade unions, student groups and new or previously marginalized political parties demanded that their voices be heard in the new political regime. But as the transition to democracy progressed—and the transition was very gradual, some people date the beginning in 1974 with Ernesto Geisel's announcement of abertura and the end in 1989 with the first president elected directly by the people—it became clear that implementing formal democracy—that is, elections—would be much easier than implementing substantive democracy. Even during the military rule, presidential elections had always been held. The military leader to be "elected" officially gave up his military position and became a civilian before accepting the presidency. The military even created an official opposition party (the Brazilian Democratic Movement, or MDB) to run against in elections, although the MDB was little more than a symbol until 1974. This may seem ridiculous, but it was necessary for the military to retain at least the outward appearance of following enlightened democratic reason, as authoritarian rule was at odds with their belief that they were governing in order to modernize Brazil according to a Western ideal of free elections and open markets.

So instituting formal elections after the military officially withdrew would not be difficult. Instituting substantive democracy, however, would be. Substantive democracy is the extension of democratic norms and practices to the arena of everyday life. This entails the development of universal citizenship rights and guaranteeing the space to organize collectively—and be heard—in pursuit of those rights. As the transition to democracy progressed, the early optimism expressed by politicians, movement leaders, academics and ordinary citizens in Brazil turned into critical accusations of "feckless democracy" and "low-intensity citizenship."[35] Scott Mainwaring, a political scientist at the University of Notre Dame who has written extensively on Brazilian politics, argued that the party system had been inadequately institutionalized and that people voted more for particular people than for particular parties.[36] At this writing in 2002, there were over thirty parties in Brazil, half of which were less than ten years old. Candidates for office regularly switched in and out of parties, reinforcing the impression that they were little more than formalities.

But even if a party system were to take hold in Brazil (and there are indications from the 2002 election that people may be increasingly voting out of a sense of party loyalty), there is still little sense of democracy "on the ground." Observers point to three sociopolitical characteristics that complicate democratic practice in Brazil: patronage, hierarchy and poverty. Patronage refers to the practice of a theoretically benign patron being personally responsible for the welfare of people within his or her circle of influence. The norms guiding patronage are very different from the norms governing democracy, because under the former system all rights are seen as "gifts" provided by the patron. These "gifts" are often things as basic as payment for labor or assistance with health care or other welfare benefits, but they are all negotiated with the understanding that receiving the gift is neither automatic nor effectively protected by a higher legal system.

This tradition of paternalism, which grew up on the large plantations in colonial Brazil, works against democracy in two ways. First, it violates the fundamental condition of universal citizenship rights codified in—and protected under—law. Second, it is a very successful means of dividing people who might otherwise organize to demand their rights. We saw this happen frequently in the settlements, particularly the ones not organized by the MST. In the northeastern sugarcane region, the MST had organized aggressively to demand the release of production credit, a move that pitted them against the city council and particularly won the anger of the head of the council. In the aftermath of the MST's mobilization, the head councilman visited settlers throughout the region and, in one case, offered the president of a settlement a handsome cart in which to carry wood. When MST leaders learned that the settlement president had accepted the cart, they were furious and insisted that this was indicative of the president's basic untrustworthiness. For his part, the president insisted equally strenuously that his accepting the cart was part of a well-thought-out ploy to deceive the head of the city council.

This is just one example of a political practice that disrupts peoples' efforts to form a consensus and mobilize in search of a collective set of rights. When people think about the best way to get running water in their houses or refrigerators or a new roof for the school, they have to choose between organizing behind a social movement that may or may not be successful and agreeing to vote for a politician who has the money and influence to promise that the water, refrigerators and school improvements will arrive in a timely fashion. When people make the latter choice, however, they lose out in two ways: they often do not receive the promised benefits once the politician has been elected or re-elected, and they have not made any progress toward having those rights guaranteed them in the future.

Hierarchical social relations also complicate the deepening of democracy in Brazil. Hierarchy in social relations stems from the extreme inequality among different classes, the members of all of which are assumed to know their place and respect the rules of the hierarchy. The rules are simple: whatever your position on the social ladder, you have some authority over those below you and none over those above, regardless of the specific situation. Brazilian anthropologist Roberto da Matta refers to this as "relational citizenship," where an individual's rights at any given time depend on his or her relationship to the other people involved.[37] Da Matta summed up relational citizenship with a phrase commonly heard in Brazil: "Do you know who you're talking to?" This phrase is employed to remind people of their place within the hierarchy, even if the particular situation would warrant a temporary reconfiguration of that hierarchy. In other words, a police officer who has a legitimate duty to pull over speeding cars might meet with "Do you know who you're talking to?" when trying to ticket someone who occupies a position considered superior to his or her own. Da Matta argues that the phrase is often met with silence, effectively deferring real citizenship rights.

A third challenge for democracy in Brazil is poverty, which has not decreased since the transition to democracy; in fact it has grown worse. The burdens of poverty are obvious, and they directly affect the democratic process by eroding people's capacity to organize collectively. It is difficult for people to campaign for running water or sanitary sewage when they must spend a full day dealing with those absences as well as working, tending the house, taking care of the children and searching for food. This is not to say that poor Brazilians have not consistently found the time to organize collectively, but poverty does not make their work any easier. And some long-term goals, like democratization, might seem less relevant than the more immediate challenges of feeding the children and staying healthy.

In light of these three factors—patronage, hierarchy and poverty—how can the MST really expect to deepen democracy in Brazil? The MST sees the work it is doing—mobilizations, demonstrations, organized occupations—as key to the construction of a political alternative in Brazil. As the movement's slogan reads, "Without agrarian reform, there is no democracy." The movement stakes out this clear position with the understanding that agrarian reform means more than just the simple redistribution of land. As we have suggested before, "true" agrarian reform means fundamentally reorganizing the structural basis of land tenure and providing basic citizenship rights to those who are scratching out their living on the land. The MST is not arguing that any democratic country should have a certain number of people living on the land, but that in the context of landlessness, poverty and exclusion in Brazil, the transition to democracy will not be complete without giving people a chance to produce and reproduce with the assurance that they can positively affect their own future.

Perhaps the most important benefit of a successful agrarian reform is the creation of an informed, educated, active citizenry. What does it mean to be part of an active citizenry or to have "effective" citizenship, as the MST argues is necessary? As Americans, we believe in certain individual freedoms—like the freedom of speech and independent thought and the freedom to elect public officials. At the most basic level, living on the settlements provides the settlers with a measure of the freedom necessary to become active citizens of the country. In the settlements, they are free from the ever-present dangers of living on the streets or in the urban slums.

In addition to getting away from the danger and violence of the slums, people who live in MST settlements have a much greater opportunity to attend school than they would in the urban slums. The 1996 Vox Populi study (cited earlier) showed that only 10 percent of all the adults on the settlement had gone past fourth grade, but that over 50 percent of all the children on the settlements were in school at the time of the study. A decent education is a basic requirement of citizenship—this belief motivated Benjamin Franklin throughout his life's work, in turn inspiring a US-led movement for universal public education that has transformed those societies that have achieved it. Education builds children who have choices later in life about what they want to do and enables adults to follow more complicated political discussions and engage with the information that comes through the television and radio.

It is difficult to imagine how one could participate in a democracy without at least a minimum level of safety and education. In 1930, only 3 percent of all Brazilians were eligible to vote because of the restrictive literacy and property requirements. Today, all Brazilians over the age of sixteen are required to vote, but how informed can that vote be if people do not have a decent education? There are regular allegations of political candidates in Brazil "stealing votes" in exchange for food, water (particularly in the arid Northeast) and other "gifts." If people are not reading newspapers and thinking critically, it is easy to see how they could be swayed by easy promises made on the campaign trail or by the apparent generosity of candidates.

In the addition to the schools that have been set up on MST settlements, the settlers also receive a basic and practical education in participatory politics. The initial land occupation requires them to literally put their lives on the line for an extended period in order to achieve a response from government. This is a political act that requires a seriousness of commitment and clarity of purpose that few in the United States—or in Brazil—ever experience. It is only the beginning of an enduring political education through practice. Settlers are required to set up settlement associations, elect officials regularly, and decide how matters will be organized.

MST settlers are also inserted into a wider political arena through contact with local government officials, particularly through the many local and state officials belonging to the Workers' Party (PT). The MST has strong ties to the PT, although the movement maintains its autonomy (the movement still abides by the decision made at its founding meeting at Cascavel in 1984 that it does not wish to become a political party or become dependent on one, which would force it to play by the rules governing conventional politics). MST settlers also have the opportunity to get involved in politics themselves, particularly when they come from large settlements with enough of a membership to get their own representatives elected. In one municipality in Santa Catarina, local elections saw no fewer than eleven MST settlers up for various positions. And remember Pacote from chapter 1, who was elected a municipal councilor after receiving land in Rio Grande do Sul.

With their increasing participation in local, regional and national politics, MST settlers are having a noticeable impact on "politics as usual." This is perhaps most evident in the realm of accountability. The cornerstone to any democracy is accountability—the transparency and the sense of responsibility for action or inaction with which the government conducts its business. With its membership of over one million people and its high visibility, the MST is forcing the government to pay attention to its constituency—people who have traditionally lacked the political and economic influence in Brazil to get their own concerns on the agenda.

One example of accountability is the punishment of people who have committed murder. Remember the massacre that happened in El Dorado dos Carajás, described in chapter 3. The people who are believed to be guilty of instigating the massacre were captured on videotape, but this documentation would not be sufficient to punish the guilty if the MST were not successful in galvanizing public opinion and pressuring the government to watch over judicial proceedings. At present, two actors in the massacre have been sentenced to life in prison, after originally having been cleared by an earlier state tribunal. The MST continues to press for trials for higher-ups they consider culpable in the massacre.

Another example of the movement's pursuit of accountability is its campaign against the World Bank's "market land reform" pilot project—called Cedula da Terra, begun in 1997. The World Bank has lent its support to a market-oriented model of agrarian reform that would receive little government intervention or assistance. Those wanting to receive land through the program apply for low-interest loans to buy land at market rates determined by willing sellers. They are aided by some other programs that are meant, as INCRA programs are meant in the established agrarian reform process, to help people become established as farmers and within communities of people participating. The government has argued that this sort of market-based and, in its terms, community-oriented agrarian reform, would be more efficient and economically viable than a predominantly state-led one prodded on by social movements such as the MST.

In 1998, the MST, along with several other social movements, filed a request for an inspection of the program on the grounds that it violated the World Bank's own mandates. The World Bank investigated both complaints and ruled that the program did not violate the Bank's rules and that many recipients of land were pleased with their participation in it, but the MST's objections were not for nothing. They made people aware of how the Cedula da Terra differed from what could be considered genuine agrarian reform according to the government's own definition. And the MST's campaign forced both the state and the public to go behind the optimistic claims about market-led agrarian reform to think about what might be lost or gained in turning the process of reform over to the market.

The market-led reforms clearly would leave most people unable to participate, because although buyers would receive low-interest loans, the purchase price of land would be at the seller's choice. If sellers are aware that the buyers are participating in such a program, they will drive particularly hard bargains. As the government itself eventually admitted, because of the expense alone, the program would benefit at

most some thousands of families, not the hundreds of thousands benefited by the process the MST has forced the government to pursue.

Just as important as the reduced number of recipients in the World
Bank–supported program is the clear intent to depoliticize the process
of agrarian reform. The MST's agrarian reform campaign has challenged
the Brazilian political system, raising issues of the disproportionate
power of rural oligarchies, legal impunity for the rich, lack of government accountability, systematic corruption of legal processes, structure
of the law itself and the legitimacy of a government and society founded
on the world's deepest social inequities. The World Bank reform would
do nothing of the kind. In contrast, it is based on the notion that the
system is fundamentally sound and that its problems can be resolved
by reducing interest rates for agricultural land purchase. Participation
in the World Bank program does nothing to educate recipients in the
nature of the political process, community responsibility and collective
action. It rests on the naive, or perhaps devious, assumption that the
problem can be solved merely by the redistribution of land within the
context of the existing political and economic arrangements.

As if to parody the idea of separating agrarian reform from the social
movements, in 2001, the Brazilian government devised an alternative
program called "agrarian reform through the mail." It invited any Brazilian to send an application for land to the land reform ministry; the
ministry would in turn assign land to qualified recipients from among
the vast tracts of unused or empty land it had identified. Not surprisingly, there were an overwhelming number of requests, but little indication that anything was being done to actually allocate land. Other
scholars told us of seeing great stacks of these applications, bound together in large batches, gathering dust in the corners of Brazilian post
offices. The process has gone nowhere and most certainly will go
nowhere in the future because, in a way analogous to but more clearly
ludicrous than the World Bank program, it tries to divorce the process
of land reform from processes of profound social change. Some have
called the Cedula da Terra and "agrarian reform through the mail" programs "agrarian reform through virgin birth."

Throughout our travels in the agrarian reform settlements of Brazil,
people told us with a sense of urgency over and over again that "the

land is only a door," "the land is only a first step," "the land is only a beginning," because to them it was absolutely clear that acquisition of
land could not succeed by itself without much deeper changes in the
society. In the Brazilian context, as in most other nations, to strip agrarian reform of that deeper political meaning would be to undermine and
destroy it.

We have emphasized throughout this book the deep historical roots
of the problem of Brazilian inequities. Without a clear-headed appreciation of those roots, one might try, as the World Bank proposes, to solve
the problem through superficial and depoliticized programs. Attacked
in this way, Brazilian inequality, like the sugarcane on which it was
originally based, can and will regenerate from the roots. Without a reform that goes to the roots, the essence of the plantation system and all
the evils that grew up around it will rise again, in old familiar forms as
well as in new ones.

The MST and its members have been relentless in exposing the shallow deceptions that the government has offered in place of a genuine,
committed reform process. The benefits of their criticism of government action go beyond the many improvements they have won in policy reform and in public support for agrarian reform. They have also
shown how even the humblest of citizens can become transformed into
a social force for more open and penetrating public debate and democratic practice. The creation of citizenship is a process of transformation of both those within the MST and those who must, like it or not,
deal with the participation of Brazil's rural poor in the affairs of the nation. The sense of irritation and impatience that many politicians, members of the press and private citizens express with the never-ending
MST critique is, in our view, the inevitable result of having to deal for
the first time with the presence of the "excluded" and the "marginalized" in the public dialog. Irritation is the predictable result of the
afflicted coming to afflict the comfortable. It is a sign of genuinely democratizing tendencies in Brazilian society.

As we suggested in chapter 1, some critics doubt whether the MST
has succeeded in democratizing its own organizational structure to the
degree the movement has argued the Brazilian State ought to democra-
tize. One critic, the Brazilian sociologist Zander Navarro, has argued
that since 1986 that the violence fostered by the struggle for land has

increasingly compelled the MST's leaders to move away from the Catholic Church's idea of a "mass movement" and toward a more centralized organization.[38] In our experience with the MST, we have noted some degree of centralization in decision making, most notably in regard to collective production in the movement's early years. The movement's push to develop large-scale collectives on the settlements was advocated by influential leaders and resisted by a significant portion of the members on the settlements. MST settlers who had left one such project in Santa Catarina complained of being shut out by local movement leaders, although they still proudly considered themselves part of the MST.

Overall, however, it is clear that participating in the movement has been an overwhelmingly positive experience in terms of political practice, one that offers MST members an example of how powerful collective organizing can be and provides a forum for actively fostering ongoing organization. The movement holds meetings every year from the settlement to the national level to find out what its members are thinking, and it is in these meetings that activities and tactics are planned for the upcoming year. This is already a significant advance over traditional political practice in Brazil. MST settlers run their own settlement associations, negotiate for access to services that they demand as their right and participate in public demonstrations that deepen the struggle for land, making it a struggle for democracy in Brazil.

## The MST and Civil Society in Brazil

The MST has not been alone in opening up Brazilian life to something more than a formalized but empty democratic political life. Throughout the 1990s, the Workers' Party (the PT, officially formed in 1980) has taken office in many of Brazil's largest cities and some of its states. With some exceptions, these PT administrations have been relatively honest and capable. Even the conservative press has expressed frequent surprise that a party founded on the union movement could manage responsible and competent administrations. The PT has drawn ideas and energy from the lively citizens' movements. As mentioned earlier, the more conservative Cardoso government and right-wing parties often adopted many of the PT's programmatic ideas as their own, such as the bolsa escola idea by which poor families are financially rewarded for keeping their children in school. The PT and the citizens' movements together have begun to prove to Brazilians that they can make real change and that much of the most effective change comes out of the favelas, the factories and the agrarian reform communities in the countryside.

The PT has also experimented with a radical system of participatory budget allocation, the Orçamento Participativo (OP), whereby people join their municipal representatives in an exhausting round of meetings to decide on the budget for the following year. Although the OP only covers a portion of any given municipality's budget, the process represents a radical and promising experiment in grassroots politics. The number of people who actually take part in the participatory budgeting process is a small fraction of those represented by the PT, but many people argue that the existence of an avenue for participation is an important step toward building a more active citizenry. The newly created municipality of Pontão in Sarandí, Rio Grande do Sul, for example, is using the participatory budgeting process, and Pacote, who is one of the municipal councilors, is very enthusiastic about the results. "When everyone participates and everyone sees how much money there is and where it is being spent, there is a lot less complaining."[39]

In addition to the PT, there has been a kind of explosion of citizen initiatives since the dying days of the dictatorship.[40] A vigorous black consciousness movement has arisen that for the first time has been effective in pointing out that Brazil is far from being a racial democracy. It has also been able to begin to erode Brazilian racism. Afro-Brazilian political figures have arisen in significant numbers and force for the first time and, as they have come to prominence, have added new life to Brazilian politics. One such person is Benedita da Silva, an Afro-Brazilian woman from one of the poorest slum communities who has shown the enormous potential for leadership and creativity that until recently has been frustrated by the exclusionist politics of class and race. After serving her term as governor of the state of Rio de Janeiro, she has just taken up a position in Lula's cabinet as minister of social services. Gilberto Gil, the songwriter and performer who has done much to popularize the black consciousness movement will be going to cabinet meetings with Benedita in his capacity as minister of culture.[41]

Community organizations, many of them closely connected to the black consciousness movement, have built on an old tradition in Brazil in which music, dance and carnival form the basis for mutual aid and representation of community interests. These newer organizations, such as Olodum and Ilé Axê in Salvador, have used the fantastic Afro-Brazilian music that comes out of poor urban areas to unite people politically, raise money for community projects and build independent community organizations. People paying twenty dollars a ticket to see Olodum performers in New York or London may not realize that they are supporting Paulo Freire schools, health clinics and community revitalization, but they are.

The feminist movement has removed barrier after barrier to women's more active participation in family and civic life. New legislation has extended a variety of protections and opportunities to women that few would have imagined possible in the Brazil of 1980. Women have become mayors of Brazil's largest cities, governors of states, and have been considered as national presidential candidates far more seriously than any woman has ever been considered for US president.

A gay-rights movement has arisen that is remarkably active and effective. AIDS activists and public health officials around the world have come to Brazil to learn from the citizen-based movement to deal with Brazil's serious AIDS epidemic. The citizens' movement to combat AIDS has led to enlightened official public policies on AIDS, including a successful campaign that prompted the Cardoso government to play a strong leading role, along with South Africa, in challenging the control multinational pharmaceutical companies were exercising over therapeutic drugs for the disease. The resulting agreement with the corporations will benefit HIV-positive people and AIDS patients all over the world.

The story of the Brazilian indigenous rights movement, as we have seen, is intimately interwoven with the story of the landless movement from its very beginning. The continuing aggressiveness of the indigenous movement in Brazil has accomplished the protection of vast areas of forest the size of major European nations. It is a daily and difficult struggle to actually defend the areas from exploitation in spite of the legal protections. That struggle is necessary, to return to our basic theme, because of the desperation of the landless poor and the impunity of the powerful. The MST and the indigenous rights movement have come into occasional conflict, but for the most part they work together as allies. The MST's strategy recognizes the wisdom of protecting indigenous rights, of reducing settlement in the Amazon as a whole, and of turning to rapacious landlords rather than Indians for land.

Linked to both the landless and the indigenous rights movement has been the rubber tappers' union begun by Chico Mendes (see chapter 3). The three movements working together have been critical in redefining the battle away from poor people quarreling with each other over pieces of a degrading environment and toward challenging the fundamental patterns of ownership that tragically despoil the Brazilian landscape at the expense of the landless, the Indians and the rubber tappers.

The Brazilian environmental movement has grown apace. Its alliances with the indigenous and rubber tappers' organizations have led many Brazilian environmentalists into an appreciation of the social foundations of ecological problems that is sometimes hard to find in the US environmental movement. In some specific cases, as we have seen above, environmentalists have found direct common cause in specific projects with MST settlers.

On the other hand, there are those in the environmental camp with a superficial understanding of the landless movement. One of the most common misperceptions is that all the landless in Brazil work through the MST. Based on this assumption, whenever landless people anywhere in Brazil chop down forests, the MST is blamed, ignoring the facts that the overwhelming share of landless in the Amazon, and a large percentage throughout Brazil, are operating outside of the MST, and that the MST analysis of the nature of the problem of the landless has led it to consistently argue against forest clearance in favor of the redistribution of existing agricultural land. Some cases of forest felling by MST settlers have been used to make unfair generalizations about the organization's policies and predominant practices. The largely urban, middle-class and upper-class base of the environmental movement has also made for some difficulties in maintaining alliances with the MST. In spite of these difficulties, many environmentalists and their organizations do understand the connection between environmental degradation and the continuing problem of landlessness and support the MST whole-heartedly.

The sem-terra, the "without-land" movement, has given rise to an urban version, called the *sem-teto* ("without-roof") movement of homeless people. The sem-teto, in some places loosely allied with the MST, in other places operating much more spontaneously and with little organization, have occupied empty buildings and lots, conducted sit-ins in government offices and otherwise followed tactics adapted to an urban environment but clearly inspired by the MST.

People have started numerous organizations to assist the street children of Brazil. Contrary to popular belief, most of the street children have families and homes; unfortunately the homes and families are so filled with stress, hunger and conflict that the street begins to seem like a better alternative than staying home. Some organizations try to offer charity to simply address the immediate needs of the children and have little impact on the political or economic problems that give rise to the problem. Others have grown into raising serious questions about the origins of the problem, in the terrible inequities of the society in general and of public policies and private investment strategies more particularly. Each inquiry into the problem inevitably leads back to a significant degree to the situation of the rural poor migrating to cities for lack of a better alternative, and then finding few alternatives in city life.

Many of the new organizations have broken out of old cultural and political patterns in a way that begins to make democracy a living practice rather than simply a stale electoral formality that in itself seldom seems to offer much hope. In spite of Brazil's depressing poverty and injustices, it is wonderfully alive with imaginative, good-hearted and politically serious efforts to make Brazil a better country. The very image of the poor and the socially excluded—who they are, what they are capable of and what they can do for Brazil—is undergoing a gradual but profound change. Though there is a very long way to go, and no assurance that the present direction might not be reversed, the atmosphere of Brazil is exciting and often very hopeful.

The MST is not operating in a vacuum, nor is it working alone. It should not be understood nor evaluated outside of the context of the wider movement for social change and democratization of which it is a part. If the MST is seen as an isolated phenomenon, it is easy to see its work as doomed, quixotic, unrealistic. As isolated communities of poor farmers in the vast Brazilian landscape, MST members might reasonably expect that the old rule of the ruthless land barons, the corrupt city politicians and the multinational corporations will sooner or later convert them again into landless laborers and sharecroppers.

Seen as part of a broader set of political alliances and of a larger set of social changes, however, the movement looks much more hopeful. Throughout our story of the MST, we have seen how it has been linked to and benefited from parallel movements among people in churches, labor unions, indigenous organizations, the rubber tappers' union and political parties. The MST has played a leadership role among all of these people at many junctures. On the other hand, without these others, there would be no MST now and there would be no hope for the MST's future.

## The MST in the International Context

Nor is this simply a story of Brazil. The MST has always worked with international organizations and in an international context. Some of that context has been highly negative, such as the implementation of "the Washington consensus" through which the US government and international organizations press constantly for low social expenditures, permissive regulatory policies and trade policies that tend to favor large and international investors over small farmers and local entrepreneurs. The agricultural research agenda favored by the Washington consensus and by US agencies and universities has an enormous worldwide influence; again, it favors capital-intensive, large-scale farming over small farmers. It argues that genetically engineered crops are the answer for the world's poor, while the MST and small farm organizations see these crops largely as a way for corporations to gain further control over agricultural production in ways that will make it difficult for poor farmers to stay in business.

However, much in the international context has been helpful to the MST and the cause of Brazilian land reform. The Catholic Church and the reforms initiated by Vatican II and Pope John XXIII in the 1960s established an international foundation for local clerics and lay workers in Brazil to help bring the landless together to defend themselves and assert their interests. Of course, conservatives in the church have opposed this work, and, unfortunately, they apparently include the present pope, who has been very active in punishing leading Brazilian liberation theologians and clerical activists. Nonetheless, the National Conference of Brazilian Bishops continues to provide direct assistance to the CPT and indirect aid to the MST.

Many organizations throughout the world have lent moral support to the MST, and some have provided advice and money. Cuba has provided some training for MST personnel in health and education. Several European governments have included the MST in foreign assistance grants and projects, and the MST has been honored by the Swedish parliament and various international organizations. A US-based group called Friends of the MST has been organized to build solidarity between grassroots activists in the United States and the MST.

As important as this assistance has been, the degree to which the MST as a national organization has avoided dependence on assistance is striking. This is even more remarkable in the individual settlements, where virtually all resources come from the settlers themselves or have been extracted from the government's agrarian reform ministry. Some state governments have also provided important resources.

Nonetheless, on most settlements, people are at least somewhat aware of the negative effects that such organizations as the IMF and World Bank can have on their fate. But they also take great courage from the support, even if only verbal, from foreigners and foreign organizations. On the settlements and in the state and national offices, it is important to people that they participate in international coalitions supporting agrarian reform and policies favorable to poor people and poor nations. Participation in the international alliance of family farmer organizations, Via Campesina, is a way for the MST to work actively with like-minded organizations around the world and to share experiences about reform. Within Via Campesina and other international organizations in which it participates, the MST is widely respected and admired. Organizations from other countries have studied the MST's actions and policies carefully.

The memory of the military government and US support for it is

still fresh in the minds of Brazilians with any degree of political awareness. On the day of this writing, the Brazilian government announced
that it would finally release police archives detailing the arrests, tor-
tures and murders carried out by the regime. Without question, this
will revive the sense of anger and pain of that era. The US Contra War
in Nicaragua and the US invasions of Panama and Grenada are also
worrisome. The thinly disguised counterinsurgency campaign of the
Colombian government financed by the US "Plan Colombia" is read by
MST members as continued US intervention on behalf of Latin American elites and US financial and geopolitical interests.

The Gulf War on Iraq, the UN sanctions on Iraq and the 2003 US
war in Iraq have also come at a high cost to the Brazilian economy, because Iraq was a major trading partner of Brazil, exchanging Iraqi oil
for Brazilian-made machinery, small arms, poultry and other agricultural products. Such losses to other nations as a result of US foreign
policy actions are not accounted for in the US calculus, which continues to worry Brazilians from all political positions, even those who
share US concerns about Saddam Hussein. The Bush administration's
aggressive statements and actions in asserting that the US is the only
superpower and will take any steps to preserve that Olympian status,
now in the name of the war on terrorism rather than as previously in
the name of the Cold War, are also worrisome. Bush's statements that
anyone who is not with the US is against it concern MST members and
many other Brazilians.

The first week after September 11, 2001, the cover of the weekly
magazine *Veja* showed a photo of one of the planes crashing in a ball of
flame into the World Trade Center, with the caption "The Vulnerable
Empire." For Brazilians, and especially MST members, the US government now seems to be acting like an empire aroused to anger and
vengeance in self-defense. Pair that with the memory that the US was
prepared to support a military coup and the long-lived dictatorship
that followed it, to a large degree because of fears of agrarian reform
and radical rural movements, and one has a formula for deep distrust
and fear of US actions in response to any serious agrarian reform in
Brazil. In this context, it is very important to MST members that people in the US be familiar with the MST and be prepared to reduce the
likelihood and force of US intervention in Brazil.

When asked about what others can do to help the MST, members and leaders give many different answers. The MST welcomes financial assistance and volunteers to work in Brazil or abroad on MST needs and projects. We have been struck, however, that most of these emphasize the importance of people working for positive social and political change in their own countries. There is surprisingly little expectation or solicitation of direct support for the MST. The assumption is that the MST will benefit most when its allies in other countries improve their own societies. Of course, part of this has to do with improving the way other governments, especially the United States, exert their influence in the world. But just as the MST has always insisted on charting its own ideological and political direction, it does not presume to tell others how to make progressive political change. That is our task and we must find our own way.

## Children of the MST and the Future

There is one question that nearly everyone interested in the MST finds fascinating and important. Above all, the settlers themselves are deeply concerned about it. Will the children growing up in MST settlements stay on the settlements in sufficient numbers to keep agrarian reform alive? Most of these children, with all the problems they face, are enjoying healthier, more comfortable lives than their parents did as children, and they are being far better prepared to do well in a wider world. Won't they leave in droves when they grow up? Won't this make the MST and agrarian reform at best a poorly remembered episode in Brazil's history?

We did not come up with any firm answer to this question. Nor has anyone else. All our information on it is contradictory. Some children express a real understanding of what the MST is all about and a fierce loyalty to the organization and its ideals. Since 1996, the movement has organized an annual meeting of *sem-terrinha* (little landless ones), which brings together the children of MST settlers and educates them about the ongoing struggle for the land. The children sing the movement's songs and tell its stories. Many have even literally confronted face-to-face the police lines and hired thugs who have come to destroy their communities. More than a few have seen the violent death of loved ones defending their homes. To one degree or another, all are receiving an education in the history of their parents' battles in the MST and their hopes for the future of the landless movement. Most love the animals and the freedom to wander as they please—we saw children playing video games, of course, but we also saw a young teenager with a special pouch made for the purpose carrying a spurred cock across the fields to the Saturday fights. Some have learned what it is to succeed in farming and would love to continue making their farm a better place.

A lot of other kids on the settlement are preoccupied with getting an education so that they can leave the settlement and have a good job and pleasant life in the city.[42] Many parents are even more determined than their children to see this happen—they see their triumph in getting land as the mechanism that paves a superhighway for their children to speed away from the countryside as soon as possible. As the MST children are growing up in more prosperous families than their parents did, they are far more exposed to television, movies and computers, the One Big Advertisement for urban life. A constant preoccupation of many in the MST is that the families, parents and children, have a tendency to become individualistic and unconcerned about the movement once they have received their piece of land.

Yet again, some children, as they get more education, come to appreciate the MST more than ever for the extraordinary thing it is. But then, there is that insistent pull. . . . Our observations would seem to support the idea, not a surprising one, that most parents want their children to stay home to be a help and comfort for the family, the community and the movement, while simultaneously hoping their children find a better life elsewhere. Most children are torn between their loyalty to family and community and their love of country pleasures and their hopes for another kind of life in the city. How the balance of this ambivalence tips for each family and child will depend a great deal on unforeseeable events.

We take a little encouragement for the future from watching two children in Sarandí on a Sunday in midsummer that had turned surprisingly cold and rainy. They were part of the family who cared for the MST-affiliated school and research center that was providing us room and board. The family had a flourishing farm alongside the schoolhouse with cows, pigs, rabbits, some row crops, a big organic garden and facilities for making endless quantities of preserves and cheese. Everyone in the family of hefty German-Brazilians worked hard, but at least most of the time with good cheer. The two boys had been left at home while the parents went to town to do errands. They had finished their chores taking care of the animals and had time on their hands.

They began to talk about what they could do with their time. In the way we all remember from our childhood, they turned over many alternatives, finding something wrong with each, in a slightly whiny debate. Finally, the eleven-year-old said with enthusiasm, "I know, let's watch videos!" The eight-year-old agreed enthusiastically, and the older boy said he would set up the school's television and VCR while the other went to fetch the tapes. There was a little conversation we didn't hear about which tape to get.

Without much to do ourselves, we carried on a quiet debate and guessing game about what videos they might be anticipating with such zeal. Since everything from Schwarzenegger movies to Hollywood romances to animated features is easily available in this region of Brazil, we made a lot of guesses, in which, to our best recollection, *Terminator II* and cartoon anthologies featured most prominently.

When the tape was put in the machine, the boys watched it intently, making occasional intelligent comments on it, through all two hours of the show. It was called *The Management of Small-Scale Agricultural Systems.*

# Postscript: The Lula Government

As we put the final touches on this manuscript, Luis Inácio da Silva, Lula, has taken office as president of Brazil. It has been over twenty years since Lula's visit to the Acampamento Natalino, in the first days of the creation of the landless movement. At that time, he encouraged the people living in tents made of plastic sheeting and wood scraps to think of themselves as part of Brazil's most important social movement.

Lula's words were much more than just political rhetoric. He himself had been born to a poor farm family in Pernambuco and had traveled to São Paulo as a young child to become a shoe-shine boy on the streets and later a drill press operator. But he was always active in labor politics—even though the country was under the rule of an authoritarian military government. In 1978 and 1979, Lula led the massive autoworkers' strikes in the São Paulo industrial region that had so much to do with ending the military dictatorship. In 1980, Lula helped to organize the Workers' Party (PT) and became its first president. From the beginning, Lula was a strong supporter of the MST and of the need for agrarian reform in Brazil.

In the first twenty-two years after the Workers' Party was formed, Lula ran for president of Brazil four times (1989, 1994, 1998, 2002). As Lula campaigned for the presidency over the years and tried to widen his appeal, the MST voiced its support for the party but stressed the movement's autonomy vis-à-vis formal politics. MST leaders repeatedly stated that the movement would continue to aggressively fight for agrarian reform no matter who was in the executive office. At the same time, movement leaders and members alike enthusiastically supported candidates and policies from the Workers' Party. Movement leaders in the Northeast organized busloads of settlers to hear Lula speak during his famous tour of the region in 1993.

In 2002, as Lula's campaign gathered steam and it seemed increasingly likely that he would win the presidency (although people were reluctant to voice their hope out loud because Lula had gotten close before), the MST's official stance was mixed. On one hand, João Pedro Stédile gave repeated interviews in which he expressed the movement's support for the ideology behind Lula's campaign. In an interview published in the *Folha de São Paulo*, he said: "Our preoccupation is not with the discourse of the candidates. Our concern is with the social forces each represents. Thus, it is evident that . . . the only candidate that represents the social forces that want real change in this country is Lula."[43] In the same interview, João Pedro said that he was going to vote for Lula, and "although there were no deliberations of congresses, all of the social militants, the MST, like other movements of Via Campesina, are involved and committed to the campaign and to a Lula victory."

On the other hand, MST leaders had several concerns about a Lula presidency—concerns that led them to support a different candidate during the nomination period. They did not want to be seen as a PT lapdog, and activists who came to the United States emphasized the movement's political independence when faced with eager questions about the 2002 elections. The movement also worried that Lula would have little room to maneuver if he won the election. All four of the presidential candidates had been compelled by President Cardoso and the IMF to signal their willingness to continue payments on the foreign debt if they were elected. The high level of indebtedness that confronts Lula will make it very difficult for him to carry out the promises he made regarding social change—and the MST worries that agrarian reform will be one casualty of Lula's induction into "real politics."

Despite some of their doubts, MST members—as well as other people involved in Brazil's growing social movements—are declaring the beginning of a new political project in Brazil now that their longtime supporter has taken office as the country's president. Will Lula be able to meet their expectations? Will he make agrarian reform a priority when he has so many constituents to make happy? Or will he become hopelessly trapped between their expectations and the demands for austerity of international banking institutions?

Although it is still early (we are writing this in the spring of 2003), the signals from the Lula administration regarding agriculture and agrarian reform are decidedly mixed. On one hand, Lula has appointed Miguel Rossetto as cabinet minister to oversee agrarian reform. A member of the Workers' Party, Rossetto is considered a friend of the MST, and he has long been a strong advocate of small-scale agriculture and serious land reform. In addition, Lula's most highly publicized program to date, Fome Zero (Zero Hunger) is under the direction of José Graziano da Silva, a prominent professor of rural development who has been known as a friend of agrarian reform. Some people worry, however, about Graziano da Silva's repeated assertions that agrarian reform should be considered a social project and policy rather than an economic one. On New Year's Day, 2003, Lula himself made an impassioned and relatively lengthy call for agrarian reform as the first main topic of his inaugural address. Miguel Rossetto has subsequently said that he expects to see more land occupations, and the Lula government is expected to be more sympathetic to them than the Cardoso government was.

On the other hand, Lula has appointed Roberto Rodriguez as minister of agriculture. Rodriguez is associated with international agribusiness and speaks vigorously on behalf of large-scale, highly capital intensive, export-oriented agricultural policies. The government's focus on such policies is likely to continue given that Brazil depends heavily on agricultural exports for the foreign currency to finance its debt payments. It is difficult to see how these policies can be made consistent with a strong emphasis on agrarian reform.

In early 2003 interviews with MST members, including João Pedro Stédile and farmers on MST settlements, as well as in talks with academic specialists, we heard a similar analysis. This analysis also appeared in newspapers and magazines. The first point was that while Lula's political party is a socialist party and Lula a socialist, the government is not a socialist government. Rather, it was said to be a government of "national unity" that owes its power in part to the support of an important sector of Brazil's most influential capitalists, who support Lula because they agree that inequality is Brazil's greatest problem. They agree that inequality retards national development for all the reasons that we have discussed in this book. Ironically, many of the most highly productive, large-scale producers are said to be among Lula's supporters. In this analysis, economic growth is considered essential to creating the wealth necessary to afford social reforms, including agrarian reform.

In this view, there is another sector of approximately twenty-seven thousand large landholders who make poor use of their land and whose land is legally subject to expropriation. "This is enough land," says Stédile, "to provide all the land we need for the agrarian reform we are prepared to carry out over the next few years." The more productive producers, in this analysis, have no interest in protecting these twenty-seven thousand. In the view of the people we talked to on the settlements who described the situation in these terms, "It is well understood that within a year, we will be mobilizing to give the Lula government the strength it needs to carry out the reforms. We will be giving him the support he needs in the streets and in a wave of land occupations."

In elaborating on this view, João Pedro Stédile said that the real confrontation between the MST and the Lula government (and between

Rossetto and Rodriguez) will come when small farmers throughout Brazil realize that the country's whole structure of price supports, credit and production incentives is highly discriminatory against family farms and that land reform cannot survive without major structural reforms in those areas. The minister in charge of agrarian reform will have to confront the minister of agriculture in a battle which it is likely only one can win. João Pedro Stédile continued: "That confrontation will come, but it need not come yet." In the meantime, in this scenario, there will be a major redistribution of land.

What is clear from this rough consensus is that there are indeed contradictions within Lula's government and contradictory views and interests among those who support it. At the beginning of the Lula administration, many people with very different goals shared a nearly euphoric optimism about what the government could accomplish. There was at least a feeling of remarkable national unity that has been rare in Brazilian history. What will happen as this feeling of unity is tested against Brazil's stubborn problem of inequality? The next chapter in the history of Brazil's fragile democracy will without question be a tense and exciting one. There seems little doubt that the people of the MST will play a significant role.

# Notes

## Introduction

1. Ricardo Mendonça. 2002. "O paradoxo da miseria." *Veja* 23, January: 82–93. Figures taken from IPEA (Instituto de Pesquisas de Economia Aplicada), Ministerio de Planejamento, Brasil.

2. IBGE (Instituto Brasileiro de Geografia e Estastica). 1990. *Estatisticas Historicas do Brasil*, 2nd ed. Rio de Janeiro: IBGE, 318–319. These figures are for 1985, the year of the founding of the MST. For an updated version with further detail and discussion, see INCRA/FAO (Instituto Nacional de Colonialização e Reforma Agraria/Food and Agriculture Organization, United Nations), 2000, coords. Carlos Enrique Guanziroli and Silvia Elizabeth de C.S. Cardim, "Novo Retrato da Agricultura Familiar: O Brasil Redescoberto," Brasília: INCRA, 16–26.

## Chapter One

1. José and Anir Placotnik. Interviews by authors. Sarandí, January 2001.

2. Argemiro Jacob Brum, 1988, *Modernizacão da Agricultura: trigo e soja*, Petrópolis, Rio de Janeiro: Vozes; José de Souza Martins, 1984, *A militarizacão da questão agricola*, Petrópolis, Rio de Janeiro: Vozes; José Graziano da Silva, 1983, *Modernizacão dolorosa*, Rio de Janeiro: Zahar.

3. Discussions of the years leading up to the military dictatorship and of the dictatorship itself can be found in Thomas Skidmore, 1967, *Politics in Brazil: An Experiment in Democracy: 1930–1964*, New York: Oxford; Thomas Skidmore, 1988, *The Politics of Military Rule in Brazil, 1964–1985*, New York: Oxford; Ronald M. Schneider, 1991, *Order and Progress: A Political History of Brazil*, Boulder, Colo.: Westview Press; Joseph M. Page, 1972, *The Revolution That Never Was: Northeast Brazil, 1955–1964*, New York: Grossman; Phyllis R. Parker, 1979, *Brazil and the Quiet Intervention, 1964*, Austin: Univ. of Texas;

Maria Helena Moreira Alves, 1985, *State and Opposition in Military Brazil*, Austin: Univ. of Texas.

4. For details on the repressive activities of the regime, see Dom Paulo Evaristo Arns, et al., 1985, *Brasil: Nunca Mais*, Petrópolis, Rio de Janeiro: Vozes; and Maria Helena Moreira Alves, *State and Opposition in Military Brazil*. For press censorship, see Joan Dassin, 1982, "Press Censorship and the Military State in Brazil," in Jane L. Curry and Joan Dassin, eds., *Press Control around the World*, New York: Praeger Publishers. Thomas Skidmore has an account of repression under the Médici government in *The Politics of Military Rule in Brazil*, 125–135, and Ronald M. Schneider has a shorter discussion in *Order and Progress*, 259–264.

5. Maria Helena Moreira Alves. *State and Opposition in Military Brazil*, 103–138.

6. Jaime Sautchuk, et al., 1978, *A Guerrilha do Araguaia*, São Paulo: Editora Alfa Omega; Fernando Portela, 1979, *Guerra de Guerrilhas no Brasil*, São Paulo: Global Editora; Wladimir Pomar, 1980, *Araguaia, O Partido e a Guerrilha*, São Paulo: Editora Brasil Debates; Maria Helena Moreira Alves, *State and Opposition in Military Brazil*, 120–123.

7. A treatment of the church's role in the Brazil of the 1960s can be found in Emanuel de Kadt, 1970, *Catholic Radicals in Brazil*, London: Oxford. A later work is Zilda Gricoli Iokoi, 1996, *Igreja e camponeses: Teologia da Libertacão e Movimentos Sociais no Campo Brasil e Peru, 1964–1986*, São Paulo: Hucitec. A basic work of one of Brazil's most influential liberation theologists is Leonardo Boff, 1987, *Teologia do Cativeiro e da Libertacão*, Petrópolis: Vozes. Perhaps the most widely read work on liberation theology is Gustavo Gutierrez, 1987, *Teologia da Libertacão*, Petrópolis: Vozes (also available in Spanish and English editions). For a discussion focused on the church and its specific relationship to the origins of the MST, see João Pedro Stédile and Bernardo Mançano Fernandes, 1999, *Brava Gente: A Trajetoria do MST e a luta pela terra no Brasil*, São Paulo: Editora Fundacão Perseu Abramo.

8. For figures on Brazilian landholding, see IBGE (Instituto Brasileiro de Geografia e Estatistica), 1990, *Estatisticas Historicas do Brasil*, 2nd ed, Rio de Janeiro: IBGE; IBGE, *Censo Agropecuario, 1995/1996*, Rio de Janeiro: IBGE.

9. José Armando da Silva (Zezinho). Interview by authors. Sarandí, January 2001.

10. For varying interpretations of political changes in this era, see Ronald M. Schneider, *Order and Progress*; Thomas Skidmore, *The Politics of Military Rule in Brazil*; Maria Helena Moreira Alves, *State and Opposition in Military Brazil*.

11. A series of essays that addresses the shortcomings of the military's economic policies and the economic and political challenges they created for subsequent regimes can be found in Lawrence S. Graham and Robert H. Wilson, 1990, *The Political Economy of Brazil: Public Policies in and Era of Transition*, Austin: Univ. of Texas.

12. The account of the events at Encruzilhada Natalino that comprise this section are drawn primarily from four sources: the most detailed account of the events, on which we have relied most heavily, is Telmo Marcon, 1997,

*Acampamento Natalino: Historia da Luta pela Reforma Agraria*, Passo Fundo, Rio Grande do Sul: Editora da Universidade de Passo Fundo; Bernardo Mançano Fernandes, 2000, *A Formacão do MST no Brasil*, Petrópolis: Vozes; João Pedro Stédile and Bernardo Mançano Fernandes, 1999, *Brava Gente: A trajetoria do MST e a luta pela terra no Brasil*, São Paulo: Editora Fundacão Perseu Abramo; and a series of interviews we conducted with participants in Sarandí in January 2001, as cited. See also Sue Branford and Jan Rocha, 2002, *Cutting the Wire: The Story of the Landless Movement in Brazil*, London: The Latin American Bureau. Although the sources are largely consistent with one another, where minor conflicts appear we have relied on Marcon as the most detailed story, except for his dating of the original *acampamento* at Encruzilhada Natalino, which is apparently in error in Marcon, judging both by other sources and his own dating of other events.

13. Telmo Marcon. *Acampamento Natalino*, 49.
14. Eleu Shepp. Interview by authors. Sarandí, January 2002.
15. Padre Arnildo Fritzen. Interview by authors. Ronda Alta, 2003.
16. Telmo Marcon. *Acampamento Natalino*, 56.
17. José Armando da Silva. Interview by authors. Sarandí, January 2002. See also Stédile and Fernandes, *Brava Gente*, 15–30.
18. Telmo Marcon. *Acampamento Natalino*, 53.
19. Analysis of the history of Brazil's land law comes from Angus Wright, "The Origins of the Brazilian Movement of Landless Rural Workers," a paper delivered at Latin American Studies Association in September 2001, Washington, D.C. Sources used in that work include Paulo Guilherme de Almeida, 1990, *Aspectos Juridicos da Reforma Agraria no Brasil*, São Paulo: Hucitec; Fabio Alves, 1995, *Direito Agrario: Politica Fundiara no Brasil*, Belo Horizonte: Editora del Rey; Paulo Tominn, 1991, *Institutos Basicos do Direito Agrario*, São Paulo: Saraiva; James Holston, 1991, "The Misrule of Law: Land and Usurpation in Brazil," *Comparative Studies in Society and History* IV: 695–725; Raymundo Laranjeira, 1999, *Direito Agrario Brasileiro: em homenagem a Memoria de Fernando Pereira Sodero*, São Paulo: Ed. LTr.; Fernando Pereira Sodero, 1990, *Esboco historico da formacão do direito agrario no Brasil*, Rio de Janeiro: FASE; Juvelino José Strozake, org., 2000, *A Questão Agraria e a Justica*, São Paulo: Ed. Revista dos Tribunais; Giralomo Domenico Trecanni, 2001, *Violencia e Grilagem: Instrumentos de Aquisacão da Propriedade da Terra no Pará*, Belém: Universidade Federal do Pará; Emilia Viotti da Costa, 1985, *The Brazilian Empire: Myths and Histories*, Chicago: Univ. of Chicago; Angus Wright, 1976, *Market, Land, and Class: Southern Bahia, Brazil, 1890–1942*, Ann Arbor, Mich.: University Microfilms.
20. Republica Federativa do Brasil, Ministerio do Desenvolvimento Agrario, Instituto Nacional de Colonizacão e Reforma Agraria. 2001. *Grilagem de Terra, Balanco 2000/2001*. Brasília. The study is available on the ministry's web site, www.incra.gov.br
21. Special agrarian supplement of *Estadão de Sao Paulo*, August 26, 2002.
22. Angus Wright. *Market, Land, and Class*, 67–77.

23. Warren Dean. 1995. *With Broadax and Firebrand: The Destruction of the Brazilian Atlantic Coast Rainforest*. Berkeley: Univ. of California, 147–148.

24. Emilia Viotti da Costa, *The Brazilian Empire*, chapter 4; Angus Wright, *Market, Land, and Class*, chapter 3.

25. Aurelio Buarque de Hollanda Ferreira. 1964. *Pequeno Dicionario Brasileiro da Lingua Portuguesa*, 11th ed. Rio de Janeiro: Ed. Civilizacão Brasileiro.

26. James Holston. "The Misrule of Law," 695, 722.

27. Fernando Pereira Sodero. *Esboco historico da formacão do direito agrario no Brasil*, 25.

28. Fernando Pereira Sodero. *Esboco historico da formacão do direito agrario no Brasil*, 25.

29. Raymundo Laranjeiro. *Direito Agrario Brasileiro*, a collection of articles by various legal scholars in homage to Sodero, who took these arguments in this direction.

30. José Carlos Garcia. 2000. "O MST entre desobedencia e democracia." In Juvelino José Strozake, *A Questão Agrario e a Justica*. Other articles in Strozake explore similar approaches.

31. 2002. "All about the MST: Interview with João Pedro Stédile." *New Left Review* 15, May/June.

32. João Pedro Stédile and Bernardo Mançano Fernandes. *Brava Gente*, 23–29.

33. João Pedro Stédile and Bernardo Mançano Fernandes. *Brava Gente*, 23–29.

34. João Pedro Stédile and Bernardo Mançano Fernandes, *Brava Gente*, 23–29; José Armando da Silva, interview by authors, Sarandí, January 2001; Telmo Marcon, *Acampamento Natalino*, 42–47.

35. João Guimaraes Rosa. 1971. *The Devil to Pay in the Backlands*, trans. James L. Taylor and Harriet de Onis. New York: Knopf. Rosa had been an army doctor with troops fighting private armies led by landowners in the backlands and later served as a diplomat.

36. Telmo Marcon. *Acampamento Natalino*, 77–79.

37. Emilia Viotti da Costa. *The Brazilian Empire*, chapter 4.

38. Stuart B. Schwartz, 1996, *Slaves, Peasants, and Rebels: Reconsidering Brazilian Slavery*, Urbana, Ill.: Univ. of Illinois, chapter 3; Arthur Ferreira Filho, 1965, *Historia Geral do Rio Grande do Sul*, 3rd edition, Pôrto Alegre: Editora Globo.

39. Elimar and Marileni Dalcin. Interviews by authors. Sarandí, January 2001.

40. Valdimirio Busa. Interview by authors. Sarandí, January 2001.

41. José and Anir Placotnik. Interviews by authors. Sarandí, January 2001.

42. Elimar and Marileni Dalcin, interviews by authors, Sarandí, January 2001; José and Anir Placotnik, interviews by authors, Sarandí, January 2001.

43. Maria Helena Moreira Alves, author of *State and Opposition*, who wrote prophetically in the last days of the dictatorship, concluded that the opposition was encircled by repressive policies of the state and various dilemmas facing all oppositional work: "To continue to develop influence and organization, the opposition will have to find ways to escape the circle that surrounds it. Mechanisms must be developed to allow social and political participation in the decisions of the state in order to transform, from the bottom, the struc-

tures of political and economic society in such a way that it becomes responsive to the needs of the population. The dialectic of state and opposition has
become a prison to both." In our view, the MST has provided one of the most
compelling answers to this dilemma so well summarized by Alves.

44. Maria Helena Moreira Alves. *State and Opposition*, 122.

45. See Gricoli Iokoi, 1996, *Igreja e Camponeses*, Editora Hucitec: Sao Paulo; Roseli
Salete Caldert, 2000, *Pedogogia do Movimento Sem Terra*, Petrópolis: Vozes;
Paulo Freire, 1983, *Pedogogia do oprimido*, Rio de Janeiro: Paz e Terra (available
in English as *Pedagogy of the Oppressed*, New York: Herder and Herder, 1972.
Original copyright in Portuguese is 1968).

46. Thomas Skidmore. *Politics in Brazil*, 39–40.

47. Thomas Skidmore, *Politics in Brazil*, 163–173; José Maria Bello, 1966, *A History of Modern Brazil, 1889–1964*, Stanford: Stanford Univ., 297–308.

48. Ronald M. Schneider. *Order and Progress*, chapters 5–6.

49. Telmo Marcon. *Acampamento Natalino*, 179–181.

50. Telmo Marcon. *Acampamento Natalino*, 182–183.

51. Sue Branford and Jan Rocha. *Cutting the Wire*, 20.

52. Telmo Marcon. *Acampamento Natalino*, 198.

53. Bernardo Mançano Fernandes. *Formacão do MST*, 88–93.

54. MST figures from João Pedro Stédile, September 2002. INCRA figures as cited
here can be found at www.incra.gov.br/_serveinf/_htm.balanco/balanco1.htm.

55. Sue Branford and Jan Rocha, *Cutting the Wire*, 22–25; Bernardo Mançano
Fernandes, *Formacão do MST*, 79–87.

56. Sue Branford and Jan Rocha, *Cutting the Wire*, 22–24; Bernardo Mançano
Fernandes, *Formacão do MST*, 79–87.

57. Sue Branford and Jan Rocha, *Cutting the Wire*, 25; Bernardo Mançano
Fernandes, *Formacão do MST*, 7987.

58. Most of the stories of the "contras" came from the interview with José
Armando da Silva, January 2002. Pacote elaborated on his observations. The
rest of the information from da Silva comes from the same interview.

59. For an exploration of the concept of agro-ecology see Miguel Altieri, 1995,
*Agro-ecology: The Science of Sustainable Agriculture*, Boulder, Colo.: Westview
Press.

## Chapter Two

1. For information on the rise of social movements during the transition to
democracy in Brazil, see R. C. L. Cardoso, "Popular Movements in the Context
of the Consolidation of Democracy in Brazil," in A. Escobar and S. E. Alvarez,
eds., 1992, *The Making of Social Movements in Latin America: Identity, Strategy
and Democracy*, Boulder, Colo.: Westview Press, 291–303; S. Mainwaring,
1984, *New Social Movements, Political Culture and Democracy: Brazil and Argentina*, Notre Dame, Ind.: Helen Kellogg Institute for International Studies,
University of Notre Dame. For a Brazilian source, see I. Scherer-Warren, 1993,
*Redes de Movimentos Sociais*, São Paulo: Edições Loyola. For a source that covers Latin America in general, see D. Slater, ed., 1985, *New Social Movements*

*and the State in Latin America*, Amsterdam: CEDLA; S. Eckstein, 1989, *Power and Popular Protest: Latin American Social Movements*, Berkeley: Univ. of California.

2. For Gomes da Silva's discussion of the PNRA, see J. Gomes da Silva, 1987, *Caindo por Terra: Crises de Reforma Agrária na Nova República*, São Paulo: Busca Vida. Also see J. Gomes da Silva, 1989, *Buraco Negro: A Reforma Agrária na Constituinte de 1987–1988*, Rio de Janeiro: Paz e Terra.

3. Quoted in the *Folha de São Paulo*, May 28, 1985.

4. W. Selcher. 1986. *Political Liberalization in Brazil: Dynamics, Dilemmas and Future Prospects*. Boulder, Colo.: Westview Press.

5. For an excellent discussion of the UDR, see L. A. Payne, 2000, *Uncivil Movements: The Armed Right Wing and Democracy in Latin America*, Baltimore, Md.: Johns Hopkins University Press. Also see R. Bruno, 1997, *Senhores de Terra, Senhores de Guerra: A Nova Face Política das Elites Agroindustriais no Brasil*, Rio de Janeiro: Editora Universidade Rural.

6. P. C. D. Oliveira and C. P. del Campo. 1985. *A Propriedade Privada e a Livre Iniciativa no Tufão Agro-Reformista*. São Paulo: Editora Vera Cruz Ltda., 13.

7. P. C. D. Oliveira and C. P. del Campo. *A Propriedade Privada e a Livre Iniciativa no Tufão Agro-Reformista*, 18.

8. J. Vidal. 1997. "The Long March Home." *The Guardian Weekend Magazine*, April 26, 14–20.

9. N. P. Peritore and A. K. G. Peritore. 1990. "Brazilian Attitudes Toward Agrarian Reform: A Q–Methodology Opinion Study of a Conflictual Issue." *Journal of Developing Areas* 24(3): 377–405.

10. A. L. Hall. 1990. "Land Tenure and Land Reform in Brazil." *Agrarian Reform and Grassroots Development: Ten Case Studies*, R. Prosterman, M. Temple, and T. Hanstad, eds. Boulder, Colo.: Lynne Reiner Publishers.

11. Organization of American States. 1997. *Report on the Situation of Human Rights in Brazil*. Washington, D.C.: Inter-American Commission on Human Rights, 116.

12. R. A. Garcia Jr. 1989. *O Sul: Caminho do Roçado*. São Paulo: Editora Marco Zero, 11–12.

13. W. Dean. 1995. *With Broadax and Firebrand: The Destruction of the Brazilian Atlantic Forest*. Berkeley: Univ. of California, 276.

14. For a full copy of Pero Vaz de Caminha's "Carta," see: http://atelier.hannover2000.mct.pt/~pr324/. Also see John Hemming's (1978) partial analysis of the Carta in *Red Gold: The Conquest of the Brazilian Indians, 1500–1760*, Cambridge, Mass.: Harvard Univ.

15. For good information on the colonization of Brazil, see L. Bethell, ed., 1987, *Colonial Brazil*, New York: Cambridge Univ.

16. For a very good account of the history of sugarcane in northeastern Brazil, see S. B. Schwartz, 1985, *Sugar Plantations in the Formation of Brazilian Society: Bahia, 1550–1835*, New York: Cambridge Univ.

17. E. Pinto. 1963. *O Problema Agrário na Zona Caniviera de Pernambuco*. Recife: Joaquim Nabuco Instituto de Pesquisa Social, 61.

18. T. E. Skidmore. 1999. *Brazil: Five Centuries of Change*. Oxford: Oxford Univ., 23.

19. S. B. Schwartz. 1985. *Sugar Plantations in the Formation of Brazilian Society: Bahia, 1550–1835*. New York: Cambridge Univ., 67.

20. For a thorough account of the encounter between European explorers and the indigenous peoples of Brazil, see J. Hemming, 1978, *Red Gold: The Conquest of the Brazilian Indians, 1500–1760*, Cambridge, Mass.: Harvard Univ.

21. J. Hemming. *Red Gold*.

22. Robert M. Levine and John J. Crocitti. 1999. *The Brazil Reader*. Durham, N.C.: Duke Univ., 121.

23. G. Freyre. 1967. *The Masters and the Slaves: A Study in the Development of Brazilian Civilization*. New York: Alfred A. Knopf.

24. Quoted in R. M. Levine and J. J. Crocitti, eds. 1999. *The Brazil Reader: History, Culture and Politics*. Durham, N.C.: Duke Univ., 91–92.

25. R. E. Sheriff. 2001. *Dreaming Equality: Color, Race and Racism in Urban Brazil*. New Brunswick, N.J.: Rutgers Univ.

26. G. Ramos. 1984. *Vidas Secas*. São Paulo: Record.

27. J. De Castro. 1969. *Death in the Northeast*. New York: Random House.

28. S. Quinn. 1998. Brazil's Northeast Rural Poverty Alleviation Program. Case study presented at the Transfers and Social Assistance for the Poor in the LAC Regional Workshop, February 24–25, 1998.

29. Unless otherwise indicated, all interview quotes cited in this chapter come from field research done by the authors in 1998, 1999, and 2001. With the exception of highly visible movement leaders and politicians, all names have been changed, in accordance with the Protocol Number 99-4-76 filed with the Committee for the Protection of Human Subjects at the University of California at Berkeley.

30. "Arrães responde a ACM." *Jornal da Tarde*, May 25, 1998.

31. K. Bond. 1999. "A Drought Ravages Northeast Brazil." *North American Congress on Latin America (NACLA)* 32 (4): 7–10.

32. B. J. Chandler. 1978. *The Bandit King: Lampião of Brazil*. College Station, Tex.: Texas A&M Univ. Also see G. M. Joseph, 1990, "On the Trail of Latin American Bandits: A Reexamination of Peasant Resistance," *Latin American Research Review* 25(3): 7–52.

33. R. M. Levine. 1997. *Brazilian Legacies*. Armonk, N.Y.: M. E. Sharpe.

34. S. B. Schwartz. 1992. *Slaves, Peasants and Rebels: Reconsidering Brazilian Slavery*. Chicago, Ill: Univ. of Illinois, 123–124.

35. Read the statement entitled "The Black Face of Multicultural Brazil," by Dulce Maria Pereira, when she was president of the Palmares Cultural Foundation. For a historian's take on the increasing number of quilombos found, see S. B. Schwartz, 1992, *Slaves, Peasants, and Rebels: Reconsidering Brazilian Slavery*, Urbana, Ill.: Univ. of Illinois.

36. R. M. Levine. 1992. *Vale of Tears: Revisiting the Canudos Massacre in Northeastern Brazil, 1893–1897*. Berkeley: Univ. of California.

37. For a fascinating account of the government's decision to engage Conselheiro

in battle and the subsequent military operations, see the translation by Samuel Putnam and Euclides Da Cunha, 1944, *Rebellion in the Backlands (Os Sertões)*, Chicago: Univ. of Chicago.

38. For different perspectives on the Peasant Leagues, see A.W. Pereira, 1997, *The End of the Peasantry: The Rural Labor Movement in Northeast Brazil, 1961–1988*, Pittsburgh, PA: Univ. of Pittsburgh; S. Forman, 1975, *The Brazilian Peasantry*, New York: Columbia Univ.; C. Morães, 1970, "Peasant Leagues in Brazil," in R. Stavenhagen, ed., *Agrarian Problems and Peasant Movements in Latin America*, Garden City, N.Y.: Doubleday; J. A. Page, 1972, *The Revolution That Never Was: Northeast Brazil, 1955–1964*, New York: Grossman.

39. For an excellent account of the sugarcane industry in the late 1800s, see P. L. Eisenberg, 1974, *The Sugar Industry in Pernambuco: Modernization without Change, 1840–1910*, Berkeley: Univ. of California.

40. Luiz de Carvalho Pães de Andrade, 1864, cited in P. L. Eisenberg, 1974, *The Sugar Industry in Pernambuco: Modernization without Change, 1840–1910*, Berkeley: Univ. of California.

41. For information on the sugarcane industry in Northeast Brazil after the 1950s, see L. Sigaud, 1979, *Os Clandestinos e os Direitos: Estudo Sobre Trabalhadores da Cana-de-açúcar de Pernambuco*, São Paulo: Livraria Duas Cidades.

42. For information on the Rural Workers' Statute, see A. W. Pereira, 1997, *The End of the Peasantry: The Rural Labor Movement in Northeast Brazil, 1961–1988*, Pittsburgh, Penn.: Univ. of Pittsburgh.

43. The report by the United States Department of Labor, Bureau of International Labor Affairs, is entitled *International Child Labor Program, Section III: Child Labor In Commercial Agriculture*. The document is not dated. See: http://www.dol.gov/ILAB/media/reports/iclp/sweat2/commercial.htm.

44. T. C. W. Corrêa de Araujo, N. L. Vieira de Mello, and A. A. Vieira de Mello. 1994. *Trabalhadores Invisíveis: Crianças e Adolescentes dos Canaviais de Pernambuco*. Recife: Centro Josué de Castro.

45. For an excellent article that discusses the desire for land among rural plantation workers, see L. Sigaud, 1977, "A Idealização do Passado numa Área de Plantation," *Contraponto* 2(2): 115–126.

46. C. J. C. Lins. 1996. *Programa de Ação Pará o Desenvolvimento da Zona da Mata do Nordeste*. Recife: SUDENE.

47. A 1998 government report read: "The crisis of the sugarcane industry in the northeastern tropical forest region is a crisis of the [productive] model. The crisis provides a unique opportunity to carry out sweeping structural changes that will eliminate the concentration of landholdings and monocultural production, in order to benefit the economic development of the region with equality and social justice." Ministerio Extraordinario da Política Fundiária (MEPF). 1998. *Programa Integrado de Reforma Na Zona da Mata Nordestina*. Recife: MEPF.

48. S. C. Buarque. 1997. "Proposta de Reestruturação do Setor Sucro-Alcooleiro e Negociação de Divida Por Terra Para Assentamentos de Reforma Agrária." Text prepared for discussion at the Working Group Meeting on: Reestruturação do

Setor Sucro-Alcooleiro e Reforma Agrária na Zona da Mata de Pernambuco. Recife: INCRA.

49. For journalistic coverage of the expropriation of Catalunha, see "MST Já Criou Cooperativa de Assentados," *Jornal do Commercio*, Recife, November 1, 1998; "Um Assentamento de R$16 Milhões," *Jornal do Comercio*, Recife, November 1, 1998. For an official report requested by INCRA on the viability of Catalunha for smallholder agricultural production, see a preliminary report by A. Hurtado and G. Marinozzi entitled "Projeto de Assentamento na Fazenda Catalunha: Estudo Preliminar de Viabilidade Econômica," completed in Brasília on October 1, 1997. This document is not published, but is available on the web at: www.incra.gov.br/fao/tpnp3.htm.

## Chapter Three

1. Although Barbalho fought back aggressively, the mounting evidence would lead within a matter of weeks to his resignation in disgrace and to his eventual imprisonment in Tocantins and seizure of his assets by federal prosecutors. At this writing, he is out of prison and has reasserted himself as leader of his state political machine, announcing his plans to run for federal deputy and his wife's plans to run for his old senate seat. *Folha de Sao Paulo*, June 27, 2001, "Desocupacao pacifica na Chao de Estrelas"; *O Liberal de Belem*, June 27, 2001, "PM retira sem-terra de forma pacifica"; *Folha de Sao Paulo*, July 29, 2001, "Fazendeiro nega encontro com Jader em SP; August 4, "Documento de procuradores complica situacao de Jader."

2. *O Liberal do Belem*, July 12, 2001, "PF vai ajudar na investigacao do assassinato do sindicalista"; July 14, "Fazendeiro nega envolvimento na morte da familia em Maraba"; July 15, "Mortes atualizam lista de marcados," by Carlos Mendes.

3. *O Liberal do Belem*, July 12, 2001, "Agronomo depoe e contradiz Jader"; July 13, "Jader diz que nao inteferiu na desapropriacao da fazenda"; July 21, "Jader se licencia do Senado por 60 dias."

4. Telmo Marcon. 1997. *Acampamento Natalino: Historia da Luta pela Reforma Agraria*. Passo Fundo: Universidade de Passo Fundo.

5. For an overview of the biological richness of the region see Michael Goulding, ed., 1995, *Floods of Fortune*, New York: Columbia Univ.

6. Phillip M. Fearnside, 2000, "Deforestation Impacts, Environmental Services, and the International Community," in Anthony Hall, ed., *Amazonia at the Crossroads: The Challenge of Sustainable Development*, London: Institute of Latin American Studies; John O. Niles, 2002, "Tropical Forests and Climate Change," in *Climate Change Policy: A Survey*, Washington, D.C.: Island Press.

7. Phillip M. Fearnside. "Deforestation Impacts, Environmental Services, and the International Community," 11–12.

8. Solon Barraclough and Krishna B. Ghimire. 2000. *Agricultural Expansion and Tropical Deforestation*. London: Earthscan.

9. Anna Luiza Ozorio de Almeida. 1992. *The Colonization of the Amazon*. Austin: U. of Texas, 76–84.

10. Susana Hecht and Alexander Cockburn, 1989, *The Fate of the Forest: Developers,*

*Destroyers, and Defenders of the Amazon*, New York, London: Verso, 113–115, 141, 176–178; Anthony Anderson, 1990, "Smokestacks in the rainforest: Industrial development and deforestation in the Amazon Basin, *World Development* 18(9): 191–205.

11. Shelton Davis. 1977. *Victims of the Miracle: Development and the Indians of Brazil*. New York: Cambridge Univ.

12. Rural Advancement Fund International (RAFI), 1994, *Conserving Indigenous Knowledge: Integrating Two Systems of Innovation*, New York: UNEP; Nigel J. H. Smith, 2000, "Agroforestry Development and Prospects in the Brazilian Amazon," in Anthony Hall, *Amazonia at the Crossroads*.

13. Rosineide da Silva Bentes, Lea Lobato de Carvalho, et al. 1992. *A Ocupacão do solo e subsolo paraenses*, special edition of *Pará Agrario*. We are indebted to Rosineide da Silva Bentes for further discussions on these issues.

14. Phillip Fearnside, 1989, "The Charcoal of Carajás: A Threat to the Forests in the Brazilian Eastern Amazon Region," *Ambio* 18 (2): 141–143; Nader Nazmi, 1991, "Deforestation and Economic Growth in Brazil: Lessons from Conventional Economics," *Centennial Review* 35 (2): 315–322; Anthony Anderson, 1990, "Smokestacks in the rainforest."

15. Susanna Hecht and Alexander Cockburn. *Fate of the Forest*, 141.

16. Ozorio de Almeida. *The Colonization of the Amazon*; Girolamo Domenico Trecanni, 2001; *Violencia e Grilagem: Instrumentos de Acquisacão da Propriedade da Terra no Pará*, Belém: UNFPA; Ronaldo Barata, 1995, *Inventario da Violencia: Crime e Impunidade no Campo Paraense*, Belém: Cejup.

17. Anna Luiza Ozorio de Almeida. *The Colonization of the Amazon*, 44–52.

18. Jorge Vivan, 1998, *Agricultura e Florestas: Principios de uma Interacão Vital*, Guaiba, Rio Grande do Sul: Livraria e Editora Agropecuaria (available from Assessoria e Servicos a Projetos em Agricultura Alternativa, Rio de Janeiro); Susanna Hecht and Alexander Cockburn, *Fate of the Forest*, 37–42; Arturo Gomez-Pompa, T. C. Whitmore, and M. Hadley, 1991, *Rainforest Regeneration and Management*, Park Ridge, N.J.: Parthenon.

19. Michael Goulding. 1980. *The Fishes and the Forest: Explorations in Amazonian Natural History*. Berkeley: Univ. of California.

20. Susanna Hecht and Alexander Cockburn. *Fate of the Forest*, 42–43.

21. For an essay considering various population estimates of Brazilian aboriginal population, with a more conservative conclusion than here, see John Hemming, 1995, *Red Gold: The Conquest of the Brazilian Indians*, 2nd ed., London: Papermac.

22. For the history of the colonial impact on Indians, see John Hemming, *Red Gold*.

23. Anna Luiza Ozorio de Almeida. *The Colonization of the Amazon*, chapters 3–5, esp. pp. 58–59.

24. Anna Luiza Ozorio de Almeida. *The Colonization of the Amazon*, 140–144.

25. The news on this subject was carried in Brazilian newspapers and magazines for months, cf. *O Estado de São Paulo*, July 11, 2001; *O Liberal de Belém*, June 12, June 21, 2001.

26. Girolamo Domenico Trecanni, *Violencia e Grilagem*; on the economics of cattle, with conclusions substantially different from earlier studies, see M. D. Faminow, 1998, *Cattle, Deforestation and Development in the Amazon: An Economic, Agronomic, and Environmental Perspective*, New York: CAB International.

27. Some books have been devoted to analyzing and comparing these perspectives, e.g., Hecht and Cockburn, *Fate of the Forest*; Bunker, *Underdeveloping the Amazon: Extraction, Unequal Exchange, and the Failure of the Modern State*, Urbana: Univ. of Illinois; Emilio F. Moran, "Deforestation in the Brazilian Amazon," in Leslie Sponsel, et al., *Tropical Deforestation: The Human Dimension*, New York: Columbia Univ. A very detailed and interesting treatment that explores the military perspective on economic development and conservation planning in the Amazon is Ronald A. Foresta, 1991, *Amazon Conservation in the Age of Development: The Limits of Providence*, Gainesville, Fla.: Univ. of Florida.

28. Girolamo Domenico Trecanni. *Violencia e Grilagem*, 163–196.

29. M. D. Faminow, *Cattle, Deforestation and Development*; Carlos Felipe Jaramillo and Thomas Kelly, 1999, "Deforestation and Property Rights," in Kari Keipi, ed., *Forest Resource Policy in Latin America*, Washington, D.C.: Inter-American Development Bank; Philip Fearnside, "Land Tenure Issues as Factors in Environmental Destruction in Brazilian Amazonia: The Case of Southern Pará," *World Development* 29(8): 1361–1372.

30. Bernardo Mançano Fernandes, 2000, *A Formacão do MST no Brasil*, Petrópolis: Vozes, 209; Gabriel Ondetti, 2001, "Brazil's Landless Movement in Comparative Historical Perspective," paper presented at the Latin American Studies Association Annual Meeting, Sept. 6–8, Washington, D.C.

31. Girolamo Domencio Trecanni. *Violencia e Grilagem*.

32. Bernardo Mançano Fernandes. *A Formacão do MST no Brasil*, 206.

33. Interview by authors. Belém, July 2001.

34. Interview by authors. Belém, July 2001.

35. Alfredo Wagner Berno de Almeida. 1995. *Quebradeiras de Coco Babaçu: Identidade e Mobilizacão*. São Luis de Maranhão: Estacão Publicidade e Marketing Ltda.

36. Anthony Anderson, "Smokestacks in the rainforest"; François le Tacon and John Harker Harley, 1990, "Deforestation in the Tropics and Proposals to Arrest It," *Ambio* 19(8): 372 ff.

37. David Cleary. 2000. "Small-Scale Gold Mining in Brazilian Amazonia," in Hall, *Amazonia at the Crossroads*.

38. For the church's view of its own history in the region, as well as a series of articles on the general situation of settlers, agrarian reform, deforestation and violence, see José Aldemir de Oliveira and Padre Humberto Guidotti, orgs., 2000, *A Igreja Arma sua Tenda na Amazonia: 25 anos de encontro pastoral na Amazonia*, Manaus: Universidade da Amazonas.

39. Alex Shoumatoff, 1988, *The World Is Burning: Murder in the Rainforest*, New York: Avon Books; Augusta Dwyer, 1990, *Into the Amazon: The Struggle for the Rain Forest*, San Francisco: Sierra Club Books.

40. J. Redwood III. 1993. *World Bank Approaches to the Environment in Brazil: A Review of Selected Projects.* Washington, D.C.: World Bank.

41. See a study done of government credit to settlers in the Amazon, Leticia Rangel Tura and Francisco de Assis Costa, orgs., *Campesinato e Estado na Amazonia: Impactos do FNO no Pará*, Belém: Brasília Juridica Ltda.

## Chapter Four

1. *Veja*, November 11, 1998, 56–57.

2. A. M. Buainain and H. M. de Souza Filho. 1998. *PROCERA: Productive impacts and payment capabilities.* Brasília: INCRA/FAO.

3. Food and Agriculture Organization of the United Nations. 1992. *Principais Indicadores Sócio–Econômicos dos Assentamentos de Reforma Agrária: Versão resumida do relatório final do Projeto BRA 87 022.* Brasília: FAO/PNUD.

4. Vox Populi. 1996. *Relatório de Pesquisa de Opinião Pública e Caracterização Sócio-Econômica em Projetos de Assentamento do INCRA no País.* Belo Horizonte: Vox Populi.

5. The quote is from an undated document titled "Impactos Regionais da Reforma Agrária no Brasil: Aspectos Políticos, Economicos e Sociais," written by Sergio Leite for a conference called Seminário Sobre Reform Agrária e Desenvolvimento Sustentável, held in Fortaleza, Ceará, March 1998.

6. The figure of 1,711 settlements was changed three times in INCRA's own accounting during the research conducted for the census. The figure presented in the census is 1,711, which includes all settlements created before 1997, including colonization projects. This figure was different, however, from the number given to researchers at the beginning of the census research, which was 1,647. INCRA has also furnished official figures that do not include the colonization projects, and these figures were used by some state governments in conducting the research.

7. For Chayanov's analysis of the Russian peasantry, see A.V. Chayanov, translated by D. Thorner, et al., 1986, *A. V. Chayanov on the Theory of Peasant Economy*, Madison, Wis.: Univ. of Wisconsin. For what would become the official interpretation of the Russian peasantry, see V. Lenin, 1977, *The Development of Capitalism in Russia*, Moscow: Progress Publishers.

8. For Bahian settlements, see Salvador Trevizan, 2000, *Sociedade–Natureza: uma concreta e necessaria integracão*, Rio de Janeiro: Papel Virtual Editora. Also, for an earlier look, see Angus Wright, 1992, "Land Tenure, Agrarian Policy, and Forest Conservation in Southern Bahia, Brazil—A Century of Experience with Deforestation and Conflict Over Land," a paper presented at Latin American Studies Association, Los Angeles.

9. The document can be found at www.presidencia.gov.br/publi_04/COLECAO/REFAGRI.HTM.

10. Steven M. Helfand and Gervasio Castro de Rezende. 2001. "The Impact of Sector-Specific and Economy-Wide Reforms: The Case of Brazilian Agriculture, 1980–1998." Nemesis papers at www.nemesis.org.br/artigoi.htm

11. Perhaps the most articulate expression of this opinion is by José Graziano da

Silva, 1996, *A Nova Dinamica da Agricultura Brasileira*, Campinas, São Paulo: Instituto de Economia da UNICAMP. One of Graziano's most ardent debators is José Eli da Veiga, whose approach to small family farming can be found in a document titled "Diretrizes Para Uma Nova Política Agrária" written for a conference called Seminário Sobre Reform Agrária e Desenvolvimento Sustentável, held in Fortaleza, Ceará, March 1998.

12. Steven M. Helfand and Gervasio Castro de Rezende. "The Impact of Sector-Specific and Economy-Wide Reforms."

13. The so-called "Washington Consensus" was a term coined in 1998 by John Williamson. The WC was essentially a list of ten governing principles that Williamson argued would generate a consensus. The WC came to be a catch-word for neoliberal doctrine and was seen as an imposition of Western philosophy on developing countries. For a summary of the debate, see C. Gore, 2000, "The Rise and Fall of the Washington Consensus as a Paradigm for Developing Countries," in *World Development*, 28(5).

14. On general value of land reform in post World War II era, see Russell King, 1977, *Land Reform: A World Survey*, Boulder, Colo: Westview; Hung-chao Tai, 1974, *Land Reform and Politics: A Comparative Analysis*, Berkeley: Univ. of California. Also see A. Amsden, 1989, *Asia's Next Giant: South Korea and Late Industrialization*, New York: Oxford Univ.

15. See A. Amsden, *Asia's Next Giant: South Korea and Late Industrialization*.

16. See George Collier and Elizabeth Quaratiello, 1999, *Basta! Land and the Zapatista Rebellion in Chiapas*, revised edition, Oakland, Calif: Food First Books.

17. For good overviews of agrarian reform in Latin America, see A. De Janvry, 1981, *The Agrarian Question and Reformism in Latin America*, Baltimore, Md.: Johns Hopkins Univ.; M. Grindle, 1985, *State and Countryside: Development Policy and Agrarian Politics in Latin America*, Baltimore, Md.: Johns Hopkins Univ.; Peter Dorner, 1992, *Latin American Land Reform in Theory and Practice: A Retrospective Analysis*. Madison, Wisc.: Univ. of Wisconsin; R. Prosterman, M. Temple, and T. Hanstad, eds., 1990, *Agrarian Reform and Grassroots Development: Ten Case Studies*, Boulder and London: Lynne Reiner; A. De Janvry, E. Sadoulet, and W. Wolford, 1998, "The Changing Role of the State in Latin American Land Reforms," in A. De Janvry, G. Gordillo, J. P. Platteau, and E. Sadoulet, eds., *Access to Land, Rural Poverty, and Public Action*, Oxford: Oxford Univ.

18. See Cardoso's influential statement on what came to be called dependency theory: F. H. Cardoso and E. Faletto, 1978, *Dependency and Development in Latin America*, Berkeley, Calif.: Univ. of California. For a concise statement on Cardoso's theoretical revisions, see F. H. Cardoso, 1995, "From 'Dependencia' to Shared Prosperity," in *New Perspectives Quarterly* 12(1): 42–45.

19. Carlos Enrique Guanziroli and Silvia Elizabeth de C. S. Cardim, coords. 2001. *Novo Retrato da Agricultura Familiar: O Brasil Redescoberto*. Brasília: INCRA/FAO.

20. Angus Wright. 1992. "Land Tenure, Agrarian Policy, and Forest Conservation in Southern Bahia, Brazil—A Century of Experience with Deforestation and

Conflict Over Land." Latin American Studies Association Meeting, Los Angeles.

21. See John Vandemeer and Ivette Perfecto. 1995. *Breakfast of Biodiversity*. Oakland, Calif.: Food First.

22. *Time Magazine*, August 26, 2002, A27.

23. For a write-up of this research and policy recommendations, see C. Valladares-Pádua, S. Pádua, and L. Cullen Jr., 2002, "Within and Surrounding the Morro do Diabo State Park: Biological Value, Conflicts, Mitigation and Sustainable Development Alternatives," in *Environmental Science & Policy* 5, 69–78.

24. Two very good sources on rural elites and their contemporary political influence are L. A. Payne, 2000, *Uncivil Movements: The Armed Right Wing and Democracy in Latin America*, Baltimore, Md.: Johns Hopkins Univ.; and R. Bruno, 1997, *Senhores da Terra, Senhores da Guerra: A Nova Face Política das Elites Agroindustriais no Brasil*, Rio de Janeiro: Forense Universitaria: Editora Universidade Rural.

25. B. Moore. 1966. *Social Origins of Dictatorship and Democracy: Lord and Peasant in the Making of the Modern World*. Boston: Beacon Press.

26. C. Prado, Jr. 1945. *História Econômica do Brasil*. São Paulo: Brasiliense.

27. The quote comes from J. P. Stédile and B. M. Fernandes, 1999, *Brava Gente: A Trajetória do MST e a Luta pela Terra no Brasil*, São Paulo: Editora Fundação Perseu Abramo, 36. The interview with Stédile and Ilse Scherer-Warren is published in J. Rossiaud and I. Scherer-Warren, eds., 2000, *A Democratização Inacabável: As Memórias do Futuro*, Petrópolis, Rio de Janeiro: Vozes.

28. J. P. Stédile and B. M. Fernandes. *Brava Gente,* 35.

29. The Brazilian Communist Party changed its name to the Popular Socialist Party (PPS) in 1993.

30. Ademar Bogo. *O Jornal Sem Terra*, January 1991: 3.

31. *O Jornal Sem Terra* vol. 102: 3.

32. *O Jornal Sem Terra* vol. 97: 3.

33. On social movements becoming professional organizations, see J. D. McCarthy and M. N. Zald, 1973, *The Trend of Social Movements in America: Professionalization and Resource Mobilization*, Morristown, N.J.: General Learning Press.

34. For a full copy of Osmar Dias's statement, see www.senado.gov.br/web/senador/odias/trabalho/Discursos/Discursos/Discurso1997/970522.htm.

35. K. Weyland. 1996. *Democracy without Equity: Failures of Reform in Brazil*. Pittsburgh: Univ. of Pittsburgh.

36. S. Mainwaring. 1994. *Democracy in Brazil and the Southern Cone: Achievements and Problems*. Notre Dame, Ind.: University of Notre Dame, Helen Kellogg Institute for International Studies.

37. R. Da Matta. 1991. *Carnivals, Rogues and Heroes: An Interpretation of the Brazilian Dilemma*. Notre Dame, Ind.: University of Indiana Press.

38. See Z. Navarro, "Mobilização Sem Emancipação: as Lutas Sociais dos Sem-Terra no Brasil," in *Produzir Para Viver: Os Caminhos da Produção Não Capitalista*, Boaventura de Sousa Santos, ed. Rio de Janeiro: Civilização Brasileira, 2002, 189–232.

39. See W. R. Nylen, "The Problem of Low and Declining Rates of Participation in Participatory Mechanisms of Public Administration: Lessons from the Participatory Budgets of Betim and Belo Horizonte, Minas Gerais," a paper prepared for delivery at the Brazilian Studies Association (BRASA) VI International Congress, Atlanta, GA, April 4–6.

40. L. S. D. Medeiros. 1989. *História dos Movimentos Sociais no Campo*. Rio de Janeiro: FASE; A. Escobar and S. E. Alvarez, eds. 1992. *The Making of Social Movements in Latin America: Identity, Strategy, and Democracy*. Series in Political Economy and Economic Development in Latin America. Boulder, Colo.: Westview Press.

41. For Benedita da Silva's autobiography (as told to Medea Benjamin and Maisa Mendonça, 1997), see *Benedita da Silva: An Afro-Brazilian Woman's Story of Politics and Love*, Oakland, Calif.: Food First Books.

42. See a collection of pieces documenting challenges of keeping young people in the Brazilian countryside: R. Abramovay, ed. 1998. *Juventude e Agricultura Familiar: Desafios dos Novos Padrões Sucessórios*. Brasília: Unesco/Fão/Incra/Epagri.

43. João Pedro Stédile. Interview. *Folha de São Paulo*, September 16, 2002.

# Further Reading

I N ORDER TO SHED LIGHT on the MST's formation and development, this
list begins with works that examine the geographical and historical roots
of Brazilian development. Two very good general histories of Brazil are
Bradford Burns' popular book, *A History of Brazil* (Columbia University
Press, 1993) and Boris Fausto's *A Concise History of Brazil* (Cambridge University
Press, 1999). An edited collection that brings together primary documents
from the historical archives and scholarly analyses is *The Brazil
Reader: History, Culture, Politics*, edited by Robert M. Levine and John J.
Crocitti (Duke University Press, 1999). For a comprehensive study of the
military period, see Thomas Skidmore's *The Politics of Military Rule in
Brazil, 1964–1985* (Oxford University Press, 1988).

One of the best histories of rural politics and political actors in the countryside
is by sociologist José de Souza Martins, *Os Camponeses e a Política
no Brasil: As Lutas Sociais no Campo e Seu Lugar no Processo Político* (Editora
Atica, 1981). The book by Leonilde Medeiros, *História dos Movimentos Sociais
no Campo* (FASE, 1989), is an excellent and more focused account of
the formation and mobilization of rural social movements. Anthony
Pereira's *The End of the Peasantry* (University of Pittsburgh Press, 1997) analyzes
rural militancy in northeastern Brazil during the military period.

For information on the political economy of land distribution in Brazil,
we recommend Caio Prado Júnior's famous work, *The Colonial Background
of Modern Brazil* (originally published in Portuguese in 1945; English edition
published by University of California Press in 1967), which should be

read in conjunction with Ignácio Rangel's article "Iniciativa Pública e Privada." (Econômica Brasileira 2[3], 1966) for two different perspectives on the need for land redistribution. Stuart Schwartz' book, *Sugar Plantations in the Formation of Brazilian Society: Bahia, 1550–1835* (Cambridge University Press, 1985), focuses on the colonial economy of northeastern Brazil and provides insight into the relationship between plantations and the nation-state. An excellent source on the modernization of agriculture under the military government (1964–1985) is *A Modernização Dolorosa: Estrutura Agrária, Fronteira Agrícola e Trabalhadores Rurais no Brasil* by José Graziano Da Silva (Zahar: 1982). An essay that situates agrarian reform in the context of globalization is "A Reforma Agrária em Tempos de Democracia e Globalização," by Bernardo Sorj (1998) in *Novos Estudos* (no. 50: 23–40). It is also very interesting to read the official statement regarding reform policies by a Brazilian president who was also one of the country's foremost sociologists, Fernando Henrique Cardoso (1995–2003): *Reforma Agrária: Compromisso de Todos* (1997, available at www.presidencia.gov.br/publi_04/COLECAO/REFAGR3.htm). A recent analysis of agrarian reform programs in Brazil from a gender perspective is *Towards a Gendered Analysis of the Brazilian Agrarian Reform* by Carmen Diana Deere and Magdalena León (Center for Latin American and Caribbean Studies, University of Connecticut, 1999).

In addition to these general pieces, there are many good sources on the movement itself. Because of the MST's increasing popularity and importance, several studies have been done that document the movement's extraordinary rise and address particular aspects of the movement's formation and character. Here we have included some of the most important sources on the movement, although we are focusing primarily on general studies. We have put references to books and articles on specific aspects of the movement in the endnotes for each chapter.

One of the most comprehensive sources on the movement was written by an academic working at the State University of São Paulo, Bernardo Mançano Fernandes, and an MST activist, João Pedro Stédile. Their book is titled *Brava Gente: A Trajetória do MST e a Luta Pela Terra no Brasil* (Editora Fundação Perseu Abramo, 2000). Bernardo Mançano Fernandes has also written another book that describes the MST's history and development in each state of Brazil where the movement has gained access. The book, *MST, Movimento dos Trabalhadores Rurais Sem-Terra: Formação e Territorialização* (Editora Hucitec, 1999), is filled with detailed information gathered by someone who has been involved in movement politics since the very beginning. A collection of essays edited by João Pedro Stédile, *A Questão Agrária Hoje* (Editora da Universidade Federal do Rio Grande do Sul, 1994), is extremely interesting because it brings together several different authors, some of whom challenge the MST's position. Another collection of essays with good material on assorted aspects of agrarian reform settlements in Brazil is a book called *Assentamentos Rurais: Uma Visão Multidisciplinar*, edited by Leonilde Medeiros (Editora Unesp, 1995).

There are several good sources on the MST in English as well. The most comprehensive account to date was written by Jan Rocha and Sue Branford, two newspaper correspondents with long histories in Brazil. The book, titled *Cutting the Wire: The Story of the Landless Movement in Brazil* (Latin American Bureau, 2002), is a journalistic account of the movement's rise and regional formation. It is comprehensive, easy to read, and filled with personal narratives collected on settlements around the country. For a more academic account on how the movement fits into the broader context of globalization, see an article written by Lucio Flávio De Almeida and Félix Ruiz Sánchez, "The Landless Workers' Movement and Social Struggles Against Neoliberalism," in *Latin American Perspectives* (27 [5], no. 114 [September 2000]: 11–32). Also see two articles written by James Petras "Latin America: The Resurgence of the Left" in *New Left Review* (223 [1997]: 17–47) and "The Political and Social Basis of Regional Variation in Land Occupations in Brazil" in *Journal of Peasant Studies* (254 [1998]: 124–133). Two short but interesting articles on the movement appeared recently in *NACLA Report on the Americas* (33, no. 5 [2000]). The articles are interesting because they were written by two Brazilian academics (translated into English) who are very familiar with the MST. Good information can also be found on the website of a non-governmental organization in San Francisco, Global Exchange (www.globalexchange.org/campaigns/brazil/mst/). Global Exchange has been working closely with the MST for several years and runs several ongoing exchange programs with the movement.

# Index

# Food First Books of Related Interest

## Benedita da Silva: An Afro-Brazilian Woman's Story of Politics and Love
*As told to Medea Benjamin and Maisa Mendonça*
*Foreword by Jesse Jackson*
The inspiring memoir of a woman who overcame poverty and tragedy to become one of the most prominent policians in Brazil. Benedita da Silva shares the story of her life as an advocate for the rights of women, people of color, and the poor, and argues persuasively for economic and social human rights in Brazil and everywhere. **Paperback, $15.95 ISBN: 0-935028-70-6**

## Basta! Land and the Zapatista Rebellion in Chiapas
*Revised edition*
*George A. Collier with Elizabeth Lowery Quaratiello*
*Foreword by Peter Rosset*
The classic on the Zapatistas in a revised edition, including a preface by Rodolfo Stavenhagen, a new epilogue about the present challenges to the indigenous movement in Chiapas, and an updated bibliography.
**Paperback, $14.95 ISBN: 0-935028-79-X**

## The Future in the Balance: Essays on Globalization and Resistance
*Walden Bello*
*Edited with a preface by Anuradha Mittal*
A new collection of essays by Third World activist and scholar Walden Bello on the myths of development as prescribed by the World Trade Organization and other institutions, and the possibility of another world based on fairness and justice. **Paperback, $13.95 ISBN: 0-935028-84-6**

## Views from the South: The Effects of Globalization and the WTO on Third World Countries
*Foreword by Jerry Mander*
*Afterword by Anuradha Mittal*
*Edited by Sarah Anderson*
This rare collection of essays by Third World activists and scholars describes in pointed detail the effects of the WTO and other Bretton Woods institutions.
**Paperback, $12.95 ISBN: 0-935028-82-X**

Call our distributor, CDS, at (800) 343-4499 to place book orders. All orders must be pre-paid.

# About Food First

Food First, also known as the Institute for Food and Development Policy, is a nonprofit research and education-for-action center working to expose the root causes of hunger in a world of plenty. It was founded in 1975 by Dr. Joseph Collins and Frances Moore Lappé, author of the best selling *Diet for a Small Planet*. Food First research has revealed that hunger is created by concentrated economic and political power, not by scarcity. Resources and decision-making are in the hands of wealthy few, depriving the majority of land, jobs, and therefore food.

Food First has grown to profoundly shape the debate about hunger and development. Through books, reports, videos, media appearances, and speaking engagements, Food First experts reveal the often hidden roots of hunger, and show how individuals can get involved in ending the problem. Food First inspires action by bringing to light the courageous efforts of people around the world who are creating faming and food systems that truly meet people's needs.

## BECOME A FOOD FIRST INTERN

Check our web site for information, www.foodfirst.org.

## BECOME A MEMBER OF FOOD FIRST

ndividual member contributions provide more than half of the funds for Food 'rst's work. Because Food First is not tied to government, corporate, or uni-._rsity funding, we can speak with a strong, independent voice. The success of our program depends on dedicated volunteers and staff, as well as financial support from our activist donors. Your gift will help strengthen our effort to improve the lives of hungry people around the world.

........................................................................................................

I would like to become a Food First member! Enclosed is my tax-deductible contribution of:

❏ $35    ❏ $40    ❏ $50*    ❏ $100*          *All gifts are tax-deductible.*
❏ $500*    ❏ $1,000*    ❏ Other: $_____

## Method of Payment

❏ Check or money order enclosed. All foreign orders must be in US funds. Make checks out to Food First. Send to: 398 – 60th Street, Oakland, CA 94618, (510) 654-4400, FAX (510) 654-4551, www.foodfirst.org.

❏ Visa          ❏ MC          ❏ AmEx

Name on card _____

Card number _____ Expiration date_____

Name _____

Address _____

City _____ State _____ Zip_____

Tel: (day) _____ Tel: (eve) _____

*A donation of $50 or more includes a FREE one-year subscription to the *New Internationalist*.

# Take Action...Support the MST!

Join the growing network of Friends of the MST, working together with the Landless Workers Movement (MST) since 1997.

- Visit our web site at www.mstbrazil.org
- Receive updates and urgent action alerts via our listserve
- Host an MST representative in your area
- Volunteer to translate between Portuguese and English
- Make a donation to support the work of the MST and the US-based Friends of the MST (online donations accepted on our www.mstbrazil.org web site)
- Organize viewings of the MST documentary "Strong Roots" (available for purchase online at http://store.globalexchange.org/ strongroots.html)
- Organize a Friends of the MST chapter in your area
- Get involved in the Nourish the New Brazil Campaign (www. nourishnewbrazil.org), working in conjunction with the national mobilization in Brazil for the Zero Hunger Campaign to end hunger through real agrarian reform and sustainable agriculture

For more information about how to get involved with the Friends of the MST and the Nourish the New Brazil Campaign, contact:

Friends of the MST
c/o Global Exchange
2017 Mission Street, #303
San Francisco, CA 94110
(415) 255-0795
www.mstbrazil.org
dawn@mstbrazil.org